Mathematics for Programming Computers

Mathematics for Programming Computers

Third Edition

Frank J. Clark

A Reston Book
PRENTICE HALL
Englewood Cliffs, N. J. 07632

Library of Congress Cataloging-in-Publication Data

Clark, Frank James
  Mathematics for programming computers.

  Includes index.
  1. Electronic data processing--Mathematics.
I. Title.
QA76.9.M35C58 1988   004'.0151   87-42985
ISBN 0-13-563180-7

Editorial/production supervision
and interior design: Editing, Design & Production, Inc.
Cover Design: George Cornwall
Manufacturing buyer: Cindy Grant

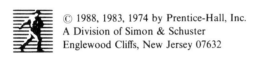

© 1988, 1983, 1974 by Prentice-Hall, Inc.
A Division of Simon & Schuster
Englewood Cliffs, New Jersey 07632

Printed in the United States of America

10 9 8 7 6 5 4 3 2

ISBN 0-13-563180-7

Prentice-Hall International (UK) Limited, *London*
Prentice-Hall of Australia Pty. Limited, *Sydney*
Prentice-Hall Canada Inc. *Toronto*
Prentice-Hall Hispanoamericana, S. A., *Mexico*
Prentice-Hall of India Private Limited, *New Delhi*
Prentice-Hall of Japan, Inc., *Tokyo*
Simon & Schuster Asia Pte. Ltd., *Singapore*
Editora Prentice-Hall do Brasil, Ltda., *Rio de Janeiro*

Contents

Preface

This text is written for students preparing for careers as programmers and for others who need a background in mathematics for information processing. The purpose of the book is to acquaint students with the mathematics that is used functionally in computer programs and with some basic concepts that are needed in a technological society. Mathematics is applied to many real-life programming situations where various problem scenarios are interpreted and expressed in algorithms and flowcharts along with the appropriate coding.

The emphasis on mathematics that is used in solving problems for computer applications provides a continuity from one chapter to the next and presents the material in a meaningful picture as a whole rather than as a series of separate and disjoint topics. Abundant exercise material and short applications programs help to increase mathematical skills and to ensure immediate reinforcement.

With computers now in use in widely diversified business and commercial applications, it is becoming easier to describe the mathematical background for a student seeking an entry occupation in programming. This mathematical background can probably best be described in terms of the expectations of future employers. Applicants for entry occupations as programmers should

Have a thorough foundation in the decimal, binary, octal, and hexadecimal numeration systems and the arithmetic operations performed in these systems

Be familiar with the computer's internal coding schemes and data representation

Understand logic operations, Boolean algebra, and some set theory

Since algebraic methods are frequently used in the solution of business and commercial problems, the text provides a strong foundation in linear, nonlinear, and logarithmic functions. Matrices are presented as a method of organizing data and solving equations. These are reinforced with short computer programs.

Probability and statistics are also commonly used as methods for predicting future trends and for presenting large amounts of data in a summarized and coherent form, and as tools for decision making. A student should understand and be able to write simple programs for measures of central tendency and measures of dispersion.

Because most entry-level jobs in the main-frame and midrange computer environment are Fortran and COBOL, examples are given in these computer languages. Because BASIC is commonly found on educational systems and typically found on the personal computer work stations or smaller systems, many of the sample programs in this text are in BASIC.

The scope of *Mathematics for Programming Computers* is to provide sufficient material and skills for students to become proficient in entry-level programming positions.

I would like to express my thanks and appreciation for the helpful suggestions of my colleagues, Dr Peter Lindstrom, Dr Bernard Hoerbelt, Jim Hofmann, and John Von Hold.

Frank J. Clark

Frank J. Clark has been a director of two Federal programs in data processing, director of a computer center, and has taught programming language courses at Dutchess and Genesee Community Colleges and at the Rochester Institute of Technology. Experience in industry includes working for AT & T, Radio Shack, and Bell Communications Research.

1

Introduction

ABOUT NUMBERS

Computer programmers are always working with numbers—from numbers to compute and represent bank balances to numbers that calculate the orbits of satellites. Even the letters of the alphabet are represented in the computer's internal memory by a number system—and numbers and letters are all stored in memory locations that are addressed by numbers. Therefore, a discussion of the different number systems used by computers and an understanding of the various classifications of numbers are essential.

We will use sets to aid us in beginning our study of number classifications. A *set* is a collection of objects and is often denoted by an upper-case letter. A collection may include such things as people, inanimate objects, numbers, or anything else. Any one item in a collection or set is called an *element* in that set.

LISTING ELEMENTS IN A SET

A set is often denoted by a capital letter and the elements in a set are usually enclosed in brackets and separated by commas. We will use set notation to describe the various types of numbers used in programming. Following is an example of set notation called the *listing* format:

$$\text{Set } A = \{1, 2, 3, 4\}$$

where A is a set or collection containing only the counting numbers 1, 2, 3, and 4, *listed* within brackets and separated by commas. To denote 3 as an element of set A, we write $3 \in A$. To indicate that an element is not a member of a set, we write $5 \notin A$, where 5 is not a member of the set A.

SET-BUILDER NOTATION

Consider another way of representing the elements in a set called *set-builder* notation. Lower-case alphabetic characters (e.g., a, b, c, x, y, etc.) may be used to indicate the elements in a set:

$$C = \{x | x \text{ is any natural number and } x > 10\}$$

This means that set C contains every x such that x is any counting number greater than 10. The vertical line is read "such that." If we had wanted to write set C in the listing format mentioned previously, we could have written: $C = \{11, 12, 13, \ldots\}$. The three trailing dots denote that the sequence continues indefinitely.

NUMBER CLASSIFICATION

Computer programming is often involved with solving problems by using several types or classes of numbers, which include counting numbers or natural numbers, integers, rational numbers, and irrational numbers.

Natural numbers consist of counting numbers. The set of natural numbers can be written as $N = \{1, 2, 3, \ldots\}$.

Integers are a set of numbers that includes the natural numbers, their negatives, and zero. $J = \{\ldots -3, -2, -1, 0, 1, 2, 3, \ldots\}$. Note that N is included in J; that is, each element of N is also an element of J. We can express the integers in set-builder notation, such as $J = \{a | a = -b, 0, \text{ or } b, \text{ where } b \in N\}$.

Rational numbers are those numbers that can be represented as a fraction or a quotient of two integers x/y, where $y \neq 0$. An example of a rational number is $\frac{1}{2} = 0.5000$, where any expansion after 0.5 yields zero. Similarly, $\frac{1}{4} = 0.2500$. Rational numbers that terminate or yield zero after a finite number of steps are called terminating decimals. Consider other examples where expansions never terminate but repeat themselves in groups as follows:

$$\frac{2}{3} = 0.666\ldots$$

$$\frac{1}{7} = 0.142857142857\ldots$$

When a digit or group of digits is repeated, the decimal fraction is called a repeating decimal expansion.

Terminating decimals and repeating decimals belong to the set of rational numbers that can be represented as x/y where $y \neq 0$. The letters x and y are variables, which means that they can be used to represent different values. In the preceding examples x and y are integers and y is not equal to zero. We can express rational numbers in set-builder notation as $Q = \{x/y | x, y \in J \text{ and } y \neq 0\}$.

Irrational numbers are those numbers that are not rational. Such numbers would be decimal numbers that do not terminate and do not repeat. Some examples of irrational numbers are $\sqrt{2}$, π, and $\sqrt{7}$. Note that the numbers that are rational and the numbers that are irrational form two sets with no elements in common. Such sets that have no elements in common are said to be disjoint. We can express irrational numbers in set-builder notation as

$$H = \{h | h \text{ represents a decimal expansion that does not repeat and does not terminate}\}$$

For example: $\sqrt{2} = 1.41421356\ldots$ and $\pi = 3.141592654\ldots$.

Real numbers include all rational and irrational numbers and can be expressed as

$$R = \{x | x \in Q \text{ or } x \in H\}$$

Thus, the set of rational numbers is a subset of real numbers and the set of irrational numbers is also a subset of real numbers but these two subsets are disjoint. Refer to Figure 1.1.

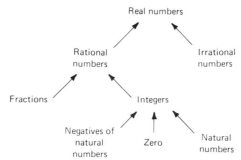

Figure 1.1

EXERCISES 1-1

1. Write the numbers of each set, using the listing format. Use three trailing dots (...) where appropriate.
   (a) Natural counting numbers from 3 to 8
   (b) Integers less than 4
   (c) Integers between -20 and -15
   (d) Natural numbers less than 4
   (e) Nonnegative integers
   (f) Natural numbers greater than 7
2. Let $X = \{3, \sqrt{2}, -4, 6, \frac{1}{2}, -8, \pi\}$. Denote with braces the following sets, using the listing method.
   (a) Natural numbers in X

    (b) Real numbers in X
    (c) Integers in X
    (d) Rational numbers in X

3. Use the set-builder format, $\{n|\text{the conditions of } n\}$, to represent each of the following sets:
    (a) Real numbers
    (b) Natural numbers greater than 6
    (c) Rational numbers between $\frac{1}{4}$ and $\frac{5}{2}$
    (d) Nonnegative rational numbers
    (e) Integers less than zero

ARITHMETIC OPERATIONS AND CLOSURE

The four arithmetic operations $+$, $-$, $\times$, and $\div$ can be performed on the sets of numbers in Fig. 1-1 with the exception that zero cannot be used as a divisor. (Note that the symbols for division may be written as $\div$ or $/$ and the symbols for multiplication may be written as $\cdot$ or $\times$.) When considering subtraction, the difference between two natural numbers may not always be a third natural number. For example, in $5 - 7$, we need to express the difference as a number preceded by a minus sign, or a number in the set of integers, -2.

For arithmetic operations in the set of integers, the result of addition, subtraction, and multiplication, will always be an integer. A set is *closed* under an operation if and only if whenever the operation is applied to proper element(s) in that set, the result is an element in that set. We can state that closure is true or that the set of integers is closed for the operation of addition, subtraction and multiplication.

$$\text{In:} \quad 5 + 16 = 21$$
$$81 - 6 = 75$$
$$4 \times 26 = 104$$

21, 75, and 104 are members of the set of integers.
The same is not always true for the operation of division on the set of integers.

$28 \div 2 = 14$; 14 is a member of the set of integers but

$28 \div 3 = 9.33\ldots$; 9.33 is a rational number with a repeating
                 and non-terminating decimal fraction.

Thus, we can state that closure is not true for division in the set of integers or that the set of integers is not closed for division and this is why we need the set of real numbers.

Under the four arithmetic operations $+$, $-$, $\times$, and $\div$, the set of real numbers is closed, that is, the result will always be a number in the set of real numbers.

Closure does not exist for arithmetic operations on all the sets of numbers. The result of $\sqrt{-4}$ is not in the set of real numbers.

There is another set of numbers that are not usually found in most business data processing problems. It is the set of complex numbers expressed in the form $x + yi$ where $x \in R$, $y \in R$ and $i = \sqrt{-1}$. If $x = 0$, the complex number can be written as yi

and denotes a pure imaginary number. If $y = 0$, the imaginary term drops out and in this case the number $x + yi$ is a real number. Since imaginary numbers are not part of typical business problems, we will not discuss them in this text.

EXERCISES 1-2

1. Is $\{(x + 2)|x \in N\}$ closed under addition? (N is the set of natural numbers.)
2. Is $\{0, 1, -1\}$ closed under multiplication?
3. Is R (the set of real numbers) closed under division?
4. Is $\{2n|n \in Q\}$ closed under addition? (Q is the set of rational numbers.)
5. Is $\{3, 4, 8\}$ closed under division?
6. Are natural numbers closed under subtraction?
7. Are natural odd numbers closed under division?
8. Are nonnegative integers closed under division?
9. Is $\{2, -2, J\}$ closed under multiplication? (J is the set of integers.)

THE NUMBER LINE

Real numbers may be visualized as points on a line and a pictorial representation of such points is called a graph of a number line. Graphs are important because they can visually summarize results of many computations as we will see in later chapters.

Zero divides the number line into positive and negative numbers. By convention, positive numbers are placed to the right of the zero and negative numbers are to the left. Note that there is a direct relationship between distance and magnitude. For example, on any given number line, the distance between 0 and 3 must be the same as the distance between 2 and 5.

Figure 1.2

The point that represents a number will be that many units distant from the point that represents zero, where the distance is a directed distance (left or right). Each number in the set of real numbers has one and only one point on the line, and this point can be described as the graph of a number. We also note that each point on the line corresponds to one and only one real number. A number line helps to illustrate the relations among the elements in the set of real numbers. Note that the horizontal line in Figure 1.2 contains three disjoint subsets:

$$\{\text{negative real numbers}\}, \quad \{0\}, \quad \{\text{positive real numbers}\}$$

If x is a real number, then one and only one of the following is true:

$$x \text{ is negative}, \quad x = 0, \quad \text{or} \quad x \text{ is positive}$$

Inequalities

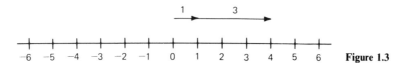

Figure 1.3

Since distance is relative to magnitude, the number line can help us visualize inequalities. Consider the points 1 and 4. There exists a positive real number 3 such that $1 + 3 = 4$. 1 is less than 4, since the positive number 3 must be added to 1 to obtain 4. Note that for any given number on the line, all numbers to the right of that number are greater than the given number and all numbers to the left are less than the given number. Following is an example using negative numbers:

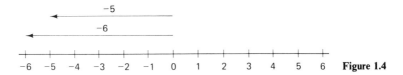

Figure 1.4

Where -5 is greater than -6 because it is to the right of -6.

The concept of "less than" can be denoted by the symbol $<$ where $1 < 4$. Similarly, we can write $4 > 1$, where the symbol $>$ denotes "greater than." The symbols $\geq$ and $\leq$ mean "greater than or equal to" and "less than or equal to," respectively. For any pair of real numbers a and b, only one of the following is possible:

$$a < b, \quad a = b, \quad \text{or} \quad a > b$$

Because of these relationships, the set of real numbers is said to be *ordered*.

Absolute Value

The number line also helps to describe the absolute value of a number in terms of its magnitude and definition. To express the absolute value of a number we write the symbol $|x|$ where $|x| \in R$ and is defined as:

$$|x| = x, \quad \text{if } x > 0$$

$$|x| = -x, \text{ if } x < 0$$

$$|x| = 0, \quad \text{if } x = 0$$

In the following examples we will write the absolute value in the context of a line segment. Let $x = b - a$ on the number line.

Example 1

If $b = 4$ and $a = 2$, then $|4 - 2| = 2 = |x|$, or using the number line in Figure 1.5

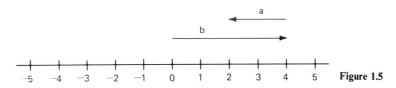

Figure 1.5

Example 2

If $b = 1$ and $a = 5$, then $|1 - 5| = -(-4) = 4 = |x|$, or using the number line in Figure 1.6

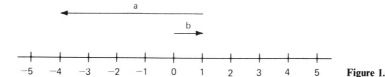

Figure 1.6

Example 3

If $b = 7$ and $a = 7$, then $|7 - 7| = 0 = |x|$, or using the number line in Figure 1.7

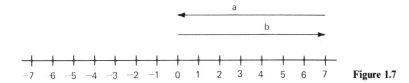

Figure 1.7

EXERCISES 1-3

1. If $a = 2$, $b = 4$, and $c = -2$, draw the number lines to show that:
   (a) $a < b$
   (b) $b > c$
   (c) $a - b = c$

2. Given the number line in Figure 1.8 and the graphic representation of $3 + 4 = 7$ as a model, draw the number lines for:

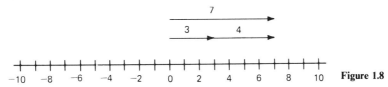

Figure 1.8

   (a) $6 + 2 = 8$
   (b) $10 - 3 = 7$
   (c) $4 + 2 = 2 + 4$
   (d) $5 - 3 = 2$
   (e) $2 \cdot 3 = 6$

3. Find the absolute value of:
    (a) 7
    (b) 3/7
    (c) −.73
    (d) 0
    (e) $x - 2$
4. If the variable x will only take on the values 1, 2, and 4 and the variable y will always be less than zero, we can express this relationship as $x > y$. Express the relationships between the variables x and y when:
    (a) x is always greater than 4 and y will always be equal to 4.
    (b) $x < 0$ and $y > 0$.
    (c) x may only have values of 7, 8, and 9 and y will always be greater than 8.
    (d) x will never take on a value assigned to y.

DATA ITEMS

Computer programming requires computations on the different types of numbers that we have been discussing and working with. Some of these items of data are:

- signed and unsigned numbers
- constants
- variables

Computations are performed on terms and expressions which contain these types of data items.

Signed and Unsigned Numbers

A signed number is a number that is preceded by a plus or minus sign. An unsigned number is handled as a positive number. Computer applications, such as accounting programs, often require that debit amounts be signed positive and credit amounts be signed negative.

Example 1

Numbers that are signed, $+1.4$, $+6$, $+33.014$, are preceded by the "+" sign and are signed positive.

Example 2

8.981, 17, .0009 are unsigned and are handled as positive numbers by the computer.

Example 3

-3, -4.12, -2496 are numbers that are signed negative.

Note that zero is considered as a nonnegative number.

Constants

A constant is a value that remains unchanged throughout a procedure or throughout an entire computer program.

Example 4

> 3.14159, $+0.005$, -0.04, where 3.14159 is a value for π, 0.005 could be a factor used for rounding to the nearest cent, and -0.04 could be a constant used as a decrement in the price for a cash sale of a gallon of gasoline.

Variables

As noted earlier, a variable may take on different values. This may be true for a procedure or during an entire computer program. A common need for variables arises when a programmer needs to write business programs such as computing net pay where the pay rate and the hours worked are variables that can take on different pay rates and different hours for many employees. Frequently a variable is named by writing one or more capital letters. This is in contrast to algebra, where only one lower-case alphabetic letter is typically used to denote a variable.

Example 5

$$RATE = 9.50$$

In this example, RATE is a variable that we have set to 9.50 as the hourly pay rate.

Example 6

$$n = 1$$
$$n = n + 2$$

In example 6, we have initialized the variable n to 1, then added an increment of 2, or replaced n with itself $+2$.

Terms and Expressions

Constants or variables combined by multiplication are often referred to as terms.

Example 7

> $3x$, $4y$, $2abc$, $-2y$, and z are terms. ($1 \times z$ is implied in z.)

Expressions are usually described as having constants or variables combined by any of the arithmetic operators. An expression must contain at least one constant and usually includes an addition or subtraction operator.

Example 8

> $2x - 1$, $9x^2 + 3x + c$, $(x + 1)$, $2/3x^3$, and x/y are expressions.

In programming languages such as COBOL, BASIC, and others, variable names typically contain more than one character.

Example 9

RATE × HOURS − TAXES

RATE, HOURS, and TAXES are variables in an expression and may appear in an equation such as:

NETPAY = RATE × HOURS − TAXES

Being able to use more than one character in variable names makes them easier to read and understand. In this example, the value for NETPAY is computed as the product of the current values in RATE × HOURS minus TAXES.

Variables names in computer programs may also include numbers.

Example 10

X1, Y45, MASS5, ANSWER4

The data items we have described are found in the computer's internal memory in various kinds of binary-coded formats. This is the subject of the following chapters.

EXERCISES 1-4

1. A value that remains the same throughout a procedure or an entire program is called

_____ .

2. Variable names begin with _____ .

3. BALANCE + PURCHASES − PAYMENT and $mx + b$ are both examples of

_____ .

4. RATE × HOURS is an example of a _____ .

5. Zero is handled as _____ number.

6. The following variables are initialized as:

$$A = -1$$
$$B = 2$$
$$C = 3$$

Find the results for:
  (a) $X = A + B$
  (b) $X = B - A$
  (c) $C = A - C$
  (d) $B = A \times (B + C)$

7. (a) Write the equation that includes the variables and the expression to find a 10 percent discount on the price of a magazine subscription.

(b) If the variable named DAYS is initialized at 365, what does the following accomplish?

$$DAYS = DAYS \times 4 + 1$$

(c) Write the expression needed to find the time it takes to travel 20 miles at 55 miles per hour.

MINUTES = 60
MPH = 55
DISTANCE = 20
TIME = _____

2

Numeration Systems

NUMBER SYMBOLS

Communications between computers and persons require symbols on whose meanings we all agree. These symbols make up the codes through which we can exchange information.

When we wish to provide answers to questions such as "how many" or "how much," we usually use the symbols that are part of the decimal system, the most widely used system of numeration. One explanation of why a system based on ten is used is that our ancient ancestors began counting when they made a one-to-one correspondence between the objects they wanted to count and their fingers. However, there are systems with bases other than ten and we will discuss those used by computers later in this chapter.

To record their computations, early people invented number symbols. See Figure 2.1. These early counting number symbols were cumbersome and hindered

Figure 2.1

mathematical thinking for thousands of years. With the invention of zero, which may be thought of as an empty wire on an abacus, mathematical thinking was revolutionized and freed from the use of so many different symbols. Our example in Figure 2.2 shows 1000 represented on an abacus where no beads are found below the counting wire for ten thousands, hundreds, tens, and ones. In this case the ten thousands, hundreds, tens, and ones wires are considered *empty*, and therefore zeros are written for their values.

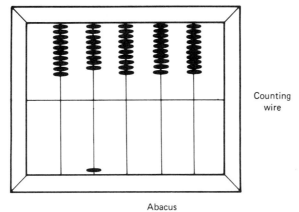

Counting wire

Abacus

Figure 2.2

Using zero, we can write any number, large or small, with a combination of ten basic symbols: 0, 1, 2, 3, 4, 5, 6, 7, 8, and 9. This greatly simplifies mathematical processes along with the use of an exponent. Exponents are a symbolic or shorthand method of writing the powers of the base. For example

$$10 \times 10 \times 10 \times 10 \times 10 = 10^5$$

In this example the exponent 5 is written as a superscript and simply indicates the number of times the base is included as a factor in the term.

Writing numbers in the decimal system of numeration means giving digits or symbols a *face value* and a *place value*. Consider the number 555. Each symbol has the same face value. However, each symbol, 5, represents a different power of base ten because each symbol has its own place value. Using exponents, the following illustrates these concepts.

The number 555 expressed in powers of base ten can be written as

$$5 \times 10^0 = 5$$

$$5 \times 10^1 = 50$$

$$5 \times 10^2 = 500$$

Note that 5×10^0 means 5×1 (five 1's) and $5 + 50 + 500 = 555$. It is clear that each successive place to the left represents a value that is ten times greater than the previous one.

We can write 7564 in powers of base ten as:

$$4 \times 10^0 = 4$$
$$6 \times 10^1 = 60$$
$$5 \times 10^2 = 500$$
$$7 \times 10^3 = 7000$$

where $4 + 60 + 500 + 7000 = 7564$. The 4 is called the units digit, 6 is the tens digit, 5 the hundreds digit, and 7 the thousands digit. Another way of describing this is to say that the 7 represents seven groups of 1000, the 5 represents five groups of 100, the 6 represents six groups of 10 and the 4 represents four 1's.

Expanded Notation

To understand the operations of addition, subtraction, multiplication, and division of numbers in the decimal system, a clear understanding of place value is required. The following examples are written in *expanded* notation and illustrate this concept.

Consider

$$\dots a_2, a_1, a_0$$

If these subscripted variables can take on values in the decimal system, then in expanded notation they may be written as

$$\dots + a_2(10^2) + a_1(10^1) + a_0(10^0)$$

Using this general format for expanded notation, we can now write the decimal number 493 as

$$493 = 4(10^2) + 9(10^1) + 3(10^0)$$

or

$$493 = 4(10)^2 + 9(10) + 3$$

We can perform all the basic arithmetic operations in expanded notation, as shown in the following examples:

Addition

$$
\begin{array}{r}
25 \\
+\ 12 \\
\hline
37
\end{array}
\quad \text{means} \quad
\begin{array}{r}
2(10)+5 \\
+1(10)+2 \\
\hline
3(10)+7
\end{array}
$$

$$
\begin{array}{r}
365 \\
+278 \\
\hline
643
\end{array}
\quad \text{means} \quad
\begin{array}{l}
3(10)^2 + 6(10) + 5 \\
+2(10)^2 + 7(10) + 8 \\
\hline
5(10)^2 + 13(10) + 13 \\
=6(10)^2 + 4(10) + 3
\end{array}
$$

(note the carries into the tens and hundreds columns)

Subtraction

$$
\begin{array}{r}
63 \\
-\ 41 \\
\hline
22
\end{array}
\quad \text{means} \quad
\begin{array}{r}
6(10)+3 \\
-(4(10)+1) \\
\hline
2(10)+2
\end{array}
$$

$$
\begin{array}{r}
463 \\
-174 \\
\hline
289
\end{array}
\quad \text{means} \quad
\begin{array}{r}
4(10)^2+\ 6(10)+\ 3 \\
-(1(10)^2+\ 7(10)+\ 4)
\end{array}
$$

we can rearrange or rename our minuend to indicate "borrowing" as follows:

$$
\begin{array}{r}
3(10)^2+15(10)+13 \\
-(1(10)^2+\ 7(10)+\ 4) \\
\hline
2(10)^2+\ 8(10)+\ 9
\end{array}
$$

Multiplication

$$
\begin{array}{r}
22 \\
\times\ 11 \\
\hline
22 \\
22 \\
\hline
242
\end{array}
\quad \text{means} \quad
\begin{array}{r}
2(10)+\ 2 \\
\times\quad 1(10)+\ 1 \\
\hline
2(10)+\ 2 \\
2(10)^2+\ 2(10) \\
\hline
2(10)^2+\ 4(10)+\ 2
\end{array}
$$

$$
\begin{array}{r}
32 \\
\times\ 18 \\
\hline
256 \\
32 \\
\hline
576
\end{array}
\quad \text{means} \quad
\begin{array}{r}
3(10)+\ 2 \\
\times\quad 1(10)+\ 8 \\
\hline
24(10)+16 \\
3(10)^2+\ 2(10) \\
\hline
3(10)^2+26(10)+16 \\
=5(10)^2+\ 7(10)+\ 6
\end{array}
$$

Division

$$
\begin{array}{r}
21 \\
4\overline{)84}
\end{array}
\quad \text{means} \quad
\begin{array}{r}
2(10)+1 \\
4\overline{)8(10)+4}
\end{array}
$$

$$
\begin{array}{r}
272 \\
14\overline{)3808} \\
28 \\
\hline
100 \\
98 \\
\hline
28 \\
28 \\
\hline
\end{array}
\quad \text{means} \quad
\begin{array}{r}
2(10)^2+7(10)+2 \\
1(10)+4\overline{)3(10)^3+8(10)^2+0(10)+8} \\
2(10)^3+8(10)^2 \\
\hline
1(10)^3+0(10)^2+0(10) \\
9(10)^2+8(10) \\
\hline
2(10)+8 \\
2(10)+8 \\
\hline
\end{array}
$$

The following are found to be essential in the description of the decimal numeration system.

1. Number symbols: 1, 2, 3, 4, 5, 6, 7, 8, and 9.
2. The symbol for zero, 0.
3. A symbol for the base, where *place* value is first introduced. When we move left to the second column (or ten's column), we create our symbol for base ten by writing 10.
4. Position values of symbols, or increasing powers of base ten.

Note that when we see the number 10 (i.e., a one followed by a zero) we assume a base ten, but we will learn that in different number systems 10 can mean eight, sixteen, or two. All that 10 means is that we have denoted the base of the number system under consideration. Further, $10°$, $2°$, $8°$, and $16°$ all mean 1 for the decimal, binary, octal and hexadecimal systems that we will be discussing.

EXERCISES 2-1

Perform the following using expanded notation.

Addition

1.	143	2.	273	3.	672
	+ 23		+419		+981

Subtraction

4.	275	5.	281	6.	543
	− 63		−102		−258

Multiplication

7.	58	8.	249	9.	428
	× 16		× 65		× 101

Division

10. $13\overline{)169}$ 11. $19\overline{)855}$ 12. $7\overline{)1000}$

Mechanical Counting

In the thirteenth century, clocks using wheels and gears were able to measure time, but it took another 400 years before someone was able to "fit" decimal numbers to wheels and gears to count "how many."

In 1642, Blaise Pascal applied this concept to an automatic adding device. Imagine the wire on the abacus forming a circle and the ten beads as ten teeth on a counting wheel. As soon as ten has been counted on any wheel, a carry is forced into the next wheel on the left. Mechanical desk calculators, adding machines, odometers, and cash registers are all examples of how the decimal system has been "fitted" onto mechanical devices.

Although the decimal system "fits" our fingers and some types of counting devices, it is not the only system devised for counting.

Leibnitz, a seventeenth-century mathematician, is credited with perfecting the binary system as we understand it today. The binary system contains two symbols, 1 and 0. Because an electric circuit can only be on or off, we can let 1 represent "on" and 0 represent "off" and fit the binary numeration system onto computers.

THE BINARY NUMERATION SYSTEM

If we read the row of lights in Figure 2.3 from right to left as a binary number, we can describe this number in base two as follows:

Lights	Binary	Decimal
on	$1 \times 10^0 = 1$	$1 \times 2^0 = 1$
off	$0 \times 10^1 = + 0$	$0 \times 2^1 = +0$
on	$1 \times 10^2 = +100$	$1 \times 2^2 = +4$
off	$0 \times 10^3 = + 0$	$0 \times 2^3 = +0$
	$\overline{101}_{(B)}$	$\overline{5}_{(D)}$

Figure 2.3

The subscript $_{(B)}$ refers to a binary number. The subscript $_{(D)}$ refers to a decimal number.

Note that in the decimal system we used the symbol 2, but in the binary system we used 10 since there is no digit 2 in the binary system. In the binary system, each time we move one place to the left, we multiply by two, or double the *place* value of a binary digit.

Binary 1111 means

Binary	Decimal
1	$1 \times 2^0 = 1$
10	$1 \times 2^1 = 2$
100	$1 \times 2^2 = 4$
1000	$1 \times 2^3 = 8$
$\overline{1111}$	$\overline{15}$

The binary system fits our description of a numeration system because it has

1. The number symbol, 1
2. A symbol for zero, 0
3. A symbol 10 for the base when we move to the second column to the left.
4. Position values of the symbols as the powers of the base increase

Note that the largest number before a "carry" in decimal is 9 and the largest number before a "carry" in binary is 1. If

$$9 + 1 = 10_{(D)}$$

and

$$1 + 1 = 10_{(B)}$$

then

$$10_{(D)} = \text{ten in the decimal system}$$

$$10_{(B)} = \text{two in the binary system}$$

By comparing our descriptions of the decimal system and the binary system, we can derive a general description of a numeration system N of base n.

Let n be the base of the numeration system. Then N has

1. Number symbols $1, 2, 3, \ldots (n - 1)$
2. A symbol for zero, 0
3. A symbol 10 for the base when we move to the second column to the left
4. Position values of the symbols as the powers of the base increase

Using this general definition, we can derive the binary system definitions by substituting two for n.

EXERCISES 2-2

1. The following example uses expanded notation and makes it easy to derive a decimal number from a given binary number.

$$1110_{(B)} = (1 \times 2^3) + (1 \times 2^2) + (1 \times 2^1) + (0 \times 2^0)$$

$$= 8 + 4 + 2 + 0$$

$$= 14_{(D)}$$

Using the procedure in the preceding example, perform the following:
(a) Express $1100_{(B)}$ as a decimal number.

(b) Express $101_{(B)}$ as a decimal number.

(c) Express $10001_{(B)}$ as a decimal number.

2. Complete the following:

    (a) $\underline{\quad}_{(B)} = (\quad) + (\quad) + (\quad) + (\quad) + (\quad)$

             $= 16 + 0 + 4 + 0 + 1$

             $= 21_{(D)}$

    (b) $110000_{(B)} = (\quad) + (\quad) + (\quad) + (\quad) + (\quad) + (\quad)$

               $= \underline{\quad} + \underline{\quad} + \underline{\quad} + \underline{\quad} + \underline{\quad} + \underline{\quad}$

               $= \underline{\quad}_{(D)}$

    (c) $\underline{\quad}_{(B)} = (1 \times 2^5) + (0 \times 2^4) + (1 \times 2^3) + (0 \times 2^2) + (1 \times 2^1) + (1 \times 2^0)$

               $= \underline{\quad} + \underline{\quad} + \underline{\quad} + \underline{\quad} + \underline{\quad} + \underline{\quad}$

               $= \underline{\quad}_{(D)}$

    (d) $10110011_{(B)} = \underline{\quad}_{(D)}$

    (e) $11011110_{(B)} = \underline{\quad}_{(D)}$

3. In a binary number, the position of the $\underline{\quad}$ or $\underline{\quad}$ indicates which $\underline{\quad}$ of base two will be multiplied by a 0 or 1.

4. Powers of the base are specified by $\underline{\hspace{4cm}}$.

The binary system is also important to programmers because it provides methods for representing computer data items in the octal and hexadecimal numeration systems.

THE OCTAL NUMERATION SYSTEM

The octal numeration system is a system based on eight. The octal number $375_{(O)}$ can be described in terms of the powers of base eight as

Octal		Decimal
5	$5 \times 10^0 =$	5
+ 70	$+7 \times 10^1 =$	+ 56
+300	$+3 \times 10^2 =$	+192
$375_{(O)}$		$253_{(D)}$

The subscript $_{(O)}$ refers to an octal number. Because the octal system is based on eight, 8 is *never* used as a symbol in octal notation. In the octal numeration system, eight is represented as 10. Each time we move one place to the left in the octal system, we multiply the place value of the octal digit by eight.

Table 2.1 shows a relationship between the decimal, binary, and octal numeration systems. The octal system fits the description of a numeration system because it has

    1. Seven number symbols: 1, 2, 3, 4, 5, 6, and 7.

    2. A symbol for zero, 0.

3. The symbol 10 for the base when we move left into the second column.

4. Position values for the symbols as the powers of the base increase.

TABLE 2.1

Decimal	Binary	Octal
0	000	0
1	001	1
2	010	2
3	011	3
4	100	4
5	101	5
6	110	6
7	111	7
8	1000	10
9	1001	11
10	1010	12
11	1011	13
12	1100	14
13	1101	15
14	1110	16
15	1111	17

The highest number we can count up to in base eight before a carry occurs is 7 and the highest number in a binary triplet is 7.

$$6 + 1 = 7_{(O)}$$

and

$$7 + 1 = 10_{(O)}$$

The octal system provides a convenient method of grouping long strings of binary numbers.

Binary 10101110111 can be written as an octal number by grouping the digits into groups of three, beginning at the right:

Binary	010	101	110	111
Octal	2	5	6	7
Decimal	$(2 \times 8^3) + (5 \times 8^2) + (6 \times 8^1) + (7 \times 8^0)$			

To provide a full triplet, we have annexed a zero to the high-order position. The octal number that is equal to the binary number in each triplet, has been written below the corresponding triplet, followed by the decimal equivalent in expanded notation.

In another example, we can write at sight any octal number as its binary equivalent by writing a binary triplet for each octal digit. Given

$$541_{(O)}$$

We can write

Octal	5	4	1
Binary	101	100	001

EXERCISES 2-3

Write the following binary numbers as octal numbers:
1. 110110011
2. 1010101
3. 1110001101
4. 1010
5. 11010
6. 100000001001
7. 1010110111111
8. 10111011
9. 1111000111011

Write the following octal numbers as binary numbers:

10.	476	14.	1001
11.	1045	15.	456
12.	201	16.	1327
13.	3321		

17. Complete the following:

(a) $\underline{\hspace{1cm}}_{(O)} = (3 \times 8^2) + (7 \times 8^1) + (0 \times 8^0)$
   $= \underline{\hspace{0.6cm}} + \underline{\hspace{0.6cm}} + \underline{\hspace{0.6cm}}$
   $= \underline{\hspace{1cm}}_{(D)}$

(b) $1011_{(O)} = (\quad) + (\quad) + (\quad) + (\quad)$
   $= \underline{\hspace{0.6cm}} + \underline{\hspace{0.6cm}} + \underline{\hspace{0.6cm}} + \underline{\hspace{0.6cm}}$
   $= \underline{\hspace{1cm}}_{(D)}$

(c) $3715_{(O)} = (\quad) + (\quad) + (\quad) + (\quad)$
   $= \underline{\hspace{0.6cm}} + \underline{\hspace{0.6cm}} + \underline{\hspace{0.6cm}} + \underline{\hspace{0.6cm}}$
   $= \underline{\hspace{1cm}}_{(D)}$

(d) $163_{(O)} = \underline{\hspace{1cm}}_{(D)}$

(e) $2042_{(O)} = \underline{\hspace{1cm}}_{(D)}$

THE HEXADECIMAL NUMERATION SYSTEM

The hexadecimal numeration system is a system based on sixteen. The hexadecimal number $134_{(H)}$ can be described in terms of the powers of the base sixteen as

Hexadecimal		Decimal
4	$4 \times 10^0 =$	4
$+ \ 30$	$+3 \times 10^1 =$	48
$+100$	$+1 \times 10^2 =$	256
$\overline{134_{(H)}}$		$\overline{308_{(D)}}$

The subscript $_{(H)}$ refers to a hexadecimal number. Because the hexadecimal system is based on sixteen, 16 is never used as a symbol for the base in hexadecimal notation. Sixteen is represented as 10 in the hexadecimal numeration system. Also, in the hexadecimal system, each time we move one place to the left, we multiply by sixteen, the place value of the hexadecimal digit.

Consider another example. Hexadecimal 1111 means

Hexadecimal		Decimal
1	$1 \times 16^0 =$	1
10	$1 \times 16^1 =$	16
100	$1 \times 16^2 =$	256
1000	$1 \times 16^3 =$	4096
$\overline{1111_{(H)}}$		$\overline{4369_{(D)}}$

We need single digits to represent numbers from ten to fifteen in the hexadecimal system. It has been conventional to use the letters A through F for this purpose. Table 2.2 shows a relationship between the decimal, binary, octal, and hexadecimal systems. Although we are using letters A through F, they are *not* used as alphabetic characters. In the hexadecimal numeration system they are considered as digits representing the decimal numbers ten through fifteen. The hexadecimal system fits our description of a numeration system because it has

1. The fifteen number symbols: 1, 2, 3, 4, 5, 6, 7, 8, 9, *A, B, C, D, E,* and *F*

2. A symbol for zero, 0

3. The symbol 10 for the base when we move left into the second column

4. Position values for the symbols as the powers of the base increase

TABLE 2.2

Decimal	Octal	Binary	Hexadecimal
0	0	0000	0
1	1	0001	1
2	2	0010	2
3	3	0011	3
4	4	0100	4
5	5	0101	5
6	6	0110	6
7	7	0111	7
8	10	1000	8
9	11	1001	9
10	12	1010	A
11	13	1011	B
12	14	1100	C
13	15	1101	D
14	16	1110	E
15	17	1111	F

An extension of Table 2.2 shows that counting in hexadecimal follows a pattern similar to the patterns found in the decimal, binary, and octal systems.

Decimal	Octal	Binary	Hexadecimal
16	20	10000	10
17	21	10001	11
18	22	10010	12
19	23	10011	13
20	24	10100	14
21	25	10101	15
22	26	10110	16
23	27	10111	17

The highest number in base sixteen before a carry is required is F, and the highest number possible in a binary quadruplet is fifteen.

$$E + 1 = F_{(H)}$$

$$F + 1 = 10_{(H)}$$

The hexadecimal system, like the octal system, provides a convenient method for grouping long strings of binary numbers to make their interpretation "easy on the eyes."

The binary number 10101101111111 can be expressed as a hexadecimal number by grouping the digits into groups of four, beginning at the right. Notice that two zeros have been annexed to the high-order position to provide a full quadruplet:

Binary	0010	1011	0111	1111
Hexadecimal	2	B	7	F
Decimal	$(2 \times 16^3) + (11 \times 16^2) + (7 \times 16^1) + (15 \times 16^0)$			

In another example, we can write any hexadecimal number as its binary equivalent using binary quadruplets. For example, in $FEED_{(H)}$ it is a simple matter to create a binary quadruplet for each hexadecimal digit, thus

$$F \quad E \quad E \quad D \quad \text{in hexadecimal}$$
$$\text{means} \quad 1111 \quad 1110 \quad 1110 \quad 1101 \quad \text{in binary}$$
$$FEED_{(H)} = 1111111011101101_{(B)}$$

The subdivision of long strings of binary numbers into quadruplets or triplets is sometimes indicated on the panels of computer consoles, thus saving computer operators and programmers the inconvenience of copying down these digits and grouping them with commas.

EXERCISES 2-4

Express the following binary numbers as hexadecimal numbers:

1. 10110110
2. 1111000000110
3. 011101
4. 1011101
5. 10111011101
6. 1111111111
7. 1010101010
8. 1001001111011
9. 1011111010101
10. 1101111011101101

Express the following hexadecimal numbers as binary numbers:

11. A12
12. CAB
13. 4F03
14. FED

15. DE161

16. 40F0B

17. Extend Table 2.2 up to decimal 35.

18. Complete the following:

(a) $3F1_{(H)} = ($ $) + ($ $) + ($ $)$

       $= $ ____ $+$ ____ $+$ ____

       $= $ ____ $_{(D)}$

(b) $ABAD_{(H)} = ($ $) + ($ $) + ($ $) + ($ $)$

       $= $ ____ $+$ ____ $+$ ____ $+$ ____

       $= $ ____ $_{(D)}$

(c) ____ $_{(H)} = (7 \times 16^3) + (0 \times 16^2) + (12 \times 16^1) + (15 \times 16^0)$

       $= $ ____ $_{(D)}$

(d) $60FAA_{(H)} = $ _____ $_{(D)}$

(e) $1CE0_{(H)} = $ _____ $_{(D)}$

(f) $307EE_{(H)} = $ _____ $_{(D)}$

THE BYTE

The grouping of binary digits into triplets or quadruplets is important and basic to the internal organization of information in computer storage. The smallest piece of information stored is a binary digit or *bit* and large numbers of bits are required to hold and process instructions and data. If instructions and data stored in binary digits are to be useful, they must be easily addressed and located so that they can be moved, added to, subtracted from, and so on.

Giving each bit its own unique address in computer storage would require very costly electronic circuitry. Therefore, bits are grouped into units called *bytes*. A byte is the smallest addressable unit of information, and each byte has its own unique internal storage address.

Typically, bytes may contain six or eight bits, depending on the computer manufacturer's choice of design:

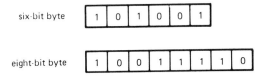

The six-bit byte contains the octal number 51. The eight bit byte contains the hexadecimal number 9E. The individual bits of a byte are linked electronically so that any unique memory address references the entire group of bits in the byte.

EXERCISES 2-5

Express the following decimal numbers as binary numbers found in a byte:
1. 362 in the six-bit format
2. 432 in the six-bit format
3. 904 in the eight-bit format
4. 1072 in the eight-bit format
5. Give the octal equivalents for 1 and 2 above.
6. Give the hexadecimal equivalents for 3 and 4 above.

3

Arithmetic Operations

To understand the contents of registers and storage maps in computers, skills must be developed in binary, octal, and hexadecimal arithmetic.

BINARY ADDITION

If we were to perform addition on a binary abacus, each wire would contain two beads. Whenever we pulled down two beads in any column, we would force a carry into the next column to the left.

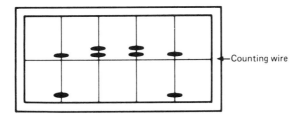

Figure 3.1

In Figure 3.1 we show the number nine as $1001_{(B)}$. If we wish to add one to nine, we must note that adding the one in the units column means exchanging two ones for a one in the next column to the left.

$$
\begin{array}{r}
1001 \\
+\ \ \ 1 \\
\hline
1010
\end{array}
$$

Describing this answer in terms of the powers of base two, we have

Binary	Decimal	
0	$0 \times 2^0 =$	0
10	$+1 \times 2^1 =$	2
0	$+0 \times 2^2 =$	0
1000	$+1 \times 2^3 =$	8
$\overline{1010}_{(B)}$		$\overline{10}_{(D)}$

Decimal equivalents are shown to the right of the next two addition examples to make the problems easier to follow:

Binary	Decimal
1010	10
$+ \quad 1$	1
$\overline{1011}_{(B)}$	$\overline{11}_{(D)}$
1011	11
$+ \ 100$	4
$\overline{1111}_{(B)}$	$\overline{15}_{(D)}$

The following contain examples of carry in binary:

Example 1

$$\text{Carry digit} \rightarrow 1$$
$$10101$$
$$+ \quad 100$$
$$\overline{11001}$$

This example may be worked out as $1 + 0 = 1$, $0 + 0 = 0$, $1 + 1 = 10$. Carry the 1 into the next column to the left, where $1 + 0 = 1$. Finally, bring down the last 1 in the fifth column to the left.

Example 2

$$\text{Carry digits} \rightarrow 11$$
$$1101$$
$$+ \quad 100$$
$$\overline{10001}$$

This example may be worked out as $1 + 0 = 1$, $0 + 0 = 0$, $1 + 1 = 10$. Carry the 1 into the next column to the left, $1 + 1$ (from the carry) $= 10$. Carry the 1 into the next column to the left.

The next example illustrates a carry into a column where two 1's already exist.

Example 3

$$
\begin{array}{r}
\text{Carry digits} \rightarrow 111 \\
1011 \\
+ \ \ 111 \\
\hline
10010
\end{array}
$$

The operation in the two's column may be expressed as $1 + 1 + 1 = 11$ or $1 + 1 + 1 = 1$, with a carry of 1. (Observe that in the first column $1 + 1 = 0$, with a carry of 1.)

You have frequently added columns of decimal numbers and mentally kept a record of the necessary carries. Although this is not a common situation in binary arithmetic, you should practice this operation to improve your skill.

Example 4

$$
\begin{array}{r}
\text{Carry digits} \rightarrow \begin{cases} 111 \\ 1111 \end{cases} \\
1001 \\
1111 \\
0111 \\
0010 \\
+ \ \ 1100 \\
\hline
101101
\end{array}
$$

In the preceding method, the carry digits were recorded at the top of each column. In binary this method is awkward because we cannot use any number greater than 1. A faster method is to form answers column by column and then add these answers together.

Example 5

$$
\begin{array}{r}
1001 \\
1111 \\
0111 \\
0010 \\
+1100 \\
\hline
\end{array}
$$

11	sum of one's column
11	sum of two's column
11	sum of four's column
11	sum of eight's column

$$
\begin{array}{r}
\hline
101101
\end{array}
$$

Binary Addition in Expanded Notation

We can also perform binary addition in terms of powers of the base or in expanded notation. Because we are using the binary system of numeration, let (10) mean two. Thus in expanded notation

$$
\begin{array}{r}
1011 \quad \text{means} \\
+ \ 100 \\
\hline
1111
\end{array}
\qquad
\begin{array}{r}
1(10)^3 + 0(10)^2 + 1(10)^1 + 1 \\
+ \qquad\qquad 1(10)^2 + 0(10)^1 + 0 \\
\hline
1(10)^3 + 1(10)^2 + 1(10)^1 + 1
\end{array}
$$

Consider another example:

$$
\begin{array}{r}
1101 \quad \text{means} \\
+ \ 101
\end{array}
\qquad
\begin{array}{r}
1(10)^3 + \ 1(10)^2 + 0(10)^1 + 1 \\
+ \ 1(10)^2 + 0(10)^1 + 1 \\
\hline
1(10)^3 + 10(10)^2 + 0(10)^1 + 10 \\
1(10)^4 + 0(10)^3 + \ 0(10)^2 + 1(10)^1 + 0
\end{array}
$$

EXERCISES 3-1

Do the following binary addition problems:

$$
\begin{array}{llllll}
\textbf{1.} & 1011 & \textbf{2.} & 11101 & \textbf{3.} & 10011 \\
 & +\ 101 & & +\ 1001 & & +\ 1111
\end{array}
\qquad
\begin{array}{ll}
\textbf{4.} & 110111 \\
 & +110111
\end{array}
\qquad
\begin{array}{ll}
\textbf{5.} & 1010101 \\
 & +\ 101011
\end{array}
$$

Add the following columns of binary numbers by either of the two methods discussed:

$$
\begin{array}{ll}
\textbf{6.} & 1011 \\
 & 0110 \\
 & 1110 \\
 & 0101 \\
 & \overline{}
\end{array}
\qquad
\begin{array}{ll}
\textbf{7.} & 01100 \\
 & 10011 \\
 & 11011 \\
 & 11100 \\
 & 10001
\end{array}
$$

Perform the following additions using expanded notation:

$$
\begin{array}{llllll}
\textbf{8.} & 1101 & \textbf{9.} & 110110 & \textbf{10.} & 11011 \\
 & +1001 & & +\ 10101 & & +\ 1011
\end{array}
$$

11. Consider each of the following binary numbers found in a byte, and perform the necessary addition:

$$
\begin{array}{ll}
\textbf{(a)} & 10110111 \\
 & +00011110 \\
 & \overline{} \\
 & \quad\text{result}
\end{array}
\qquad
\begin{array}{ll}
\textbf{(b)} & 10101011 \\
 & +10101011 \\
 & \overline{} \\
 & \quad\text{result}
\end{array}
$$

If you did example 11b correctly, your result should have "overflowed" the allotted eight bits in the resulting byte. An overflow condition like this may cause a computer program to halt.

Programmers must take care to ensure that arithmetic result fields are long enough to accommodate any possible answer. Some coding techniques for overflow handling are given in Chapter 8.

OCTAL AND HEXADECIMAL ADDITION

Recall that in base eight, the highest value before a carry is seven, and in base sixteen the highest value before a carry is fifteen. In octal:

in expanded notation where 10 means eight

$$
\begin{array}{r}
401 \\
+\ 76 \\
\hline
477_{(O)}
\end{array}
\qquad \text{means} \qquad
\begin{array}{r}
4(10)^2 + 0(10)^1 + 1 \\
+\ 7(10)^1 + 6 \\
\hline
4(10)^2 + 7(10)^1 + 7
\end{array}
$$

The next example contains a carry:

$$
\begin{array}{r}
132 \\
+\ 55 \\
\hline
207_{(O)}
\end{array}
\qquad \text{means} \qquad
\begin{array}{rl}
1(10)^2 +\ & 3(10)^1 + 2 \\
+\ & 5(10)^1 + 5 \\
\hline
1(10)^2 +\ & 10(10)^1 + 7 \\
=\ 2(10)^2 +\ & 0(10)^1 + 7
\end{array}
$$

The next examples in the octal system are written in conventional notation and also contain carries:

$$
\begin{array}{r}
\text{Carry digits} \rightarrow 1 \\
477 \\
+\ 210 \\
\hline
707
\end{array}
\qquad
\begin{array}{r}
11 \\
6741 \\
+\ 6073 \\
\hline
15034
\end{array}
$$

In hexadecimal:

in expanded notation where 10 means sixteen

$$
\begin{array}{r}
130C \\
+491 \\
\hline
179D_{(H)}
\end{array}
\qquad \text{means} \qquad
\begin{array}{r}
1(10)^3 + 3(10)^2 + 0(10)^1 + C \\
+\ 4(10)^2 + 9(10)^1 + 1 \\
\hline
1(10)^3 + 7(10)^2 + 9(10)^1 + D
\end{array}
$$

The next example contains a carry:

$$
\begin{array}{r}
A0\ 4\ B \\
+\ \ DAD \\
\hline
+ADF8\ _{(H)}
\end{array}
\qquad \text{means} \qquad
\begin{array}{rl}
A(10)^3 +\ & 0(10)^2 + 4(10)^1 + B \\
+\ & D(10)^2 + A(10)^1 + D \\
\hline
A(10)^3 +\ & D(10)^2 + E(10)^1 + 18 \\
=\ A(10)^3 +\ & D(10)^2 + F(10)^1 +\ \ 8
\end{array}
$$

The next examples in the hexadecimal system are written in conventional notation and contain carries:

$$
\begin{array}{r}
\text{Carry digits} \rightarrow 1\ \ \ 1 \\
8\,D7\,C \\
+6\,B5\,A \\
\hline
F8\ D6
\end{array}
\qquad
\begin{array}{r}
1\,1\,1 \\
E7\,AB \\
+\ 3\,FAD \\
\hline
12\,75\,8
\end{array}
$$

EXERCISES 3-2

Figure 3.2 is the decimal addition table.
1. Make an addition table for, and include zero in the three tables:
   (a) The binary system

+	1	2	3	4	5	6	7	8	9	10
1	2	3	4	5	6	7	8	9	10	11
2	3	4	5	6	7	8	9	10	11	12
3	4	5	6	7	8	9	10	11	12	13
4	5	6	7	8	9	10	11	12	13	14
5	6	7	8	9	10	11	12	13	14	15
6	7	8	9	10	11	12	13	14	15	16
7	8	9	10	11	12	13	14	15	16	17
8	9	10	11	12	13	14	15	16	17	18
9	10	11	12	13	14	15	16	17	18	19
10	11	12	13	14	15	16	17	18	19	20

Figure 3.2

(b) The octal system

(c) The hexadecimal system

2. Add in octal:

(a)	1340	**(b)**	6402	**(c)**	1326	**(d)**	63510	**(e)**	532401
	+ 207		+ 435		+5507		+ 7741		+ 65204

(f)   316   **(g)** Perform exercises 2a, b, and c in expanded notation.
             427
             553
            + 102

3. Add in hexadecimal:

(a)	1BEA	**(b)**	DEED	**(c)**	FEED	**(d)**	4795A
	+2215		+3112		+CEED		+ B04B

(e)   123456   **(f)**   4D
         +ABCDEF   3C
                             50
                            +BB

(g) Perform Exercises a, b, and c in expanded notation.

4. Describe the addition process, as it would take place in bytes of memory for Exercises 2c and 3a (if they were performed by computers).

Displacement

An important reason for studying hexadecimal and octal addition is the need to understand displacement. Before a program can be run, it must be stored somewhere in main memory. Units of main memory called bytes have their own unique addresses, and each computer instruction and each item of data begins at some address in main memory. On many computers the programmer does not know where in main memory his or her program will be stored at the time it is running. Therefore, the programmer does not know the addresses of all the bytes the program is using. However, if the address of the first byte in the program were known, then the addresses of other bytes could be calculated.

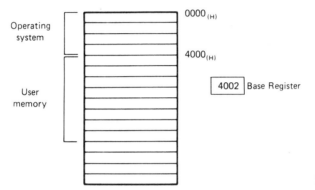

Figure 3.3

Figure 3.3 shows a map of main memory and indicates that the first $4000_{(H)}$ positions of main memory are used by the computer's operating system or the system of programs that monitor and control the operation of the computer. User memory indicates where a user's program may begin. If the operating system requires $4000_{(H)}$ bytes of memory, then, in this example, the user's program may start at the next even-numbered location, or $4002_{(H)}$. This number, $4002_{(H)}$, is placed by the operating system into a register called a base register. The idea is that by giving the programmer an absolute starting address in a register that is accessible to him, the distance between the base address and any other address in a program can be determined. This distance is called a *displacement*.

Consider $42A0_{(H)}$ as an address found by the programmer in the base register. If he or she knew that the entire program required $1030_{(H)}$ bytes of storage, then

$$
\begin{array}{r}
42A0 \\
+103\,0 \\
\hline
52D0_{(H)}
\end{array}
$$

would give the ending address of the program.

As an exercise, consider: If the programmer knew that the last $200_{(H)}$ bytes in this example were used for data items only, what would be the displacement of the first byte of data?

If these $200_{(H)}$ bytes of data contained eight records of 64 bytes each, what would be the displacement for each of the eight records? Give the answers in hexadecimal.

It is also possible for the programmer to control the displacement of individual items of data. Because this subject requires some assembly language programming skills, it is outside the scope of this book.

SUBTRACTION

The Complement Method

The complement method is a way of subtracting that does not require "borrowing." It is the procedure typically used by computers to perform binary subtraction. To get a better understanding of this method we begin first with examples in the decimal system.

A *complement* is something that fills up or completes. For example, for the number 3, $3 + 6 = 9$, and we say that 6 is the nine's complement of 3. A ten's complement is a number that, when added to a given number, will yield the complete set for a power of ten. If the given number is 8, then $8 + 2 = 10$ and 2 is the ten's complement of 8. There are mechanical counting devices and machines still in use that perform decimal subtraction by the complement method.

Sample Problem

$$\text{Subtract} \quad \begin{array}{r} 373 \\ -185 \\ \hline \end{array} \quad \begin{array}{l} \text{minuend} \\ \text{subtrahend} \end{array}$$

Take the 9's complement of the subtrahend by subtracting it from a minuend of nines.

$$\begin{array}{r} 999 \\ -185 \\ \hline 814 \end{array} \rightarrow \text{nine's complement of 185}$$

$$\text{Add in 1} \quad \begin{array}{r} 1 \\ \hline 815 \end{array}$$

815 is the ten's complement of 185, since $815 + 185$ yields a complete set for 10^3. Add the ten's complement of the subtrahend to the original minuend.

$$\begin{array}{r} 373 \\ +815 \\ \hline \end{array}$$

Carry out → $\boxed{1}\,188$
of the high
order

The carry out of the high order is detected by the circuitry, and the machine recognizes 188 as a positive number. It is helpful for the student to convert this carry out of the high order into a plus sign so that it will not be considered as a digit in an answer. A procedure demonstrating this process follows:

$$\text{Subtract} \quad \begin{array}{r} 373 \\ -185 \\ \hline \end{array}$$

$$
\begin{aligned}
373 - 185 &= 373 - 185 + (1000 - 1000) \\
&= 373 - 185 + 999 + 1 - 1000 \\
&= 373 + \underbrace{(999 - 185 + 1)}_{\substack{\text{ten's} \\ \text{complement}}} - 1000 \\
&= 373 + 815 - 1000 \\
&= 1188 - 1000 = 188
\end{aligned}
$$

Note that "borrowing" is not necessary when taking the ten's complement.

When may we expect *no* carry out of the high order?

Sample Problem

$$\text{Subtract} \quad \begin{array}{r} 425 \\ -491 \\ \hline \end{array}$$

We know that our answer will be a negative number.

	999	
Take the nine's complement	-491	
	508	nine's complement of 491
Add 1	$+\ \ 1$	
	509	ten's complement of 491
Add in original minuend	$+425$	
No carry out of high order →	934	

The machine detects the absence of a carry out of the high-order position and recognizes the answer as being negative. This also means that the answer itself is in the *complement* form. The number 934 is *not* the result of $425 - 491$, but -66 is. To get the correct answer, -66, the machine *recomplements* the answer obtained thus far.

	999	
Take the nine's complement	-934	
	65	
Add 1	$+\ \ 1$	
	66	ten's complement of 934

The absence of a carry out of the high order on the first ten's complement procedure indicated that the answer 934 was a negative number and also that it had to be *recomplemented*. After the recomplementation, the final answer can be expressed by the machine as a negative number in its true form, −66.

Sample Problem

$$\text{Subtract} \quad \begin{array}{r} 4235 \\ -\ 614 \\ \hline \end{array}$$

Note that in this problem the subtrahend is one position shorter than the minuend. If we were performing this subtraction in a four-position counter and in a manner similar to the procedures followed by an accounting machine, we would need to pad out the remaining subtrahend position with a zero and add a corresponding amount of 9's in the new minuend.[1]

$$\begin{array}{r} 4235 \\ -0614 \\ \hline \end{array}$$

	$\begin{array}{r} 9999 \\ -0614 \\ \hline \end{array}$
Nine's complement	9385
Add 1	$+\quad 1$
	$\overline{9386}$
Add original minuend	$+4235$
Convert the carry to a + sign	$+3621$

Using the same four-position counter, can we take the ten's complement of 0000?

$$\begin{array}{r} 9999 \\ -\ 0000 \\ \hline 9999 \\ +\quad 1 \\ \hline 10000 \end{array}$$

The four-position counter still contains our original 0000. Therefore, we say that the quantity zero *cannot* be complemented. Note that the ten's complement of 9999 is

$$\begin{array}{r} 9999 \\ -9999 \\ \hline 0000 \\ +\quad 1 \\ \hline 1 \end{array} \quad \text{ten's complement of 9999}$$

[1] Padding or annexing high-order zeros is done to ensure that the complement of the subtrahend has the same number of digits as the minuend.

EXERCISES 3-3

Perform decimal subtraction by the ten's complement method:

1. 3764   **2.** 7951   **3.** 7889   **4.** 8395   **5.** 6530
      −1045   − 263   −8910   − 26   −6809

6. 4096   **7.** 67552   **8.** 42031
      − 185   − 9021   − 1940

Binary Subtraction

Complement addition of binary numbers is the method by which most computers perform subtraction. The complement of a binary number is called the *two's* complement. A two's complement (of a binary number) is a number that, when added to a given number, will yield a complete set for a power of two. For example, if the given number is 1, 1 + 1 = 10. We say that 1 is the two's complement of 1.

To take the two's complement of binary numbers, begin by taking the *one's* complement of the subtrahend, then add 1 to get the two's complement.

Sample Problem

$$\text{Subtract} \quad \begin{array}{r} 1011 \\ -1001 \\ \hline \end{array}$$

This is performed by subtracting the subtrahend from a minuend of all ones:

$$\begin{array}{r} 1111 \\ 1001 \\ \hline 0110 \\ +\ \ \ 1 \\ \hline 0111 \end{array}$$

one's complement of subtrahend

two's complement of subtrahend

Another way to perform this procedure is to *invert*, or reverse, each binary digit and then add 1. If the original digit in the subtrahend is a 1, change it to zero; if zero, then change it to 1. Thus, 1001 becomes 0110 + 1 or 0111 without the operation of subtraction. Note that we have padded a zero to the left to give our complemented subtrahend the same number of positions or digits as our minuend.

Now add the two's complement of the subtrahend to the original minuend:

$$\begin{array}{r} 1011 \\ 0111 \\ \hline +0010 \end{array}$$

Carry out of the high order changed to a + sign}

If there were no carry out of the high order, our answer would be a negative number and would also be in complement form. The computer would detect this condition and recomplement the negative number.

Sample Problem

Subtract   101101
                −110001   001110
                                    +   1
                                    ──────────
                                      001111 ← two's complement of subtrahend
                                    +101101 ← original minuend
No carry out of high order   111100
                                      000011
                                    +   1
                                    ──────────
                                      −100   recomplemented answer

As an exercise, consider the following binary numbers to be found in bytes and perform the subtraction by the two's complement method:

$$10111011$$
$$−00110111$$
$$\overline{\text{result}}$$

Octal and Hexadecimal Subtraction

The complement addition operations for the octal and hexadecimal numeration systems are the same as they are for the decimal and binary numeration systems.

In the octal system, we first take the seven's complement of our subtrahend, then add one.

Sample Problem

Subtract $305_{(O)}$
              − $27_{(O)}$

Take the seven's complement of the subtrahend

                777
                027
              ──────
                750   seven's complement of subtrahend
              +   1
              ──────
                751   eight's complement of subtrahend
              +305   add in original minuend
Carry out of → +256
high order
as + sign

If there were no carry out of the high order, the answer would be a negative number in complement form. Of course, this kind of result would have to be recomplemented. For example, in octal:

$$
\begin{array}{r}
421 \\
-502 \\
\hline
\end{array}
$$

$$
\begin{array}{r}
777 \\
-502 \\
\hline
\end{array}
$$

$$
\begin{array}{rl}
275 & \text{seven's complement of subtrahend} \\
+\ \ 1 & \\
\hline
276 & \text{eight's complement of subtrahend} \\
+421 & \text{add original minuend} \\
\hline
717 & \text{no carry out of high order} \\
060 & \text{seven's complement of result} \\
+\ \ 1 & \\
\hline
-\ 61 & \text{recomplemented answer} \\
\end{array}
$$

In the hexadecimal system, we first take the fifteen's complement of our subtrahend and then add one.

Sample Problem

Subtract

$$
\begin{array}{r}
FAD_{(H)} \\
-ADD_{(H)} \\
\hline
\end{array}
$$

$$
\begin{array}{r}
FFF \\
ADD \\
\hline
\end{array}
$$

$$
\begin{array}{rl}
5\ 2\ 2 & \text{fifteen's complement of subtrahend} \\
+\ \ 1 & \\
\hline
5\ 2\ 3 & \text{sixteen's complement of subtrahend} \\
+FAD & \text{add in original minuend} \\
\hline
+4D\,0 & \\
\end{array}
$$

Carry out of
high order
as + sign

If there were no carry out of the high order, the answer would be negative and in complement form. To represent such an answer in true form requires *re*complementing. For example, in hexadecimal:

$$
\begin{array}{r}
ABE \\
-BEA \\
\hline
\end{array}
$$

$$
\begin{array}{r}
FFF \\
-BEA \\
\hline
\end{array}
$$

$$
\begin{array}{rl}
4\ 1\ 5 & \text{fifteen's complement of subtrahend} \\
+\ \ 1 & \\
\hline
4\ 1\ 6 & \text{sixteen's complement of subtrahend} \\
+ABE & \text{add original minuend} \\
\hline
ED4 & \text{no carry out of high order} \\
1\ 2\ B & \text{fifteen's complement of result} \\
+\ \ 1 & \\
\hline
-1\ 2\ C & \text{recomplemented answer} \\
\end{array}
$$

EXERCISES 3-4

1. What is the one's complement of 0? of 1?

2. Can you take the ten's complement of 000 and represent the result in three positions?

3. Subtract the following using complement addition.

In binary:

(a)	10110	(b)	1101	(c)	10101011	(d)	111011
	−10010		−1110		− 0111001		− 10110

In octal:

(e)	364	(f)	4075	(g)	32240	(h)	375
	−211		−4314		− 2051		− 26

In hexadecimal:

(i)	AFC	(j)	403B8	(k)	DEED	(l)	13FA6
	−495		− 14A9		− FEED		−10EAB

MULTIPLICATION

Binary Multiplication

Binary multiplication is perhaps the easiest of all the multiplication operations discussed in this chapter. Multiplication of binary numbers involves the simple manipulations of shift, copy, and add:

$$
\begin{array}{r}
101101 \\
\times \quad 101 \\
\hline
\end{array}
$$

Copy	101101
Shift one place left	000000
Shift one place left and copy	101101
	11100001

Octal and Hexadecimal Multiplication

Another method of multiplication sets up *partial products*. These partial products are then added together to yield the correct answer.

Sample Problem

$$
\text{Multiply in octal} \quad
\begin{array}{r}
437 \\
\times \ 25 \\
\hline
\end{array}
$$

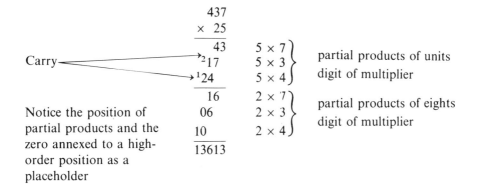

```
                    437
                  × 25
                  ____
                    43      5 × 7 ⎫
Carry————————————→²17      5 × 3 ⎬ partial products of units
                →¹24       5 × 4 ⎭ digit of multiplier
                  ____
                    16      2 × 7 ⎫
Notice the position of   06  2 × 3 ⎬ partial products of eights
partial products and the 10  2 × 4 ⎭ digit of multiplier
zero annexed to a high-  ____
order position as a      13613
placeholder
```

Sample Problem

Multiply in hexadecimal   4A2
                            × B5

```
                    4A2
                  ×  B5
                  ____
                    0A      5 × 2 ⎫
                    32      5 × A ⎬ partial products of units
                  ¹14       5 × 4 ⎭ digit of multiplier
                  ____
                    16      B × 2 ⎫ partial products of
Notice the position of   6 E  B × A ⎬ sixteens digit of
the partial products    ¹2C   B × 4 ⎭ multiplier
                  ____
                  34 6 8A
```

If the student is familiar with all the products of the various pairs of digits in a numeration system, multiplication is as easy in the binary, octal, and hexadecimal systems as it is in the decimal system.

EXERCISES 3-5

1. Construct multiplication tables in:
    (a) The binary system
    (b) The octal system
    (c) The hexadecimal system

2. Multiply the following binary numbers using the shift, copy, and add method:
    (a)   1011   **(b)**   101101   **(c)**   101110
        × 111   × 10001   × 1010

3. The following binary number is found in a byte.

$$\boxed{00001010}$$

Show the result of shifting left two positions. This is equivalent to multiplying by _____
_____. If we shifted right one position (padding one high-order zero), the result is
equivalent to _____ by _____.

4. The following is the result of multiplication:

$$\boxed{00011000}$$

If the product is derived by shifting left three positions, what was the multiplier? _____
_____. What was the multiplicand? _____.

5. Multiply the following octal numbers using the partial products method:
   (a)   137   (b)   1234   (c)   707
         × 20   × 56   × 45
         ─────   ─────   ────

6. Multiply the following hexadecimal numbers using the partial products method:
   (a)   1AD   (b)   F0F0   (c) C128
         ×   63   × DAB   × A09
         ─────   ─────   ─────

DIVISION

Binary Division

Binary division is like a series of repeated subtractions.

Sample Problem

$$\text{Divide in binary} \quad 10\overline{)11110}$$

$$
\begin{array}{r}
1111 \\
10\overline{)11110} \\
10 \\
\hline
11 \\
10 \\
\hline
11 \\
10 \\
\hline
10 \\
10 \\
\hline
\end{array}
$$

Note that division by two is similar to shifting right one position.

A remainder in a binary, octal, or hexadecimal division problem is treated in the same manner as a remainder in decimal division.

$$
\begin{array}{r}
11 \\
111\overline{)11000}
\end{array}
\quad
\frac{11}{111} \leftarrow \text{fraction}
$$

$$
\begin{array}{r}
111 \\ \hline
1010 \\
111 \\ \hline
11
\end{array}
$$

Octal and Hexadecimal Division

Using our skills in subtraction and referring to the multiplication tables from Exercise 3-5, we can perform division in the octal and hexadecimal systems.

Sample Problem

$$
\begin{array}{r}
324 \\
12\overline{)4111} \\
36
\end{array}
\quad
\frac{1}{12} \leftarrow \text{fraction}
$$

$$
\begin{array}{r}
\overline{31} \\
24 \\ \hline
51 \\
50 \\ \hline
1
\end{array}
$$

Sample Problem

$$
\begin{array}{r}
123 \\
A\overline{)B5E} \\
A
\end{array}
$$

$$
\begin{array}{r}
\overline{15} \\
14 \\ \hline
1E \\
1E
\end{array}
$$

EXERCISES 3-6

1. Divide the following binary numbers using repeated subtractions:
   (a) $11\overline{)11011}$
   (b) $110\overline{)10100}$
   (c) $101\overline{)1010101}$

2. Divide the following octal numbers using repeated subtractions:
    (a) 12⟌11174
    (b) 45⟌7200
    (c) 37⟌25376

3. Divide the following hexadecimal numbers using the repeated subtraction method:
    (a) E⟌C4
    (b) 2C⟌15088

4. Given $01011000_{(B)}$. Show the result of dividing by 2. How many positions did we shift right? Suppose the hexadecimal number 18 was the quotient (with no remainder) obtained by shifting right three times. What was the original dividend?

SHIFTING BINARY DIGITS

Multiplication and division by shifting binary bits left or right in a register present the following interesting situation.

Consider a register containing the hexadecimal value

$$\boxed{\text{0CA0}}$$

What would the result be of dividing by two, or performing one shift to the right and padding high-order zeros?

To divide by four, we must shift right two binary bits and pad high-order zeros to the left. What is the result of dividing the register above by four, that is, shifting right two positions?

Give the result for multiplying the register above by eight.

It is easy to see that we can alter hexadecimal values in registers by shifting and thereby alter the coding for instructions or data in a program. This is one method by which programmers can maintain privacy of files. For example, if at any time someone tried to read out the contents of main memory after the programmer had altered the hexadecimal values in a unique manner, no one could be sure of the program's instructions or data.

4

Conversions

Because computers can represent numbers in the three numeration systems we have been discussing, programmers need to be able to recognize these data items and to transform them if necessary from one numeration system to another. These transformations or conversions can be done quickly without expanded notation.

CONVERTING NUMBERS FROM ONE NUMERATION SYSTEM TO ANOTHER

Converting a decimal number to a number in base two, base eight, or base sixteen can be done using repeated division.

The *first dividend* is the decimal number to be converted.

The *divisor* is the base of the new numeration system, expressed as a decimal number.

The *remainder* is a digit in the new number.

Decimal to Binary

Convert $41_{(D)}$ to a binary number, following the explanation just given:

		Remainder in Binary
2	$\underline{|41}$	1
2	$\underline{|20}$	0
2	$\underline{|10}$	0
2	$\underline{|\,5}$	1
2	$\underline{|\,2}$	0
2	$\underline{|\,1}$	1
	0	

Each new quotient becomes the next successive dividend. Division ends with the last dividend greater than zero.

The digits in the remainder form a binary number when they are dropped to the right:

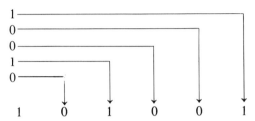

$41_{(D)}$ is 101001 in binary.

Decimal to Octal

Convert $163_{(D)}$ to an octal number:

$$
\begin{array}{ll}
8\underline{|163} & 3 \\
8\underline{\ |20} & 4 \\
8\underline{\ |2} & 2 \quad 4 \quad 3 \\
\quad\ \ 0
\end{array}
$$

$163_{(D)}$ is 243 in octal.

Decimal to Hexadecimal

Convert $285_{(D)}$ to a hexadecimal number:

$$
\begin{array}{ll}
16\underline{|285} & D \\
16\underline{\ |17} & 1 \\
16\underline{\ |1} & 1 \quad 1 \quad D \\
\quad\ \ \ 0
\end{array}
$$

$285_{(D)}$ is 11D in hexadecimal.

Octal to Decimal

Converting octal and hexadecimal numbers to decimal numbers can be done with repeated multiplications. The following rules help to convert octal numbers to decimal numbers:

1. Multiply the high-order octal digit by 8.

2. Add the next digit to the right as a decimal number, and express this sum as a decimal number.

3. Multiply this sum by 8.

4. Repeat this procedure until the units digit of the octal number has been added in, but do not multiply this last sum by 8.

Convert $324_{(O)}$ to a decimal number:

$$
\begin{array}{ccc}
3 & 2 & 4 \\
\times 8 \\
\hline
24 \\
+2 \leftarrow \\
\hline
26 \\
\times 8 \\
\hline
208 \\
+4 \leftarrow \\
\hline
212
\end{array}
$$

Checking this conversion by expanded notation, $324_{(O)}$ means

$$
\begin{array}{rl}
4 \times 8^0 = & 4 \\
+2 \times 8^1 = & 16 \\
+3 \times 8^2 = & 192 \\
\hline
& 212
\end{array}
$$

in decimal, and the result is verified.

Hexadecimal to Decimal

Following the rules for octal to decimal conversion, substituting 16 for a multiplier, and adding in hexadecimal digits as decimal numbers with decimal sums, convert $4B1_{(H)}$ to a decimal number:

$$
\begin{array}{ccc}
4 & B & 1 \\
\times 16 \\
\hline
64 \\
+11 \leftarrow \\
\hline
75 \\
\times 16 \\
\hline
1200 \\
+ 1 \leftarrow \\
\hline
1201
\end{array}
$$

Because $4B1_{(H)}$ means

$$1 \times 16^0 = \quad 1$$
$$11 \times 16^1 = \quad 176$$
$$4 \times 16^2 = \underline{1024}$$
$$1201$$

in decimal, the result is verified.

Binary to Decimal

Binary numbers may be converted to decimal numbers by first converting the binary number to its octal or hexadecimal equivalent and then converting the new octal or hexadecimal number to a decimal number.

Using binary triplets or binary quadruplets as we did in Chapter 2 convert $1011101_{(B)}$ to its octal and hexadecimal equivalents.

$$001 \ 011 \ 101_{(B)} = 135_{(O)} = 93_{(D)}$$

and

$$0101 \ 1101_{(B)} = 5D_{(H)} = 93_{(D)}$$

TABLE 4.1   POWERS

Base	0	1	2	3
Binary	1	2	4	8
Octal	1	8	64	512
Decimal	1	10	100	1000
Hexadecimal	1	16	256	4096

Table 4.1 shows a relationship of the powers of the bases of the four numeration systems under consideration in this chapter. Table 4.1 also may be used as a tool to convert binary, octal, and hexadecimal numbers to decimal numbers. For example, the octal number $435_{(O)}$ can be converted to its decimal equivalent in the following manner:

$$5 \times \ 1 = \quad 5$$
$$3 \times \ 8 = \quad 24$$
$$4 \times 64 = \underline{256}$$
$$285$$

Using Table 4.1, we find that octal 435 is equal to decimal 285. Table 4.1 may be expanded to include higher powers of the bases.

Octal and Hexadecimal Conversions

Using the binary numeration system, we are easily able to convert octal numbers to hexadecimal numbers or hexadecimal numbers to octal numbers:

Octal	4	7	3	0
Binary triplets	100	111	011	000
Regrouped as binary quadruplets		1001	1101	1000
Hexadecimal		9	D	8

Thus

$$4730_{(O)} = 9D8_{(H)}$$

As an exercise, convert $FAD_{(H)}$ to its octal equivalent by first writing the correct binary quadruplets, and then regrouping them into binary triplets.

EXERCISES 4-1

1. Convert the following decimal numbers to numbers in the binary, octal, and hexadecimal systems:
   (a)   25
   (b)   13
   (c)   81
   (d)   44
   (e)   121
   (f)   497
   (g) 5862

2. Convert the following binary numbers to octal, hexadecimal, and decimal numbers:
   (a)   1011011
   (b)   1011001101
   (c)   1011011011011
   (d)   100000111100101
   (e)   10101011011101111
   (f) 10111111110010111010

3. Convert the following octal numbers to binary, hexadecimal, and decimal numbers:
   (a)   127
   (b) 4610
   (c)   55
   (d)   103
   (e) 4200
   (f) 1111

4. Convert the following hexadecimal numbers to binary, octal, and decimal numbers:
  (a) DEED
  (b)   401
  (c)   EA2
  (d) BEAD
  (e) 129CF

5. Complete the following table:

Decimal	Binary	Octal	Hexadecimal
242			
	1101110		
		374	
			1ED4

CONVERSIONS OF FRACTIONS

The decimal fraction .534 can be represented as

$$\frac{5}{10} + \frac{3}{100} + \frac{4}{1000}$$

We can also express decimal numbers less than 1 by using negative exponents. Thus, .534 can be written as

$$.534 = (5 \times 10^{-1}) + (3 \times 10^{-2}) + (4 \times 10^{-3})$$
$$= .5 + .03 + .004$$
$$= .534$$

Each time we move one place to the right of the decimal point, the power of the base decreases by one. Using either fractions or negative powers of the base, we can convert binary, octal, and hexadecimal fractions to decimal fractions.

Binary to Decimal

Convert $.1011_{(B)}$ to a decimal fraction.
    We express each digit in the appropriate decimal equivalent of the powers of

base two. Thus

$$.1011 = (1 \times 2^{-1}) + (0 \times 2^{-2}) + (1 \times 2^{-3}) + (1 \times 2^{-4})$$

$$= \tfrac{1}{2} + 0 + \tfrac{1}{8} + \tfrac{1}{16} \qquad \text{(expressed as fractions)}$$

$$= \tfrac{11}{16} \qquad \text{(adding up the terms)}$$

$$= .6875 \qquad \text{(dividing)}$$

Octal to Decimal

Convert $.204_{(O)}$ to a decimal fraction.

$$.204_{(O)} = (2 \times 8^{-1}) + (0 \times 8^{-2}) + (4 \times 8^{-3})$$

$$= \tfrac{2}{8} + 0 + \tfrac{4}{512} \qquad \text{(expressed as fractions)}$$

$$= \tfrac{33}{128} \qquad \text{(adding up the terms)}$$

$$= .2578125 \qquad \text{(dividing)}$$

Hexadecimal to Decimal

Convert $.F8_{(H)}$ to a decimal fraction.

$$.F8 = (15 \times 16^{-1}) + (8 \times 16^{-2})$$

$$= \frac{15}{16} + \frac{8}{256} \qquad \text{(expressed as fractions)}$$

$$= \frac{248}{256} \qquad \text{(adding up the terms)}$$

$$= .96875 \qquad \text{(dividing)}$$

Binary and Hexadecimal Conversion

Given the binary number 11.111001. Annex high- and low-order zeros to complete full binary quadruplets to each side of the binary point and assign a hexadecimal digit to each quadruplet as follows:

	0011.11100100	in binary
means	3.E4	in hexadecimal

Binary and Octal Conversions

In a similar manner, we can convert binary fractions to octal fractions by grouping binary triplets starting from the binary point:

	010.101001	in binary
means	2.51	in octal

Decimal fractions can be converted to binary, octal, and hexadecimal fractions by using the base of one of these three numeration systems (written as a decimal number) as a multiplier. Multiplication is continued until the decimal fraction has been reduced to zero or until a sufficient number of binary, octal, or hexadecimal digits has been generated to approximate the original decimal fraction.

Decimal to Binary

Convert the decimal fraction 0.8125 into a binary fraction:

Decimal Fraction	Multiplier	Product	Binary Digits
.8125	× 2	= 1.6250	1
.6250	× 2	= 1.2500	1
.2500	× 2	= 0.5000	0
.5000	× 2	= 1.0000	1

Multiplying .8125 by 2 yields 1.6250. The decimal integer 1 becomes the first binary digit. The second multiplication uses the resulting decimal fraction, .6250, as its multiplicand. After the fourth multiplication, the resulting decimal fraction is .0000 and we need not multiply any more. Digits in the last column on the right are dropped to the left:

$$\begin{array}{c}\boxed{}1 \\ \boxed{}1 \\ \downarrow\downarrow\downarrow 0 \\ .1101\end{array}$$

Thus, $0.8125_{(D)} = 0.1101_{(B)}$.

Decimal to Octal

Using 8 as a multiplier, we can convert decimal fractions to octal fractions.
Convert the decimal fraction 0.975 to an octal fraction:

Decimal Fraction	Multiplier	Product	Octal Digits
.975	× 8	= 7.800	7
.8	× 8	= 6.4	6
.4	× 8	= 3.2	3
.2	× 8	= 1.6	1
.6	× 8	= 4.8	4
.8	× 8	= 6.4	6
.4	× 8	= 3.2	3
.2	× 8	= 1.6	1
.6	× 8	= 4.8	4

Dropping the octal digits to the left, we obtain the repeating octal fraction .763146314.... Nine digits are shown in this example since a sufficient number of significant digits was generated to illustrate the conversion. Converting $0.975_{(D)}$ to octal 0.763146314... provides an example of a result that is a nonterminating fraction.

Decimal to Hexadecimal

Using 16 as a multiplier, we can convert decimal fractions to hexadecimal fractions. Convert the decimal fraction 0.69921875 to a hexadecimal fraction:

Decimal Fraction	Multiplier	Product	Hexadecimal Digits
.69921875	× 16	= 11.18750000	B
.1875	× 16	= 3.0000	3

The hexadecimal digit B is placed immediately to the right of the hexadecimal point, and the 3 is placed after the B. Thus, 0.B3 is our resulting hexadecimal fraction.

EXERCISES 4-2

Complete the following table:

	Decimal	Binary	Octal	Hexadecimal
1.	0.92			
2.		1101111.10011000		
3.				1.00C
4.			276.532	
5.	.25			
6.			3.33	
7.				.A9
8.		1.11001101		

Problems do arise with the conversion of fractions. For example, there is no exact binary representation for decimal .1. Binary .00011001 converted to a decimal is represented as

$$2^{-4} = \quad .0625$$
$$+2^{-5} = +.03125$$
$$+2^{-8} = +.00390625$$
$$\overline{\quad\quad\quad .09765625}$$

and only closely approximates $.1_{(D)}$. This means that there is also no exact binary representation for $.1 + .1 = .2$ in decimal. As an exercise, try to approximate decimal .2 to eight decimal fraction positions using negative powers of base two.

On computers that performed only pure binary arithmetic, this caused adjustments to be made in important tasks such as preparing payroll checks and billing customers. In the next chapter, we will learn how binary-coded decimal numbers overcome this problem and how computations in business problems can be exact to the penny.

5

Codes and Data Representation

Various schemes have been developed, using the place value of binary digits, to create codes that relate decimal values to groups of binary digits and thus can be used to exchange information in computer-to-human communications. While all these coding schemes have their basis in the binary numeration system, they may vary from one manufacturer's model to another. Some of the most commonly used coding schemes are

Binary-Coded-Decimal or BCD, a 4-bit code

American Standard Code For Information Interchange or ASCII, which may be a 6-bit or 7-bit code

Extended Binary-Coded-Decimal Interchange Code or EBCDIC, an 8-bit code

BINARY-CODED-DECIMAL

Because ten decimal digits, 0 to 9, must be represented, a minimum of 4 binary bits (or a binary quadruplet) is needed to encode each decimal digit. Systems that translate binary data to decimal digits in this manner are called Binary-Coded-Decimal or BCD.

Table 5.1 illustrates relationships between binary digits and decimal values in several BCD codes:

TABLE 5.1

Decimal	8421-BCD	2421-BCD	Excess-3
0	0000	0000	0011
1	0001	0001	0100
2	0010	0010	0101
3	0011	0011	0110
4	0100	0100	0111
5	0101	1011	1000
6	0110	1100	1001
7	0111	1101	1010
8	1000	1110	1011
9	1001	1111	1100

8421-BCD Code

The 8421-BCD code is a commonly used 4-bit code. Refer to the 8421-BCD code in Table 5.1. Binary 0100 is equivalent to decimal 4; 1001 in binary is equivalent to decimal 9. Using this method, we find that the decimal number 72 is represented in two binary quadruplets as

$$
\begin{array}{ll}
7 \quad 2 & \text{in decimal} \\
0111 \ 0010 & \text{in 8421-BCD}
\end{array}
$$

In a simple but efficient method, the four bits are assigned or *weighted* with decimal values of 8, 4, 2, and 1. The binary quadruplets 1010 through 1111 are not used to represent decimal numbers in this particular BCD code.

Given the 8421-BCD numbers

$$0001001101000111$$

find its decimal equivalent by separating this binary number into quadruplets:

$$0001,0011,0100,0111$$

Use the values 8, 4, 2, and 1 in each quadruplet in the second column of Table 5.1 to get decimal 1347.

Note that if we convert these same binary digits using place value alone and ignoring the BCD quadruplets, we derive a different value:

$$0001001101000111 = 1 \times 2^{12} = 4096$$
$$1 \times 2^9 = 512$$
$$1 \times 2^8 = 256$$
$$1 \times 2^6 = 64$$
$$1 \times 2^2 = 4$$
$$1 \times 2^1 = 2$$
$$1 \times 2^0 = 1$$
$$\overline{4935}_{(D)}$$

When we use place values only for these binary digits, the decimal equivalent is 4935—not the value, 1347, represented in the 8421-BCD code.

Since the weight of each bit in the quadruplet becomes greater by a power of two as we move one place to the left, the 8421-BCD code is often called the *natural* BCD system.

Arithmetic in 8421-BCD

Consider the following addition example:

Example 1

8421-BCD		Decimal
0101		5
+0011		+3
1000	8421-BCD eight	8

This example is straightforward but problems arise. In decimal, a carry is forced on the tenth count. In a binary quadruplet, a carry is generated on the sixteenth count. The computer must add a binary six (0110) when a sum results in binary numbers that are greater than 1001 since binary numbers 1010 through 1111 are not permitted in *8421-BCD*. These and other correction factors can make BCD arithmetic circuits complex and their arithmetic operations take more time than the binary arithmetic operations described in Chapter 3.

Example 2

8421-BCD		Decimal
0110		6
+1000		+8
1110	binary fourteen	
+0110	correction factor	
0001 0100	8421-BCD fourteen	14

Adding a binary six "skips" over the six unused BCD codes or adds six if the result is greater than nine.

Consider an example in subtraction.

Example 3

8421-BCD		Decimal
0011 0100		34
−0001 0100		−14
0010 0000	8421-BCD twenty	20

When no "borrows" are forced, corrections are not needed. However, in our next example, a correction factor of six is needed because a borrow is made on the fifth binary digit with a weight of sixteen instead of ten.

Example 4

8421-BCD		Decimal
0010 0100		24
−0001 0111		−17
0000 1101	binary thirteen	
−0110	correction factor	
0111	8421-BCD seven	7

In the last example, an additional binary six was subtracted from binary thirteen to derive seven in 8421-BCD.

2421-BCD and Excess-3 Codes

Some other four-bit codes are 2421-BCD and excess-3 codes. *The 2421-BCD code* weights a group of four binary digits, 2, 4, 2, and 1, where the most significant bit has a value of 2 instead of 8. In this BCD code, the highest number possible is 9 since $2 + 4 + 2 + 1 = 9$. However, this creates two representations for digits 2 through 7.

In Table 5.1 note that we have selected weights so that digits 0 to 4 begin with 0 and digits 5 to 9 begin with 1.

The excess-3 code is formed by simply adding three to each BCD quadruplet as shown in Table 5.1. It is an *unweighted* code since the bit positions or place values are not assigned to a power of base two. However, the excess-3 code is useful in obtaining the 9's complement of a decimal digit. For example, 4 is the 9's complement of 5 and by a 1's complement in the excess-3 code, we can derive 4 as shown here:

Complementing	1000	excess-3	5
results in	0111	excess-3	4

Because the 9's complement is generated by complementing each bit in the excess-3 quadruplet, we can say that the excess-3 code is *self-complementing*. When the 9's complement of a decimal number is comparable to the 1's complement in binary, it is useful in performing decimal subtraction. Self-complementing is also a property of the 2421-BCD code. As an exercise, show that 3 is the 9's complement of 6 in 2421-BCD.

EXERCISES 5-1

1. The _____ code is a four-bit code.
2. Two weighted codes are _____ and _____.
3. The _____ BCD code is an unweighted code.
4. In a weighted BCD code, each binary _____ can represent a _____ number.
5. If a BCD code represents decimal 2 as 0101 and decimal 7 as 1010, it can be described as _____.

6. Why is 1010 in 8421-BCD not permitted? _____.

7. For 10000101
   (a) Give its decimal equivalent in 2421-BCD. _____
   (b) Using the powers of base two only, give its decimal equivalent. _____

8. Perform the following in 8421-BCD:
(a)	1000	(b)	0101	(c)	0110	(d)	0111	(e)	0011 0100
	+0101		+0111		+0011		+1000		+0001 0110

9. Perform the following in 8421-BCD:
(a)	0011 0010	(b)	1001 0010	(c)	0101 0001	(d)	1000 1000
	−0010 0111		−1001 0001		−0011 0110		−0111 0110

10. Find the 9's complement in the excess-3 code for the following:
    (a) 0011 (b) 1010 (c) 0111 (d) 0100 0101
11. Show why 9 + 9, 9 + 8, 9 + 7, and 8 + 8 in 8421-BCD also need the correction factor.

THE AMERICAN STANDARD CODE FOR INFORMATION INTERCHANGE OR ASCII

The ASCII code is an alphanumeric code found in many kinds of computer systems. Alphanumeric refers to all digits, alphabetic characters, and special characters such as the "*," asterisk, "?," question mark, "$," dollar sign, and the like. A 6-bit ASCII code contains codes for 64 characters or 2^6 characters, including upper-case letters, numerics, and special characters. However, the code is limited since it does not provide for lower-case letters.

With the 7-bit or full ASCII code, both upper-case and lower-case letters are included as well as the numeric, special, and control characters for operations such as printing. The 7-bit code is typically used with input and output devices and contains 2^7 or 128 character codes. Another version of the ASCII code uses an 8-bit code for 2^8 or 256 codes.

Table 5.2 shows the internal computer codes for the ASCII 7-bit code and the 8-bit Extended Binary Coded Decimal Interchange Code (EBCDIC), two very commonly used codes for representing alphanumeric data.

TABLE 5.2

Character	7-Bit ASCII	EBDIC	Character	7-Bit ASCII	EBDIC
0	011 0000	1111 0000	a	110 0001	1000 0001
1	011 0001	1111 0001	b	110 0010	1000 0010
2	011 0010	1111 0010	c	110 0011	1000 0011
3	011 0011	1111 0011	d	110 0100	1000 0100
4	011 0100	1111 0100	e	110 0101	1000 0101
5	011 0101	1111 0101	f	110 0110	1000 0110
6	011 0110	1111 0110	g	110 0111	1000 0111
7	011 0111	1111 0111	h	110 1000	1000 1000
8	011 1000	1111 1000	i	110 1001	1000 1001
9	011 1001	1111 1001	j	110 1010	1001 0001
A	100 0001	1100 0001	k	110 1011	1001 0010
B	100 0010	1100 0010	l	110 1100	1001 0011
C	100 0011	1100 0011	m	110 1101	1001 0100
D	100 0100	1100 0100	n	110 1110	1001 0101
E	100 0101	1100 0101	o	110 1111	1001 0110
F	100 0110	1100 0110	p	111 0000	1001 0111
G	100 0111	1100 0111	q	111 0001	1001 1000
H	100 1000	1100 1000	r	111 0010	1001 1001
I	100 1001	1100 1001	s	111 0011	1010 0010
J	100 1010	1101 0001	t	111 0100	1010 0011
K	100 1011	1101 0010	u	111 0101	1010 0100
L	100 1100	1101 0011	v	111 0110	1010 0101
M	100 1101	1101 0100	w	111 0111	1010 0110
N	100 1110	1101 0101	x	111 1000	1010 0111
O	100 1111	1101 0110	y	111 1001	1010 1000
P	101 0000	1101 0111	z	111 1010	1010 1001
Q	101 0001	1101 1000	Examples of several special characters follow:		
R	101 0010	1101 1001	space	010 0000	0100 0000
S	101 0011	1110 0010	.	010 1110	0100 1011
T	101 0100	1110 0011	,	010 1100	0110 1011
U	101 0101	1110 0100	$	010 0100	0101 1011
V	101 0110	1110 0101	*	010 1010	0101 1100
W	101 0111	1110 0110	+	010 1011	0100 1110
X	101 1000	1110 0111	−	010 1101	0110 0000
Y	101 1001	1110 1000	/	010 1111	0110 0001
Z	101 1010	1110 1001	=	011 1101	0111 1110

Programmers often need to look at "memory maps" or printouts of internal computer memory in order to verify their data or to analyze errors. The following is an abbreviated example of a memory map in 7-bit ASCII. Note that the leftmost column contains the addresses of the first byte in the next column to the right. These addresses are given as hexadecimal numbers. Note also that bytes are grouped in twos. This means that each line of this memory map contains a storage address and a row of sixteen bytes. This is further seen by examining the address in each succeeding row whose numbers are sixteen greater than the address in the preceding row.

Storage Address	Hexadecimal Values 7-Bit ASCII							
000400	2020	2020	2053	5953	5445	4D20	3130	3020
000410	4649	4C45	2020	2020	352F	312F	3837	2020
000420	5550	4441	5445	2020	2020	2020	2020	2020

The digits 53 found in the first row translate to

101 0011

in the 7-bit ASCII. A reference to Table 5.2 shows that 101 0011 is the binary equivalent for the letter "S." As an exercise, translate all these 7-bit ASCII codes to alphanumeric characters.

EXTENDED BINARY CODED DECIMAL INTERCHANGE CODE OR EBCDIC

The EBCDIC code is an 8-bit code that provides for 256 or 2^8 possible codes. On many main-frame computers, decimal numbers are represented in the EBDIC format and the memory maps for COBOL and Assembler language programs, for only two examples, have many similarities.

Decimal arithmetic in the BCD codes and in EBCDIC is often used for accounting and other kinds of business and banking problems where repetitious calculations must be made. Numbers ranging to millions of dollars can be computed and results given exactly to the penny.

When used in computations, the EBCDIC format is altered by removing the four high-order bits in each byte to represent numbers in a packed decimal format. Refer to Table 5.2. The number 125 is stored in the EBCDIC format as F1F2F5. When it is transformed to a packed decimal, it appears as 125F.

Packed Decimal Arithmetic

Two decimal digits are *packed* into one byte with the exception of the low-order half-byte used to contain the sign of the number. The length of a packed decimal number may be from 1 to 16 bytes long and contain 1 to 31 decimal digits, with the low-order four binary bits used for a sign. The following illustrates this arrangement of digits and sign:

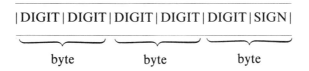

| DIGIT | DIGIT | DIGIT | DIGIT | DIGIT | SIGN |

byte   byte   byte

Each decimal digit (and the sign) is coded in four binary bits. Digits 0 to 9 are represented as binary 0000 to 1001. Binary 1010 to 1111 or hexadecimal A to F are not permitted as digits, but they may be used to sign a number. Usually the hexadecimal digits A, C, E, and F are used for positive, B and D for negative. The hexadecimal F may be found on unsigned numbers. Digits 0 through 9, or binary 0000 to 1001, are invalid signs. Thus,

00101000	00101100

is recognized as 282+ and

00110100	00011101

is recognized as 341 −.

Packed decimal arithmetic is usually performed in main storage on many mainframe computers. However, decimal points, dollar signs, and commas are not computational and do not appear in this format. The programmer must define the size of the numbers and keep track of decimal fraction positions. In programming languages such as COBOL and Assembler language, the programmer is responsible for inserting the commas, decimal points, and dollar signs after calculations have been performed.

At the end of Chapter 4, we noted that there is no binary equivalent for .1 in decimal. The next problem illustrates how packed decimal arithmetic provides results that are exactly to the nearest penny, correcting a deficiency in pure binary arithmetic. Given the numbers $1_\wedge 3197+$ and $0_\wedge 0050+$ where the "$_\wedge$," or the caret, represents an assumed decimal (or binary) point, study the following example, rounding to the nearest penny:

	Binary Numbers	Decimal
	00000000 0001$_\wedge$0011 00011001 01111100	$1_\wedge 3197+$
+	0000$_\wedge$0000 00000101 00001100	$0_\wedge 0050+$
	00000000 0001$_\wedge$0011 00011110 01111100	

The "+" sign remains unchanged but because binary quadruplet, 1110, is not permitted to represent a decimal digit, proceed as we did on page 57 by adding binary six or 0110 to this quadruplet.

$$00000000 \quad 0001_\wedge 0011 \quad 00011110 \quad 01111100$$
$$+ \qquad\qquad\qquad\qquad\qquad\qquad\qquad 0110$$
$$\overline{00000000 \quad 0001_\wedge 0011 \quad 00100100 \quad 01111100}$$

which results in $1_\wedge 3247C$ or $1_\wedge 3247+$.

Before printing this result, the programmer truncates the unwanted digits 47, the sign is retained and a decimal point inserted via editing commands. After using an edit command, this data item will appear in storage without high-order zeros as

F14BF3C2

Refer to Table 5.2 and verify these EBCDIC characters, which now appear in an "unpacked" format where each digit occupies one byte. The low-order digit is preceded by the sign after the number is "unpacked."

EXERCISES 5-2

1. The 6-bit ASCII code provides for _____ characters and the 7-bit ASCII code provides for _____ characters.

2. Why are 64 different character codes possible in the 6-bit ASCII code?

3. When is packed decimal arithmetic more useful than straight binary arithmetic?

4. Complete the following table, making the necessary conversions for alphanumeric characters.

EBCDIC	7-Bit ASCII	Character
1111 0011	011 0011	—
—— ——	—— ——	A
—— ——	101 0000	—
0101 1011	—— ——	—
—— ——	010 0000	—
—— ——	—— ——	U
1000 0010	—— ——	—
—— ——	111 1010	—

5. When memory maps are printed in EBCDIC, the 8-bit codes are not given in binary digits but as hexadecimal values. For example, the letters ASCII would appear in an 8-bit EBCDIC memory map as

C1E2C3C9C9

Refer to Exercise 4 and give the hexadecimal values for all the EBCDIC codes.

6. (a) Convert the following social security number to EBCDIC.

041-31-8765

Be sure to include the editing dashes.

(b) How many 8-bit bytes in internal storage are required for this number?

7. Give the EBCDIC representation for the following:

(a) $24.95

(b) $1,402.96

(c) 65.00

(d) *Register

(e) + or −

8. Give the packed decimal representation for the following:

(a) 1347−

(b) 203+

(c) 41863+

(d) 9600−

9. The following is a portion of a storage map in EBCDIC. Storage addresses in hexadecimal numbers are given in the column on the left. The following sixteen bytes in each row contain alphabetic data items in EBCDIC and numeric data items in packed decimal.

Address	EBCDIC Values	
017C	E2A38199A3409686	40E3818293854040
018C	0000129C0000100C	0000321C0000204D
019C	0000188C_____	_____

(a) Decode the EBCDIC characters in the first line.

(b) Complete, giving the address (in hexadecimal) of the high-order byte of the packed decimal data items.

Data Item	Address
129C	018E
100C	____
____	____
____	____
____	____

(c) Find the total for these numeric data items. Place the total in storage beginning at address 01A4 and pad out unused positions in the third line with blank spaces.

The multiplication operation in BCD arithmetic can be thought of as a series of addition and division as a series of subtractions. The number of bytes in the result must be large enough to accommodate the product in multiplication. In division, the remainder may be found in computer storage to the right of the resulting quotient. Managing arithmetic operations is discussed in Chapter 8.

REPRESENTING NUMBERS WITH EXPONENTS

When numbers of mixed and varied magnitudes are used in calculations, and when it is necessary for the computer to store as many significant digits as possible, floating-point registers are employed. This is done by storing a number in three parts:

1. The sign of the number
2. The characteristic used to determine the exponent or power of the base
3. The number represented as a binary fraction (a value less than 1)

A number is represented as a product of the binary fraction and the power (or exponent). In IBM computers, there are single, double, and extended precision numbers. The size of these numbers is measured in bits or binary digits:

Single precision numbers—32-bits

Double precision numbers—64-bits

Extended precision numbers—128-bits

To simplify our explanation and to use fewer binary digits in our description, we will discuss the 32-bit or single precision numbers. See Figure 5.1. IBM numbers the bits from 0 to 31, with bit numbered 0 used for the sign.

Bits	0	1–7	8–31
	Sign	Characteristic	Binary fraction

Figure 5.1

The sign bit is set to 0 for positive numbers, 1 for negative numbers. Both positive and negative numbers are represented in the same way in true form. When the bit numbered 1 has the value 1, the power or exponent is positive. Adding a 1 to the characteristic multiplies the binary fraction by a power of 16. Both the characteristic and the fraction are represented in true form, that is, as if positive.

Refer to Table 5.3, which shows a relationship between several binary and decimal fractions:

TABLE 5.3 BINARY AND DECIMAL FRACTIONS

Power	Binary Fraction	Decimal Fraction
2^{-1}	.1	.5
2^{-2}	.01	.25
2^{-3}	.001	.125
2^{-4}	.0001	.0625
2^{-5}	.00001	.03125
2^{-6}	.000001	.015625
2^{-7}	.0000001	.0078125
2^{-8}	.00000001	.00390625
2^{-9}	.000000001	.001953125

With the negative powers of base two represented by the number of places to the right of the binary point, it is possible to write decimal fractions as the sum of binary fractions. For example

.75 in decimal is equivalent to $2^{-1} + 2^{-2}$ in binary

.53125 in decimal is equivalent to $2^{-1} + 2^{-5}$ in binary

.375 in decimal is equivalent to $2^{-2} + 2^{-3}$ in binary

Assume the following is found in a floating-point register. The sign, 0, denotes a positive number:

$$0 \quad 1000001 \quad 00010000 \quad 00000000 \quad 00000000$$

In the preceding example, the characteristic has a 1 in bit position 1 to specify a positive exponent and a 1 in bit position 7 to multiply the binary fraction by 16^1.

The binary fraction in positions 8 to 31 is

$$_\wedge 000100 \ldots \quad \text{or} \quad .0625_{(D)}$$

where "$_\wedge$" refers to an assumed binary point. The actual binary point is assumed by the computer and is never part of the floating-point register. We can now compute the number in the single-precision floating-point register as

$$16^1 \times 2^{-4} = 16 \times .0625_{(D)}$$

$$= 1.0 \quad \text{in decimal}$$

Since the characteristic is seven positions long, and the leftmost digit is always used for the sign of the exponent, we can write a simple procedure to derive quickly a number in the floating-point register.

Given the following floating-point number

$$0 \quad 1000001 \quad 110000000000000000000000$$

the sign bit is 0; therefore, the number is positive. The characteristic is $1000001_{(B)} = 65_{(D)}$. Let c equal the characteristic and n the power on 16. Then the characteristic minus 2^6 (or 64) equals the exponent. Using x to represent the binary fraction, we can write in general terms

$$c - 64 = n$$

and

$$_\wedge x_{(B)} \times 16^n = \text{result in decimal}$$

Thus

$$65 - 64 = 1$$

and

$$_{\wedge}11_{(B)} \times 16^1 = .75_{(D)} \times 16$$

$$= 12_{(D)}$$

Refer to Table 5.4, which shows the relationship between some powers of base sixteen and decimal equivalents. This might be helpful in solving the next problem and the exercises at the end of this section.

TABLE 5.4

Power	Decimal Equivalent
16^5	1048576
16^4	65536
16^3	4096
16^2	256
16^1	16
16^0	1
16^{-1}	.0625
16^{-2}	.00390625
16^{-3}	.00024414
16^{-4}	.000015258
16^{-5}	.000000953

Given

$$1 \ 0111101 \ 101000 \ldots = ?$$

The bit zero contains a 1; therefore, the number is negative. The characteristic is 0111101, with a 0 in the leftmost position. Thus, the exponent will have a minus sign.
Then

$$c - 2^6 = 61 - 64 = -3$$

the exponent for base sixteen.

The binary fraction is $_{\wedge}101$ or $.625_{(D)}$. The number stored in the register is computed as

$$-.625 \times 16^{-3} = -.625 \times .0002441$$

$$= -.000152587$$

Reversing our procedure, find the contents of a single-precision floating-point register for 24.5:

$$24.5 = 11000.1_{(B)} = {}_{\wedge}110001_{(B)} \times 2^5$$

Next, make the exponent a multiple of 4 so that we can easily change to base sixteen by dividing 4 into an exponent on 2. Thus

$$_\wedge 110001 \times 2^5 = {_\wedge}000110001 \times 2^8$$

Then

$$24.5 = {_\wedge}000110001 \times 16^2$$

(When an exponent is not a multiple of 4, move the binary point the appropriate number of positions.)

Find the characteristic as follows:

$$c - 64 = 2$$

or

$$c = 2 + 64$$

$$c = 66 = 1000010_{(B)}$$

The 32-bit floating-point register contains

$$0 \ \ 1000010 \ \ 00011000100\ldots$$

Given -38.51, find the contents of a single-precision floating-point register:

$$38.51 = 100110.1_{(B)} \qquad \text{(approximation)}$$

Making the base two exponent a multiple of 4, we have

$$100110.1_{(B)} = {_\wedge}001001101_{(B)} \times 2^8$$

$$= {_\wedge}001001101_{(B)} \times 16^2$$

and

$$c - 64 = 2$$

$$c = 66$$

$$= 1000010_{(B)}$$

The 32-bit floating-point register contains

$$1 \ \ 1000010 \ \ 00100110100\ldots$$

As noted in Chapter 4, there is no exact binary equivalent for the decimal fraction .1 and a reference to Table 5.3 will indicate this.

Of course, we could do some or all of our computations in larger double or extended precision numbers to improve accuracy, but there will still not be an exact binary representation for some decimal fractions.

Although most round-off errors are slight, they can be computationally poor when repeated many times in business problems such as payroll checks or mortgage amortization schedules to name only two applications. Business arithmetic is performed accurately with the Binary-Coded-Decimal formats (BCD) discussed earlier.

We can summarize the discussion on coding numeric data items by stating that most main-frame computer systems represent numbers in one of three ways:

Straight binary where arithmetic is performed in general-purpose registers

Binary-coded-decimal and EBCDIC where arithmetic is performed in storage

Floating-point or exponential representation where arithmetic is performed in floating-point registers

EXERCISES 5-3

1. Express the following binary numbers as decimal fractions:
   (a) .1011
   (b) .00010001
   (c) .00101
   (d) .100000001
   (e) .00111
2. Rewrite the following as binary fractions multiplied by a power of 2 divisible by 4:
   (a) 100.11
   (b) 10110.001
   (c) 100001.1011
   (d) $.101 \times 2^{-1}$
   (e) $.0001 \times 2^{3}$
3. Express the following 32-bit single-precision numbers as decimal numbers:
   (a) 1 1000000 10000000 00000000 00000000
   (b) 0 1000010 10100000 ...
   (c) 0 1000011 11100000 ...
   (d) 0 0111111 00110000 ...
4. Represent the following decimal numbers as 32-bit single-precision numbers:
   (a) -5.25
   (b)   .625
   (c)   4.0
   (d) 2304
5. The following are hexadecimal representations for 32-bit single-precision values:

Value	Sign	Exponent	Binary Fraction
(a) 4360 0000			
(b) BE23 0000			
(c) C154 0000			

Give the sign, exponent, and binary fraction for parts (a), (b), and (c).

6

Related Topics in Algebra

This chapter reviews several basic topics in algebra that will be required to understand much of the material in the chapters that follow.

- The axioms for arithmetic operations on the set of real numbers
- Properties or behavior of real numbers with respect to those operations
- Replacement sets and solution sets in equations
- The evaluation of mathematical expressions
- The handling of inequalities

AXIOMS FOR OPERATIONS

Axioms describe the behavior of elements in the set of real numbers where at least two real numbers are assumed to exist. Operations, sometimes referred to as binary operations, are addition and multiplication, and these arithmetic operations manipulate and assign to a pair of elements in the set of real numbers another element in the set of real numbers, which is the result of that manipulation. Simple examples are

$$1 + 2 = 3$$

where 1, 2, 3 are elements in the set of real numbers.

$$3 \times 5 = 15$$

where 3, 5, 15 are elements in the set of real numbers.

The result of an operation may not always be different from the original pair of real numbers being manipulated as in

$$0 + 0 = 0$$

$$1 \times 1 = 1$$

The following hold true for all real numbers a, b and c:

1. CLOSURE AXIOM FOR ADDITION

$$a + b \text{ yields a unique real number}$$

(In the language of sets, if $a \in R$ and $b \in R$, then $a + b \in R$ where R is the set of real numbers)

2. COMMUTATIVE AXIOM FOR ADDITION

$$a + b = b + a$$

3. ASSOCIATIVE AXIOM FOR ADDITION

$$(a + b) + c = a + (b + c)$$

4. IDENTITY AXIOM FOR ADDITION
There is a real number 0 such that for any real number a,

$$a + 0 = 0 + a = a$$

5. INVERSE AXIOM FOR ADDITION
For every real number a, there is a real number $-a$ such that

$$a + (-a) = (-a) + a = 0$$

This number, $-a$, is called the *additive inverse* of a.

6. CLOSURE AXIOM FOR MULTIPLICATION

$$a \times b \qquad \text{yields a real number}$$

(If $a \in R$ and $b \in R$, then $a \times b \in R$)

7. COMMUTATIVE AXIOM FOR MULTIPLICATION

$$a \times b = b \times a$$

8. ASSOCIATIVE AXIOM FOR MULTIPLICATION

$$(a \times b) \times c = a \times (b \times c)$$

9. IDENTITY AXIOM FOR MULTIPLICATION
There is a real number 1 such that for any real number a

$$a \times 1 = a \quad \text{and} \quad 1 \times a = a, \quad \text{or} \quad a \times 1 = 1 \times a = a$$

10. INVERSE AXIOM FOR MULTIPLICATION

For every real number $a \neq 0$, there is a real number $1/a$ such that

$$a \times \frac{1}{a} = \frac{1}{a} \times a = 1$$

This number, $1/a$, is called the *multiplicative inverse* of a.

11. DISTRIBUTIVE AXIOM FOR MULTIPLICATION WITH RESPECT TO ADDITION

$$a \times (b + c) = (a \times b) + (a \times c)$$

Axioms 1 and 6 state that the sum or product of any two real numbers is a real number and that this sum or product is unique to the pair of numbers being operated on. This means that there is one and only one real number that satisfies the operation. For example

$$3 + 4 = 7$$

Seven is the unique answer. There is no other real number that satisfies the operation of addition for the numbers 3 and 4.

Axioms 2 and 7 state that the order in which a pair of real numbers is to be added or multiplied does not alter the sum or product. For example

$$4 + 3 = 7 \quad \text{and} \quad 3 + 4 = 7$$
$$4 \times 3 = 12 \quad \text{and} \quad 3 \times 4 = 12$$

Axioms 3 and 8 state that when three numbers are added or multiplied, they may be grouped in either of two ways without altering the result. For example

$$(3 \times 4) \times 2 = 12 \times 2 = 24$$
$$3 \times (4 \times 2) = 3 \times 8 = 24$$

Axiom 4 describes zero as the identity element for addition.

Axiom 9 describes 1 as the identity element for multiplication.

In Axiom 5 note that both a and $-a$ are real numbers, and that when a is added to its additive inverse, the identity element 0 results.

In Axiom 10, a given number, when multiplied by its multiplicative inverse, yields the identity element for multiplication. This holds true for any real number a except 0.

Axiom 11 states that multiplication is distributive with respect to addition. The multiplier can be distributed among the terms it multiplies. For example

$$2(3 + 5) = (2 \times 3) + (2 \times 5) = 16$$

It should be noted that addition is not distributive with respect to multiplication. Thus

$$2 + (3 \times 5) \neq (2 + 3) \times (2 + 5)$$

About Subtraction and Division

Subtraction. Earlier we described negative numbers as residing to the left of the 0 on the number line. In Axiom 5, we wrote a and its additive inverse $-a$, and thus assumed the negative of a number. For example, if $a = 3$, then $-a = -3$. However, if $a = -3$, then $-a = 3$ and $-(-3) = +3$. This concept of the negative of a number makes subtraction possible and permits such results as $2 - 5 = -3$.

The *difference* between two numbers, usually denoted as $a - b$, may also be expressed as the addition of the additive inverse. Thus

$$a - b = a + (-b)$$

Division. The operation of finding a quotient of two numbers is called division. In Axiom 10, we expressed the operation of division in the term $1/a$. If we denote the multiplicative inverse of a as a^{-1}, then $a \times 1/a = a \times a^{-1} = 1$.

This nomenclature for the multiplicative inverse makes it possible for us to express the quotient of two numbers a/b as $a \times b^{-1}$. We can define division by stating that a number x is said to be divided by a number d if there exists a number q such that $q \cdot d = x$. The number d is called the divisor, and the number q is called the quotient. The number x is called the dividend.

About Equality

In Chapter 1, the relationships between numbers was expressed as *ordered*. That is, for any pair of real numbers x and y, only one of the following relationships is possible.

$$x > y, \quad x = y, \quad \text{or} \quad x < y$$

In examining the equals, or equality relationship, we note that it can be expressed in the following laws:

$a = a$	Reflexive Law
If $a = b$, then $b = a$	Symmetric Law
If $a = b$ and $b = c$, then $a = c$	Transitive Law
If $a = b$, then a may be replaced by b and b may be replaced by a	Substitution Law

EXERCISES 6-1

1. State the axioms appropriate to each of the following:
    (a) $(x + 3) + (-b) = x + [3 + (-b)]$
    (b) $(x + y) \in R$
    (c) $x + ya + yb = x + y(a + b)$
    (d) $1 \cdot a = a$
    (e) $4(3 + 2) = (3 + 2)4$

(f) $xy = yx$

(g) $2a + 3a = a2 + a3$

(h) $(1 + m)\dfrac{x}{y} = \dfrac{x1}{y} + \dfrac{xm}{y}$

(i) $-b + 0 = -b$

(j) $cy + ab = ab + cy$

(k) $4[(5 + 3) + 2] = 4(5 + 3) + 4 \cdot 2$

(l) $\dfrac{a}{x + 2} \cdot \dfrac{x + 2}{a} = 1, (x + 2 \neq 0, a \neq 0)$

(m) $\dfrac{3}{4} + \dfrac{2}{4} = \dfrac{2}{4} + \dfrac{3}{4}$

(n) $(ab)c = a(bc)$

(o) $a + -a = 0 = -a + a$

(p) $a^{-1} \cdot a = 1$

2. State the law that applies to each of the following:

(a) $x = 4, 4 = x$

(b) If $a = b + 3$ and $b = 2$, then $a = 2 + 3$

(c) If $a - 2 = b + 3$ and $b + 3 = x^2$, then $a - 2 = x^2$

3. Is subtraction commutative for real numbers?

4. Is division commutative for irrational numbers?

5. Is the set $\{\ldots, -1, 0, 1, 2, 3, \ldots\}$ closed under division?

6. Why is $4a + bc \neq (4a + b) \times (4a + c)$?

PROPERTIES

Axioms of operations, laws governing relationships, and elements in the set of real numbers make up a mathematical system. Axioms and laws also imply *properties* or behaviors of the elements in the set of real numbers with respect to the operations. These properties can be expressed in *theorems*, which are stated by an "If..., then" statement. The "If" part of the theorem is called the hypothesis and the "then" part is called the conclusion. Proving these theorems requires showing that a conclusion is a logical result of the laws of the mathematical system.

One such property is the Addition Law for Equality, which states in a very general way that equals added to equals are equal. More specifically

$$\text{If } a \in R, \ b \in R, \ c \in R, \text{ and } a = b, \text{ then } a + c = b + c$$

Theorem 6-1

$$\text{If } a = b, \text{ then } a + c = b + c$$

Proof. By the Reflexive Law

$$(A) \ a + c = a + c$$

but $a = b$, so that (A) becomes $a + c = b + c$ by the Substitution Law.

The Multiplication Law for Equality states that equals multiplied by equals are equal:

$$\text{If } a \in R, \ b \in R \text{ and } a = b, \text{ then } ac = bc \text{ when } c \in R$$

Theorem 6-2.   Given $a \in R, \ b \in R, \ c \in R$.

$$\text{If } a = b, \text{ then } a \cdot c = b \cdot c$$

Proof. By the Reflexive Law

$$\textbf{(B) } a \cdot c = a \cdot c$$

But $a = b$ so that (B) becomes $a \cdot c = b \cdot c$ by the Substitution Law.

Two other theorems that cover familiar properties are the following:

Theorem 6-3.   Cancellation Law of Addition.

$$\text{If } a \in R, \ b \in R, \text{ and } c \in R, \text{ and } a + c = b + c, \text{ then } a = b$$

Proof. Since $a + c = b + c$ is given:

$(a + c) + (-c) = (b + c) + (-c)$	Theorem 6-1
$a + [(c + (-c)] = b + [(c + (-c)]$	associative axiom for addition
$a + 0 = b + 0$	inverse axiom for addition
$a = b$	identity axiom for addition

Theorem 6-4.   Cancellation Law for Multiplication.

$$\text{If } a \in R, \ b \in R, \ c \in R, \text{ and } ac = bc, \text{ then } a = b, \text{ when } c \neq 0.$$

Proof. Since $ac = bc$ is given

$(ac) \cdot 1/c = (bc) \cdot 1/c$	Theorem 6-2
$a(c \cdot 1/c) = b(c \cdot 1/c)$	associative axiom for multiplication
$a(1) = b(1)$	inverse axiom for multiplication
$a = b$	identity axiom for multiplication

EXERCISES 6-2

1. Write a sentence describing each of the following:
   (a) If $a \in R$, $b \in R$, and $a + b = 0$, then $a = -b$ and $b = -a$
   (b) If $a \in R$, $b \in R$, and $a \cdot b = 0$, then $a = 0$ or $b = 0$, or both a and $b = 0$
   (c) $-(-a) = a$ (where $a \in R$)
   (d) $-a + -b = -(a + b)$ (where $a, b \in R$)
   (e) $(-a)b = -(ab)$ (where $a, b \in R$)

(f) $\dfrac{-x}{-y} = \dfrac{x}{y}$ $(y \neq 0,\ x,\ y \in R)$

(g) $\dfrac{a}{b} = \dfrac{c}{d}$ if and only if $ad = bc$ (where $a, b, c, d \in R$)

2. Using the variables a, b, and c, write the algebraic expression for each of the following:
   (a) 1 divided by the multiplicative inverse of a real number yields the real number.
   (b) A negative real number multiplied by another negative real number yields a positive real number.
   (c) A positive real number divided by a negative real number yields a negative real number, and a negative real number divided by a positive real number yields a negative real number.
   (d) Every real number multiplied by zero yields zero as a result.

3. Is $\dfrac{ax}{bx} = \dfrac{a}{b}$ $(b,\ x \neq 0)$?

4. Is $\dfrac{1}{x} \cdot \dfrac{1}{y} = \dfrac{x}{y}$ $(x,\ y \neq 0)$?

5. Is $\dfrac{a}{b} \cdot \dfrac{x}{y} = \dfrac{ax}{by}$ $(b,\ y \neq 0)$?

6. Is $\dfrac{a}{x} + \dfrac{b}{x} = \dfrac{a+b}{2x}$ $(x \neq 0)$?

7. Is $\dfrac{x}{a} + \dfrac{y}{b} = \dfrac{xb - ay}{ab}$ $(a,\ b \neq 0)$?

8. Is $\dfrac{\dfrac{a}{b}}{\dfrac{x}{y}} = \dfrac{ay}{bx}$ $(b,\ y,\ x \neq 0)$?

REPLACEMENT SETS AND SOLUTION SETS FOR EQUATIONS

To understand more about equations, review the following definitions:

Definition 6-1.   An *open sentence* is a sentence that is neither true nor false; that is, it cannot be determined if it is true or false from the given information. Open sentences must have least one variable.

Examples

   (a) $2 + x = 6$
   (b) $7 + 3x > 10$
   Without introducing more information about x, these statements are open sentences.

Definition 6-2.   A *closed sentence* is a sentence that is true or false, but not both.

Examples

(a) $3 < 0.05$ (false)
(b) $3 + 2 = 5$ (true)

Definition 6-3.   An *equation* is an open sentence or closed sentence in which two quantities are equal.

Examples

(a) $4 + 5 = 9$
(b) $3x + 2 = 11,$ where $x = 3$

Definition 6-4.   The *replacement* set of a sentence is a set whose members may be used to replace a variable in an open sentence to make a closed sentence.

Example

Given the open sentence $2x + 3 = 5$ and the replacement set $I = \{\ldots, -2, -1, 0, 1, 2, \ldots\}$, then $2x + 3 = 5$ can be made true only when $x = 1$. Any other members of the replacement set will make $2x + 3 = 5$ false.

Definition 6-5.   A *solution* is an element from the replacement set that makes the sentence true.

Definition 6-6.   The *solution set* is the set whose members are all solutions of some open sentence.

Examples

(a) In $2x + 5 = 8$, the solution set is $\{\frac{3}{2}\}$.
(b) In $x^2 - 2x = 0$, the solution set is $\{0, 2\}$.
(c) In $2x + 5 > 8$, the solution set is $\{x | x = 2, 3, 4, \ldots\}$ if the replacement set contains positive integers only. A conditional equation is an equation that has a solution set. In $2x + 2 = 8$, the solution set is $\{3\}$, which contains one element.

Equivalent equations have the same solution set. For example

$$2a + 3 = 13$$

$$a + 7 = 12$$

are equivalent equations whose solution set is $\{5\}$.

An *identity* is an equation whose solution set must contain the set of all elements of the replacement set. For example

$$7x - 3x = 4x$$

is an identity because any element in the set of real numbers may replace the variable x.

If the solution set contains no members, it can be represented as $\emptyset$, the null set, and the equation is a false sentence. $y = y - 3$ is an example of a false sentence.

EXERCISES 6-3

1. Give two equations equivalent to $2x + 4 = 12$.
2. Give an example of
   (a) A conditional equation
   (b) An identity
3. Find the solution set for
   (a) $3x + 9 = 29$
   (b) $2x = 2x + 1$
   (c) $x^2 + 3x - 4 = 0$
   (d) $2x = y$
4. Find the values of $2x + 3$ for the replacement set

$$\{-1, 0, 1, 2, 3\}$$

5. Find the values of $x - 4$ for the replacement set

$$\{-6, -4, -2, 0, 2, 4, 6\}$$

6. Find the solution set for the equation $|3x + 8| = 11$.
7. (a) List the elements in the replacement set of integers

$$A = \{x \in J \mid -4 < x < 5\}$$

   (b) Find the solution set for the inequality $|x| > 2$.
8. Find the solution set for the following:
   (a) $|x| > 9$
   (b) $|x| < 9$

EVALUATING MATHEMATICAL EXPRESSIONS

A mathematical expression is a set of values and operators. Values are found in constants and variables and are called *operands*, or "that which is operated on." *Operators* are symbols used to specify some arithmetic operation. Operations may result in one and only one value.

Consider the equation

$$y = mx + b$$

The expression $mx + b$ is evaluated as follows:

1. Find the product for $m \times x$
2. Add to this product the value of b
3. Replace any previous value for y with the result of $mx + b$.

This description implies rules that govern the evaluation of mathematical expressions.

The rules that follow apply to computer programming and make coding of mathematical expressions in Fortran and BASIC a fairly easy task:

1. Operands and operators are placed on a line. The line is referred to as a *statement.* In

$$y = mx + b$$

this can be easily coded as

$$10 \ Y = M*X + B$$

where 10 is the statement number (required in BASIC, sometimes in Fortran). In many computer languages, the "+" sign denotes addition and the "*," or asterisk, is the symbol to denote multiplication. In our example, Y, on the left of the "=" sign, is replaced by the evaluation of the expression M * X + B found to the right of the "=" sign.

2. Two arithmetic operators cannot be placed adjacent to each other. However, if one operand is preceded by a minus sign (signed negative), it must be enclosed in parentheses. Thus

$$Y*(-X)$$

3. Terms and expressions in parentheses are evaluated first. In

$$2 + (A*B)$$

the product for A × B is found and then added to 2. If A = 3 and B = 4, the expression is evaluated first as 2 + 12, not as 5 × 4.

4. Without or within parentheses, the computer executes the operations according to an order or *hierarchy* of arithmetic operations as follows:

Level	Operator	Operation
1	** (Fortran) or ˆ (BASIC) + sign, − sign	Exponentiation
2	*, /	Multiplication and division
3	+, −	Addition and subtraction

Exponentiation will be performed first and signs are set on variables or constants. Multiplication and division are performed next, addition and subtraction last. Operations on levels 2 and 3 are performed from left to right in an expression. Operations on level 1 are performed from right to left. Arithmetic operators and the equal sign are separated by blank spaces. In the following examples

1. $X + Y - C$

the sum of $X + Y$ is computed first, then C is subtracted from that sum. Note that in

2. a/bc must be coded as $A/(B * C)$

where the product of $B * C$ becomes a divisor. If this expression were coded as $A/B * C$, the quotient of A/B would be multiplied by C and yield a different result.

3. Given:

$$J = 3, \quad K = 4, \quad L = -2, \quad M = 0$$

Substituting these values in the expression

$$J * K + L + M$$

yields

$$(3 \times 4) + (-2) + 0 = 12 + (-2) = 10$$

4. $y = 2x - x^2 + 1$, coded as $Y = 2 * X - X ** 2 + 1$

Exponentiation is performed first, followed by multiplication, subtraction, and addition.

EXERCISES 6-4

1. Write the Fortran statements for the following:

(a) $a = \left(\dfrac{x}{y}\right) z$

(b) $d = b^2 - 4.0ac$

(c) $\dfrac{a}{bc} = x$

(d) $\dfrac{1.5}{a + s + t^2} = y$

(e) $x = c[(a + b)(x + y)]$

Use the values of J, K, L, and M given in example 3 when you work the following Fortran problems.

2. Find the values for the following:
   (a) $J + M$
   (b) $J ** 2 + L * J$

3. If $M = J + K$ means that M is *replaced* by $J + K$, find values for M and J in the following:
   (a) $M = K * L + M + K ** 2$

(b) $J = J + 1$

(c) $J = (-J)$

4. Let $A = J$, $B = K$, $C = L$, and $D = M$. In the following problems, begin your computation with the innermost parentheses as does the computer:

(a) $A + (A * B)$

(b) $(A * (A + B)) + C$

(c) $(A + (A * B))/C$

5. Use the values given in Problem 4 for A, B, C, and D and the hierarchy of operations. If operations at the same level are computed from left to right, find X in the following:

(a) $X = B + C/A * B$

(b) $X = (B + C)/A * B$

(c) $X = D - A * B + C/B$

6. If exponentiation is performed from right to left, what is the algebraic expression for $A ** (B ** C)$?

7. The coding for $-Z \left(\frac{x}{y}\right)$ is which of the following?

(a) $(X/Y) * (-Z)$

(b) $X * Y/Z$

(c) $X/(Y * (-Z))$

(d) $(X/Y) * -Z$

Note that -6^2 can be properly coded for some BASIC compilers as $(-6)\hat{}2$. However, some other language compilers may not accept a negative quantity raised to a power of a real number since they raise values to a real power using logarithms and a negative quantity has no logarithm. (See Chapter 18.)

HANDLING INEQUALITIES

To denote inequality, comparison or *relational* operators are used. They may differ in appearance depending on the computer language employed.

Operator		Meaning
BASIC	Fortran	
$> =$	.GE.	Greater than or equal to
$>$	.GT.	Greater than
$< >$	.NE.	Not equal to
$=$	.EQ.	Equal to
$< =$	.LE.	Less than or equal to
$<$	.LT.	Less than

In Fortran, a period must appear on each side of the relational operator so that the computer will not mistake it for a variable name.

Examples

Fortran	Mathematical Expression
(X.GT.Y)	$x > y$
(X.EQ.250.5)	$x = 250.5$
(A.NE.B)	$a \neq b$

These preceding Fortran expressions are written within parentheses.

BASIC	Mathematical Expression
X < = Y	$x \leqslant y$
A > C	$a > c$
M > = N	$m \geqslant n$

These preceding BASIC expressions do not require parentheses.

Before continuing with illustrations of program statements that contain inequalities, we note the following.
In BASIC, all statements must be numbered sequentially:

$$10 \ X = 5$$
$$20 \ Y = 10$$
$$30 \ X = X * Y$$

In this short program segment, the value in X is replaced by itself times the value found in Y. In Fortran, a statement referenced by other Fortran statement(s) needs to be numbered.

```
       GO TO 40
       ─────────────
       ─────────────  other statements in program
40  A = B + C
```

GO TO is a command common to many computer languages. It causes the program to "jump" or branch to another statement in a program. That statement must be known to the program by a "label."

Definition 6-7. A *statement label* is either a number or a name given to a computer statement that contains operators and operands.

All BASIC and Fortran statement labels are numbers. COBOL statement labels are called names and typically begin with an alphabetic character. For example

			Operators		
		Operand	↓	Operand	
Statement labels	$\begin{cases} 135 \\ \text{HERE} \end{cases}$	X = Y =	A L	+ *	B Fortran or BASIC 3.14 COBOL

$$\underbrace{\qquad\qquad\qquad\qquad\qquad\qquad}_{\text{Statements}}$$

The IF Statement. The IF statement (with its variations) is used in the Fortran, BASIC, and COBOL computer languages to aid in testing variables and making programmed decisions. A general format for the IF statement is

IF (condition) (statement)

An example of the use of the IF statement in COBOL helps to illustrate the testing and decision-making procedures:

IF INVENTORY IS LESS THAN PURCHASE-ORDER GO TO BACK-ORDER.

where BACK-ORDER is a statement label.

The format for the IF statement in Fortran is similar to that of COBOL.

IF(X.LE.51) GO TO 101

is a Fortran statement that says that if X is less than or equal to 51, go to a statement whose label is 101. Other examples of Fortran statements in which the relational operators appear are

IF (XMAX.GT.10.0) GO TO 98
IF (A.EQ.B) GO TO 75

BASIC examples are

10 If A > = B THEN GO TO 30
90 IF RESULT < > BALANCE THEN GO TO 200

Consider next a data processing example in Fortran that illustrates the use of the IF statement in decision making. A car dealer makes an agreement with each of his salespeople to give them

1. A guaranteed salary of $2000 per month
2. 5% commission on all sales
3. 10% bonus on all sales over $20,000

Assume that at least one car a month is sold, and use the IF statement to test for sales, as follows:

```
        SALARY = 2000.00
        BONUS = 0.0
        COMM = SALES * 0.05
        IF(SALES .LE. 20000) GO TO 5
        BONUS = (SALES − 20000) * 0.1
      5 TOTAL = SALARY + COMM + BONUS
```

Note that we set the variable BONUS to 0.0 initially. If more than $20,000 in sales has not been achieved, our program will branch around the calculations for BONUS. If the conditions of the IF statement are not met, our program will "fall through" to the next sequential statement and calculate the BONUS.

EXERCISES 6-5

1. Code the following in Fortran.
   (a) $(a + 2.5) = c$
   (b) $i \neq j$
   (c) $(4.1x + 2.1) > y$
   (d) If base × height > 20.5 go to 50
   (e) If pay is less than 999.99 go to 100

2. Find the resulting values for X and TOTAL in the following BASIC program segment:

```
      10 X = 3
      20 TOTAL = 10
      30 TOTAL = TOTAL * X
      40 IF TOTAL < 200. GO TO 30
```

_____
_____   other statements in program
_____

3. Given the following Fortran program segment:

```
         X = A
         Y = 1.0
      10 A = A − B
         X = X + A
         Y = Y + 1.0
         IF (Y .LT. Z) GO TO 10
```

_____
_____   other statements in program
_____

If Z has a value of 15 initially, statement 10 will be executed _____ times.

4. Write the BASIC code to set X to 2, then continue squaring X until it is equal to 256.

5. Complete the Fortran statements that follow to calculate gross pay. OVRTM represents overtime and is computed as 1.5 times the number of hours greater than 40.

```
        OVRTM = 0.0
        IF (HOURS _____) _____

10 _____
 5_____ = RATE*HOURS + OVRTM
```

The IF statement is one of the simplest and yet most powerful statements used in programming. Variations of the IF statement will be discussed further in the chapter on algorithms.

7

Formatting for Arithmetic

A primary activity for programmers is handling numeric data items. This includes naming and formatting variables for computations in programming languages as well as managing arithmetic problems in overflow, rounding, and truncating.

Computer data items are stored in memory in reserved areas called *fields* and referenced in a computer program by a variable name. Fields contain one or more contiguous bytes of the same type of data. Two examples, Fortran and COBOL, require the programmer to specify the size or length of the field, thereby giving the programmer some control over the variables he or she is using. The length assigned to a variable is critical since it will determine how many *significant* digits are to be found in a field.

Significant Digits

The following five statements describe the notion of significant digits:

1. All nonzero digits are significant. For example, 134, 2.467, and .85 contain three, four, and two significant digits, respectively.

2. All zeros occurring *between* nonzero digits are significant digits. For example, 10203 is a number with five significant digits; 40.123 is a number with five significant digits.

3. Trailing zeros following a decimal point are significant digits. For example, 45.60, 4.560, .4560, and 56.00 have four significant digits each.

4. Zeros between the decimal point and preceding a nonzero digit are *not* significant digits. For example, 0.078, which can be expressed as 78×10^{-3} contains two significant digits:

0.000012 contains two significant digits.

0.012345 contains five significant digits.

0.00400 contains three significant digits.

5. Trailing zeros are not considered to be significant when the decimal point is not written. 3,000 may be written as 3×10^3 and contains only one significant digit; 4,560,000 may be written as 456×10^4 and contains three significant digits. 4,560,000.00, however, contains a decimal point and nine significant digits.

FORMATTING VARIABLES

As in algebra, numeric variables are given names and are used to represent different values.

Some Fortran systems permit one to six letters or digits in names. All variable names begin with an alphabetic character and the first letter of a variable determines which of two types of arithmetic modes are to be used. Variable names for integers must begin with one of the following letters: I, J, K, L, M, or N. Variable names for real numbers must begin with any letter except I, J, K, L, M, or N.

If the student has a computer available and writes computer code for any of the exercises that follow in this text, the user's manuals for that computer and computer language must be used as references.

FORTRAN VARIABLES

Fortran means *formula translation* and is oriented toward scientific and mathematical problems requiring numbers to be formatted by size and type using two basic arithmetic modes:

1. Fixed-point arithmetic
2. Floating-point arithmetic

Fixed-point arithmetic handles operations using integers such as 4, -35, 70192, and the like. In 70192, we note that no commas are present. Commas are not computational in any computer language.

Floating-point arithmetic handles operations using real numbers such as 4., 1.23, -0.008, 3.333, and the like. The real number, 4. will be recognized by Fortran as a floating-point number because it contains a decimal point, and this is a convenient way of distinguishing between the two modes of arithmetic.

I-Specification for Integers

The general reference format for integers is expressed in the term "Iw," where "I" specifies an integer and the "w" specifies the field length or the number of positions reserved for digits. In the integer format, the w-specifier controls the size of the field. For example, I6 refers to an integer variable that will contain six positions. In Fortran, formats are frequently associated with input/output statements.

In the following Fortran input statements:

        READ (1,20) NUMBER
    20 FORMAT (I3)

In our example, the 1 in the parenthesized expression (1,20) is a code identifying a file of disk records. The two statements describe reading a variable named NUMBER from the disk. The 20 in this expression refers to the number of the FORMAT statement that may or may not appear directly after the READ statement that references it. In statement 20, I3 specifies that NUMBER is an integer variable (fixed-point), in a field three positions long.

Refer to Table 7.1. The contents of the fields in the first three lines are correct.

TABLE 7.1

	Format	Number	Contents in Field
1.	I2	12	12
2.	I3	123	123
3.	I4	1234	1234
4.	I3	−12	−12
5.	I5	123	00123
6.	I4	−1234	1234
7.	I2	1234	34

If a minus sign is required, a space must also be reserved for it in the field as in line 4.

In line 5, the integer format is greater than the number. When this occurs, the number is right-justified in the field. Note also that some Fortran systems will regard the extra spaces as zeros.

Errors can occur in formatting the size of integer variables. If the field length is too short, the minus sign and significant digits in the high-order positions can be truncated and lost as shown in the last two lines of the table. On the other hand, some Fortran systems will truncate low-order positions when the length is too short.

The fixed-point mode permits only integer results. A problem such as $\frac{7}{2}$ results in a quotient of 3. The decimal fraction .5 is truncated and lost.

F-Specification for Real Numbers

The format for real numbers is referred to as the floating-point format and is expressed in the general description "Fw.d," where F specifies the floating-point format for real numbers, w specifies the field width, and d specifies the number of decimal positions to the right of the decimal point.

The "d" specifier controls the number of positions to the right of the decimal point and must always be less than the "w" specifier. The "w" specifier must allow for the actual decimal point and a sign if necessary. F6.3 refers to a real variable six positions long with three positions to the right of the decimal point. F3.6 will cause an error condition since "d" is greater than "w."

The following Fortran statements describe printing a variable named RATE, which is five positions long including a decimal point with two positions to the right of the decimal point:

WRITE (2,30) RATE
30   FORMAT (F5.2)

The parenthesized expression in the WRITE statement contains (2,30) where the 2 is the code to identify a printer (in our example) and 30 is the number of the FORMAT statement.

Refer to Table 7.2. Positions must be reserved in the field for the minus sign, for the decimal point and for each digit in the real number as shown in lines 1 to 4.

TABLE 7.2

	Format	Number	Contents in Field
1.	F4.1	22.3	22.3
2.	F7.2	− 388.56	− 388.56
3.	F4.3	.345	.345
4.	F6.0	− 1234.	− 1234.
5.	F7.5	24.56771	4.56771
6.	F4.2	− 62.34	2.34
7.	F5.2	45.345	45.35
8.	F5.2	61.001	61.00

Errors can occur when variables are incorrectly formatted. If no positions are reserved for the sign, for the decimal point, and for all the digits to the left of the decimal point, significant digits and the sign are truncated and lost as shown in lines 5 and 6. In cases like this, one asterisk may be printed for each position in the field.

If the positions to the right of the decimal point are too few to represent the number in the variable as in the last two lines of Table 7.2, the number may be rounded if possible to the nearest decimal in order to fit into the field. Significant digits in the low-order positions will be lost. (Note that some Fortran systems will truncate and *not* round.)

To avoid errors in formatting variables, the programmer must provide for what will be the largest possible number that is required to occupy the field. In a payroll example, consider that no check will be printed for an amount greater than 999.99. A variable named PAY can then be formatted as F6.2.

The student should be aware not only of restrictions in a programming language such as Fortran, but also of the distinctions between Fortran and a few other commonly used programming languages.

COBOL VARIABLES

COBOL is the language frequently used for business and commercial data processing applications. Variables in COBOL are given a "PICTURE" clause that specifies the type and size attributes in a manner that is easily understood. The READ and WRITE statements in COBOL are not associated with format statements such as those in Fortran.

An example of a variable named for integer values is

SPARE-PARTS   PICTURE 999.

Note that a period ends each COBOL statement. The digit 9 is used to specify a place in a field reserved for any digit. In our example, the variable named SPARE-PARTS references a field of integers three positions long. The first letter in a COBOL name has no effect on the type of variable being defined.

An example of a variable used for real numbers is

PRICE PICTURE 999V99.

The variable named PRICE reserves a field in memory for a real number five positions long and including two decimal fraction positions. The "V" is the symbol to indicate the location of an assumed decimal point, not the actual decimal point. Editing the decimal point in COBOL (including any necessary signs) is done by the programmer after calculations.

The *sign* of a number in COBOL will be a part of a data item when the S-specifier is used in a PICTURE clause:

ACCOUNT-BALANCE   PICTURE   S999V99.

The S-character is useful when handling debit amounts that may be signed positive and credit amounts that may be signed negative, for example, in accounting programs used to create balance sheets. The S-character does not represent a position in storage but if it is omitted, a data item is treated as having a positive value. In the unpacked decimal format

F2F3C5 will be recognized as 235+

and

F6F2D3 will be recognized as 623−

As in Fortran, size errors can occur. Significant digits to the left or the right of the implied decimal point can be lost. On the other hand, if too many positions are specified, zeros will be padded to the left or right in a field where appropriate. Refer to Table 7.3. The "∧", or caret, means an assumed decimal point and the numeric data items are aligned on the decimal point.

TABLE 7.3

	PICTURE	Number	Contents in Field
1.	99V99	23∧00	23∧00
2.	999V99	23∧0	023∧00
3.	999V99	1287∧44	287∧44
4.	99V9	45∧67	45∧6
5.	S999	123−	123−
6.	999	123−	123

In line 2 of Table 7.3, a zero has been padded in the low- and high-order positions. In line 3, the most significant digit is truncated, and in line 4, the least significant digit is truncated (with no rounding). In line 6, the sign has not been retained and the absolute value is stored in the field because the S-character was omitted.

EXERCISES 7-1

1. Identify the following constants and variables as a Fortran fixed-point or floating-point:
  (a) 0.666
  (b) 666.0
  (c) −123
  (d) GROSS
  (e) NET
  (f) VOLTS
  (g) K80
  (h) ANSWER
2. Give the Fortran format for the following numbers:
  (a) 678
  (b) −7988

(c) 9786
(d) 101.1
(e) 555.
(f) .0023
(g) −7.254
(h) 509.756

3. Correct any errors in the following table:

	Number	Fortran Format
(a)	420	I5
(b)	−2.36	F5.2
(c)	23.54	F5.3
(d)	6.7	F3.4
(e)	8.1244	I7
(f)	34.7076	F6.4
(g)	−6.8950	F7.4

4. Give the PICTURE clause for the following numbers:

	Number	COBOL PICTURE
(a)	001	
(b)	1∧2−	
(c)	37∧45	
(d)	239∧01	
(e)	8∧236	
(f)	495	

5. Give the value or the contents in the following fields and identify any significant digits that may have been truncated.

	Number	PICTURE	Contents in Field
(a)	32105	99999	
(b)	14∧56	9V	
(c)	54372−	S99999	
(d)	50∧90	99V9	
(e)	674∧51	99V999	
(f)	23	9999	

6. Give the Fortran format for the following:
  (a) The maximum number of miles on an automobile odometer
  (b) The price of a gallon of gasoline
  (c) A charge account where the maximum purchase cannot exceed five hundred dollars
  (d) A baseball batting average
  (e) Fahrenheit temperatures for your city

Notes on BASIC

BASIC is the language found on most computer systems, from main-frame to personal computers. It handles integers and numbers containing decimal fractions without the need to format variables and BASIC systems will keep track of decimal points. For example

```
100 N = 34.2
110 L = N*2
120 PRINT L
```

will display 68.4 for the variable L.

SCIENTIFIC NOTATION

Problems in engineering, astronomy, and other sciences require a compact method of writing very large and very small numbers and quantities that must be expressed in a format that is easily read and understood. For example, the speed of light

$$186,000 \text{ miles per second}$$

can also be written as

$$186000 = 1.86 \times 10^5$$

A few other examples are

$$3.16 \times 10^7 \text{ seconds in a year}$$
$$1.44 \times 10^3 \text{ minutes in a day}$$
$$2.09 \times 10^7 \text{ feet, radius of the earth}$$
$$2.01 \times 10^{-30} \text{ pounds, mass of an electron}$$

In scientific notation, numbers are written with one nonzero digit to the left of a decimal point, followed by any other digit(s) to the right of the decimal point. The number is multiplied by some power of base ten.

When changing from decimal notation to scientific notation, *positive* exponents may be determined by the number of places the decimal point must be moved to the left.

Example 1

$$\begin{array}{cc}\text{Decimal} & \text{Scientific} \\ 432.10 & 4.321 \times 10^2\end{array}$$

Negative exponents may be determined by the number of places the decimal point must be moved to the right.

Example 2

$$\begin{array}{cc}\text{Decimal} & \text{Scientific} \\ .00017 & 1.7 \times 10^{-4}\end{array}$$

When changing from decimal notation to scientific notation: Numbers that already have a single nonzero digit to the left of the decimal point have a zero exponent. Numbers that are 10 or greater have positive exponents. Numbers less than 1 have negative exponents. The following examples illustrate this practice:

$$234,000 = 2.34 \times 10^5$$
$$0.234 \times 10^6 = 2.34 \times 10^5$$
$$0.0234 = 2.34 \times 10^{-2}$$
$$0.567 = 5.67 \times 10^{-1}$$
$$0.0000567 = 5.67 \times 10^{-5}$$
$$0.0789 \times 10^3 = 7.89 \times 10^{-2} \times 10^3$$
$$= 7.89 \times 10$$
$$.03 \times 10^2 = 3 \times 10^0$$

Exponential Notation

When exponents are needed in computer programs, numbers are expressed in a format called *exponential notation*, which differs from scientific notation by not having a nonzero digit to the left of the decimal point. The formats for exponential notation used in this chapter are available in the Fortran language.

A real number multiplied by a power of 10, for example, 0.65×10^2, cannot be input to the computer on a single typed line because the exponent is raised above the line. To indicate the exponent, we use the letter "E." Refer to Table 7.4.

TABLE 7.4

Decimal	Scientific Notation	Exponential Notation
456000.	4.56×10^5	.456E+6
.123	1.23×10^{-1}	.123E0
2.85	2.85×10^0	.285E+1
.045	4.5×10^{-2}	.45E−1

Note that exponents in exponential notation are one greater than exponents in scientific notation and no significant (non-zero) digit(s) are found to the left of the decimal point.

E-Specification

To express real numbers in exponential form, we use the E-specification. It is written in the general format as "Ew.d," where E specifies the exponential format, w specifies the field width (including the signs and decimal point), and d specifies the number of decimal positions to the right of the decimal point. The "w" must always be greater than "d" and allow for a sign on the number if necessary and the decimal point. For example, E8.3 refers to a floating-point variable eight positions long with three positions to the right of the decimal point. In the "E" format, the length of the field also includes a position for the letter "E," the exponent, and a sign on the exponent if required.

The following Fortran statements describe reading a variable which is eight positions long including the decimal point, three decimal positions, the letter "E," and a two-digit exponent with a sign.

READ (1,50) POUNDS
50 FORMAT (E8.3)

If this statement reads the mass of the earth in pounds, the data item for input should appear as

.132E+26

If used in computations, the data item may be found in a floating-point register in the binary exponential format described in Chapter 5.

Refer to Table 7.5. Numbers are converted to exponential notation to determine their E-specifications or formats.

TABLE 7.5

Number	Exponential Form	Format	Input Data Item
.00303	$.303 \times 10^{-2}$	E7.3	.303E$-$2
1.45	$.145 \times 10^{1}$	E7.3	.145E+1
$-26.$	$-.26 \times 10^{2}$	E7.2	$-.26$E+2
6000	$.6 \times 10^{4}$	E5.1	.6E+4
.00036	$.36 \times 10^{-3}$	E6.2	.36E$-$3

In the first line in Table 7.5, the zero is included when it appears between significant digits.

As with the I- and F-specifications, errors occur when the length of the variable is not long enough to include all elements that are required for a data item written in exponential form. In .456E+ 03, the space between the + sign and the exponent can be interpreted as a zero on some Fortran systems. This would be a serious problem if that Fortran system only accepted two digits for the exponent.

In Fortran, the format for printing numbers in exponential notation may be the same as those given in the READ or input statement. A leading zero to the left of the decimal point may also be printed and the E-specification for a WRITE statement must be long enough to accommodate it. Further, on some Fortran systems, exponents such as +1 will be printed as +01 and the format for the WRITE statement must provide for it.

EXERCISES 7-2

1. Write the following numbers as they would appear after multiplication by a power of base ten:
  (a) $.576 \times 10^6$
  (b) $.1001 \times 10^{-3}$
  (c) $.33345 \times 10^5$
  (d) $.751 \times 10^{-2}$
  (e) $.7564 \times 10^3$
  (f) $.9 \times 10^{-7}$

2. Change the following to exponential form:
  (a) 100300
  (b) 64.907
  (c) .0000045
  (d) .00573467
  (e) 600000

3. Complete the following table. (Do not include nonsignificant zeros.)

Number	Scientific Notation	Exponential Notation
10030		
.000045		
		.321E+0
		.95E−3
	7.01×10^5	
	5.75×10^{-2}	
		.7E−1
.005734		
	1.9×10^{-7}	
		.1645E+2

4. Write the E-specification for the following:

  (a) $.5 \times 10^3$

  (b) $.1983 \times 10^{-2}$

  (c) .0034

  (d) .000078

  (e) .001004

  (f) .51E + 2

  (g) .837E − 7

  (h) .14145E + 3

  (i) The number of hours in a week

  (j) The speed of light in miles per second

  (k) One tenth of a cent

5. Write the results in exponential notation for the following:

  (a) .32E−2 + .104E+2

  (b) .6E−3 − .52E−1

  (c) .146E+2 × .72E+3

  (d) 3.14159 ÷ .9E−2

Notes on BASIC

Care must be taken in BASIC. On some systems the following events are possible:

$$100 \text{ PRINT} \quad 4.2E-1 + 4.2E-1$$

yields a result of .84, which may not be what the programmer wants. However, as another example

$$100 \text{ PRINT} \quad 10E+10 * 1000E+20$$

yields a result of 1E + 34. In this case, the operands and the results are in the same notation, or the E-format (exponential format).

To force the result into an E-format when it is desirable to do so, programmers must write field specifiers. Consider the following program, where "ˆ" is the circumflex mark, not the caret:

$$100 \ N = 54.2$$
$$110 \ T\$ = "\# \# \#.\# \# \# \ ^\wedge \ ^\wedge \ ^\wedge \ ^\wedge "$$
$$120 \ N = N*10E + 1$$
$$130 \ \text{PRINT USING } T\$;N$$

OUTPUT   54.200E+02

(*Note:* Not all BASIC compilers support USING.)

In statement 110 we define field specifiers in T$, "forcing" the system to print the result in E-format. Field specifiers are contained in quotes and assigned to a variable with an equals sign.

The # sign is a placeholder for any digit to the right or left of the decimal point.

In other words, # signs will be replaced by digits in the result. The position of the decimal point must be specified by the programmer.

The "^" symbols specify that the E-format is to be used. The number of "^" symbols indicates the number of positions that are required to print the exponential part of the result. One caution is always to be noted: When writing BASIC programs that require computations, the programmer should reference the manual for the computer being used.

8

Managing Arithmetic Operations

Arithmetic is a binary operation that manipulates and assigns to a pair of operands or elements an element that is formed as a result of that binary operation. Arithmetic includes

A symbol to denote a specific operation

Two operands

A result

Symbols for arithmetic operations in computers were presented earlier in Chapter 6. They are " + " for addition, " − " for subtraction, " * " for multiplication, " / " for division, " ** " or " ^ " for exponentiation.

Operands (in this text) are variables or constants in the set of real numbers that are operated on.

Results are values in the set of real numbers that are the consequences of operations. However, there are times when the results of arithmetic operations are values that need to be modified, especially when the consequences result in the overflow of the most significant digits. Other results may need modifications for precision and accuracy and rounding and truncating.

In managing arithmetic operations, the programmer has the responsibility to keep track of decimal points (actual or implied); define proper field sizes; provide for signs, especially when negative results are anticipated; and modify results of computations when necessary.

ADDITION

The sum or result field should contain as many positions as the largest value to be added and at least two more positions in the high order for a possible carry and sign.

When adding real numbers, the number of digits to the right and left of the decimal point are considered as shown in the following example:

		Fortran Format	COBOL PICTURE
999.99	addend	F6.2	999V99
+ 99.999	augend	F6.3	99V999
1099.989	sum	F8.3	9999V999

(It is sometimes useful to use 9's for determining the maximum lengths of fields when adding, subtracting, and multiplying.)

As an exercise show the sum fields for adding a positive number to a negative number and for adding two negative numbers. Allow for a sign if a negative result is anticipated.

Overflow in Addition Problems

The size of a result field should be large enough to hold the largest anticipated value, that is, the greatest possible purchase, the highest or lowest temperature, and so on. However, when account balances are totaled up in applications such as banking or retail purchases, hundreds of amounts may be operated on at the end of every month. If the number of accounts is known in advance, the format of the result or total field can be easily determined by multiplying the highest possible amount by the maximum number of accounts.

Example

99.99	highest possible amount
× 1525.	number of accounts
152484.75	highest possible total

It is not always possible to be this exact when formatting the size of total amounts in a system where customers are being added or dropped each month. If the result field is too large, nothing is lost; if it is too small, truncation of a serious nature occurs.

To prevent the loss of high-order significant digits, the programmer may test for an overflow condition and give a warning that remedial action is needed.

In a COBOL example, assume that two data items were defined as

```
BALANCE   PICTURE   99V99.
TOTAL     PICTURE   999V99.
```

And also assume that values for BALANCE and TOTAL were 95.50 and 971.39, respectively, and that these values were unknown to the programmer. After the statement

ADD BALANCE TO TOTAL.

is executed, the most significant digit in the sum 1066.89 would be truncated and the TOTAL field would contain 066.89, an obvious *size* error. No indication of this transformation would be given by the computer.

A COBOL option, ON SIZE ERROR is used to handle these situations.

ADD BALANCE TO TOTAL ON SIZE ERROR GO TO OVERFLOW.

OVERFLOW can be the name of a COBOL routine to correct the problem, saving BALANCE by adding it to a second field and printing a message:

OVERFLOW.   ADD BALANCE TO TOTAL2.
            DISPLAY BALANCE UPON PRINTER-OUT.
            DISPLAY "OVERFLOWED" UPON PRINTER-OUT.

where the balance that caused the overflow and an appropriate message are both printed.

It is also possible to *subtract out* the addend that caused the overflow condition, as we shall see in the following Fortran example. Before coding the example, however, we note that for one Fortran compiler, the highest possible positive integer is 32767 or $(2^{15} - 1)$, and the lowest possible negative integer is $-(2^{15})$. Study the following and note that

$$X = X + Y$$

means that X is replaced by its value plus the value in Y.

$$X = X - Y$$

means that X is replaced by its value minus the value in Y:

```
      INTEGER X,Y
      X=32767
      WRITE(2,100)X
      Y=9
  2   X=X+Y
      WRITE(2,100)X
100   FORMAT(1X,I6)
      IF (X) 3,1,1
  1   GO TO 4
```

(continued)

```
3   X=X−Y
    WRITE(2,100)X
    OFLO=OFLO+X
    X=0
    GO TO 2
4   CALL EXIT
    END
    32767
   −32760
    32767
         9
```

Note that 1X in statement 100 will put a blank space before the value in X.

A general description of the activities in this Fortran program follows.

X is declared to be an integer, initialized to 32767, and printed out at the bottom of the listing. Y, declared to be an integer, is initialized to 9 and added to X, causing a negative result of -32760. This result occurred in the following manner:

$$32767 + 1 = -32768$$
$$+ 1 = -32767$$
$$+ 1 = -32766$$
$$+ 1 = -32765$$
$$+ 1 = -32764$$
$$+ 1 = -32763$$
$$+ 1 = -32762$$
$$+ 1 = -32761$$
$$+ 1 = -32760$$

When 9 was added to 32767, X went first to the lowest possible negative number, -32768, and then increased in value to -32760. The statement

$$IF (X) \; 3, 1, 1$$

tested X and found it to be negative, and program control was given to statement 3. At statement 3, Y was subtracted from X. Next, X was added to an overflow counter, and then set to zero. Program control was given to statement 2, where Y could be added to X yielding 9.

Note that in this form of the Fortran IF statement, a variable or expression is enclosed in parentheses followed by three statement numbers. If after the variable or expression is tested, a result is found to be

- Negative, control is given to the first statement
- Zero, control is given to the second statement
- Positive, control is given to the third statement

SUBTRACTION

The number of digits on either side of the decimal point must also be considered in subtraction.

Example 1

		Fortran	COBOL PICTURE
9999.9	minuend	F6.1	9999V9
− 999.999	subtrahend	F7.3	999V999
8999.901	difference	F8.3	9999V999

In the event that the subtrahend is greater than the minuend, a position for the sign must be included in the length of the result or "difference" field.

Example 2

	Fortran	COBOL PICTURE
999.999	F7.3	999V999
− 9999.9	F6.1	9999V9
−8999.901	F9.3	S9999V999

It is also possible to subtract a negative number from a positive number or to subtract a negative or positive number from a negative number. As an exercise, show how these possibilities affect the length of the result fields.

When negative results are unwanted, tests must always be made after subtraction. Consider a payroll situation where, due to sickness or other reasons, an employee missed a great amount of time and pay. Voluntary deductions such as union dues, savings plans, and United Fund contributions may actually amount to more than the money earned for the period. In this situation, gross pay will be smaller than these deductions. To avoid a negative net pay the following Fortran statement compares the variables for pay and deductions.

$$\text{IF (PAY − DEDUCT) 20,20,10}$$

If it is true that PAY is less than or equal to DEDUCT or the variable representing voluntary deductions, program control is given to the statement numbered 20, which should contain an instruction to bypass subtraction of these deductions. IF statements to test conditions like this also exist in COBOL and BASIC.

EXERCISES 8-1

1. Using the letter "n" as a placeholder to describe a reasonably formatted variable, complete the following:
   (Use a minus sign where required.)

(a) nn.nn   + _____ = nnn.nn
(b) .nn   + −nn.n = _____
(c) nnn.n   − _____ = nnn.nnn
(d) −nn.nn − nn.nn   = _____
(e) nn.n.   − −nnn.nn = _____
(f) −nnn.n − −nn.nn   = _____

2. The following Fortran statement can be used to sum four quiz grades.

$$SUM = A + B + C + D$$

Format SUM for the highest possible result.

3. Should a negative result be possible in
   (a) INCOME − Taxes   _____
   Can a negative result be possible in
   (b) CHECKING-ACCOUNT-BALANCE − SERVICE-CHARGE   _____
   (c) CASH + SUPPLIES + EQUIPMENT − EXPENSES   _____

4. A savings bank has 2453 depositors. To total the interest paid each quarter and avoid an overflow condition, what should the format of the result field be if the highest possible interest for any account is $999.99?_____.

5. Overflow conditions can be detected in COBOL with the _____ option and with the _____ statement in Fortran.

6. Write the Fortran statements to read a checking account balance and to test for an overdrawn condition.

MULTIPLICATION

The length of the product field must be equal to the length of the multiplicand plus the length of the multiplier when multiplying integers.

Example 1

		Fortran	COBOL PICTURE
999	multiplicand	I3	999
× 99	multiplier	I2	99
98901	product	I5	99999

For multiplication of numbers with decimal fractions, this also means adding up the number of digits to the right and to the left of the decimal point in both the multiplier and multiplicand.

Example 2

		Fortran	COBOL PICTURE
99.999	multiplicand	F6.3	S99V999
× −99.9	multiplier	F5.1	S99V9
−9989.9001	product	F10.4	S9999V9999

As with addition and subtraction, when a sign is anticipated, the format should allow for it.

In some situations, programmers subtract a field from itself to ensure that it will contain zeros. Next, this field can be used as a result field for any arithmetic operation, and any unused positions will be certain to contain zeros and no other digit from a previous operation. Usually, however, this is not necessary. When results of arithmetic contain fewer digits than positions in a result field, the computer may "pad" zeros to the left or right of the decimal point where needed. For example

$$
\begin{array}{rcl}
2451 & 4 & \text{digits} \\
\times \quad .12 & 2 & \text{digits} \\
\hline
0294.12 & 6 & \text{digits}
\end{array}
$$

On the other hand, in the operations of multiplication and division, there are times when the decimal fraction part of a real number is longer than necessary. This is frequently true when only two positions are required in a result containing the cents portion of a dollar. Discounts on bonds, tax abatement rates, and results of some statistical measurements are some examples. When programmers need to handle these types of applications, they must determine the *precision* and *accuracy* required in their result fields.

Precision refers to the number of decimal positions.
$\frac{2}{7} = .28571428571$ has a greater precision than $\frac{2}{7} = .285714286$.

Accuracy refers to the number of significant digits.
$\pi = 3.14159$ is accurate to six significant digits. $\sqrt{2} = 1.4142$ is accurate to five significant digits.

The numbers 123.45, 1.23, and 0.12 are all expressed to two decimal places and have the *same* precision. However, they do not contain the same number of significant digits and, therefore, differ in accuracy.

Precision

In an example illustrating precision, consider that a municipality will give a tax abatement rate of .375985 to a landlord who promises to install insulation in all windows of a large apartment building. If the annual tax on this building was $6123.55 then the TAX would be formatted as F7.2 and the RATE (of abatement) would be formatted as F7.6. The coding to reduce this landlord's taxes would be

```
      READ (1,30) TAX, RATE
   30 FORMAT (F7.2,F7.6)
      ABATE = TAX*RATE
      TXDUE = TAX - ABATE
```

ABATE could be formatted large enough to include all of the digits to the right of the decimal point or as F13.8:

WRITE (2,40) ABATE

40 FORMAT (F13.8)

As an exercise, write a reasonable format for the variable named TXDUE as it might appear on a tax bill.

Care must be taken with decimal fraction positions. Some Fortran systems will only accept a maximum of nine positions to the right of the decimal point. With numbers requiring greater precision than this it might be better to use the exponential format discussed earlier.

Accuracy

Multiplication of approximate numbers often gives an incorrect impression of the accuracy of quantities. Assume that after the programmer rounded to the nearest cent, the following two values were multiplied. In

Variable Name	PICTURE	Value
FIRST	V99	.88
SECOND	V99	× .22
FRACTION-PART	V9999	.1936

after the COBOL statement

MULTIPLY FIRST BY SECOND GIVING FRACTION-PART.

was executed, the accuracy of each operand is to two significant digits, whereas the result has an accuracy to four significant digits. Since .88 and .22 may have been rounded off in previous calculations, their actual values could have been in the ranges of .875 − .884 and .215 − .224, respectively. Taking the *least* possible values and the *largest* possible values for each and multiplying, we get

Least	Largest
.875	.884
× .215	× .224
.188125	.198016

Rounding these two products to two significant digits yields .19 for the least and .20 for the largest possible values, respectively. Although these products have the same number of significant digits, they differ by one cent. Are they then *accurate* to two significant digits? While one cent may be a trivial amount for one operation, repetitious calculations of this type can compound differences. As with precision, care must be taken with the accuracy of results. The question of how many significant digits and when to round to the nearest cent should be determined by the policy of the organization for which the programmer is working.

DIVISION

Since division by zero is not permitted on the computer, all divisors should be tested before the division operation is executed:

IF (DIVSR.EQ.0.00) GO TO 2

is a Fortran statement that will cause program control to be transferred to statement 2 if DIVSR has a value of zero. Statement 2 should contain remedial activity or another instruction to bypass the division operation.

Zero divisors in COBOL can be trapped very simply by means of the statement

IF DIVISOR = 0 GO TO BY-PASS.

where BY-PASS is the name of a paragraph containing the instruction(s) to perform some corrective action.

Because the smallest possible number of positions for any divisor field is one, it follows that the largest possible number of digits in these quotients must equal the number of digits in the dividend.

Example 1

$$\frac{2222}{1} = 2222$$

Example 2

$$\frac{88.888}{2} = 44.444$$

Note that .444 is *not* a remainder.

Example 3

$$\frac{985.68}{44.4} = 22.2$$

If the programmer knows these values before the division operation, the Fortran format and the COBOL PICTURE clause for this example are

Divisor	F4.1	99V9
Dividend	F6.2	999V99
Quotient	F4.1	99V9

In business applications, where the same operation is performed repetitiously, values for each item of data are not known but a maximum field length must be determined. The number of integer and decimal fraction positions in the dividend could be the same as that in the quotient.

If the divisor or dividend were negative, the Fortran format would need to be large enough to accommodate a sign and the COBOL PICTURE clause would contain the S-specifier.

When the divisor has decimal fractions, a rule often used is to shift them to the right or multiply both the divisor and the dividend by an appropriate power of 10. This means shifting right one decimal position if the divisor has one digit for a decimal fraction, two places right if the divisor has two digits for a decimal fraction, and so on. This is based on the theorem in Chapter 6 where "equals multiplied by equals are equal." Thus

Example 4

$$\frac{9.999}{.1} = \frac{9.999 \times 10}{.1 \times 10} = \frac{99.99}{1.} = 99.99$$

Example 5

$$144 \div .12 = 1200$$

is equivalent to

$$(144 \times 10^2) \div (0.12 \times 10^2) = 1200$$

As an exercise, write the Fortran formats and the COBOL PICTURE clauses for the operands in this example.

Remainders

A division operation can be expressed in terms of divisor, dividend, quotient, and remainder, where

$$\frac{\text{Dividend}}{\text{Divisor}} = \text{quotient} + \text{remainder}$$

Dividing

$$\begin{array}{r} .80 \\ 2\overline{\smash{)}1.61} \\ \underline{1.6} \\ .01 \quad \text{remainder} \end{array}$$

We note that although this remainder is often written as the fraction $\frac{1}{2}$, the remainder contains the same amount of decimal fraction positions as the dividend.

Rewriting the equation for division, we have

$$(\quad .80 \quad \times \quad 2.0 \quad) + \quad .01 \quad = 1.61$$
$$(\text{quotient} \times \text{divisor}) + \text{remainder} = \text{dividend}$$

Remainders can be located in storage maps but high-level ANS COBOL provides an instruction to capture them separately from quotients and to make them available for further computations or printing. If A = 2.0 and B = 1.61, we could then write

DIVIDE A INTO B GIVING C REMAINDER D.

to have the remainder available in the variable named D. If we wrote an equivalent Fortran statement

C = B/A

and formatted C as F5.3, the result of 1.61/2.0 would be .805 where the remainder may appear as the decimal fraction .005. If C were formatted as F5.2, the result would be .81 where the remainder may be automatically rounded by the constraints of the field size (depending on the Fortran system being used).

Remainders are sometimes the unusable results of division as in repeating decimal expansions:

$$1 \div 7 = 0.142857142857\ldots$$

or in

$$1 \div 3 = 0.33333\ldots$$

In cases like these, the programmer must format the result field to capture as many significant digits in the quotient as are required for the accuracy that is needed in the application. Remaining decimal fractions may be unused and ignored.

Rounding

Conventionally, rounding has been performed by adding 5 in the column to the right of the number to be rounded and truncating the unwanted digits.

Examples

Rounding to the nearest cent

```
      2.407
    +  .005
    ─────────
      2.41│2     ← digit to be dropped
```

Rounding to the nearest dollar can mean dropping more than two digits:

```
     42.803691
   +    .500000
   ────────────
     43.│303691     ← digits to be dropped
```

Other examples are

$$
\begin{array}{ccc}
\text{(a)} & \begin{array}{r} -\ 147 \\ +\ -\ \ 5 \\ \hline -\ 15|2 \end{array} &
\text{(b)} \begin{array}{r} 14296 \\ +\ \ \ \ 50 \\ \hline 143|46 \end{array} \quad
\text{(c)} \begin{array}{r} 191 \\ +\ \ \ \ 5 \\ \hline 19|6 \end{array}
\end{array}
$$

In example (a), we rounded to the nearest two digits. In example (b), we rounded to the nearest three digits. In example (a), we added in a negative 5 because the number to be rounded was negative. In example (c), there is no carry because the digit to be eliminated is less than 5.

If we know that a field named X has five positions, including dollars and cents, we can round to the nearest positive or negative dollar amount. The following coding illustrates this procedure in Fortran:

```
        ROUND = .50
        IF (X)20,10,10
    10 RESLT = X + ROUND
        _____

        _____         other statements in program

        _____

    20 ROUND = −ROUND
        GO TO 10
```

A Packed Decimal Format

A different procedure may be followed in Assembler languages, where programmers can actually access the bytes containing the digit to be rounded and the digit(s) to be truncated. Instead of adding $+5$ or -5 to the digit(s) to be dropped, the digit(s) under consideration may be added algebraically to itself or themselves.

Examples

$$
\begin{array}{ll}
\text{(a)} \begin{array}{r} 2.34+ \\ +\ .04+ \\ \hline 2.38+ \\ 2.3+ \end{array} &
\text{(b)} \begin{array}{r} 4.78- \\ +\ .08- \\ \hline 4.86- \\ 4.8- \end{array} \\[2em]
\text{(c)} \begin{array}{r} 24.5673+ \\ +\ .0073+ \\ \hline 24.5746+ \\ 24.57+ \end{array} &
\text{(d)} \begin{array}{r} 18.4321- \\ +\ .4321- \\ \hline 18.8642- \\ 18- \end{array}
\end{array}
$$

(*Note:* The sign of the number appears next to the low-order position.)

Consider a situation where the programmer does not round off to the nearest cent but, rather, truncates the least significant digit.

Variable	PICTURE	Value
ADDEND	999V999	045ᴧ659
SUM	9999V99	4321ᴧ05

In

ADD ADDEND TO SUM.

the SUM field does not contain enough decimal fraction places. After the instruction is executed, the least significant digit is truncated and lost and the variable SUM will contain 4366.70.

Using the ROUNDED option in COBOL, we can derive a more acceptable answer for a business problem:

ADD ADDEND TO SUM ROUNDED.

which would result in a value for SUM of 4366.71. The ROUNDED option can be used in all four arithmetic operations in COBOL.

Truncating

From the notion of significant digits we can state that since $3000 = 3 \times 10^3$, the number 3000 contains one significant digit. Numbers such as 3456.78 can be reduced by successive truncation to one significant digit in the following manner:

Data Item	Significant Digits
3456.78	6
3456.7	5
3456	4
3450	3
3400	2
3000	1

The process of truncation resembles an approximation when amounts need to be given roughly in the hundreds, thousands, or millions. Approximations in these amounts are typical in government budgets, lists of outstanding shares, corporate expenses, and the like, except that they are usually made more reasonable by rounding.

Assume that at a certain point in time, a corporation had 14,867,624 shares of stock outstanding and that the programmer had to report outstanding shares that were expressed to the nearest thousands. The procedure to prepare this information would be

$$\frac{14867624}{10^3} = 14867.624$$

$$\begin{array}{r} 14867.624 \\ +\quad\quad .500 \\ \hline 14868.124 \end{array} \quad \text{rounding}$$

Truncating the decimal fractions yields 14868 or the approximate number of outstanding shares to the nearest thousands.

Truncation of decimal fractions can be done with the integer or INT function in Fortran and BASIC. The following statements

$$X = 14868.124$$
$$N = INT(X)$$

assign the value of 14868 to the variable named N.

Approximations to any number of significant digits can be done by dividing a number by an appropriate power of 10, rounding, and truncating.

The INT function is useful in another situation. The next statements

$$X = 27.94$$
$$I = INT(X) \qquad \text{value in I is 27}$$
$$Y = I \qquad\qquad \text{value in Y is 27.00}$$
$$Z = X - Y \qquad \text{value in Z is   .94}$$
$$SUM = SUM + Z$$

illustrate subtracting the integer portion of a number from itself to select the decimal fractions, then totaling these decimal fractions in the variable named SUM. If I should represent balances truncated to the dollar, then these instructions would capture the discarded pennies.

The INT function is not available in COBOL but the programmer can truncate unwanted digits. Given:

A PICTURE 99V99.
B PICTURE 99.

The statement

MOVE A TO B.

will cause the truncation of unwanted decimal fraction positions.

EXERCISES 8-2

1. Using the letter "n" as a placeholder, to describe a reasonably formatted variable, complete the following exercises. (Indicate a minus sign where needed and exclude extra positions for a remainder in division.)

   (a) nnnn.nn × nnnn.nn = _____

   (b) _____ × −nnn.nn = nnnn.nnnn

   (c)   n.n   × _____ = nnn.nnnn

   (d) nnn.nnn /   n.nn = _____

   (e)   nn.nn   /   .nn = _____

2. Which of the following has the greatest precision?

   (a) 1.2304 (b) 1.23 (c) 1.2304064

3. What is the accuracy of each of the following?

   (a) 400 (b) .00035 (c) 4030.101

4. Find the accuracy of the following to six significant digits:

   (a) 13/7   (b) 11/9   (c) 1/9   (d) 18/11

   (e) .3401E+3 (f) .324001E−4

   (g) Format (in Fortran) the result field for parts (a), (b), (c), and (d).

5. Rewrite the formula for division by computing the value of the remainder.

   REMAINDER = _____

   Be sure to indicate the operation to be performed first by enclosing it in parentheses.

6. Using the formula in Exercise 5, find the remainder in

   (a) 37/3

   (b) 14.5/5

   (c) 19/3.3

7. A retail store orders items by quantity. In order to determine the price per item for a customer, the store must first determine their cost per item. Which of the next two COBOL statements will do this?

   (a) DIVIDE QUANTITY INTO COST-OF-ORDER GIVING COST-PER-ITEM REMAINDER FRACTION-PART.

   (b) DIVIDE QUANTITY INTO COST-PER-ORDER GIVING COST-PER-ITEM ROUNDED.

8. A formula expressing the relationship of Centigrade temperatures to Fahrenheit temperatures is

$$\frac{C}{5} = \frac{F - 32}{9}$$

Complete

```
         READ (1,20) F
     20 FORMAT (_____)
         C = _____
         WRITE (2,30) C
     30 FORMAT (_____)
```

9. A furniture wholesaler is willing to give discounts of 40% to all retail stores. If the highest possible price for a piece of furniture is formatted as F7.2
   (a) Format the variables for the discounted price and the discount rate.
   (b) Write the Fortran statement(s) to compute the difference between the original price and the discounted price.

10. A price/earnings per share of stock or P/E ratio is computed by first dividing the outstanding shares into earnings less taxes to get the earnings per share.

$$\frac{\text{Earnings after taxes}}{\text{Shares outstanding}} \quad \frac{1{,}234{,}912.80}{561{,}324} = 2.20$$

   where $2.20 is the earnings per share.
   If the price of the stock is quoted at 23 and $\frac{3}{8}$, the P/E ratio is computed as the price of the stock divided by the earnings per share, or

$$\frac{23\frac{3}{8}}{2.20}$$

   (a) Give the COBOL PICTURE clause for PRICE per share, EARNINGS per share, and the P/E RATIO.
   (b) Write the COBOL DIVIDE statement to find the P/E RATIO.

11. Describe the rounding activity in the following report of daily deposits. Note that the columns called "Ratio to Total" and "Decimal %" do not yield the desired 100%, but that the last column, denoted "%," does.

Day	Amount Deposited	Ratio to Total	Decimal %	Rounding	%
Mon.	$ 1,062.25	.094653	9.4	.095153	9.5
Tue.	437.62	.038995	3.8	.039148	3.9
Wed.	118.00	.010515	1.0	.010663	1.0
Thur.	1083.52	.096549	9.6	.097212	9.7
Fri.	8521.15	.759289	75.9	.759501	75.9
	$11,222.54	1.000001	99.7%	1.001677	100.0

12. Truncate the following four significant digits
    (a) 0.00045672
    (b) 0.1234
    (c) 679.0
    (d) 0.14784
    (e) 1271000

13. Approximate by rounding and truncating 3,478,395.788 to the nearest
    (a) tens
    (b) tenths
    (c) thousands
    (d) hundreds

    (e) millions

    (f) hundreths

14. A state government has a budget of 45,658,760.85. Show how this can be approximated to the nearest million dollars.

15. Describe the error in logic in the following Fortran statement:

$$NET = RATE * HOURS + (HOURS - 40.0 * 1.5)$$

9

Handling Powers and
Roots

Problems as varied as determining compound interest and finding the side of a triangle require algebraic expressions that contain powers or roots of some real number.

POWERS

An example in compound interest illustrates how powers of a number can simplify calculations and reduce the programming effort. Assume that $1000 in a five-year investment pays 7% interest compounded annually. If the interest is not withdrawn, the manual and repetitious calculations for the five-year period could be as shown in Table 9.1:

TABLE 9.1

Year	Calculations
1	$1000.00 \times .07 = 70.00$
2	$(1000.00 + 70.00) \times .07 = 74.90$
3	$(1070.00 + 74.90) \times .07 = 80.14$
4	$(1144.90 + 80.14) \times .07 = 85.75$
5	$(1225.04 + 85.75) \times .07 = 91.76$

The total value after five years is $1310.79 + 91.76 = 1402.55$.

Using the distributive axiom for multiplication from Chapter 6, we can generalize the calculations as follows:

Let

P = principal
i = interest rate per annum
n = number of years
A = principal plus interest, where A is the amount or value of the investment

After one year the interest is Pi and the amount is $P + Pi$ or $P(1 + i)$. After the second year, interest is $iP(1 + i)$ and the amount is $P(1 + i) + iP(1 + i)$, or

$$A = P(1 + i)(1 + i)$$
$$= P(1 + i)^2$$

In general, the amount after n years is

$$A = P(1 + i)^n$$

and we can take the value of any principal forward in any amount of time using powers of some real number.

By placing an exponent on the real number, 1.07, we simplify calculations in Table 9.1. Thus

$$A = 1000.00(1.07)^5$$
$$A = 1402.55$$

Exponents

Definition 9-1.   When two or more numbers are multiplied together, each one of them is called a factor. If all factors are equal to each other, the number of factors is called a *power* of that factor.

For example, the factors $a \cdot a$ may be written as a^2, $a \cdot a \cdot a \cdot a$ can be written as a^4, and, in general, we write a^n, where a is called the base and n is called the power or exponent of the base. The term a^4 is described as "a to the fourth power"; a^n is called "a to the nth power."

Some general statements about exponents are

1. Let a equal any real number; then $a^1 = a$ and $a^1 \cdot a^1 \cdot a^1 = a^3$.
2. $a^n = 1$ for $a = 1$ and any n.
3. 0^0 is undefined.
4. $a^{-n} = \dfrac{1}{a^n}$.

Arithmetic Operations

When coding for *addition and subtraction* of numbers that have different exponents, we do not need to take any preliminary steps as the next examples in BASIC illustrate. (The "^" is BASIC's exponentiation symbol.)

Example

$$100 \ A = .37$$
$$110 \ B = 2.65$$
$$130 \ X = A\hat{\ }2 + B\hat{\ }3$$
$$140 \ Y = B\hat{\ }3 - A\hat{\ }2$$
$$150 \ PRINT \ X,Y$$

This results in X = 18.74653 and Y = 18.47273. The PRINT command displays these values on the computer's monitor or screen.

Simplifying the coding for *multiplication and division* of numbers that have exponents can be accomplished using the laws that govern the use of exponents. The following laws apply to any real numbers a, b, m, and n where b > 0.

1. $a^m \cdot a^n = a^{m+n}$
Let m = 3, n = 4. Then

$$a^3 \cdot a^4 = (a \cdot a \cdot a) \cdot (a \cdot a \cdot a \cdot a)$$
$$= a^{3+4}$$
$$= a^7$$

In this case, the BASIC coding is simplified from

$$A\hat{\ }M \cdot A\hat{\ }N \ \text{to} \ A\hat{\ }(M + N)$$

2. $a^m \cdot b^m = (a \cdot b)^m$
Let a = 4, b = 3, m = 2. Then

$$4^2 \cdot 3^2 = (4 \cdot 3)^2$$
$$= 144 \quad \text{(Likewise, } 16 \cdot 9 = 144)$$

The coding is $(A * B)\hat{\ }M$. Parentheses are important in this case since under the hierarchy rules exponentiation will be performed first. If parentheses were omitted, the result would be

$$4 \times 3^2 = 36$$

3. $a^m/a^n = a^{m-n}$ for $a \neq 0$ and all $m, n \in R$
Let m = 5, n = 3 (m > n). Then

$$\frac{a \cdot a \cdot a \cdot a \cdot a}{a \cdot a \cdot a} \quad \text{means} \quad a^{5-3} = a^2$$

and can be coded as $A\hat{\ }(M - N)$.

4. $a^m/a^n = 1$ when $m = n$ and $a \neq 0$. If $m = n = 4$

Then

$$\frac{a^1 \cdot a^1 \cdot a^1 \cdot a^1}{a^1 \cdot a^1 \cdot a^1 \cdot a^1} = 1$$

or

$$a^{4-4} = a^0 = 1$$

and coding for exponents may not be needed in this situation.

5. $a^m \div a^n = \dfrac{1}{a^{n-m}}$ if $m < n$, $a \neq 0$, and $\dfrac{1}{a^{n-m}} = a^{-(n-m)}$

Let $a = 10$, $m = 2$, $n = 3$. Then

$$\frac{10 \cdot 10}{10 \cdot 10 \cdot 10} = \frac{1}{10^{3-2}} \quad \text{or} \quad \frac{1}{10} = 10^{-1}$$

The coding for this expression is $A\,\hat{}\,-(N - M)$.

6. $a^m \div b^m = \left(\dfrac{a}{b}\right)^m$ if $b \neq 0$

Let $a = 6$, $b = 4$, $m = 3$. Then

$$6^3 \div 4^3 = \left(\frac{6}{4}\right)^3$$

$$= \frac{27}{8}$$

Likewise

$$\frac{6^3}{4^3} = \frac{216}{64}$$

$$= \frac{27}{8}$$

This can be coded as $(A/B)\,\hat{}\,M$.

7. $(a^m)^n = a^{mn}$

Let $m = 3$, $n = 4$. Then

$$(a \cdot a \cdot a)^4 = (a \cdot a \cdot a) \cdot (a \cdot a \cdot a) \cdot (a \cdot a \cdot a) \cdot (a \cdot a \cdot a)$$

$$= a^{3 \cdot 4}$$

$$= a^{12}$$

This can be coded as $A\,\hat{}\,(M * N)$.

EXERCISES 9-1

1. Simplify the following operations wherever possible, coding answers $a - 1$ in BASIC or Fortran:
   (a) $x^5 \cdot x^6$
   (b) $a^3 \cdot a^4 \cdot (2a)^2$
   (c) $y^4 \cdot z^4$
   (d) $a^6 \div a^2$
   (e) $a^x \div b^x$
   (f) $x(12^3 \div 6^3)$
   (g) $3^4 \div 3^6$
   (h) $5(4^2 \div 4^2)$
   (i) $2v \cdot (v^3)^2$
   (j) $8^2 \cdot 16^3 \cdot 64 = 2^?$
   (k) $a^{-1} =$
   (l) $3^4 \cdot 9^2 \cdot 3^{-1} \cdot 27 = 3^?$

   (m) $\dfrac{x^n}{x^{-n}}$

   (n) $\dfrac{x^{n-1}}{x^n} \div \dfrac{x^{-n}}{x^{n+1}}$

2. Use the law of exponents and the commutative axiom for multiplication where needed to simplify the following:
   (a) $(2.30 \times 10^{-4}) \times (1.86 \times 10^5)$

   (b) $\dfrac{(1.36 \times 10^5) \times (4.5 \times 10^6)}{(7.8 \times 10^6)}$

3. The distance to a certain star is 7×10^{13} miles. If the speed of light is 1.86×10^5 miles per second, how long will it take the light from this star to reach earth?

4. The exponentiation operator in Fortran and COBOL is the "**" or double asterisk. Assume that in determining the area of frisbees for packaging, a manufacturer uses the formula, area $= \pi r^2$, and wants an accuracy for pi to five significant digits or PI = 3.1416. The radius in inches is 10.25. Complete the following coding:

   READ (1, 10) _____

   10 FORMAT (_____)

   AREA = _____

   where the variable AREA is assigned the result of the calculations on the right side of the equals sign.

5. Use $A = P(1 + i)^n$ and one of the general statements about exponents. Solve for P by taking the value of A backward in time to find how much must be deposited today to receive $1000 in five years at 6% compounded annually. (Refer to the general statements about exponents if necessary.)

6. Simple interest is not compounded; that is, interest is not paid on previous year(s) interest.

For a \$1000 Certificate of Deposit, what is the difference between a five-year 10.77% simple interest and a five-year compound interest account at 9%? (Compounded annually)

7. If the average distance from the earth to its moon is about 240,000 miles, how long would it take to travel this distance at 55 miles per hour? Express the answer with an accuracy of six significant digits.

8. If it took a service bureau one-fourth of a year to complete a payroll system of programs, for how many minutes of time would the programmer charge? Use an 8-hour day, 40-hour week, and express the answer with a precision of five digits.

RADICALS

Definition 9-2. "The nth root of x is y," denoted as $\sqrt[n]{x} = y$, if and only if $y^n = x$.

Example

If $n = 2$ and $x = 4$, then $y = \sqrt{4} = \pm 2$ since $(\pm 2)^2 = 4$. We describe $\sqrt{4}$ as the second, or square root of 4.

If $n = 3$ and $x = -8$, then $y = \sqrt[3]{-8} = -2$ since $(-2)^3 = -8$. We describe $\sqrt[3]{-8}$ as the cube root of -8.

A radical is any indicated root. The symbol that denotes a root to be taken is $\sqrt{}$. If any root other than 2 is to be taken, the number specifying that root is written in the radical sign ($\sqrt[3]{27}$) and is called the *index*. The number under the radical sign is called the *radicand*. The nth root of a radicand x can be expressed as $\sqrt[n]{x}$.

There are four basic laws that govern operations on radicals:

1. $\sqrt[n]{x^n} = (\sqrt[n]{x})^n = x$, for $\sqrt[n]{x} \in R^*$
   states that the order in finding the power or the root is not important. That is, $\sqrt[3]{27^3} = (\sqrt[3]{27})^3 = 27$.

2. $\sqrt[n]{a} \cdot \sqrt[n]{b} = \sqrt[n]{a \cdot b}$ for $\sqrt[n]{a}$ and $\sqrt[n]{b} \in R$
   states that radicals with the same index can be multiplied.

3. $\sqrt[n]{a} \div \sqrt[n]{b} = \sqrt[n]{a/b}$ and $\sqrt[n]{a}$ and $\sqrt[n]{b} \in R$
   states that radicals with the same index can be divided.

4. $x\sqrt{a} + y\sqrt{a} = (x + y)\sqrt{a}$ for $x\sqrt{a}$ and $y\sqrt{a} \in R$

states that radicals that have the same index and radicand can be added or subtracted. Thus,

$$2\sqrt{a} + 3\sqrt{a} = 5\sqrt{a}$$
$$2\sqrt[3]{x} - 3\sqrt[3]{x} = -\sqrt[3]{x}$$

*Note that $\sqrt[2]{-4^2} = (\sqrt[2]{-4})^2$, but $\sqrt[2]{-4} \notin R$, where R represents the set of real numbers.

Some roots are elements in the rational set of numbers, for example

$$\sqrt[4]{16} = \pm 2, \qquad \text{since } (\pm 2)^4 = 16$$

$$\sqrt{a^2 \cdot b^4} = \pm(ab^2), \quad \text{since } (\pm ab^2)^2 = a^2 b^4$$

$$\sqrt[3]{1/8} = \tfrac{1}{2}, \qquad \text{since } (\tfrac{1}{2})^3 = \tfrac{1}{8}$$

If the root cannot be represented by an integer or a rational (fractional) number, it is called an irrational number.

Examples

$$\sqrt{2}, \quad \sqrt[3]{100}$$

Other roots, such as the root for $\sqrt{-1}$, are not typical of data processing problems and are not discussed here.

Finding Roots

To find the square root of a number, both Fortran and BASIC use the *mathematical functions*

> SQRT in Fortran
> SQR in BASIC

To find the square root of a variable named SQUARE, we can write in Fortran

> ANSWER = SQRT(SQUARE)

and the variable ANSWER will be assigned the value computed as the square root of the value found in the variable SQUARE.

Library functions or mathematical functions like INT and SQRT conceal from the programmer the complicated arrangement of computations taken by the software. They should be used whenever possible to simplify the programmer's efforts.

The function SQRT (or SQR) requires that its argument "SQUARE" be enclosed in parentheses and the argument must be a positive real number.

The argument for the square root function may also be an arithmetic expression. The hypotenuse in a right triangle is computed as

$$c^2 = a^2 + b^2$$

where c = the hypotenuse, and a and b are the base and height, respectively. In BASIC, we can code

> 10 HYPOTENUSE = SQR(BASE^2 + HEIGHT^2)
> 20 PRINT HYPOTENUSE

(As in algebra, terms and expressions enclosed in parentheses are computed first.)

Since the symbol for the radical "$\sqrt{}$" is not on computer keyboards, and since there is no mathematical function for finding roots except for the square root, roots must first be converted by the programmer to fractional powers. If $\sqrt[3]{8} = 2$, then $2^3 = 8$ and we can write:

$$8^{1/3} = 2$$

Refer to Definition 9-2.

In general terms, we can state that the nth root of x is y if and only if $y^n = x$, and code

$$X = Y\hat{}N \text{ or}$$
$$Y = X\hat{}(1/N)$$

This means that both roots and powers can be coded using exponents, and because terms in parentheses are computed first, it is possible to write

$$X = Y**(.5)$$

as another way of taking the square root. Consider Fortran examples:

$$T = P**(1./4.) \text{ or } T = P**(.25)$$
$$R = S**(1./5.) \text{ or } R = S**(.20)$$

In the Fortran expression, P**(1/4), the fraction 1/4 can cause truncation of decimal fractions. Therefore, the exponent can be written as 1./4. to avoid mixing fixed-point and floating-point modes.

When the exponent yields repeating decimal fractions or irrational numbers it is best to code

$$B = D**(1./7.)$$

and

$$C = A**(1./3.)$$

rather than

$$B = D**(.142857)$$

or

$$C = A**(.3333)$$

because the computer will use its own precision and probably provide the greatest accuracy.

For convenience in manual operations, as well as in computer programming, it is always helpful to simplify a radical expression to one that can be easily operated on. The following transformations are frequently used:

Example 1

Use as small a radicand as possible.

In $\sqrt{250}$

$$\sqrt{250} = \sqrt{25 \cdot 10} = \sqrt{25} \cdot \sqrt{10} = 5\sqrt{10}$$

and code

$$5.0 * SQRT(10.0)$$

Example 2

Use a rational denominator.

In $3/\sqrt[3]{9}$, we can use the property of the multiplicative identity:

$$\frac{3}{\sqrt[3]{9}} \times \frac{\sqrt[3]{81}}{\sqrt[3]{81}} = \frac{3\sqrt[3]{3 \cdot 27}}{\sqrt[3]{9 \cdot 9 \cdot 9}}$$

$$= \frac{9\sqrt[3]{3}}{9}$$

$$= \sqrt[3]{3} = 3^{1/3}$$

and code

$$3.0 ** (1./3.)$$

Example 3

Use an element from the set of integers as a radicand.

In $\sqrt{\frac{3}{7}}$, we can again use the multiplicative identity:

$$\sqrt{\tfrac{3}{7} \cdot 1} = \sqrt{\tfrac{3}{7} \cdot \tfrac{7}{7}}$$

$$= \sqrt{\tfrac{21}{49}}$$

$$= \sqrt{\tfrac{1}{49}} \cdot \sqrt{21}$$

$$= \tfrac{1}{7}\sqrt{21}$$

and code

$$(1./7.) \cdot SQRT(21.0)$$

At times, it may be desirable to reverse the procedures found in example 1.

Example 4

Use a coefficient of 1 or 2.
In $5\sqrt{5}$, we can apply the second law for radicals. Thus

$$5\sqrt{5} = \sqrt{5^2} \cdot \sqrt{5}$$
$$= \sqrt{25} \cdot \sqrt{5}$$
$$= \sqrt{125} \quad \text{or} \quad 1\sqrt{125}$$

and code

SQRT(125.0)

Before continuing with transformations of radicals, we note that the notions of exponents and integral roots are related in Definition 9-2.

Understanding that a number in radical form is another way of expressing the same number in exponential form makes it possible to write the *eighth law of exponents.*

8. $\sqrt[n]{a^m} = (\sqrt[n]{a})^m = a^{m/n}$ for $\sqrt[n]{a} \in R$ and $m, n \in R$.

Example

Let

$$a = 16, \quad m = 4, \quad n = 2$$

Then

$$\sqrt[2]{16^4} = (\sqrt[2]{16})^4$$
$$= 16^{4/2}$$
$$= 256$$

Likewise,

$$\sqrt{65536} = 256$$

and

$$\sqrt[2]{(256)^2} = 256$$

Using the eighth law of exponents, we can now complete our methods of simplifying radicals.

Example 5

Use as low an index as possible.

$$\sqrt[6]{16} = \sqrt[6]{2^4}$$
$$= (\sqrt[6]{2})^4$$
$$= 2^{4/6}$$
$$= 2^{2/3}$$
$$= \sqrt[3]{2^2}$$
$$= \sqrt[3]{4} = 4^{1/3}$$

and code

$$4.0 \cdot \cdot (1./3.)$$

EXERCISES 9-2

1. Simplify the following wherever possible:

(a) $3\sqrt[3]{27}$

(b) $4^2 + 2\sqrt{64} + 3\sqrt{64}$

(c) $\sqrt{3} - 2\sqrt{3}$

(d) $2^5 + \sqrt{2} + 16^{3/2} + 16^{3/2} \cdot 4^0$

(e) $9\sqrt{5} + 6\sqrt{125}$

(f) $\dfrac{3}{2\sqrt{3}} + \dfrac{7}{\sqrt{3}} - \dfrac{6}{4\sqrt{3}}$

(g) $\sqrt{x^4}$

(h) $\sqrt[x]{4^2}$

Using fractional (rational) exponents, show that

(i) $\sqrt[n]{a} \cdot \sqrt[n]{b} = \sqrt[n]{ab}$, where $a \geq 0$, $b \geq 0$.

In general, if $a \neq 0$, $a^{-n} = 1/a^n$ for n any positive integer. Where exponents are fractional (rational) and negative, take the reciprocal and proceed as before.

Example

$$\left(\frac{1}{27}\right)^{-2/3} = (27)^{2/3} = 9$$

Perform the following:

(j) $\left(\dfrac{8}{125}\right)^{-2/3}$

(k) $\dfrac{36^{-1/2} \cdot 9^{-1/2}}{81^{1/4}}$

(l) $\left[4\sqrt[4]{\dfrac{x^8}{16}}\right]^{-1/2}$

(m) $\left(\sqrt{x^{-3}}\right)^{-2/3}$

2. Simplify, if possible, and write the Fortran expressions for the following:

(a) $\sqrt{72}$ (e) $\sqrt{x} \cdot \sqrt{xy}$

(b) $\frac{1}{3}\sqrt{45}$ (f) $A\sqrt{C} + B\sqrt{C}$

(c) $\dfrac{5}{\sqrt[4]{16}}$ (g) $\sqrt{\frac{5}{8}}$

(d) $\sqrt[3]{81^2}$

3. When $a = -1$, what is a^n when n is odd? When n is even?

4. Is
   (a) B**3./2. = B$^{1.5}$
   (b) $(-5.)$**2.
   a valid expression?

5. Let A = 2, B = 3, and C = 5. Find the following:
   (a) A^B + C
   (b) A^(B + C)
   (c) A^ − B + A^(C − B)
   (d) C^(A * (−B))

6. Write the Fortran or BASIC statements for the following:
   (a) X = A to the fifth power
   (b) X = the fourth root of B
   (c) $a = \sqrt{x/y}$
   (d) $c = x^2 - 4x + 9$
   (e) $a = (x/y)^{1/3}$
   (f) $a^{1/5} + b = f$
   (g) $a = \dfrac{a^5}{5}$
   (h) $b - \sqrt{(b^2 - 4ac)}$

7. Find the solution set for the following:
   (a) $\sqrt{x^2 + 3} = 8 + x$ (Try squaring both sides)
   (b) $2\sqrt{x + 4} - x = 1$
   (c) $\sqrt[3]{x + 1} = 3$

8. Complete the following, using the $>$, $<$ or $=$ signs, for $x > 1$:
   (a) If $b > 1$, then b^x_____1.
   (b) If $0 < b < 1$, then 0_____b^x_____1.
   (c) If $b^{1/x} = a$, then a^x_____b.

9. A maker of clocks needs to know the time in seconds it takes a pendulum to swing from one side to the other and uses the formula

$$\text{Time} = \frac{\pi}{4}\sqrt{l}$$

where pi = 3.14159 and l is length in inches. If the lengths of the pendulums are from 10 to 20 inches and are found in the variable named XLEN, complete the following using reasonable formats.

```
        READ (1,20) XLEN
    20  FORMAT(_____)
        TIME = _____
        WRITE (2,30) TIME
    30  FORMAT(_____)
```

10. Code the following in Fortran or BASIC:
    (a) An aircraft h feet above the earth's surface can be seen for m miles. This is expressed in the following formula: $m = \sqrt{3h/2}$. Code the formula making h the subject of the program statement.

    $$H = \text{\underline{\hspace{6cm}}}.$$

    (b) The air pressure in pounds per square foot equals the velocity of the wind given in miles per hour squared times .003. Code the appropriate formula making the velocity the subject of the program statement.

11. A TV antenna post is secured to a roof with four bracing wires. Each wire is connected to the post at a point 2.5 feet above the roof and to the roof 2.5 feet from the post. How long is each wire?

12. The approximate number of seconds a falling object takes to fall f feet is given in the formula

    $$\text{Time} = \tfrac{1}{4}\sqrt{f}$$

    If it takes a desk 3 seconds to hit the ground after being dropped, how far did it fall?

ABOUT COBOL

The COBOL verbs ADD, SUBTRACT, MULTIPLY, and DIVIDE correspond to the operators "$+$," "$-$," "$*$," and "$/$," respectively. The exponentiation operator "$**$" in COBOL has no associated verb and is only used with the COMPUTE verb. Thus

$$\text{COMPUTE X} = \text{C}**2,$$

for squaring C or

$$\text{COMPUTE X} = \text{C}**.5.$$

for the square root of C.

Although these facilities enhance the usefulness of the COMPUTE verb, COBOL has limited computational capabilities and because its evaluation of long formulas is slow and inefficient, COBOL programs are seldom used for complex computations. COBOL is used primarily for business data processing tasks.

10

Algorithms and Flowcharts

ALGORITHMS

An *algorithm* is a finite set of instructions or commands designed to accomplish a specific task. An algorithm should satisfy the following criteria:

1. One or more *input* values must be present for processing.
2. Each *processing* instruction or command is clear and precise.
3. At least one value is produced as *output*.
4. The algorithm performs the required task efficiently and completely.
5. The algorithm terminates after a finite number of instructions.

Although computer programs vary from simple to very complex, they have three things in common with our description of an algorithm: input, processing, and output. Most applications that are programmed for computers should be written efficiently and completely and terminate after a finite number of instructions are executed.

Instructions are given to computers sequentially or one after the other. It is this sequence or serial arrangement of instructions and a level of detail that affects the creation of algorithms and the approach to the solutions of problems in information processing. Therefore, a process must be described as completely as possible. To do this, we begin by (1) understanding the problem, (2) stating what is known, and (3) stating what is unknown.

Consider a simplified problem—updating your savings account.

Understanding the problem. This is a matter of knowing that at the end of a period of time the bank will pay a certain amount of interest based upon the balance in the account and the rate of interest the bank is willing to pay.

What is known. The balance that appears in the bank's records (and in your passbook) and the interest rate promised by the bank. The balance and the rate of interest are *inputs*.

What is unknown. The amount of interest to be added to the balance. The amount of interest is the desired *output*.

Consider the *processing* steps needed to link input and output in this problem.

The bank's computer must find your account record in its disk or tape storage; take the balance and multiply it by a specified rate. This result or the amount of interest due is then added to the current balance to create your updated balance in storage. This amount will also appear in your updated (printed) bank statement, and the interest amount will probably be printed on a form and mailed to you with a copy for the Internal Revenue Service.

The language of algorithms is an English-like pseudo-code, which in a very general way resembles the computer instructions used to process a given task. For the savings account problem, we can write the following:

Take the interest on the savings account record

Write the updated record to disk

Print statements

To break these general statements down into a more satisfactory level of detail, we can write

Input savings account record

Compute interest = balance × rate

Add interest to balance

Write new balance to disk

Print bank statement

Print 1099 Form (Statement of Earnings Form)

The processing commands that give the necessary level of detail in this example are input, multiply, add, write (to disk), and print. The program control is given to one command at a time in this top-down sequence.

We can clarify the algorithm by illustrating the sequence of commands in a diagram or flowchart (see Figure 10.1).

Input savings account record

Compute interest = balance × rate

Add interest to balance

Write new balance to disk

Print bank statement

Print 1099 Form
(Statement of Earnings)

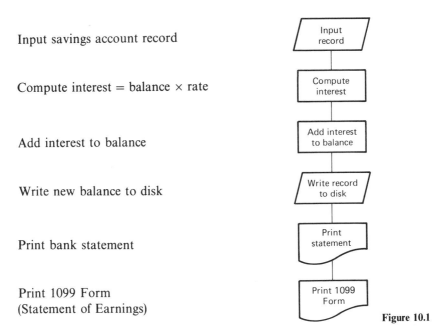

Figure 10.1

FLOWCHARTS

Flowcharts are frequently used to describe graphically program control and data flow because they make processing steps easy to visualize and follow. In the preceding flowchart, the parallelogram is the symbol to indicate input or output. The rectangle is the symbol used to indicate processing. The last symbols in this flowchart represent the printing function. Flowcharts contain symbols, annotations within the symbols, and flow lines.

> *Symbols* represent functions such as input/output commands, arithmetic operations, and program modifications.
>
> *Annotations* within a symbol describe a specific type of command, operation, or modification that is to take place.
>
> *Flow lines* connect the symbols and indicate the directions of the sequential steps. Flow lines may include arrowheads.

To set the order in which processing commands are to be carried out in algorithms and flowcharts, we need three basic formats, two of which are needed for control.

> *Sequence*—where one command sequentially follows another until the algorithm terminates.

Decision-Making Control—where one and only one set of command(s) is to be executed depending on whether a given condition is found to be "true" or "false."

Loop or Iteration Control—where one or more sequential commands are to be repeated while a given condition is "true." The repetition is terminated or fails when this condition is "false."

Sequence

Algorithms and flowcharts for sequential commands are easy to write since we all are familiar with doing simple tasks, particularly the arithmetic in the savings account problem discussed earlier. Consider another example.

You are renting an apartment and learn that your monthly payment is .5% of the present value of the house. Also assume that you have lived in the apartment for two years, what percent of the value of the house have you paid in rent? Write the algorithm and flowchart to find the value of the house (see Figure 10.2).

Input monthly rent

Compute value = monthly rent/0.005
Print value
Compute total rent = 24 × monthly rent
Compute percent = total rent ÷ value
Print percent

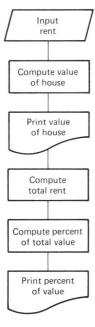

Figure 10.2

Decision-Making Control

The control elements for decision making indicate that a *choice* must be made. Therefore, we need the terms

IF THEN ELSE IF-END

in an algorithm to indicate that the sequence of commands will change depending on specified conditions. The flowchart symbol for decision is diamond shaped, as shown in Figure 10.3.

Figure 10.3

The shape of the decision symbol makes possible a choice among three alternatives. In the following example, however, we only need to make one of two choices.

    Consider that an inventory system in an automotive parts store has a reorder number assigned to the number of parts kept in each bin. The record of the number of windshield wipers, for example, is kept in a computer storage area that has the variable name COUNT. When a customer places an order, the quantity of windshield wipers ordered is subtracted from COUNT. When the bin count of windshield wipers is less than 100, a reorder message is printed; otherwise, the value in COUNT is printed. We can construct an algorithm as follows:

```
Input quantity
Subtract quantity from COUNT
IF COUNT is less than 100
     THEN
          print re-order message
     ELSE
          print value in COUNT
IF-END
_____
_____ any other program statements
_____
```

The keywords in this algorithm are IF THEN and ELSE. The IF statement is found in programming languages such as Fortran, COBOL, and BASIC, but the syntax varies from one language to another. If the student codes any of the examples in this chapter, the appropriate manuals must be referenced. We have included an IF-END to denote the end of these control statements. It is not part of the syntax of the IF statement in most programming languages.

Note that IF THEN ELSE IF-END are arranged in a specific pattern. IF and IF-END are lined up together as are THEN and ELSE. The indentation improves readability of this algorithm. The IF and IF-END define the limits of the decision control elements, and after the test is made on the bin counter and one of the print commands has been executed, program control is given to any statements that might follow the IF-END.

Using a flowchart, we can indicate that the control elements have forced a clear choice between two sets of commands. (See Figure 10.4.)

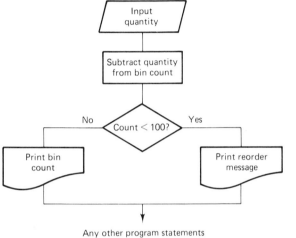

Any other program statements

Figure 10.4

It is possible to omit the ELSE clause when the choice is to process only one set of command(s) or *not* to process them. For example, if only the reorder message were required, we could write the algorithm as follows:

```
Input quantity
Subtract quantity from COUNT
IF COUNT is less than 100
        THEN
                print re-order message
IF-END
                                        any other program statements
```

The flow line leaving the left side of the decision symbol in the flowchart indicates that program control will be given to statements after the IF-END if the bin count is equal to or greater than 100, thus omitting the instructions to print COUNT. (See Figure 10.5.)

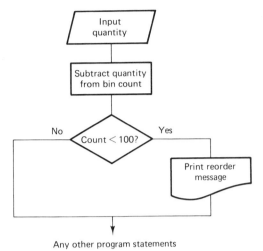

Any other program statements   **Figure 10.5**

Nesting Decision-Making Control

Either the THEN or the ELSE clauses may contain another IF. An IF statement may then be "nested" within another IF. Using the previous example, we could modify the algorithm and flowchart by writing

```
Input quantity
Subtract quantity from COUNT
IF COUNT > 100
     THEN print bin counter greater than 100
     ELSE
          IF 100 > COUNT
               THEN
                    print bin counter less than 100
               ELSE
                    print bin counter equal to 100
          IF-END
     IF-END
```

(See Figure 10.6.)

Before coding nested IFs, the student should refer to the manual for the language to be used. In BASIC, if an IF statement does not contain the same number of ELSE and THEN clauses, each ELSE is matched with the nearest unmatched THEN. For example

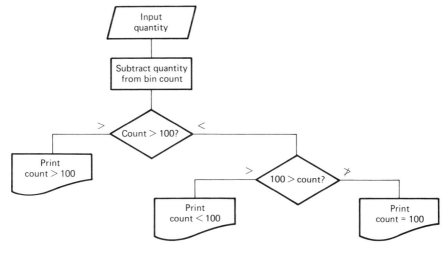

Figure 10.6

```
IF COUNT = 100
    THEN
        IF 100 = quantity
          THEN
              print bin counter = quantity
          ELSE
            print quantity not equal to bin counter
        IF-END
    IF-END
```

In this case, "quantity not equal to bin counter" will not print when COUNT is not equal to 100 and program control will fall through to any statement following the ELSE clause.

Loop or Iteration Control

The control elements for iteration are

DO WHILE and DO-END

They indicate that a set of commands are to be executed over and over until some specified condition is no longer true. The word DO is used in Fortran and the word WHILE is used in BASIC. COBOL has the PERFORM UNTIL for this type of iteration. The word DO-END is used here to denote the end of the iteration and functions much like the WEND (or WHILE END) in BASIC.

Consider that a manufacturer of rectangular metal plates must determine the area of these items before they can be sold. All plates are 48 inches long and their widths vary from 6 to 36 inches in increments of 1 inch. (The area of a rectangle is computed as length × width.) We can write the algorithm as follows:

```
Set length = 48
Set width = 6
DO WHILE width is less than 37
    Compute area = width × length
    Print area
    Add 1 to width
DO-END

_____
_____ any other statements in program
_____
```

The flowchart for this algorithm contains a flow line that returns above the decision symbol, as shown in Figure 10.7.

Width is initialized to 6 inches. As long as the width is from 6 to 36 inches, the process will be repeated. That is, control of the commands begins with the first computation and continues through to the command to increment the widths. At this point, control is returned or "loops back" to the DO WHILE statement (see flow line)

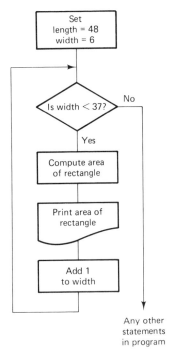

Any other statements in program   **Figure 10.7**

where a decision is made. When the width is greater than 36, the condition "width is less than 37" is no longer true, and the loop is broken. Program control is then given to any statement following the DO-END statement. The DO WHILE and DO-END statements determine the limits of the loop.

Care must be taken with the DO WHILE DO-END. It is possible to write an endless loop or to process the loop forever.

Consider that every month a retail store processes a file that contains many records for charge account customers. New purchases are added to any existing balances due and bills are mailed. The following illustrates this procedure in general terms:

```
Open the file
     Input a customer's record
     DO WHILE a customer record is found in the file
          Add new purchases to balance due
          Print bill
     DO-END
Close the file
```

In this arrangement, we print the same customer's bill over and over again. In other words, we never read and process more than one record in the file. We never break out of the loop and get past the DO-END. The following flowchart, shown in Figure 10.8, makes this clear.

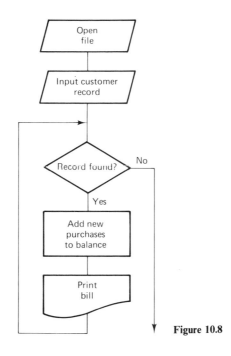

Figure 10.8

One way to get out of this loop is to write an instruction to input the record after the
DO WHILE statement:

```
Open the file
    DO WHILE a customer's record is found in the file
        Input a customer's record
        Add new purchases to balance due
        Print bill
    DO-END
Close the file
```

To execute properly, we must construct each loop with an entry point, a processing
section, and an exit point.

The flowchart for this algorithm indicates an entry point to the loop at the DO
WHILE statement. Since the customer records are input and processed within the
loop, processing steps will be executed once for each customer. When the computer
determines an *end-of-file* condition, the exit point will have been reached and program
control will be given to any statements following the DO-END.

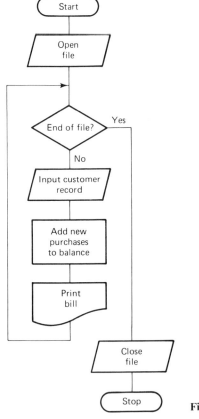

Figure 10.9

Note the symbol at the top and bottom of the next flowchart (see Figure 10.9). It is the *terminal* symbol used to indicate the start, stop, or interrupt of a program or procedure.

Summarizing the control elements, we can state that

Sequential statements that do not contain control elements will not alter the arrangement of processing commands.

Decision-making control elements, IF THEN ELSE IF-END, force a choice between different sets of sequential commands depending on specified conditions.

Iteration control elements, DO WHILE and DO-END, cause a process or sequence of commands to be repeated until a specified condition is no longer true.

Flowchart symbols frequently used with these control elements are illustrated in Figure 10.10.

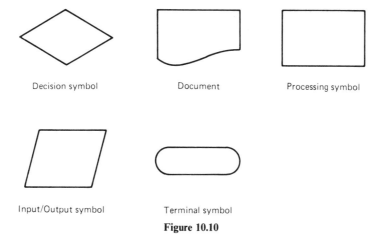

Decision symbol   Document   Processing symbol

Input/Output symbol   Terminal symbol

Figure 10.10

The normal flow of information in a flowchart is from top to bottom and from left to right. When this normal flow changes from bottom to top or from right to left, arrow heads should be used.

EXERCISES 10-1

1. Describe the activities in the following algorithms.
   (a) Set n = 1
       Set x = 1
       Set y = 1

```
DO WHILE N < 5
    compute x = x + y
    compute y = y + x
    print x and y
    add 1 to n
DO-END
```

(b) Set R = 0.5
Input A
IF A > 0
    THEN
        A = A + R
    ELSE A = A + (−1∗R)
IF-END

2. Translate the following scenarios into the appropriate algorithms using one of the three formats discussed in this chapter:

(a) To get a student driver's permit, an applicant must be 16 years old.

(b) Using all the receipts from a business trip, prepare an expense voucher with total expenses.

(c) Input a number. If the number is negative print CREDIT ELSE IF the number is positive, print DEBIT.

(d) Input records in an employee file and print out their names and addresses until there are no more records in the file.

(e) Convert the following Fahrenheit temperatures to Centigrade: 20, 30, 40, 50, 60. Use the formula

$$C = 5\frac{F - 32}{9}$$

3. Identify the following formats (see Figures 10.11, 10.12, 10.13, and 10.14):

(a)

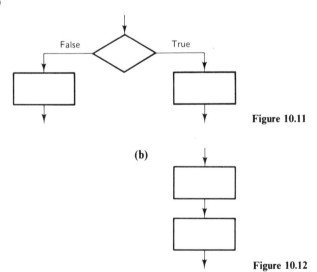

Figure 10.11

(b)

Figure 10.12

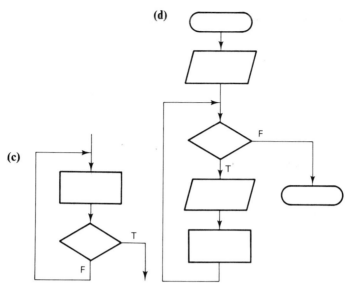

Figure 10.13   **Figure 10.14**

4. Use flow lines, and

    (a) Arrange the following symbols in appropriate places in a flowchart:

    (b) Write the algorithm associated with the flowchart. (See Figure 10.15.)

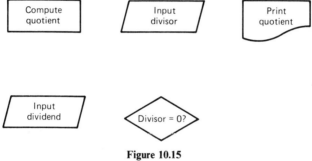

Figure 10.15

5. Write the flowcharts for the following algorithms:

(a) IF employee is not married
       THEN
              set tax exemption to single
       ELSE
              set tax exemption to married
    IF-END

(b) Open the file
    DO WHILE a record is found in the file
       Input salesperson's record
       Compute commission = sales × 8%
       Print check for commission
    DO-END
    Close file

(c) Input mileage
    Input gallons of gasoline
    Compute miles per gallon = mileage ÷ gallons
    Write miles per gallon to disk

6. Study the following algorithm. It contains an IF THEN IF-END construct nested inside a DO WHILE. Write the flowchart that illustrates this algorithm. (Each record in the file contains one number to be tested.)

                    Open file
                    DO WHILE there is a record in the file
                       Input record
                       IF number is greater than zero
                           THEN
                                  add number to total
                       IF-END
                    DO-END
                    Print total
                    Close file

7. The next flowchart (Figure 10.16) uses the full capability of the decision symbol by providing three choices. In general and simplified terms, this illustrates the way a programmer might prepare a Trial Balance for a business organization. The balances are found in storage as signed packed decimal numbers. Debits are signed positive. Credits are signed negative. Balances with a value of zero are bypassed in this example. Write the algorithm for this activity.

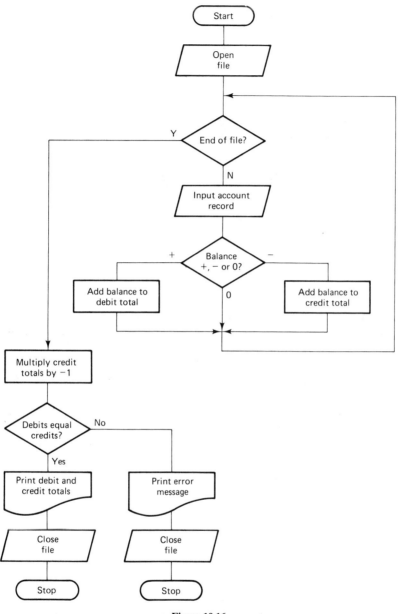

Figure 10.16

11

Programming
Considerations

When considering the various programming languages, the question arises as to why there is no one universally accepted language? With the exception of machine language, these languages allow the programmer to concentrate on the nature of the problem to be solved rather than on the characteristics of a particular machine, that is, programming in COBOL for business applications, Fortran for scientific problems, for only two examples.

Whatever the language, and whatever the application, programmers need to apply the control elements described in Chapter 10, with the logic required for good electronic record keeping, and to develop and maintain programs for activities such as

- Counting records
- Input and output verification
- Sorting records
- Creating tables and table lookup
- File maintenance

The logic to process these activities is the same in nearly all computer languages, and in BASIC, Fortran, and COBOL the coding is similar. The logic for table handling in COBOL is simple, but the coding becomes more complex and requires some experience when using the many options of the PERFORM verb.

These activities often involve reading an entire file, repeating the same processing activity over and over again for each record until an entire file has been read, processed, and written to some medium as we have discussed in the last chapter.

Computer code has to be written **from** algorithms and flowcharts. This code often includes programmed *counters* that are frequently used to keep track of repetitions or iterations in the algorithms that are needed for good electronic record keeping.

COUNTERS

Counters control iterations or loops. Counters, sometimes called index variables, take on *initial* values, an optional *incrementing* or *decrementing* factor and a *limit* or final value.

In BASIC, counters can control iteration using the FOR NEXT instructions: In a problem similar to Exercise 6-5, 4, consider

```
10 N = 0
20 FOR I = 1 TO 5
30 N = N + 2
40 M = N^2
50 NEXT I
```

Here there is a controlled loop with the counter I, in statement 20, initialized at 1 and incremented by 1. When no incrementing factor is given, the counter is automatically incremented by 1 in the NEXT statement. In our example, the NEXT I statement increments counter I by 1.

The statement FOR I = 1 TO 5 tests the value of I. If I has a value from 1 to less than 6, statements in the loop are executed. When I has a value greater than 5, control is given to the command after the NEXT I statement and the loop is exited.

A Fortran example of a "programmed" counter follows:

```
N = 0
DO 20 I = 1, 5
N = N + 2
20 M = N**2
```

This is similar to the BASIC example where even numbers 2, 4, 6, 8, and 10 are squared. The DO statement is followed by a statement number, which is in turn followed by an index definition, I = 1, 5. The index (or index variable) must be written as a fixed-point variable, in our example the letter I, and will take on successive values from 1 to 5.

The DO statement tells the computer to cycle through a loop or to execute repeatedly a following sequence of instructions up to and including the statement it references. The number of iterations or cycles is controlled by the values found to the right of the equals sign.

In COBOL, iteration is controlled through the use of the PERFORM verb.

```
                    MOVE ZEROS TO N.
                    PERFORM PARA1 UNTIL M = 100.
                    GO TO DONE.
            PARA1.
                    ADD 2 TO N.
                    COMPUTE M = N**2.
            DONE.
```

COBOL programming examples are nearly self-documenting. The preceding example can easily be read as accomplishing the same result as the previous Fortran and BASIC examples. Note that in all examples, iteration is performed only while a specified condition is true. As noted in the last chapter, when this condition becomes false, iteration is terminated.

Counters are important when controlling the number of records to be read or written in a file or when counting data items to be processed.

Note that for most business applications, a *record* is a collection of related data items (here a data item is simply a fact). A *payroll record*, for example, contains facts such as employee name, rate of pay, hours worked, employee identification number, and the like. A *file* is a collection of records that have common characteristics or similar functions.

INPUT VERIFICATION

All input must be valid, or else processing and output are meaningless. Keyboard operators, clerks, bookkeepers, accountants, tellers, salespeople, and customers; all make errors when writing numbers. One method of verifying data items such as identification or payroll numbers uses check digits. Gasoline credit cards may contain examples of check digits.

There are various methods of determining a check digit, and sometimes much is left to the ingenuity of the programmer. Two examples are given here:

Example 1

Let n = an account number; then $n/m = q + r$, where r, a remainder, becomes the check digit. This check digit is annexed to the low-order position of the account number. For example, let $n = 4587$, $m = 6$. Then

$$\frac{4587}{6} = 764 + 3/6$$

Annexing r to the low-order position of n, we get the account number with its check digit, or 45873.

Example 2

Let 121234567 be an employee social security number. Add the digits in the social security number *casting out* nines as we add. Annex the resulting digit to the low-order digit of the social security number as a check digit:

$$1 + 2 + 1 + 2 + 3 + 4 + 5 + 6 + 7$$

Casting out nines means $1 + 2 + 1 + 2̸ + 3̸ + 4̸ + 5̸ + 6̸ + 7̸ = 4$. The check digit, 4, is annexed to the social security number after the low-order digit. Thus 1212345674.

An algorithm for casting out nines can be written using a counter described in the following.

```
Input first digit—(variable to be used as result field)
Set counter to 1
DO WHILE counter is less than 9
Input next digit
result = result + next digit
IF result is greater than or equal to 9
      THEN subtract 9 from result
Add 1 to counter
IF-END
DO-END
```

We can code our algorithm in BASIC as follows:

```
10 INPUT M
20 FOR I = 1 TO 8
30 INPUT N
40 M = M + N
50 IF M > = 9
        THEN
              M = M − 9
60 NEXT I
70 PRINT M
80 END
```

The first INPUT statement is a request for the operator to enter a value for the variable M. After the first digit is typed in at the keyboard, the variable M will later be used to derive the resulting check digit.

Statement 30 contains the INPUT request for the remaining digits in the social security number. Statements 40 and 50 develop the check digit and statement 70 prints the check digit on the terminal screen.

The statement FOR I = 1 TO 8 tests the value of I. If I has a value from 1 to less than 9, statements in the loop are executed. When I has a value greater than 8, control is given to the command after the NEXT I statement as the loop is exited. The next flowchart in Figure 11.1 illustrates this type of control.

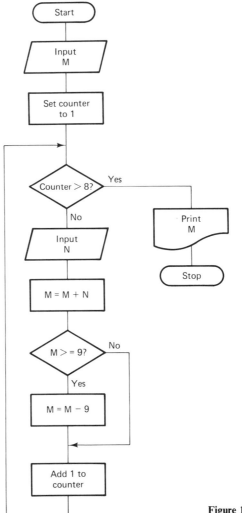

Figure 11.1

More About Counters

Care must be taken when setting upper and lower limits on counters. This upper limit was set at 8. Since the first digit of the nine-digit social security number was input before the loop was entered; only eight more digits needed to be processed.

The next example uses the counter, and its initial and final values as variables used in computations within the loop. The decrementing factor is − 1. Incrementing or decrementing factors are preceded by the word STEP in BASIC.

```
100 N = 1
110 INPUT X
120 FOR Y = X TO N STEP −1
130 N = Y*N
140 NEXT Y
150 PRINT N
160 END
```

This loop finds *n*! or *n factorial* for integers of any value of *x*. For example, if *x* = 5, then *n*! is computed in this loop as

$$5 \times 4 \times 3 \times 2 \times 1$$

Other integer values may be used for X and N.

OUTPUT VERIFICATION

Errors must be corrected before they spread throughout a business system. Catching these errors cannot always be done visually. When data items are found on magnetic tapes or disks, for example, other methods are used.

Hash Totals

A *hash total* can be taken on a data item that is not normally used in calculations, and thus is not subject to change. Hash totals can be used to ensure that all records in a file have been processed and serve better in this regard than a simple count of the records in a file.

Consider item numbers in an inventory system. Each item number is placed at the beginning of a record in a tape file of inventory records. Refer to Figure 11.2 and note that each record contains a *collection of related data items*.

Figure 11.2

Each record in the inventory file contains an item number, a description, and a level number, i.e., a number denoting the amount on hand. Inventory levels are checked periodically to determine whether they are overstocked or understocked. To be certain that each record has been interrogated, a "hash" total is taken. This means adding up each of the item numbers each time the tape is read. To make certain that each record is read, the computed hash total is compared to the hash total written at the end of the tape file. If the hash totals agree, each record has been read and processed. If the hash totals are not equal, an error situation exists.

Proof Numbers

In some payroll situations, such as those found in educational and other public institutions, the same gross pay is usually given to each employee each week. This means that federal and state tax amounts and voluntary deductions will always remain constant (unless there is a change in dependents or tax laws). By signing alternately "+" and "−," and by algebraically adding such amounts as gross pay, federal tax, state tax, United Fund, and so on, a unique *proof* number can be assigned to each employee each pay period. This proof number can be used to verify that each employee's check has been correctly processed. (See Table 11.1.)

TABLE 11.1

+ Employee number	− Gross pay	+ Fica tax	− Federal tax	+ State tax	− United fund	Proof number
110412	960.00	68.64	108.00	52.00	2.00	015476
132164	1040.00	74.36	120.00	62.00	2.00	029600

Note the signs placed above each column. Each of these fields is algebraically added together for each employee to produce a proof number. (Decimal points are ignored.)

Crossfoot Totals

Taking crossfoot totals is a procedure used to verify the addition of rows and columns of numbers.

Assume that an input file of Accounts Receivable with customer records has data items containing amounts for quarterly purchases as shown in Table 11.2. Totals are given by customer. A report in Table 11.3 totals the amounts billed quarterly. Although the file and the report contain the same amounts, their totals are computed differently and must agree. Let Q1 represent purchases from January through March, Q2 purchases from April through June, and so on. Taking crossfoot totals of these amounts in Table 11.2 means

- Adding up the totals for each quarter for each customer and creating an annual grand total of purchases by customers.
- Totaling quarter purchases, then taking the grand total of purchases for the four quarters.

TABLE 11.2 DATA FROM CUSTOMER FILE

Customer	Q1 total	Q2 total	Q3 total	Q4 total	Annual total
1	124.30	30.95	35.65	56.00	246.90
2	189.75	290.00	0.00	15.20	494.95
3	54.45	0.00	120.25	75.36	250.06
4	109.75	85.65	32.12	125.66	353.18
5	0.00	15.10	295.88	0.00	310.98
					1656.07

In Table 11.3 totals are taken by quarter and then added together.

TABLE 11.3 REPORT FROM BILLING

Customer	March	June	September	December	
1	124.30	30.95	35.65	56.00	
2	189.75	290.00	0.00	15.20	
3	54.45	0.00	120.25	75.36	
4	109.75	85.65	32.12	125.66	
5	0.00	15.10	295.88	0.00	
	478.25	421.70	483.90	272.22	1656.07

To make certain that no errors were made in the report, the programmer

(1) writes the algorithm for crossfooting totals
(2) flowcharts the algorithm
(3) codes and tests the program.

The algorithm to take crossfoot totals in this situation follows. Note that the fields used to accumulate totals have been set initially to zeros in the event that these variables may contain data from a previous operation.

```
Set total counters to zero
Open the file
DO WHILE there is a record in the file
    Input an Accounts Receivable record
    Take quarterly totals by each customer to create
        final annual grand total by customer
```

(Continued)

DO-END

Input totals for each quarter from report

Take grand total of quarters

Print totals by customer and by quarters

IF totals not equal

    THEN print error message

IF-END

Close file

The preceding algorithm and the flowchart in Figure 11.3 contain two types of control elements. The DO WHILE and the IF THEN.

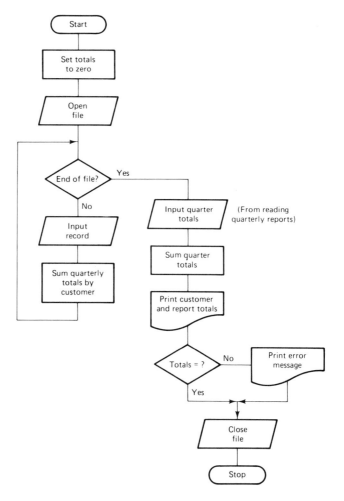

Figure 11.3

Adding columns vertically for each quarter and summing the quarterly totals should yield the same result as summing the rows or quarterly totals horizontally for each customer and taking the annual grand total for all customers.

Coding from the Flowchart and Algorithm

File handling is much easier in BASIC than in Fortran or COBOL. If the student has BASIC available, the following program creates the file of customer quarterly totals, then takes crossfoot totals. It can be run to prove out the algorithm. (The logic for the other computer languages is the same and the coding is similar for this organization of control elements.

```
40 OPEN "C:CROSSFOOT" FOR OUTPUT AS #1
50 FOR I = 1 TO 5
60 INPUT "ENTER CUSTOMER TOTALS BY QUARTER ", Q1,Q2,Q3,Q4
70 PRINT #1, Q1; Q2; Q3; Q4
90 NEXT I
100 CLOSE #1
110 '...INITIALIZE VARIABLES FOR TOTALS TO ZERO...
120 QT = 0
130 CHECKSUM = 0
140 OPEN "C:CROSSFOOT" FOR INPUT AS #1
150 WHILE NOT EOF(1)
160     INPUT #1, Q1, Q2, Q3, Q4
170     QT = QT + Q1 + Q2 + Q3 + Q4
180 WEND
190 INPUT "ENTER REPORT TOTALS ",QONE,QTWO,QTHREE,QFOUR
200 CHECKSUM = QONE + QTWO + QTHREE + QFOUR
210 PRINT QT;"Annual total of sales by customer totals"
220 PRINT CHECKSUM;"Grand total of sales by quarters"
230 IF QT < > CHECKSUM
        THEN
            PRINT"Totals in error"
240 CLOSE #1
250 END


RUN
ENTER CUSTOMER TOTALS BY QUARTER 124.30,30.95, 35.65, 56.00
ENTER CUSTOMER TOTALS BY QUARTER 189.75,290.00,0.00,15.20
ENTER CUSTOMER TOTALS BY QUARTER 54.45,0.00,120.25,75.36
ENTER CUSTOMER TOTALS BY QUARTER 109.75,85.65,32.12,125.66
ENTER CUSTOMER TOTALS BY QUARTER 0.00,15.10,295.88,0.00
ENTER REPORT TOTALS 478.25,421.70,483.90,272.22
    1656.07 Annual total of sales by customer totals
    1656.07 Grand total of sales by quarters
```

Creating the File

Before data can be sent from a program to a file on another medium, the output file must be OPENed. In our example, statement 40 OPENs the file named "CROSSFOOT" FOR OUTPUT. C: refers to the disk drive on which the file is to be created. The # 1 in our example specifies the file number, a convenient method for referring to this file in later file-related statements. Statement 50, FOR I = 1 TO 5, has as an upper limit, the number of customer records to be created in the file.

The INPUT command in statement 60 contains a message or prompt in quotation marks that requests the operator to enter the quarter totals for one customer. (This message appears at the bottom of the program listing.) At this point, program execution pauses while customer totals are typed, separated by commas. After four totals for one customer have been entered, the operator presses the carriage return key, program execution resumes and the command, PRINT # 1, moves one record containing these totals from the program to the disk file named CROSSFOOT (which is now simply referred to by # 1).

After the file has been created, it is closed in statement 100. Statement 110 is nonexecutable. It begins with a single quote, which specifies that a comment on the program may appear on that line. The next lines in the program are from the algorithm for taking crossfoot totals.

Processing the File

Before the file CROSSFOOT can be used for *input* to a program it must be OPENed as shown earlier in statement 140. INPUT # 1 means input to the program for processing, the four data items, Q1, Q2, Q3, Q4 in one customer's record from the file CROSSFOOT.

Statement 150, the WHILE statement (useful when reading all the records in a sequential file without the need to specify the number of records) begins the control for iteration. As long as it is true that we have NOT read the *End-Of-F*ile marker for the file CROSSFOOT (referred to as 1 in a WHILE statement), we can proceed with the sequential commands that follow.

Statement 160 causes one customer record to be brought from disk storage into the program for processing. QT accumulates totals one record at a time for all customers. When the EOF condition occurs, program control passes to the statements that follow the WEND statement.

The INPUT statement in line 190 asks for totals to be entered from the report. The message "ENTER REPORT TOTALS " appears as output from statement 190. (See the bottom of the program listing.) At this point the program pauses while totals are entered at the keyboard separated by commas. After the report totals have been entered, the carriage return key is pressed. QONE, QTWO, QTHREE, and QFOUR are the variables to take on the values of these report totals by quarter. CHECKSUM accumulates the grand total for all four quarters.

Totals are printed, a test is made on them, an appropriate message is printed if necessary, the file is CLOSEd, and the program is terminated with the END statement. After the program has been typed in, the word RUN is typed followed by a carriage return and the program begins execution.

The next section describes the use of counters in sorting records.

SORTING RECORDS

After a new file has been created and its records verified for accuracy and completeness, it is often the programmer's task to sort the records in a logical sequence to present information in an orderly and meaningful manner.

Consider the following file of customer records that are sorted in ascending order on a customer number. This organization of data is useful for filing records on disk or permanent storage, but when reporting the best customers, we might need to re-sort on the balance field:

Customer number	Balance
48	428.65
50	321.96
67	805.00
85	38.40
91	102.45

In BASIC, the DIM (for Dimension) statement is used to reserve storage for an array of data items.

DIM BALANCE(5)

Reserves an area named BALANCE in storage for five adjacent numeric data items. To access one of these data items or element in an array, subscripts are used. Subscripts may be whole numbers or variables with whole number values. BALANCE can now be coded as a subscripted variable.

Examples:

BALANCE(4) refers to the 4th element in BALANCE

BALANCE(J) refers to the Jth element in BALANCE where J cannot be greater or less than the number of elements in BALANCE.

BALANCE(J + 2), BALANCE(J − 3)

and so on as long as the subscript is within the bounds of the array that is, not less than 1 or greater than the upper bound − in our example, five elements.

The following BASIC code loads the array named BALANCE using the letter I as a subscript. Note that customer balances are found in the DATA statement and that the data items are separated by commas.

```
10 DIM BALANCE(5)
20 DATA 428.65,321.96,805.00,38.40,102.45
30 FOR I = 1 TO 5
40     READ BALANCE(I)
50 NEXT I
```

The READ statement reads values from the data statement and assigns them to locations in BALANCE on a one-to-one basis, in our example, to successive locations 1 through 5 as specified by the index variable I.

Assume that we have loaded the array BALANCE with customer balances. The following algorithm and flowchart for the sort contain two nested control elements within a DO WHILE.

```
Set N = number of elements in array
Set counters: J = 1, H = 1
DO WHILE counter J is less than or equal to N
    DO WHILE counter H is less than or equal to N − J
        IF an element is greater than the next sequential
            element, exchange elements
        IF-END
        Add 1 to counter H
    DO-END
    Add 1 to counter J set H = 1
DO-END
```

Note the use of the circle as a connector symbol and arrowheads in the flowchart. (See Figure 11.4.) The connector symbol is sometimes used instead of flowlines to simplify the appearance of a flowchart.

With a few modifications, the following sort program in BASIC can be run in Fortran with the DO statement or in COBOL with the PERFORM verb and will place customer balances in ascending order.

```
70 N = 5
80 FOR J = 1 TO N
90     FOR H = 1 TO (N − J)
100 IF BALANCE(H) > = BALANCE(H + 1) THEN 150 ELSE 180
150 SAVEB = BALANCE(H)
160 BALANCE(H) = BALANCE(H + 1)
170 BALANCE(H + 1) = SAVEB
180 NEXT H
190 NEXT J
```

```
200 FOR J = 1 TO 5
210     PRINT BALANCE(J)
220 NEXT J
230 END
```

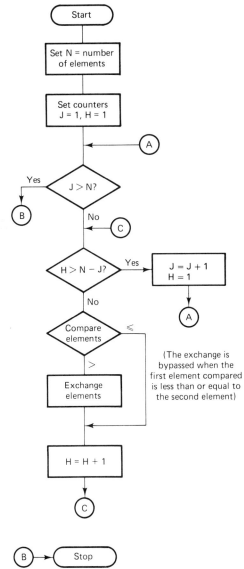

Figure 11.4

(In BASIC or COBOL we can use the letter H or any other letter for index variables and whole number subscripts. In Fortran letters I through N should be used.) Using a loop within a loop, the program compares adjacent elements in the array, reversing them if the numbers are not in ascending sequence and bypassing an exchange when the first element compared is less than or equal to the second element. The variable SAVEB is needed to temporarily save a number when an exchange is made.

On the first pass through the inner loop, the first element is compared to the second. On the second pass the second element is compared to the third and so on. No matter where the largest number is found, by the time the inner loop has completely cycled, it will be placed in the last position in the array.

After the inner loop is completely cycled, the outer loop's counter is incremented by 1 and the inner loop begins again with a new final value for its counter or 1 less than before. This means that one less comparison needs to be made since the highest number in the array is already in the correct position. Each complete cycle of the inner loop will cause the next highest number to be placed in the next highest position in the array thus placing all the elements in ascending order.

To place the best customer or the highest balance first, the "$>$" symbol can be changed to the "$<$" symbol.

In COBOL, sorting can be done with the COBOL SORT statement.

CREATING TABLES

Tax tables are needed in payroll programs, amortization schedules are prepared for loans and mortgages and so on. Very often it is the programmer who prepares these tables from mathematical formulas.

Earlier in an exercise in Chapter 9 we suggested that finding a value backwards in time included the operation of taking the reciprocal of:

$$\frac{1}{(1 + i)^n} \quad \text{or} \quad (1 + i)^{-n}$$

We can use one of these expressions in a formula to determine an annual loan payment and help to develop an amortization schedule or table.

$$\text{Payment} = \text{loan}/((1 - (1 + i)^{-n})/i)$$

Where i = the interest rate and n = the number of years. Given

Amount of loan = \$4000.00
The interest rate is 8% compounded annually.
Payments are made annually for 5 years.

Using this formula

$$\text{annual payment} = 4000.00/((1 - (1 + .08)^{-5})/.08)$$
$$= 4000.00/((1 - .6805832)/.08)$$
$$= 1001.83 \text{ (rounded)}.$$

The amortization schedule for this loan can be prepared by creating Table 11.4.

TABLE 11.4

Period	Annual payment	Interest on outstanding principal	Amortization of principal	Principal outstanding
0				4000.00
1	1001.83	320.00	681.83	3318.17
2	1001.83	265.4536	736.3764	2581.7936
3	1001.83	206.54349	795.28651	1786.5071
4	1001.83	142.92057	858.90943	927.59767
5	1001.83	74.207813	927.62219	− 0.02452
		1009.125473	4000.02453	

The difference in the original principal and the final amortization of principal is only two cents but a difference often occurs due to rounding after only four or five decimal digits.

The first column is the period or time frame for interest. Column 2 contains the payment due at the end of every period. Computing the next three columns, we have

$$0.08 \times 4000.00 \quad = 320.00$$

$$1001.83 - 320.00 = 681.83$$

Thus, 320.00 of the first payment is the first year's interest and 681.83 is used to reduce the debt:

$$4000.00 - 681.83 = 3318.17$$

or the amount still owed.

The remaining periods are computed in a similar manner as the algorithm and flowchart for this table-building process illustrate. (See Figure 11.5.)

```
Set loan to 4000.00
Set interest to 8%
Set payment to 1001.83
Set payment period to 5
Set counter I to 1
DO WHILE counter I is less than or equal to number of periods
    Compute interest on current principal amount
    Compute reduction of principal
    Compute remaining principal
    Print a line in loan schedule
    Add 1 to counter
DO-END
```

The control elements are for *iteration*. (Iteration can be performed using the DO WHILE or FOR NEXT statements.)

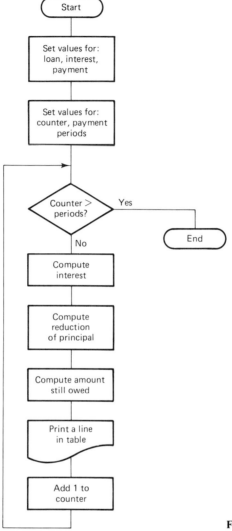

Figure 11.5

The BASIC program that follows prepares the amortization schedule and totals the amounts in the third and fourth columns of Table 11.4. The total in the third column is 1009.13 (rounded) and reveals that the true cost of this loan in five years is about 25% of its principal.

```
100 '...AMORTIZATION PROGRAM...
110 PAYMENT = 1001.83
115 AMOUNT = 4000.00
120 PRINT "PERIOD","PAYMENT","INTEREST","AMORTIZATION","PRINCIPAL"
```

```
125 PRINT "----------","----------","----------","----------","----------"
130 PRINT , , , ,AMOUNT
135 FOR I = 1 TO 5
140 INTEREST = AMOUNT * .08
145 REDUCTION = PAYMENT − INTEREST
150 AMOUNT = AMOUNT − REDUCTION
155 PRINT I,PAYMENT,INTEREST,REDUCTION,AMOUNT
160 TOTALINTEREST = TOTALINTEREST + INTEREST
165 TOTALREDUCTION = TOTALREDUCTION + REDUCTION
170 NEXT I
175 PRINT , ,"----------","----------"
180 PRINT , ,TOTALINTEREST, TOTALREDUCTION
185 END
```

TABLE LOOKUP

Frequently, a specific record must be retrieved from computer storage to be verified or modified. Consider Table 11.5, which contains entries for automobile part numbers and prices. A table *entry* is a collection of related facts treated as a unit.

TABLE 11.5

	Part number	Price
Entry 1	10025	300.00
Entry 2	11620	475.81
Entry 3	20009	300.00
Entry 4	36125	029.00
Entry 5	40201	750.25

Over a period of time, prices may vary with inflation or special sales. However, the part number will probably not change and can serve as a key or identification number. This key is also called the *table argument*. A table *argument* is a unique number found in an entry in a table. The table argument serves as a key to reference other related facts in the table entry. The table *function* is the information contained in a table entry and referenced by the table argument.

Each table argument can have one corresponding function but a function may have more than one table argument. In Table 11.5, more than one part has a price of $300.00. Assume that Table 11.5 exists on magnetic tape and that an inquiry was made on part number 36125 from a keyboard. The part number entered from an input device can be described as the *search argument*. A *search argument* is a value given in input data. It is used to locate an equal comparison between itself and the table argument.

The logic used to find the part number on the tape is as follows:

1. Compare the search argument to a table argument.
2. If the comparison finds the two arguments to be equal, branch to a routine in the program to process the function.
3. If the comparison finds the two arguments not to be equal, have we examined each table argument in the tape?
4. If we have not compared every part number to the number in the search argument, move ahead one entry to compare the next table argument to the search argument.
5. If we have examined every table argument and found unequal comparisons, the search argument is invalid; that is, there is no corresponding entry in the tape, and the inquiry should be bypassed.

We can flowchart the logic for table lookup in Figure 11.6.

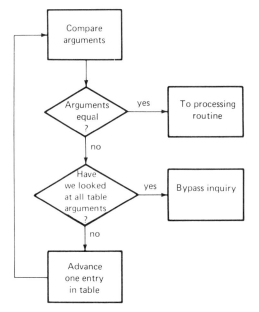

Figure 11.6

Julian Dates and Computing Elapsed Time

Files have retention dates. Tax files must be retained a number of years specified by state and federal laws. Overdue accounts are handled by 30-, 60-, or 90-day elapsed time and time periods are also important in annuities and mortgages. Julian dates are often used to compute elapsed time. A *Julian date* is a unique number assigned to each day in a year.

If we assign to each successive day in a year a unique number from 1 to 365, it is a simple matter to determine elapsed time by subtraction. For example

Day-Number	Calendar date
71	March 12
−38	February 7
33	

Using this technique, we can quickly determine that 33 days have elapsed between February 7 and March 12.

To create a table of days with each table argument containing the month and day (Jan. 1, Jan. 2, etc.) and each table function containing 001, 002, and so on, would be costly in terms of computer storage and table lookup time. Instead, we use a smaller table containing one table argument for each month and a function containing accumulated days. (See Table 11.6.)

TABLE 11.6

Argument (month)	Function (accumulated days)
01	000
02	031
03	059
04	090
05	120
06	151
07	181
08	212
09	243
10	273
11	304
12	334

If we are interested in 0815, or August 15, we search for 08 and add 15 to 212. August 15 is the 227th day of the year. Assume that a date found on a tape file was 156 and a search argument contained the date 0815, or August 15; the elapsed time can be determined by a table lookup routine and the operations of addition and subtraction:

$$
\begin{array}{cc}
212 & 227 \\
+\ 15 & -156 \\
\hline
227 & 71 \quad \text{days elapsed time}
\end{array}
$$

Assume that a loan was made on November 20 and paid in full on January 20. Subtracting

$$
\begin{array}{r}
20 - \quad \text{January 20} \\
-324 - \quad \text{November 20} \\
\hline
-304
\end{array}
$$

yields a negative number. By adding 365 to a negative result field, we add in a full year, or 365 days, and correct. Thus

$$365 + (-304) = 61 \text{ days}$$

This is the elapsed time between November 20 and January 20.

One algorithm and flowchart (see Figure 11.7) for computing elapsed time are

Input beginning month and day
Compute Julian date
Input ending month and day
Compute Julian date
Compute elapsed time

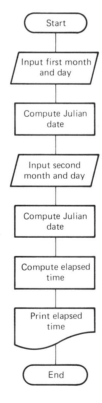

Figure 11.7

In the BASIC program that follows, the DATA statement contains the first Julian date for each of 12 months. These dates are read into the array named JULIAN in the FOR NEXT statements. Note that data items in the DATA statement are separated by commas and that the subscripts MONTH1 and MONTH2 act as search arguments. (This program assumes no negative results.)

```
100 '...JULIAN DATE PROGRAM...
125 DIM JULIAN(12)
127 DATA 0,31,59,90,120,151,181,212,243,273,304,334
130 FOR I = 1 TO 12
140     READ JULIAN(I)
150 NEXT I
160 INPUT "ENTER FIRST MONTH ", MONTH1
165 INPUT "ENTER DATE ",DAY1
170 DATE1 = JULIAN(MONTH1) + DAY1
180 INPUT "ENTER SECOND MONTH ",MONTH2
185 INPUT "ENDING DAY ",DAY2
190 DATE2 = JULIAN(MONTH2) + DAY2
200 ELAPSED = DATE2 − DATE1
210 PRINT DATE2 " − " DATE1 " = " ELAPSED "Days elapsed"
215 END
```

To include the years in a Julian date, input data and the table argument may include two high-order digits for the last two digits of the year.

$$87001 \quad \text{means January 1, 1987} \quad \text{or} \quad 87 \times 10^3 + 001$$

and

$$89063 \quad \text{means March 4, 1989} \quad \text{or} \quad 89 \times 10^3 + 063$$

Leap years require additional coding by the programmer.

Binary Search

For large tables containing 100 or more entries, a more efficient technique for table searching can be used. The technique, known as *binary search*, begins searching at the middle of the table instead of at the beginning and continues to divide the remaining entries in half until the desired entry is located.

For convenience of illustration, we shall use a table of only 30 entries. (See Table 11.7.) In this table, inventory item numbers are the table arguments and prices are the functions. Note that if our table contained 100 inventory items, an average of 50 comparisons would be required to find each desired entry. Further, table lookup for each entry (see Figure 11.6) may require five or six computer instructions, so that in a 100 element table, searching under table lookup routines could require that six instructions be repeated a costly 100 times if we began at the top.

TABLE 11.7

Entry	Item No.*	Price
1	01	1.25
2	02	2.00
3	03	3.45
4	06	6.98
5	08	0.65
6	10	1.58
7	12	2.76
8	15	2.50
9	17	2.85
10	19	1.90
11	21	4.15
12	22	0.95
13	28	2.13
14	40	1.04
15	42	2.16
16	45	1.81
17	51	4.45
18	60	8.00
19	63	8.50
20	70	9.00
21	71	1.05
22	79	2.18
23	80	6.43
24	83	7.04
25	88	4.02
26	90	5.14
27	91	5.58
28	94	6.35
29	98	1.23
30	99	8.50

*In ascending sequence.

To begin the search at the middle of the table, we take the first and last entry and average them:

$$\frac{1 + 30}{2} = 15\tfrac{1}{2}$$

Because no entry can be accessed by $\tfrac{1}{2}$, we truncate the fractional part of our answer and start searching at the fifteenth entry, which is the item numbered 42. Three things are possible at this point:

1. The search argument equals the table argument.
2. The search argument is lower than the table argument.
3. The search argument is higher than the table argument.

If the search argument equals the table argument, we have found the required item. If the search argument is higher than the table argument, the required item is in the upper half of the table. If the search argument is lower than the table argument, the required item is in the lower half of the table.

Suppose the search argument is 21:

$$\frac{1 + 30}{2} = 15\frac{1}{2}$$

After truncation occurs, comparison between the search argument, 21, and the table argument, 42, reveals 21 to be in the lower half of the table since $21 < 42$. (See Table 11.7.)

Next, take the lower half of the table and divide this group of table entries in half:

$$\frac{1 + 15}{2} = 8$$

Comparing 21 to Item No. 15, we find that table argument to be in the second quarter of the table. Averaging gives

$$\frac{8 + 15}{2} = 11\frac{1}{2}$$

and truncating the $\frac{1}{2}$ yields 11. The search argument and the table argument are now equal, and we have found the required item 21.

EXERCISES 11-1

1. (a) Numeric data items may be verified for completeness and accuracy by a _____.
   (b) Files may be verified for completeness by _____ .
   (c) Check digits are used to verify _____ .
   (d) A file is a collection of _____ that have similar _____ .
   (e) A record is a collection of _____ .
2. The DO statement in Fortran is similar to the FOR NEXT construct in BASIC. In the following program, DO 30 I = 1,5 means execute the successive instructions down to and including statement numbered 30. After statement 30 is reached, counter I is incremented by 1. A test on the value in I is made before the loop is executed again and when I > 5 program control is given to the statement that follows statement 30. Write the code to complete the following Fortran program:

Fortran	BASIC
DO 30 I = 1,5	10 FOR I = 1 TO 5
READ _____	20 INPUT #1, Q1,Q2,Q3,Q4
20 FORMAT _____	30 QT = Q1 + Q2 + Q3 + Q4
QT = QT + Q1 + Q2 + Q3 + Q4	40 NEXT I
30 CONTINUE	50 PRINT QT
WRITE _____	60 END
50 FORMAT _____	
70 STOP	
75 END	

(The CONTINUE statement provides a reference number for the DO statement.) STOP terminates the execution of a Fortran program and END specifies the end of the program.

3. If the variables $X = 3$, $Y = 2$, and $Z = 1$ initially, what will their values be after the activities in the flowchart in Figure 11.8 are completed?

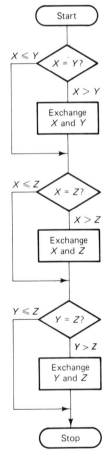

Figure 11.8

4. In the flowchart shown in Figure 11.9 there are two counters named CTR1 and CTR2.
  (a) How many records are read? _____
  (b) How many records are printed? _____

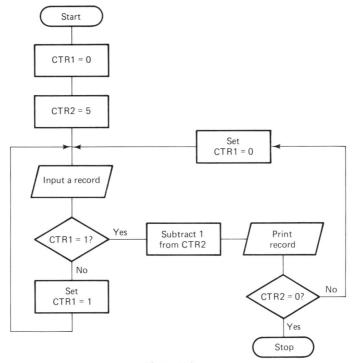

Figure 11.9

5. In a file of inventory records, each record contains a part number, description of the item in inventory, a price, the quantity-on-hand, and a level number. Write the algorithm to read this file, and take the "hash" total on a data item that will not be used in calculations. In the same iteration, compare the quantity-on-hand to a reorder number and print a message for any item when the quantity-on-hand is too low.

6. A file of N numbers is read into an array as shown in the next BASIC program segment. Because the programmer does not know exactly the number of elements on the disk file, ARRAY is dimensioned as high as reasonably possible.

```
70 DIM ARRAY(100)
80 OPEN "C:TEST" FOR INPUT AS #1
90 I = 0
110 WHILE NOT EOF(1)
120 INPUT #1,N
130 I = I + 1
140 ARRAY(I) = N
150 WEND
160 CLOSE #1
```

Write the code in BASIC or Fortran to find the highest number in the array. It is not necessary to sort the array in ascending or descending order.

7. Using the binary search technique, and one decision symbol, flowchart the logic to find one table argument in Table 11.7. (If the student writes the program for this problem, the INTeger function should be used for truncation.) The flowchart can be expanded to input n number of search arguments and to handle invalid search arguments.

8. A couple with $10,000 for a down payment wants to purchase a home with a 15-year mortgage at 9% interest, believing that they will sell the house within that time. Aware that monthly payments on shorter loans may be higher than for conventional 30-year mortgages, they decide to compare the cost of the 15-year mortgage to interest on the $10,000 that might be otherwise invested. Given

$$\begin{aligned}
\text{Cost of home} &= \$75,000 \\
\text{Less down payment} &\quad - 10,000 \\
\text{Amount of loan} &= 65,000
\end{aligned}$$

Let

$$n = \text{the number of years to pay back the loan}$$
$$m = \text{the number of monthly payments per year}$$
$$r = \text{the interest rate}$$

where 9% compounded monthly = 9%/12 months is equivalent to 0.75% 12 times a year.

The monthly payment is computed as

$$\text{Amount of loan}/[(1 - (1 + r/m)^{-mn})/(r/m)]$$

Now consider an alternative savings plan for the $10,000 with 6.5% interest compounded quarterly. A formula that computes the amount in this savings account after 15 years is

$$\text{Savings} = 10,000(1 + r/m)^{mn}$$

Let

$$r = \text{interest rate}$$
$$m = \text{number of interest periods per year}$$
$$n = \text{number of years}$$

Write the algorithm to compute the actual cost of the loan and the return on savings. If BASIC or Fortran is available, write a program to compare these two amounts.

9. Using a table of Julian dates, write the algorithm and BASIC or Fortran program to find the elapsed time for
   (a) 3/21/87 to 2/1/88
   (b) 2/20/87 to 1/20/88

10. The following COBOL statements read like an algorithm. Describe the activities taking place. Assuming that records in DRIVER-FILE and LICENSE-FILE are sorted in ascending order, how are first and last records handled?

```
      OPEN DRIVER-FILE. OPEN LICENSE-FILE.
      READ LICENSE-FILE.
      MOVE LICENSE-NUMBER TO SAVE.
BEGIN.
      READ DRIVER-FILE AT END GO TO NEXT-SEARCH.
      IF PLATE-NUMBER < SAVE GO TO BEGIN.
      IF PLATE-NUMBER = SAVE GO TO FOUND-IT.
      IF PLATE-NUMBER > SAVE GO TO INVALID-PLATE.
FOUND-IT.
      WRITE FOUND-CAR-RECORD FROM LICENSE-RECORD.
      CLOSE DRIVER-FILE, LICENSE-FILE.
INVALID-PLATE.
      DISPLAY "LICENSE-NUMBER OUT OF SEQUENCE OR
      ILLEGAL-PLATE-NUMBER VERIFY RECORDS".
      CLOSE DRIVER-FILE, LICENSE-FILE.
```

If you are familiar with COBOL, you can easily change the GO TO's to PERFORM, modify the program in a more structured manner, and compare all the PLATE-NUMBERs to LICENSE-NUMBERs.

11. Write an algorithm to create a check digit for a seven-digit employee number.

12. Flowchart the three steps in the following scenario. Use one decision symbol with three choices and connector symbols to simplify the drawing.

FILE MAINTENANCE

One of the most important activities in processing information is file maintenance. For example, in order to prepare bills for customers, all transactions for purchases must be recorded within a reasonable amount of time. Typically, two files must be processed:

- A master file of all customers containing data items such as name, customer number, and balance due.
- A transaction file of purchases made within the last billing period (one or more per customer).

When updating a master file in this manner, we find that three events are possible (assuming records in both files are sequenced in ascending order on customer number):

1. A record on the master file contains a customer number that is less than the transaction customer number. This indicates that the master record is inactive. No purchases were made in this period, and no processing should take place for that customer.

2. The customer numbers in the master file and on the transaction record are equal. This means the customer has made purchases during the period and this balance must be updated.

3. The customer number in the master file is greater than the customer number on the transaction record. This indicates a new customer whose record must now be merged into the new master file and processed in the next billing period.

12

Set Theory

We noted in Chapter 1 that a *set* is a collection of elements. These elements can be numbers, persons, objects, or anything else. The tires on a car form a set, the days of the week, all the negative numbers, all students in a class, and so on. Typically, a set is a number of things grouped in such manner as to form a whole.

PROPERTIES OF ELEMENTS IN A SET

Properties of elements in sets are

1. A statement must exist that states whether an element is or is not in a set.
2. The order in which the elements appear in a set is not important.
3. Elements in a set are distinct.

Definition 12-1. Two sets are equal if and only if they contain the same, that is, identical elements.

This means the same as the following: If two sets are equal, then they contain the same elements; and if they contain the same elements, then the two sets are equal. Thus, if

$$A = \{1, 3, 5\}$$

and

$$B = \{5, 1, 3\}$$

then $A = B$ by Definition 12-1, and by property 2.

Sets are typically referred to by upper-case letters A through Z. Two sets may contain the same *number* of elements, yet not be equal.

One-to-One Correspondence

It is believed that our ancient ancestors made a one-to-one correspondence between objects they were interested in (or a set of things) and the fingers of their hands (another set). Today, the meaning for a one-to-one correspondence is much the same.

For example, let $A = \{1, 2, 3, 4\}$ and $B = \{a, b, c, d\}$; then we can show a one-to-one correspondence between A and B in the following manner:

$$\{1, \ 2, \ 3, \ 4\}$$
$$\updownarrow \quad \updownarrow \quad \updownarrow \quad \updownarrow$$
$$\{a, \ b, \ c, \ d\}$$

This is only one of several one-to-one correspondences possible between A and B.

Definition 12-2.   Two sets are *equivalent* if each element of the first set can be paired with one and only one element of the second set and if each element of the second set can be paired with one and only one element of the first set. That is, if there is a one-to-one correspondence between the elements of the two sets, the sets are equivalent.

Equivalent sets are sets that contain the same number of elements. If two sets are equal then they are equivalent. However, the converse is not necessarily true because the definition for equality states that identical elements must exist in both sets.

Example 1

$$A = \{\Delta, \$, ?\}$$
$$B = \{\text{red, green, blue}\}$$

Since the elements in A and B can be put into a one-to-one correspondence, A and B are equivalent sets by Definition 12-2; but $A \neq B$.

Example 2

$$A = \{1, 2, 3\}$$
$$B = \{3, 2, 1\}$$

In this example, A and B are equal and equivalent sets by Definitions 12-1 and 12-2, respectively.

A set may contain no elements, a finite number of elements, or an infinite number of elements.

Definition 12-3.   A set containing no elements is called the *null* set or empty set and may be written as either $A = \{\ \ \}$ or $A = \varnothing$, but not $\{\varnothing\}$, which denotes a set containing the empty set.

A set containing a finite number of elements can be written in the *listing format*

$$A = \{4, 5, 6\}$$

or by the *set-builder* notation:

$$A = \{x | 3 < x < 7, x \text{ is a natural number}\}.$$

The preceding notation reads: set A = the set of all x such that x is a natural number greater than 3 and less than 7.

Definition 12-4. A set is said to contain an infinite number of elements if it can be put into a one-to-one correspondence with

$$A = \{1, 2, 3, \ldots\}$$

where A is the set of all of the counting, or natural, numbers.

The use of three dots may also indicate omitted elements in a set containing a finite number of elements. In the set $B = \{1, 2, 3, \ldots, 50\}$, the three dots are a short-cut method to indicate the missing natural numbers from 4 through 49.

When discussing sets, it is useful to have some general reference in mind from which all the elements of the sets can be drawn. Consider, for example, the set of all programmers. This consists of COBOL programmers, Fortran programmers, Assembly language programmers, and, in general, people who simply want to increase their skills in getting computers to help them solve problems. There are also American programmers, French programmers, and so on. Therefore, from a general set of all programmers, we can draw any one of a number of different subsets of programmers. A general set is sometimes referred to as a universal set.

Universal Set

The term *universal set* is used to designate the entire collection of things under consideration. To demonstrate this concept in a practical data processing situation, assume that the entire collection under consideration is the set of data items in a pay check. Then

Paycheck = {gross pay, hours worked, rate of pay, medical insurance, savings bonds, social security number, state taxes, federal taxes, FICA, net pay}

Paycheck is the total collection of items under consideration, but it is clear that there are smaller collections of items within the larger collection. Involuntary deductions or taxes such as state and federal taxes and FICA deductions and voluntary deductions such as medical insurance and savings bonds make up two smaller collections called *subsets*.

TABLE 12-1

	Name	Gross Pay	Hours	Rate	Medical Insurance	State Tax	Fed Tax	Fica	Savings Bonds	Net Pay
Record 1	A	960.00	80	12.00	25.75	52.00	108.00	68.64	92.31	613 30
Record 2	B	1040.00	80	13.00	25.75	62.00	120.00	74.36	100.00	657.89

Table 12-1 represents a simplified data base for employees or the collection of data items needed to prepare payroll checks. In a payroll situation, sets are a useful concept. Observe that the elements of the set, gross pay, are calculated for each individual by multiplying elements in two other sets: hours and rate. Net pay is calculated by subtracting out the deductions for medical insurance, savings bonds, state, federal, and FICA taxes. Further, the subsets comprising taxes must be totaled for all employees and checks have to be sent to the appropriate government agencies.

Using our nomenclature of upper- and lower-case letters, let U represent the total collection of paycheck elements, and let g = gross pay, w = hours worked, r = rate of pay, m = medical insurance, b = savings bonds, n = social security number, s = state taxes, f = federal taxes, t = FICA, and p = net pay. Then

$$U = \{g, w, r, m, b, n, s, f, t, p\}$$

The symbol U is often used to represent the Universal Set.

Subsets

If we let T represent a smaller collection of items that make up the involuntary deductions called taxes, then

$$T = \{s, f, t\}$$

where all the elements of T are included in U. However, there are elements in U not found in T.

Definition 12-5. If every element of a given set A is an element of a given set B and at least one element in B is not found in A, then A is said to be a *proper subset* of B. This can be denoted as $A \subset B$.

In the paycheck universe, we can write $T \subset U$, or $\{s, f, t\} \subset \{g, w, r, m, b, n, s, f, t, p\}$. The symbol $\subset$ is read "is a proper subset of."

The null set, $\{\ \}$ or $\varnothing$, is a *proper* subset of every set except itself. For example

$$\varnothing \subset T$$

Definition 12-6. Set A is said to be a subset of set B if and only if each element of A is an element in B. This is denoted as $A \subseteq B$.

This means that

$$\{s, f, t\} \subseteq \{s, f, t\}$$

where the symbol $\subseteq$ is read "is contained in," or "is a subset of." Therefore, every set is a subset of itself.

EXERCISES 12-1

1. Write each of the following sets using braces and listing the elements or members:
   (a) Days of the week
   (b) Natural numbers between 7 and 12
   (c) Natural numbers less than 3 and greater than 8
   (d) Even natural numbers

2. A is the set of all counting numbers less than or equal to 10. State which of the following expressions are true, and which are false.
   (a) $8 \in A$ (f) $12 \in A$
   (b) $.5 \in A$ (g) $\frac{1}{4} \notin A$
   (c) $25 \notin A$ (h) $0 \subseteq A$
   (d) $\emptyset \in A$ (i) $-1 \in A$
   (e) $\emptyset \subset A$

3. Which of the following sets are finite? Which are infinite?
   (a) The natural numbers
   (b) The population of Missouri
   (c) The decimal places for π
   (d) All the money in America

4. If $U = \{\$, a, ?\}$, list all the possible subsets in U.

5. Which pairs of sets are equivalent? Which are equal?
   (a) $\{a, b, c\}$ and $\{c, a, b\}$
   (b) $\{1, 2, 3, 4\}$ and $\{5, 6, 7, 8\}$
   (c) $\{\frac{1}{2}, \frac{2}{3}, \frac{7}{8}\}$ and $\{x, y, z\}$
   (d) $\{R, w, *\}$ and $\{\text{dogs, cats}\}$

6. Let $U = \{1, 2, 3, 4, 5, 6, 7\}$, $A = \{1, 2, 3\}$, and $B = \{2, 3, 4, 5\}$. Using $\in, \notin, \subset, \subseteq, \not\subset,$ and $\not\subseteq$, describe the relationship of the following. (Example: The relationship of A and U is $A \subset U$.)
   (a) B, U (d) $1, A$
   (b) A, B (e) $\emptyset, B$
   (c) $7, B$

7. Let $A \subset U$, $B \subset U$, $C \subseteq B$, $x \in A$, and $y \in B$.
   (a) Can $x \in B$?
   (b) Must $y \in A$?
   (c) Can $y \in C$?
   (d) Is $C \subset U$?

8. List all subsets of each set:
  (a) $A = \{1, 2\}$ set of two elements
  (b) $B = \{1, 2, 3\}$ set of three elements
  (c) $C = \{1, 2, 3, 4\}$ set of four elements

9. Based on your answers to Exercise 8, determine the number of subsets in a set of five elements. Can you determine a formula for the number of subsets in a set of n elements?

10. Is there a set that has only one subset?

11. Describe the following sets:
  (a) $\{\quad\}$
  (b) $\varnothing$
  (c) $\{\varnothing\}$

12. List the subsets for a, b, c in Exercise 11.

Venn Diagrams

Venn diagrams are helpful when describing relationships between sets. (See Figure 12.1.)

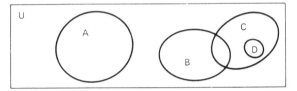

Figure 12.1

Although the compartments vary in many possible ways, there is no section that can remain unspecified as to membership. If an element is common to more than one set in the rectangle, it will only appear once in an operation on the sets to which it belongs. (See Figure 12.2.) If the element is employee deductions, for example, the Venn diagram is only concerned with this logical type, not how many employee deductions there are. In Figure 12.1, the universe or entire collection of things under discussion is indicated by all points inside the rectangle U.

The different shapes indicate the subsets of U, and in Figure 12.1 $A \subset U, B \subset U$, $C \subset U, D \subset U$, and $D \subset C$. All shapes A, B, C, and D are "properly contained" in U. D is also properly contained in C. B and C have some commonality, and A has no elements common to B, C, or D.

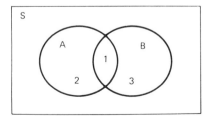

Figure 12.2

Definition 12-7. If two sets A and B are not empty sets and contain no common elements, they are said to be *disjoint sets*.

Let $A = \{1, 2\}$ and $B = \{3, 4\}$. Then

$$1 \in \{1, 2\}$$

and

$$2 \in \{1, 2\};$$

but

$$1 \notin \{3, 4\}$$

and

$$2 \notin \{3, 4\}$$

Thus, A and B are disjoint sets because they have no elements in common.

OPERATIONS ON SETS

There are two operations on subsets in a given universe that are important to us, *union* and *intersection*.

Union

Definition 12-8. The *union* of two subsets, A and B, is a *binary operation* that yields a third subset C formed by the elements found in either A or B, or in both A and B.

The symbol $\cup$ indicates the union of two subsets, and $A \cup B$ is read "A union B," or "the union of A and B."

To illustrate the properties of the operation of union, we use the universal set, $S = \{1, 2, 3\}$,[1] with the following proper subsets:

$$A = \{1, 2\}$$
$$B = \{1, 3\}$$
$$C = \{2, 3\}$$
$$D = \{1\}$$
$$E = \{2\}$$
$$F = \{3\}$$
$$\varnothing = \{\ \ \}$$

[1]We use the letter S instead of U to designate the universal set to avoid confusion with the union symbol, $\cup$.

Then

$$A \cup B = \{1, 2, 3\}$$

see Figure 12.2.

The elements in $A \cup B$ are listed only once because two sets have been joined, not added in any numerical sense. This conforms to the third property of sets. Because we are interested only in classes of objects, the repetition of the digit 1 is redundant. In the example, we are interested only in the fact that the digit 1 is an element in either A or B or in *both* A and B.

Table 12.2 called a union table, shows the results for all possible unions in the universe S, where $S = \{1, 2, 3\}$.

Because the union of any two sets produces a subset of the universal set, the operation of union has the property of *closure*. (That is, the union of any two sets in the universal set yields a set in the universal set or the universal set.) Studying Table 12-2, note that $B \cup C = C \cup B$, $F \cup D = D \cup F$, $A \cup B = B \cup A$, and so on; that is, the commutative law holds true for the union of sets. See Definition 12-8.

The commutative property.   Inspection of the elements in the subsets being operated on also demonstrates the *commutative property* of union.

TABLE 12.2

$\cup$	S	A	B	C	D	E	F	$\emptyset$
S	S	S	S	S	S	S	S	S
A	S	A	S	S	A	A	S	A
B	S	S	B	S	B	S	B	B
C	S	S	S	C	S	C	C	C
D	S	A	B	S	D	A	B	D
E	S	A	S	C	A	E	C	E
F	S	S	B	C	B	C	F	F
$\emptyset$	S	A	B	C	D	E	F	$\emptyset$

Since $B \cup C = C \cup B$

$$\{1, 3\} \cup \{2, 3\} = \{1, 2, 3\}$$

and

$$\{2, 3\} \cup \{1, 3\} = \{1, 2, 3\}$$

Therefore

$$\{1, 3\} \cup \{2, 3\} = \{2, 3\} \cup \{1, 3\}$$

Since in Table 12.2 the arrangement of sets is symmetrical, the left diagonal ($\backslash$), sometimes called the major diagonal, provides a way of locating the sets that demonstrates the commutative law. Thus, if we place a pencil along the diagonal, we can see that the subsets to the right of the pencil form a mirror image of the subsets on the left. (See Table 12.2a.)

TABLE 12.2a

$\cup$	S	A	B	C	D	E	F	$\varnothing$
S	S	S	S	S	S	S	S	S
A	S	A	S	S	A	A	S	A
B	S	S	B	S	B	S	B	B
C	S	S	S	C	S	C	C	C
D	S	A	B	S	D	A	B	D
E	S	A	S	C	A	E	C	E
F	S	S	B	C	B	C	F	F
$\varnothing$	S	A	B	C	D	E	F	$\varnothing$

From this inspection, we can see that $B \cup A = A \cup B$, $E \cup B = B \cup E$, and so on.

The associative property.   Consider $(D \cup E) \cup F = D \cup (E \cup F)$, where D, E, and F are as shown in Table 12.2. As in algebra, the parentheses indicate the operation to be performed first.

Since

$$(D \cup E) = A \quad \text{and} \quad (E \cup F) = C$$

and

$$A \cup F = D \cup C$$

Also, since

$$A \cup F = S \quad \text{and} \quad D \cup C = S$$

then

$$(D \cup E) \cup F = D \cup (E \cup F)$$

The Venn diagrams in Figure 12.3 graphically illustrate this associative property.

From Table 12.2, it can be shown that the associative property holds for the union of all sets in the universe S.

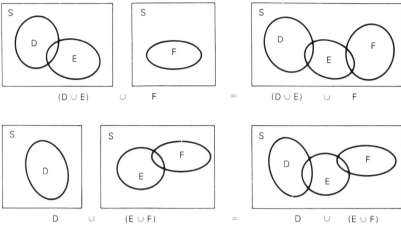

Figure 12.3

The identity property.   The identity property for union can also be derived from Table 12.2, where

$$S \cup \varnothing = S$$
$$A \cup \varnothing = A$$
$$B \cup \varnothing = B$$
$$C \cup \varnothing = C$$
$$D \cup \varnothing = D$$
$$E \cup \varnothing = E$$
$$F \cup \varnothing = F$$
$$\varnothing \cup \varnothing = \varnothing$$

From this we see that $\varnothing$ serves as the identity for the union operation.

Observe from the last column to the right or in the bottom row of Table 12.2, the union of a given set and the null set always yields the given set.

EXERCISES 12-2

1. Given (see Figure 12.4)
   Name the pairs of disjoint sets.
2. Draw the Venn diagram to illustrate the commutative law for union in $A \cup B = B \cup A$.

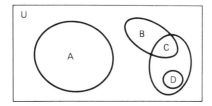

Figure 12.4

3. Find the result for the following:
   (a) $\{1, 2, 3\} \cup \{2, 3, 4\}$
   (b) $\{x | 6 < x \leqslant 9\} \cup \{0, 3, 80\}$ (where x is a natural number)
   (c) $\{a, b, c, d\} \cup \{a, c, e\}$
4. Verify the associative property for

   $A = \{\$, \#\}, B = \{11\}, C = \{/, \#\},$

   where $(A \cup B) \cup C = A \cup (B \cup C)$
5. Using Venn diagrams, prove that $\varnothing \cup A = A$, for any set.
6. Given $S = \{\Delta, 0\}$, list the four subsets of S and construct the appropriate union table.
7. When does
   (a) $A \cup D = A$
   (b) $A \cup \varnothing = U$
8. Each customer of the XYZ Retail Store has two types of records in the store's files: Record 1, which contains the customer's name, address, and customer identification number and is used for mailing lists when advertising sales; and Record 2, which contains the customer's identification number, purchases for the last month, date and amount of the last payment, and balance due. This record type is used to bill customers.
   Consider each record as a collection of data items.
   (a) Use the listing format to indicate all the elements formed by the union of these sets (or records).
   (b) Does the union of these two sets demonstrate the property of closure?
   (c) Draw the Venn diagram to illustrate the elements, showing any elements common to the two sets.

Intersection

If set $B = \{1, 2, 3, 4\}$ and set $C = \{2, 3, 4, 5\}$, the elements common to both B and C are 2, 3, and 4. If $E = \{2, 3, 4\}$, then set E contains only those elements found in both B and C.

Definition 12-9. The *intersection* of two subsets A and B is a binary operation that yields a third subset C formed by the elements found in both of the subsets A and B.

The symbol $\cap$ indicates the intersection of two subsets, and $A \cap B$ is read "A intersect B," or "the intersection of A and B." For the sets given in the preceding example, we can write

$$\{1, 2, 3, 4,\} \cap \{2, 3, 4, 5\} = \{2, 3, 4\} \quad \text{or} \quad B \cap C = E$$

To illustrate the properties of the operation of intersection, we use the universal set $S = \{\$, \#, /\}$ with the following proper subsets:

$$A = \{\$, \#\}$$
$$B = \{\$, /\}$$
$$C = \{\#, /\}$$
$$D = \{\$\}$$
$$E = \{\#\}$$
$$F = \{/\}$$
$$\varnothing = \{ \ \}$$

Then

$$A \cap B = \{\$\} \quad \text{or} \quad A \cap B = D$$

TABLE 12.3

$\cap$	S	A	B	C	D	E	F	$\varnothing$
S	S	A	B	C	D	E	F	$\varnothing$
A	A	A	D	E	D	E	$\varnothing$	$\varnothing$
B	B	D	B	F	D	$\varnothing$	F	$\varnothing$
C	C	E	F	C	$\varnothing$	E	F	$\varnothing$
D	D	D	D	$\varnothing$	D	$\varnothing$	$\varnothing$	$\varnothing$
E	E	E	$\varnothing$	E	$\varnothing$	E	$\varnothing$	$\varnothing$
F	F	$\varnothing$	F	F	$\varnothing$	$\varnothing$	F	$\varnothing$
$\varnothing$	$\varnothing$	$\varnothing$	$\varnothing$	$\varnothing$	$\varnothing$	$\varnothing$	$\varnothing$	$\varnothing$

In the Venn diagram shown in Figure 12.5, the shaded area indicates the subset resulting from the intersection of A and B.

The results for all possible intersections in the universe S are shown in Table 12.3.

The operation of intersection, like the operation of union, has the property of closure, because the intersection of any two sets produces a subset of the universal set.

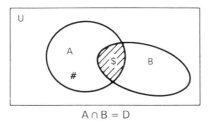

A ∩ B = D   **Figure 12.5**

The Commutative Property. Inspection of Table 12.3 reveals that $D \cap C = C \cap D$, $B \cap F = F \cap B$, $B \cap E = E \cap B$, and so on. Thus, the commutative property holds for the intersection of sets. This follows from the definition of the intersection operation and can be observed by inspection of the elements in the subsets being operated on.

Example

$$E \cap A = A \cap E:$$

$$\{\#\} \cap \{\$, \#\} = \{\#\}$$

and

$$\{\$, \#\} \cap \{\#\} = \{\#\}$$

Therefore

$$\{\#\} \cap \{\$, \#\} = \{\$, \#\} \cap \{\#\}$$

In Table 12.3, the arrangement of sets is symmetrical. Thus, in this table, like in the union Table 12.2a, the left diagonal (\\) provides a way of locating the sets that demonstrate the commutative law. We find $B \cap A = A \cap B$, $C \cap A = A \cap C$, and so on. Compare Table 12.2, which illustrates the union operation, to Table 12.3, which illustrates the intersection operation. The left diagonal in Table 12.3 is the same as it appeared in Table 12.2a, but in Table 12.2, the right diagonal (/), sometimes called the minor diagonal, contains only the universal set, S. This same diagonal in Table 12.3 contains only the null set.

When two subsets have no elements in common, their intersection yields the null set, $\varnothing$. Such sets, as we have seen in Definition 12-7 are commonly called *disjoint*.

The Associative Property. The associative property also holds true for the intersection of sets. Refer to Table 12.3 and consider the example

$$(C \cap B) \cap F = C \cap (B \cap F)$$

Since

$$C \cap B = F \quad \text{and} \quad B \cap F = F$$

we have

$$F \cap F = F \quad \text{and} \quad C \cap F = F$$

Therefore

$$(C \cap B) \cap F = C \cap (B \cap F)$$

The Venn diagrams in Figure 12.6 show associativity for $(A \cap B) \cap D = A \cap (B \cap D)$.

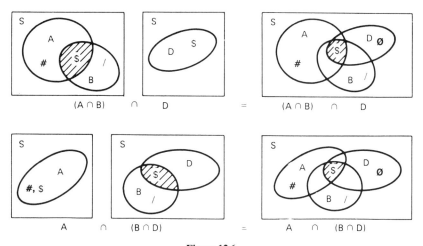

Figure 12.6

The Identity Property.   The identity property for intersection can be noted in Table 12.3 where

$$A \cap S = A$$

$$B \cap S = B, \text{ and so on}$$

The universal set S serves as the identity for the intersection operation. This can be determined by inspection of the sets in the second row or in the second column from the left, where the intersection of a given set with the universal set always yields the given set.

Note also that the intersection of a given set with itself yields the given set.

Example

$$A \cap A = A$$

As an exercise, the student should demonstrate why sets A, B, C, D, E, and F cannot be called the identity for intersection operations in Table 12.3.

COMPLEMENT

For every subset in a universal set, there is another subset that contains just those elements that the first one does not.

For example, in $U = \{1, 2, 3, 4\}$, if $A = \{3, 4\}$, then a set B exists such that $B = \{1, 2\}$. This relationship is called the *complement*.

Definition 12-10.   The complement of a set A in U is another set containing all the elements in U not found in A.

The symbol $\bar{A}$ or A' denotes the complement of A. We can illustrate this distinction in Venn diagrams. In Figure 12.7, the shaded portion is identified as $\bar{A}$ and represents those elements not found in A.

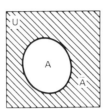

Figure 12.7

DISTRIBUTIVE LAWS

Earlier we learned about a distributive law in which multiplication was distributive with respect to addition. Consider

$$x(y + z) = xy + xz$$

If

$$x = 2, y = 3, z = -1$$

then

$$2[3 + (-1)] = 2 \cdot 3 + 2 \cdot (-1)$$

or

$$4 = 4$$

Operations on sets involve two distributive laws.

First Distributive Law

The Venn diagrams in Figure 12.8 graphically illustrate that intersection is distributive with respect to union. In the algebra of sets, we can also state that intersection is distributive with respect to union:

$$X \cap (Y \cup Z) = (X \cap Y) \cup (X \cap Z)$$

This says that intersecting the union of two sets Y and Z by a third set X yields the

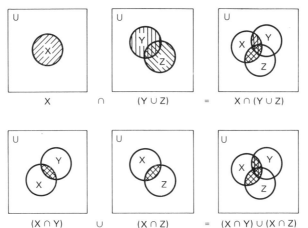

$$X \quad \cap \quad (Y \cup Z) \quad = \quad X \cap (Y \cup Z)$$

$$(X \cap Y) \quad \cup \quad (X \cap Z) \quad = \quad (X \cap Y) \cup (X \cap Z) \qquad \textbf{Figure 12.8}$$

same set as intersecting sets Y and Z by set X and joining the resulting sets by the union operation.

Second Distributive Law

In conventional algebra, we do not have the equality $x + yz = (x + y)(x + z)$. (Addition is not distributive with respect to multiplication.) Substituting as before, we can demonstrate that

$$2 + (3 \times -1) \neq (2 + 3)(2 - 1)$$

However, in the algebra of sets, we can state that $A \cup (B \cap C) = (A \cup B) \cap (A \cup C)$, or that union is distributive with respect to intersection. This is illustrated in Figure 12.9.

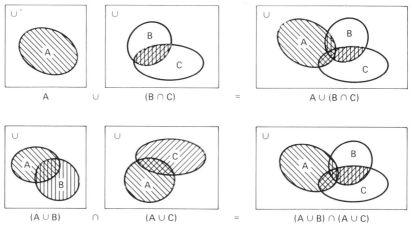

Figure 12.9

It is called the second distributive law. It means that joining by union set A to the set formed by the intersection of sets B and C yields the same set as joining by union sets B and C with set A and intersecting the resulting sets. Note that interchanging the union and intersection operations of the first distributive law results in the second distributive law.

EXERCISES 12-3

1. Form the intersection of the following sets:
   (a) $\{1, 2, 4\} \cap \{1, 3, 5, 6\}$
   (b) $\{\#, ?, @\} \cap \{\#, ?, !\}$
   (c) $\{x | 7 \geqslant x \text{ or } x > 9\} \cap \{1, 2, 3\}$ where x is a natural number
   (d) $\{$Even natural numbers less than 21$\} \cap \{$Odd natural numbers less than 10$\}$

2. Given $U = \{a, b, c, d, e, f, g, h\}$
   $A = \{b, d, f, h\}$, $B = \{a, b, c, d\}$
   $C = \{a, c, e, g\}$
   List the elements in the following:
   (a) $A \cap B$
   (b) $A \cup C$
   (c) $\bar{A}$
   (d) $\bar{B}$
   (e) $\overline{(A \cup B)}$
   (f) $\bar{A} \cap C$
   (g) $\bar{B} \cap \bar{C}$
   (h) $A \cup (B \cap C)$
   Perform the operation inside the parentheses first.

3. Given $S = \{1, 2, 3, 4\}$, list all the subsets and construct the intersection table for all intersection operations on this set.

4. Given (see Figure 12.10)

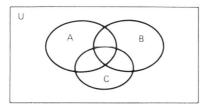

Figure 12.10

   Shade those parts of the diagram denoted by the following:
   (a) $A \cap B$ (d) $\bar{C} \cap \bar{B}$
   (b) $A \cap \bar{B}$ (e) $(A \cup B) \cap \bar{C}$
   (c) $\bar{A} \cup B$ (f) $(A \cap B) \cup \overline{(A \cap C)}$

5. When does
   (a) $A \cap B = A \cup B$?
   (b) $A \cap \varnothing = \varnothing$?

(c) $\bar{A} \cup \varnothing = \varnothing$?

(*Hint:* always, sometimes, never)

(d) Why does $A \cap U = A$?

6. Verify the commutative law for intersection for the sets

$A = \{\triangle, 0, \square, \diamondsuit\}$

$B = \{\triangle, 0, 11\}$

7. True or false?

(a) $A \cap B = A$ if $A \subseteq B$

(b) $A \cap \bar{A} = U$

(c) $A \cup (B \cap C) = (A \cup B) \cap (A \cup C)$

(d) If $C \subset A$ and $C \subset B$, then $A \subseteq (C \cap B)$

8. Given (see Figure 12.11)

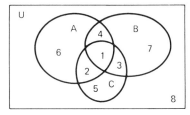

Figure 12.11

where $A = \{1, 2, 4, 6\}$, $B = \{1, 3, 4, 7\}$, $C = \{1, 2, 3, 5\}$. Find

(a) $\{1, 2, 4, 6\} \cup \{1, 2, 3, 5\}$

(b) $\{1, 3, 4, 7\} \cap \{1, 2, 4, 6\}$

(c) $A \cap B \cap C$

(d) $A \cup (B \cap C)$

(e) $\bar{A} \cap (B \cup C)$

9. Mr. Jones owns an automobile parts warehouse. He has the option of buying, at discounts, the following items from dealers A, B, and C:

Dealer A	headlights
Dealer B	fan belts, headlights, spark plugs
Dealer C	headlights, spark plugs, motor oil

Use the second distributive law to illustrate buying only the headlights and spark plugs. Let $A = \{h\}$; $B = \{f, h, s\}$; $c = \{h, s, m\}$.

13

Logic

Logic is the study of the principles of valid reasoning using rules that operate on a statement or several statements to reach a correct conclusion. In mathematical logic, exact terms are used in restricted ways and symbols are used to represent statements and to express relationships between them.

Restrictions

The following types of statements are not used.

1. Ambiguous or nonsensical statements
2. Interrogative statements that ask questions
3. Exclamatory statements or imperative statements

A simple declarative statement can be used and may be true or false but not both at the same time. These statements may be combined by connectives to form a compound statement.

Symbols

Consider

> It is Friday.
> The checks are out.

It is possible to combine these two simple declarative statements by using the connective *and* or the connective *or*:

1. It is Friday *and* the checks are out.
2. It is Friday *or* the checks are out.

Using a lower-case alphabetic character as a placeholder or symbol for each simple statement, we can substitute as follows:
Let

$$p = \text{It is Friday.}$$

$$q = \text{The checks are out.}$$

Using the symbols ∧ for the connective "*and*" and ∨ for the connective "*or*," we can now write the following two compound statements:

Compound statement (1) $p \wedge q$: It is Friday and the checks are out.
Compound statement (2) $p \vee q$: It is Friday or the checks are out.

∨ means the *inclusive* use of *or*; that is, either or both. When it is necessary for the *exclusive* use of *or*, we mean either, *but not both*, and use the symbol <u>∨</u>.

Conjunction

A sentence containing "and" is a conjunction of two simple statements. It is expressed in the form of "*p* and *q*" and is written symbolically as $p \wedge q$.
In the two following simple declarative statements

$$2 < n \quad \text{and} \quad m = 2$$

Let

$$p = 2 < n$$

$$q = m = 2$$

where $m, n \in R$; that is, m and n are any real numbers. Let T represent true, and F represent false and consider all the possibilities for p and q:

When p is T and q is T, then $p \wedge q$ is T.
When p is T and q is F, then $p \wedge q$ is F.
When p is F and q is T, then $p \wedge q$ is F.
When p is F and q is F, then $p \wedge q$ is F.

Table 13.1, a truth table for *conjunction*, groups all the possibilities for the compound statement p and q.

TABLE 13.1

p	q	$p \wedge q$
T	T	T
T	F	F
F	T	F
F	F	F

Note that the conjunction of two statements is true only when both statements are true. Truth tables simplify compound statements and make results easy to understand.

Disjunction

A sentence containing *or* is a disjunction of two simple statements. It is expressed in the form of "*p* or *q*" and is written symbolically as $p \vee q$. The disjunction of two statements is true if either one or both of the statements is true. We see this in Table 13.2, the truth table for disjunction.

In the statements "x is a prime number or $x < 6$," let $p =$ the number x is a prime and $q = x < 6$ (where x is a natural number). Then all the possibilities for $p \vee q$ can be expressed in the truth table for disjunction.

TABLE 13.2

p	q	$p \vee q$
T	T	T
T	F	T
F	T	T
F	F	F

Negation

The negation symbol is $\sim$. If we let p represent the statement "the light is on," then $\sim p$ means "the light is not on." Since we have made the restriction that all statements must be true or false, if p is true then $\sim p$ must be false. Table 13.3 shows the two possibilities for negation.

TABLE 13.3

p	$\sim p$
T	F
F	T

It is possible to construct a truth table combining the three symbols used so far. Consider

$(p \wedge q) \vee \sim p$

p	q	$(p \wedge q)$	$\sim p$	$(p \wedge q) \vee \sim p$
T	T	T	F	T
T	F	F	F	F
F	T	F	T	T
F	F	F	T	T

To construct this table, we first enter the values for p and q and complete the column for conjunction $(p \wedge q)$. Next, enter values for $\sim p$ by negating the values under the column headed p. The columns headed $(p \wedge q)$ and $\sim p$ represent, respectively, the values for p and q in Table 13.2. Using the table for disjunction, we complete the column headed $(p \wedge q) \vee \sim p$.

EXERCISES 13-1

1. In the following, identify the simple statements, assign lower-case letters to them, and rewrite the entire sentence in symbolic notation.
   (a) $y = 3$ and $x = 4$,
   (b) $c < 1$ or $a = c^2$,
   (c) TYPE = SALARIED AND NETPAY = GROSS − TAXES.
   (d) The triangle has no right angle or its angles are equal.
   (e) $z = 10$ and $y = 9$ and $x = 8$.

2. Write the truth tables for the following:
   (a) $p \vee \sim q$
   (b) $\sim p \wedge \sim q$
   (c) $\sim p \vee (p \wedge q)$
   (d) $(\sim p \wedge q) \vee (p \wedge \sim q)$
   (e) $\sim \sim q$

3. The truth table for disjunction describes the *inclusive* meaning of *or*. If $p \veebar q$ is defined as p or q but not both, construct the truth table for this *exclusive* meaning of *or*.

4. Two statements are equivalent if their truth values are the same. Are the following equivalent statements? (Construct the truth tables.)
   (a) $\sim p \vee \sim q$ and $\sim(p \vee q)$
   (b) $\sim p \wedge \sim q$ and $\sim(p \wedge \sim q)$

5. The prerequisite for a position as a COBOL programmer trainee is:
   A two-year degree in data processing. One year's experience in programming in COBOL is acceptable but not necessary. Write the truth table for this situation.

6. Prerequisites for a position as a Fortran programmer are as follows:
   (1) Two-year college degree in data processing AND
   (2) One year's experience in programming OR
   (3) Three years' experience as a Fortran programmer.
   (a) Complete the following truth table for this situation. (*Note:* Three "placeholders," p, q, and r are required for the three preceding simple statements. There are 2^n entries needed in any truth table, where n is the number of placeholders.

p	q	r
T	T	T
T	T	F
T	F	T
T	F	F
F	T	T
F	T	F
F	F	T
F	F	F

etc.

   (b) Construct the truth table for (p OR q) AND r

OTHER TYPES OF COMPOUND STATEMENTS

Conditional Statement

Many statements in logic are characterized by the words IF THEN. They can be expressed symbolically as $p \rightarrow q$, which is read "if p, then q" or "p implies q," where p and q are two simple statements. The symbol $\rightarrow$ is the implication symbol and is the connective used to form this type of compound statement. Calling the "if clause" the *antecedent* and the "then clause" the *consequent*, we can name the two parts of the conditional statement:

  If A is a bicycle, then A has two wheels.

   Antecedent: $p = A$ is a bicycle.
   Consequent: $q = A$ has two wheels.

We will examine the four possible truth values of: if p then q, or $p \rightarrow q$.

1. If the antecedent is true and the consequent is true, then the statement $p \rightarrow q$ is true.

2. If the antecedent is true and the consequent is false, then the statement $p \rightarrow q$ is false.

3. If the antecedent is false (or A is not a bicycle) and the consequent is true, then $p \rightarrow q$ is true. A may be any other two-wheeled vehicle such as a motorcycle.

4. If the antecedent is false and the consequent is false, then $p \rightarrow q$ is true.

A summary of this analysis is shown in Table 13.4, the truth table for conditional statements. We see from this that $p \rightarrow q$ is false only when p is true and q is false. In every other case it is true.

TABLE 13.4

p	q	$p \rightarrow q$
T	T	T
T	F	F
F	T	T
F	F	T

Biconditional Statement

When we state both "If p, then q" and "if q, then p," we use a sentence with "double implication," or a biconditional statement. A biconditional statement is symbolized as $p \leftrightarrow q$, where $p \leftrightarrow q$ means the same as $(p \rightarrow q) \wedge (q \rightarrow p)$. In

p: The triangle is an equilateral triangle.
q: The triangle has three equal angles.

The biconditional statement, $p \leftrightarrow q$, is read "The triangle is an equilateral triangle if and only if the triangle has equal angles."

Using the truth tables for conjunction statements and conditional statements, we can derive the biconditional truth table.

Given

p	q	$p \rightarrow q$		q	p	$q \rightarrow p$
T	T	T		T	T	T
T	F	F	and	F	T	T
F	T	T		T	F	F
F	F	T		F	F	T

then

$p \rightarrow q$	$q \rightarrow p$	$(p \rightarrow q) \wedge (q \rightarrow p)$
T	T	T
F	T	F
T	F	F
T	T	T

From these two truth tables, we can find $(p \rightarrow q) \wedge (q \rightarrow p)$. Since $(p \rightarrow q) \wedge (q \rightarrow p)$ means the same as $p \leftrightarrow q$, we then have the truth table for the biconditional statement, Table 13.5.

If either, but not both, p or q is false, then $p \leftrightarrow q$ is false. If p and q are both true or both false, then $p \leftrightarrow q$ is true.

TABLE 13.5

p	q	$p \leftrightarrow q$
T	T	T
T	F	F
F	T	F
F	F	T

Two statements are equivalent if and only if they have identical values in the last column of their truth tables. For example, $p \rightarrow q$ and $\sim q \rightarrow \sim p$ are equivalent statements.

p	q	$p \rightarrow q$	$\sim q$	$\sim p$	$\sim q \rightarrow \sim p$
T	T	T	F	F	T
T	F	F	T	F	F
F	T	T	F	T	T
F	F	T	T	T	T

From these two truth tables, we see that the last columns are identical; hence, the two statements $p \rightarrow q$ and $\sim q \rightarrow \sim p$ are equivalent statements.

Other Forms of the Conditional Statement

Given $p \rightarrow q$, three other related statements are possible.

1. The converse, $q \rightarrow p$: If q, then p.
2. The inverse, $(\sim p) \rightarrow (\sim q)$: If not p, then not q.
3. The contrapositive, $(\sim q) \rightarrow (\sim p)$: If not q, then not p.

Example

Write the converse, inverse, and contrapositive for the statement "If $a^2 - b^2 = 1$, then $(a + b)(a - b) = 1$."

Converse: If $(a + b)(a - b) = 1$, then $a^2 - b^2 = 1$.
Inverse: If $a^2 - b^2 \neq 1$, then $(a + b)(a - b) \neq 1$.
Contrapositive: If $(a + b)(a - b) \neq 1$, then $a^2 - b^2 \neq 1$.

Consider the statement "If we run, then we will tire." Accepting this statement as true, study its converse: "If we tire, then we ran." Being tired is not necessarily a result of running. Likewise, the inverse, "If we do not run, we will not tire, is also not necessarily true. The contrapositive, "If we do not tire, then we did not run," is equivalent to the original statement: If you did not tire, you could not have been running.

The following truth table (Table 13.6) summarizes all the possibilities for the three variations of the conditional statements we have been discussing. Do you see how the columns for the converse, inverse, and contrapositive were obtained? Note that the contrapositive of a statement may be formed by the converse of the inverse, or the inverse of the converse, of the original statement.

TABLE 13.6

		Statement	Converse	Inverse	Contrapositive
p	q	$p \rightarrow q$	$q \rightarrow p$	$(\sim p) \rightarrow (\sim q)$	$(\sim q) \rightarrow (\sim p)$
T	T	T	T	T	T
T	F	F	T	T	F
F	T	T	F	F	T
F	F	T	T	T	T

TAUTOLOGIES

A *tautology* is a compound declarative sentence that is true regardless of the truth values assigned to its individual component statements. A tautology is identified by all T's in its final column in a truth table. Tautologies are basic tools in determining the validity of arguments. For example, consider the truth table for $p \rightarrow (p \vee q)$, Table 13.7:

TABLE 13.7

p	q	$p \vee q$	$p \rightarrow (p \vee q)$
T	T	T	T
T	F	T	T
F	T	T	T
F	F	F	T

Under p and q enter the values for p and q as before. Under $p \vee q$ list the values found in the truth table for disjunction. Combine the columns under p and $p \vee q$ using the conditional truth table to form the last column $p \rightarrow (p \vee q)$. Because there are no F's in the last column, $p \rightarrow (p \vee q)$ is a tautology. If we change the symbol $\vee$ to $\wedge$ then $p \rightarrow (p \wedge q)$ is shown in Table 13.8.

TABLE 13.8

p	q	$p \wedge q$	$p \rightarrow (p \wedge q)$
T	T	T	T
T	F	F	F
F	T	F	T
F	F	F	T

The truth table for $p \rightarrow (p \wedge q)$ contains one F in its final column; therefore, $p \rightarrow (p \wedge q)$ is not a tautology.

CONTRADICTIONS

When the last column contains all F's, we have a *contradiction*, as shown in Table 13.9.

TABLE 13.9

p	q	$(p \vee q)$	$\sim(p \vee q)$	$(p \vee q) \leftrightarrow \sim(p \vee q)$
T	T	T	F	F
T	F	T	F	F
F	T	T	F	F
F	F	F	T	F

Consider the truth table for $(p \vee q) \leftrightarrow \sim(p \vee q)$. Because the last column contains all F's, $(p \vee q) \leftrightarrow \sim(p \vee q)$ is called a contradiction. (In this last example $(p \vee q)$ was treated as the p and $\sim(p \vee q)$ was treated as the q in the biconditional truth table.)

EXERCISES 13-2

1. Rewrite the following in the form if..., then...:
   (a) Equilateral triangles have equal sides.
   (b) Friday is payday.
   (c) A stitch in time saves nine.
2. Which of the following are conditional statements and which are biconditional?
   (a) $y = mx + b$ if and only if $b = y - mx$.
   (b) If it is a quadrilateral, then it is a polygon.
   (c) If it is snowing, the temperature is below $33°$.
   (d) $x^2 - x - 6 = 0$ if and only if $x = 3$.
3. Write the examples in Exercise 2 in symbolic notation.
4. Given

$$p = A \text{ is tall}$$
$$q = B \text{ is short}$$
$$r = C \text{ is medium}$$

Write the truth tables for the following:
   (a) $\sim p \rightarrow \sim q$
   (b) $(q \wedge r) \rightarrow p$
   (c) $(q \wedge r) \leftrightarrow (r \wedge q)$
   (d) $\sim p \rightarrow r \vee (q \vee r)$
   (e) $(p \rightarrow q) \leftrightarrow (\sim r \vee \sim q)$
   (f) $p \rightarrow (\sim p \rightarrow q)$

5. (a) Is $p \leftrightarrow (p \vee q)$ a tautology?

   (b) Construct a contradiction in symbolic notation and prove it by its associated truth table.

6. Write the converse, inverse, and contrapositive for the following:

   (a) $p \rightarrow q$

   (b) $p \rightarrow \sim q$

7. Write an equivalent statement for $(p \rightarrow q) \wedge (q \rightarrow p)$. Construct the truth tables to prove your answer.

8. Verify the following tautologies by constructing their truth tables:

   (a) $p \wedge q \rightarrow p$

   (b) $[p \wedge (p \rightarrow q)] \rightarrow q$

   (c) $\sim(p \wedge q) \leftrightarrow \sim p \vee \sim q$

   (d) $\sim(p \vee q) \leftrightarrow \sim p \wedge \sim q$

   (e) $\sim(p \rightarrow q) \leftrightarrow p \wedge \sim q$

9. Describe the activities of the flowcharts in Figure 13.1 and express these activities by writing the appropriate statements in symbolic notation.

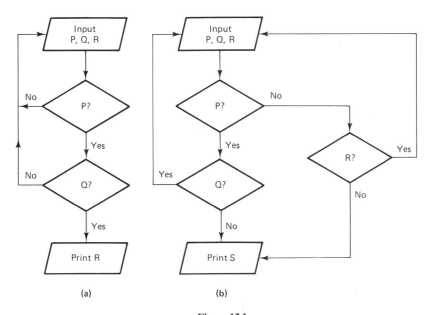

(a)   (b)

Figure 13.1

PROGRAMMING LOGIC OPERATORS

The symbols in mathematical logic for $\wedge$, $\vee$, and $\sim$ can be easily translated to the logical operators AND, OR, and NOT, which are used in computer languages such as

Fortran, BASIC, and COBOL. In Fortran, these operators can be separated from constants, variables or expressions by periods and written as

.AND.
.OR.
.NOT.

These operators may be used within the control elements for decision making or in the IF THEN ELSE statements. When expressions contain either the AND or the OR operators, the expressions on each side of the operator are evaluated and then compared for their truth values.

The general format is

$$\text{expression}_1 \qquad \text{operator} \qquad \text{expression}_2$$

For example, if expression$_1$ were

$$X + Y > A$$

and expression$_2$ were

$$X/Y = 2$$

we could arrange these two expressions with the AND operator as follows:

$$X + Y > A \quad \text{AND} \quad X/Y = 2$$

Now if

$$X = 4$$
$$Y = 2$$
$$A = 1$$

then

$$4 + 2 > 1 \quad \text{AND} \quad 4/2 = 2$$

is true. However, X, Y, and A may have other values in a computer program. As shown in Table 13.1 for conjunction, there are four possible events for *AND*. Consider Table 13.10.

TABLE 13.10 TRUTH TABLE
FOR "AND"

Truth Value of Expression$_1$	Truth Value of Expression$_2$	Result
1	1	1
1	0	0
0	1	0
0	0	0

Although this is a truth table, we have not used T and F. Instead, a true expression is represented by 1 and a false expression by 0.

In the examples that follow in this chapter, we use the binary digits 1 for *True* and 0 for *False*.

Study the following BASIC routine:

```
30 A = 3
40 B = 4
50 C = −5
60 IF A + B < C AND C < A
        THEN
                PRINT "TRUE"
        ELSE
                PRINT "FALSE"
```

For the result to be true and have a value of 1, the expressions on each side of the *AND* operator must be true. If either or both expressions are false, the result is false and represented by 0.

Analyze the code as follows:

Example 1

Let

$$A = 3, B = 4, C = −5$$

If

$$A + B < C \quad AND \quad C < A$$
$$3 + 4 < −5 \quad AND \quad −5 < 3$$
$$7 < −5 \quad AND \quad −5 < 3$$

We have truth values of   0   AND   1
Thus, the result is   0
Hence, since one expression is false, the result is false,
and program control will be given to the ELSE clause.

In Table 13.2 for disjunction, there are four possible events for *OR*. For the result to be true, either or both of the expressions must be true. If both sides are false, the result is false.

In a similar manner, Table 13.11 illustrates that there are only four possible events for the OR operator.

TABLE 13.11   TRUTH TABLE
FOR "OR"

Truth Value of Expression$_1$	Truth Value of Expression$_2$	Result
1	1	1
1	0	1
0	1	1
0	0	0

Study the following **BASIC** routine.

```
70 I = 7:K = 0:N = 3
80 IF I*3 > N*N OR N + K = 3
        THEN
              PRINT "TRUE"
        ELSE
              PRINT "FALSE"
```

Analyze the code as follows:

Example 2

Let

$$I = 7, K = 0, N = 3$$

If

$$I \times 3 > N \times N \text{ OR } N + K = 3$$

$$7 \times 3 > 3 \times 3 \text{ OR } 3 + 0 = 3$$

$$21 > 9 \quad \text{OR} \quad 3 = 3$$

We have truth values of   1   OR   1
and the result is   1

If we change I to 2 in the example and retain the same values for K and N, the result is still true. However, if I = 2, N = 7, K = 3; the result will be false.

The NOT operator reverses the truth value of the expression it operates on. The next BASIC routine uses the negation operator.

```
IF NOT (I > K + N)
    THEN
          PRINT "I NOT GREATER THAN K + N"
```

In BASIC, the NOT operator is placed before an expression in parentheses as in some Fortran systems. In COBOL, the NOT operator is placed before a logic operator within an expression. If the student codes and tests any of these routines, the appropriate manuals should be referenced.

Using NOT, we can write a series of instructions for an EXCLUSIVE OR situation where our result is true (or 1) if one and only one of the expressions is true (or 1).

Example 3

Let E = (A AND B) OR (A OR B) where E will contain the truth value for the entire statement.
First try A = 0, B = 0.

$$E = (A \text{ AND } B) \quad OR \quad (A \text{ OR } B)$$
$$0 \text{ AND } 0 \quad OR \quad 0 \text{ OR } 0$$

The truth values are   0   OR   0
and the result in E is   0

If we try A = 1 and B = 1, then

$$E = (A \text{ AND } B) \quad OR \quad (A \text{ OR } B)$$
$$1 \text{ AND } 1 \quad OR \quad 1 \text{ OR } 1$$

We have truth values of   1   OR   1
and the result in E is   1

But by our definition of EXCLUSIVE OR. only one of the expressions may be true, not both. We need statements that will yield a 0 truth value when both A = 1 and B = 1. Hence

let
$$C = (A \text{ AND } B)$$
$$D = (A \text{ OR } B)$$

where C will contain the truth value for (A AND B) and D will contain the truth value for (A OR B) in E = (A AND B) OR (A OR B). Let

$$K = 1$$
$$L = 0$$

Then, using the IF statement, which tests a condition, we can write in a general way:

```
        IF A = K GO TO TEST
XOR     E = C OR D
        —
        —    other statements in program
        —
TEST    IF B NOT = L GO TO NEXT
        GO TO XOR
NEXT    E = L
```

The GO TO causes a branch to the statement whose label follows; that is, GO TO XOR means that the computer will branch to the statement labeled XOR, namely, E = C OR D, and execute it.

If A = K; that is, A has a value of 1, and B also has a value of 1, we cannot have the necessary conditions for the EXCLUSIVE OR, and program control is transferred out of the IF statements to the statement labeled NEXT, so that E is set to a truth value of 0. If A or B, but not both, has a truth value of 1, the necessary conditions for the EXCLUSIVE OR will have been met.

As an exercise, write your own EXCLUSIVE OR routine using IF, AND, OR, and NOT with appropriate statements and their accompanying labels.

The complete hierarchy of operations follows. It may be useful in working out the problems in Exercise 13-3.

1. $+$ sign, $-$ sign, exponentiation, NOT
2. Multiplication, division
3. Addition, subtraction
4. Relational operators
5. AND
6. OR

where AND and OR are both evaluated from left to right. In the hierarchy of operations, some systems place the NOT operator after relational conditions. Before programming any of the examples in this chapter, refer to appropriate manuals for the system you are using.

EXERCISES 13-3

1. Verify example 3, the EXCLUSIVE OR, using the four possible combinations of $A = 1$, $A = 0$, $B = 1$, $B = 0$ and construct the truth table.
2. Let $A = 3$, $B = -2$, $C = 4$. Find the resulting truth values for the following:
   (a) $A - B > C$ AND NOT $(C > 0)$
   (b) $C*2. < =6$ OR $A*B = A*C$
   (c) $(C + 2.)/B$ .NE. 10. .OR. C .LE. $A + A$
   (d) $A + 1. > B + 1.$ AND $C + 1. < 1.0E + 6$
3. Let $X = 0$, $Y = 2$, $Z = -1$. Find the truth values for the following:
   (a) $X = Y$ OR $Y > Z$
   (b) $Z**2$ .LE. Y .AND. $X + Y + Z = 1.$
   (c) $2^Y < x$ and $y(z/2) = -1$
4. Flowchart the EXCLUSIVE OR routine.
5. Given the following COBOL statements;

IF INVENTORY IS LESS THAN PURCHASE-ORDER GO TO TEST-PRICES.

-------------------   Other statements in program

TEST-PRICES.
      IF VENDOR-ONE-PRICE IS LESS THAN VENDOR-TWO-PRICE
      GO TO NEXT-TEST ELSE GO TO READ-NEXT-VENDOR.
NEXT-TEST.
      IF VENDOR-ONE-PRICE IS LESS THAN VENDOR-THREE-PRICE
      GO TO BACK-ORDER-ONE.

(a) What are the only conditions possible to go to the statement BACK-ORDER-ONE?

(b) Describe (in English) how the AND operator can be used to simplify testing for the lowest price.

6. Assume that distinct values have been computed for three variables X, Y, and Z. If the value of X is

(a) Greater than Y and greater than Z, go to statement number 10.

(b) Less than Y but greater than Z, go to statement number 20.

(c) Greater than Y but less than Z, go to statement number 30.

(d) Less than Y and less than Z, go to statement number 40.

Write a sequence of IF statements to make the decisions previously outlined.

LOGICAL OPERATORS AND BINARY OPERANDS

Assembler language programmers can access binary digits for logical operations. The relationship of the binary numeration system to *AND* and *OR* instructions on binary operands is easy to follow and has many practical applications.

Example 1

AND

When two values are "ANDed" together, their truth values are compared column by column (or position by position):

```
        1 0 1 1 0 0 1 1    value A
  AND   0 1 0 1 0 1 0 1    value B
        ───────────────
        0 0 0 1 0 0 0 1    result
```

The resulting bit for each column is 1 if and only if the corresponding bits for value *A* and value *B* are both 1; otherwise the resulting bit is 0.

Example 2

OR

When two values are "ORed" together, their bits are compared column by column:

```
        0 1 1 0 1 1    value A
  OR    1 0 1 0 0 0    value B
        ───────────
        1 1 1 0 1 1    result
```

The resulting bit is 1 if either or both corresponding bits from value *A* or value *B* is 1; otherwise the resulting bit is 0.

Example 3

EXCLUSIVE OR

When two values are "EXCLUSIVE ORed" together, their bits are compared column by column.

$$
\begin{array}{r}
1\ 0\ 1\ 1 \quad \text{value } A \\
\text{EXCLUSIVE OR} \quad 0\ 1\ 0\ 1 \quad \text{value } B \\
\hline
1\ 1\ 1\ 0 \quad \text{result}
\end{array}
$$

The resulting bit is 1 if one and only one of the corresponding bits from value A or value B is 1; otherwise the resulting bit is 0.

The next BASIC program segment "proves out" the results for the last three examples using decimal equivalents for the binary operands A and B. Results are printed out as decimal numbers.

```
100 A = 179:B = 85
110 PRINT A AND B
120 A = 27:B = 40
130 PRINT A OR B
140 A = 11:B = 5
150 PRINT A XOR B
RUN
    17
    59
    14
```

Practical Application

A practical application of these computer instructions is found in the following problem.

Assume the following descriptions for housing:

$$
\text{Type}\begin{cases}
\text{within city limits} \\
\text{public} \\
\text{private} \\
\text{multiple units}
\end{cases}
$$

$$
\text{Ordinances}\begin{cases}
\text{screens} \\
\text{porch railings} \\
\text{water pipes} \\
\text{electrical outlets}
\end{cases}
$$

The first four items describe the type of housing: the last four items refer to city ordinances governing the conditions of all housing.

These descriptions can be expressed in a binary format.

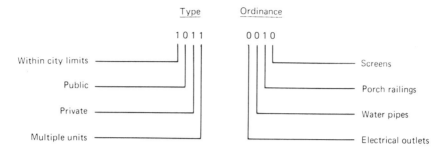

The property in the preceding example is indicated as an in-city, privately owned, multiple-unit building with porch railings. Suppose that to meet the requirements of the law, the items under ordinance must all contain ones.

Let value A be the constant for in-city, private multiple units that meet the requirements of the law, and let value B represent the reference value for any property under consideration. In

$$
\begin{array}{r}
10111111 \qquad \text{value } A \\
\text{AND} \quad 10110010 \qquad \text{value } B \\
\hline
10110010 \qquad \text{result}
\end{array}
$$

the result of the AND operation clearly shows that the property under consideration has three violations, or three 0s where there should be 1s.

If we use the EXCLUSIVE OR operation

$$
\begin{array}{r}
10111111 \qquad \text{value } A \\
\text{EXCLUSIVE OR} \quad 10110010 \qquad \text{value } B \\
\hline
00001101 \qquad \text{result}
\end{array}
$$

the precise violations are indicated as 1s.

The OR operation can also be used to indicate violations:

$$
\begin{array}{r}
10111111 \qquad \text{value } A \\
\text{OR} \quad 10110010 \qquad \text{value } B \\
\hline
10111111 \qquad \text{result}
\end{array}
$$

If the owner of value B knows what he has, the result of the OR can reveal what he needs to meet the requirements of the city ordinances.

EXERCISES 13-4

1. Evaluate the following for AND:
   (a) 10110110
       01010101
   (b) 110110
       111111
   (c) 10011111
       00000000

2. Evaluate the following for OR:
   (a) 10101001   **(b)** 101010   **(c)** 11110101
       00110110   111111   00000000

3. Evaluate the following for EXCLUSIVE OR:
   (a) 10101110   **(b)** 110010   **(c)** 11000101
       10010111   111111   00000000

4. (a) Describe the effect of the results in *b* and *c* in Exercises 1, 2, and 3.
   (b) What is the effect of EXCLUSIVE OR on an operand with itself?

5. In each of the following describe the operation as AND, OR, EXCLUSIVE OR, addition, or subtraction:
   (a) 10101010   **(b)** 10010111   **(c)** 11101011
       11001100   10001001   01010111
       10001000   00001110   10111100

   (d) 00011010   **(e)** 110110
       01101101   100001
       10000111   110111

6. Programmers often do error analysis from printed representation of the contents of internal storage. Given the hexadecimal numbers

	0C	4D	29	3E
Byte numbers	0	1	2	3

found in a printout of internal storage, consider each hexadecimal number as a binary quadruplet and give the result in hexadecimal for
   (a) ORing bytes 0 and 1
   (b) ANDing bytes 0 and 1
   (c) EXCLUSIVE ORing bytes 2 and 3 (*Note:* Each underline indicates a byte.)

7. Refer to the housing problem on page 210 of this chapter. Assume that the buildings under consideration were multiple public units and within city limits. Write the hexadecimal constant (as a byte) to identify possible violations.

8. Design an eight-position binary operand that will make decisions for the following situations:
   (a) An electronics company is interested in male or female employees with at least a two-year college degree or four years of experience. A passing grade on an aptitude test is also required.
   (b) A special research project requires a graduate student who was on the dean's list at least in his senior year and has had four years of mathematics and one year of physics.

9. Before preparing quarterly reports on FICA taxes, the previous quarterly amount fields must be set to zeros. Name the logic operator and an operand needed to perform this. (Do not use the EXCLUSIVE OR.)

14

Boolean Algebra

We are interested in Boolean algebra because it relates to the circuitry in a computer system. Historically, Boolean algebra was related to the formal study of logic by George Boole in 1854. Claude Shannon, in 1938, applied Boolean principles to electrical circuits.

Logic circuits perform the logic and counting operations in a computer. Consider switch A in Figure 14.1 as a logic variable or electrical signal that can have one of two distinct states *on* or *off*. We refer to these values as 1 or 0 or true or false. A switch is either open or closed. If switch A is 0 or false for an open condition, then it is 1 or true for a closed condition.

In Figure 14.1, the *on/off* condition of the light bulb is dependent on the open or closed condition of switch A. By letting 1 represent the on-condition and 0 represent the off-condition, we can apply Boolean algebra to switching circuits. The set of elements operated on in Boolean algebra are $\{0, 1\}$. The binary operations in Boolean algebra are

"$+$" which denotes a *sum* of two variables

Example

$A + B$

"$\cdot$" which denotes a *product* of two variables

Example

$A \cdot B$ or simply AB

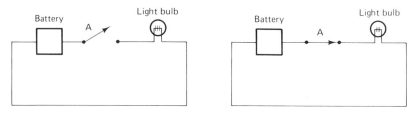

Figure 14.1

The operations "+" and "·" are commutative and each operation is distributive over the other. The set of elements and operations have the following constraints:

1. Negative numbers are not permitted.
2. All variables exist to the zero (or first) power.
3. There are no roots.
4. Variables may be complemented and appear with a bar placed over them, for example, $\bar{A}$.

For the following arbitrarily named variables A, B, and C, there are basic properties of circuits.

COMMUTATIVE LAWS

1(a) $A + B = B + A$
1(b) $AB = BA$

ASSOCIATIVE LAWS

2(a) $A + (B + C) = (A + B) + C$
2(b) $A(BC) = (AB)C$

DISTRIBUTIVE LAWS

3(a) $A(B + C) = AB + AC$
3(b) $A + BC = (A + B)(A + C)$

IDENTITY LAWS

4(a) $A + 0 = A$
4(b) $A \cdot 1 = A$

COMPLEMENT LAWS

5(a) $A + \bar{A} = 1$
5(b) $A \cdot \bar{A} = 0$

TAUTOLOGY LAWS

6(a) $A + A = A$

6(b) $A \cdot A = A$

Thus, terms like $2x$ and x^2 are not permitted.

EXAMPLES OF OPERATIONS WITH VARIABLES AND 1 AND 0

7(a) $A + 1 = 1$

7(b) $A \cdot 0 = 0$

ABSORPTIVE LAWS

8(a) $A + A \cdot B = A$

8(b) $A \cdot (A + B) = A$

DE MORGAN'S LAWS

9(a) $\overline{AB} = \bar{A} + \bar{B}$

9(b) $\overline{A + B} = \bar{A}\bar{B}$

The logic used in an electronic switching circuit can be illustrated with the IEEE Standard Symbols. (See Figure 14.2.)

OR gate   AND gate   NOT circuit
                                       (inverter)   **Figure 14.2**

OR is the symbol for the "$+$" operation and is referred to as an OR "gate." AND is the symbol for the "$\cdot$" operation and is referred to as an AND "gate." NOT represents the complement.

THE SUM

This operation corresponds with the parallel circuit shown in Figure 14.3a.

Figure 14.3a

The circuit is represented as a Boolean operation and a symbol in Figure 14.3b.

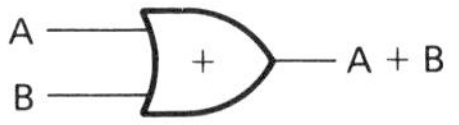

Figure 14.3b

In Figure 14.3a, if an electrical signal is available at i, then either A or B or both must be closed to produce output at o. Since A or B may be open or closed at any given time, there are four possible results for $A + B$. These results are summarized in Table 14.1, which is similar to the truth table for disjunction.

TABLE 14.1

A	B	$A + B$	Result
1	1	$1 + 1$	1
1	0	$1 + 0$	1
0	1	$0 + 1$	1
0	0	$0 + 0$	0

THE PRODUCT

This operation is associated with the series circuit shown in Figure 14.4a.

Figure 14.4a

This circuit is represented as a Boolean operation and a symbol in Figure 14.4b.

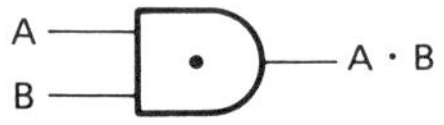

Figure 14.4b

In Figure 14.4a, if a pulse of electricity is available at i, then both A and B must be closed to produce output at o. Since A and B may be open or closed at any given time, there are four possible results for $A \cdot B$. These results are given in Table 14.2, which is similar to the truth table for conjunction.

TABLE 14.2

A	B	$A \cdot B$	Result
1	1	$1 \cdot 1$	1
1	0	$1 \cdot 0$	0
0	1	$0 \cdot 1$	0
0	0	$0 \cdot 0$	0

COMPLEMENT

Complementation refers to the change in the condition of a switch from *on to off* or from *off to on*. Complementing is associated with the symbol for an inverter and denoted in a Boolean expression by placing a bar over a variable. Thus, $\bar{A}$ means *not A*.

If A is on, then $\bar{A}$ represents the off-condition.
If A is off, then $\bar{A}$ represents the on-condition.
$\bar{A}$ is the complement of A.

A complete set of events consists of two electrical conditions (see Table 14.3). This table is similar to negation in logic statements, where $T = 1$ and $F = 0$. $A + \bar{A}$ can be drawn in a parallel arrangement as shown in Figure 14.5.

All possible states of electricity for this operation are shown in Table 14.4. The result for $A + \bar{A}$ will always be 1.

Figure 14.5

TABLE 14.3

A	$\bar{A}$
1	0
0	1

TABLE 14.4

A	$\bar{A}$	$A + \bar{A}$	Result
1	0	$1 + 0$	1
0	1	$0 + 1$	1

Figure 14.6

$A \cdot \bar{A}$ can be drawn in a series arrangement. This is shown in Figure 14.6. Table 14.5 shows all the possible states of electricity for this arrangement.

The result for $A \cdot \bar{A}$ is always 0.

TABLE 14.5

A	$\bar{A}$	$A \cdot \bar{A}$	Result
1	0	$1 \cdot 0$	0
0	1	$0 \cdot 1$	0

The inverter symbol takes one input but the AND, OR gates may take more than two inputs as shown in Figure 14.7.

Figure 14.7

Combining Circuits

Figure 14.8 shows the inverter, AND, and OR gates combined in one circuit diagram. The Boolean expression for this combination is $B \cdot (A + \bar{B})$ and the possible conditions are given in Table 14.6.

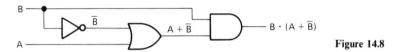

Figure 14.8

In this case, $B \cdot (A + \bar{B})$ has 2^2 or 4 possible conditions, since $\bar{B}$ is not a new variable but represents the complement of B.

TABLE 14.6

A	B	$\bar{B}$	$B \cdot (A + \bar{B})$	Result
1	1	0	$1(1 + 0)$	1
1	0	1	$0(1 + 1)$	0
0	1	0	$1(0 + 0)$	0
0	0	1	$0(0 + 1)$	0

EXERCISES 14-1

1. The complete set of elements to be operated on in Boolean algebra is _____ : name the two operations permitted.

2. Give the results for the following:
   (a) $B \cdot 0 =$ _____
   (b) $1 + A =$ _____
   (c) $\bar{1} + 0 =$ _____
   (d) $\bar{0} + 1 =$ _____
   (e) $C + \bar{C} =$ _____

3. What does "$\bar{A}$ is the complement of A" mean?

4. Draw the circuit for each of the following and write a table of the appropriate on/off conditions and results:
   (a) $A + B + C$
   (b) $A \cdot B \cdot C$

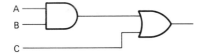

Figure 14.9

5. Refer to Figure 14.9 to answer the following:
   Give the results when
   (a) $A = 1, B = 1, C = 0$
   (b) $A = 0, B = 1, C = 0$
   (c) $A = 1, B = 1, C = 1$
   (d) $A = 0, B = 0, C = 1$

6. Given: $A + \bar{A}B$.
   (a) Draw the appropriate circuit.
   (b) Write the corresponding table.

7. If a circuit contains n variables, how many possible results exist?

8. Given Figure 14.10:

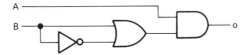

Figure 14.10

   (a) Write the Boolean expression for Figure 14.10.
   (b) Is output at o dependent on B, $\bar{B}$, or A?

9. Complete the following table:

A	$\bar{A}$	B	$A \cdot B + \bar{A}$	Result
1	0	1	$1 \cdot 1 + 0$	
1	0	0		
0	1	1		
0	1	0		

10. Complete the following table:

A	B	$\bar{B}$	$B \cdot ($	Result
1	1	0		1
1	0	1		0
0	1	0		0
0	0	1		0

11. Draw the circuits and truth tables for the following:
    (a) $\bar{A}(A + B)$

(b) $\bar{A}B(A + B)$
(c) $AB + A(B + C)$

12. Write the Boolean expressions for the following parts of Figure 14.11:

(a)

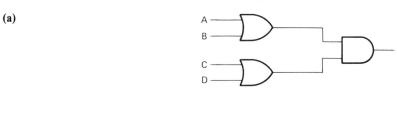

(b)

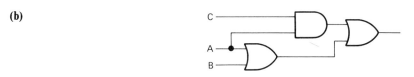

(c)

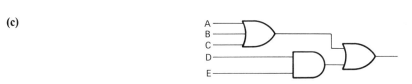

Figure 14.11

13. If A is a necessary two-year degree in data processing and B means an optional one year's experience as a programmer, select the correct logic circuit for meeting job prerequisites, as shown in Figure 14.12.

(a)

(b)

(c)

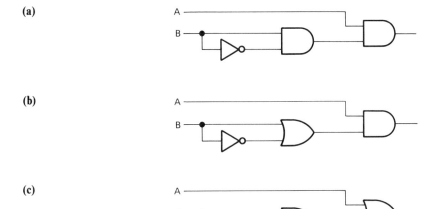

Figure 14.12

14. Draw the circuit diagrams for the following:
    (a) $(AB) + \bar{C}$
    (b) $\bar{A} + BC$
    (c) $A(B + \bar{A})$
    (d) $\bar{A}\bar{B} + AB$

15. Let $\rightthreetimes$ = NOR, "not (A or B)," the Boolean expression is $\overline{A + B}$.

    = NAND, "not (A and B)," the Boolean expression is $\overline{AB}$. (The "o" negates the sum or product and generally represents complementation.)
    Draw the circuit diagrams for the following:
    (a) $\overline{AB} + \overline{A}\overline{B}$
    (b) $\overline{A + B} + C$

16. A ribbon cable interfacing a printer with a microprocessor contains a number of wires, several of which communicate information such as the following:

    • Printer is on.
    • Printer is "on-line" with the computer.
    • Printer is ready to accept data.
    • Paper is in the printer.

    (a) Draw the appropriate circuit to show that printing can start when the preceding conditions are met.
    (b) How many 1's are in the last column of the truth table for this situation?

FIRST DISTRIBUTIVE LAW

In $A \cdot (B + C) = A \cdot B + A \cdot C$, the distributive property exists as it does in conventional algebra. Equivalent circuits for this property for each side of the equals sign are shown in Figure 14.13.

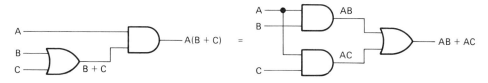

Figure 14.13

The result columns in Tables 14.7 and 14.8 prove the equivalency of the two preceding circuits. Tables can also be used to demonstrate equivalency for the commutative, associative, and absortive laws.

TABLE 14.7

A	B	C	$A \cdot (B + C)$	Result
1	1	1	1(1 + 1)	1
1	1	0	1(1 + 0)	1
1	0	1	1(0 + 1)	1
1	0	0	1(0 + 0)	0
0	1	1	0(1 + 1)	0
0	1	0	0(1 + 0)	0
0	0	1	0(0 + 1)	0
0	0	0	0(0 + 0)	0

TABLE 14.8

A	B	C	$A \cdot B + A \cdot C$	Result
1	1	1	$1 \cdot 1 + 1 \cdot 1$	1
1	1	0	$1 \cdot 1 + 1 \cdot 0$	1
1	0	1	$1 \cdot 0 + 1 \cdot 1$	1
1	0	0	$1 \cdot 0 + 1 \cdot 0$	0
0	1	1	$0 \cdot 1 + 0 \cdot 1$	0
0	1	0	$0 \cdot 1 + 0 \cdot 0$	0
0	0	1	$0 \cdot 0 + 0 \cdot 1$	0
0	0	0	$0 \cdot 0 + 0 \cdot 0$	0

Before discussing the second distributive property, we will use tables and circuits to examine briefly the properties of identity and tautology.

Identity Laws

In the first identity law, 4a: $A + 0 = A$, the result is entirely dependent on the condition of the variable (see Table 14.9).

TABLE 14.9

A	0	$A + 0$	
1	0	1 + 0	1
0	0	0 + 0	0

Thus, 0 is the identity element for the " + " operation.

Similarly, in the second identity law, 4b: $A \cdot 1 = A$, the result is also dependent on the condition of the variable A (see Table 14.10).

TABLE 14.10

A	1	$A \cdot 1$	Result
1	1	$1 \cdot 1$	1
0	1	$0 \cdot 1$	0

Thus, 1 is the identity element for the "·" operation.

Tautology Laws

Sometimes called idempotent laws, the laws of tautology state that variables remain unchanged after they have been added to or multiplied by themselves, that is, the result is the same as the original value of the variable. For example, in conventional algebra, the formula $A + A = 2A$ contains the coefficient 2. In Boolean algebra, only 1 and 0 are permitted as coefficients.

The following circuit clarifies the expression $A + A = A$, property 6(a). In Figure 14.14, output is dependent only on the condition of A.

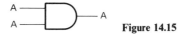

Figure 14.14

In conventional algebra, $A \cdot A = A^2$. However, in Boolean algebra, no powers (or roots) are permitted.

The following circuit illustrates this Boolean property 6(b): $A \cdot A = A$. In Figure 14.15, output is dependent only on the condition of A.

Figure 14.15

SECOND DISTRIBUTIVE LAW

Using some of the basic properties of Boolean algebra, we can show that

$$A + BC = (A + B)(A + C) \qquad \text{(property 3(b))}$$

or that the next two circuits are equivalent (see Figure 14.16).

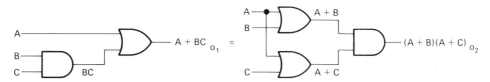

Figure 14.16

to prove:	$A + BC = (A + B)(A + C)$	
Step 1	$(A + B)(A + C) = AA + AB + AC + BC$	(property 3(a))
Step 2	$= A + AB + AC + BC$	(property 6(b))
Step 3	$= A(1 + B + C) + BC$	(properties 3(a), 4(b))
Step 4	$= A(1) + BC$	(property 7(a))
Step 5	$= A + BC$	(property 4(b))

Note that this is not demonstrable in conventional, non-Boolean algebra.

An explanation of the proof is as follows:

Step 1 performs the algebraic multiplication on the given, $(A + B) \cdot (A + C)$.

In Step 2, $A \cdot A = A$ by the second law for tautology.

Step 3 "factors out" the variable A.

In Step 4, $1 + B = 1$ and $1 + C = 1$ by property 7(a).

In Step 5, $A \cdot 1 = A$ by the identity law for "$\cdot$".

Inspection of the circuits for the second distributive law shows that output at o_1 and o_2 are the same for the corresponding conditions of the variables A, B, and C. The outputs of a logic circuit or of a combination of logic circuits are the *functions* only of the inputs at any given time. As an exercise write the truth tables for Figure 14.16.

Note that in Figure 14.16, the network on the left contains fewer "gates" than its equivalent network on the right. If there are fewer gates (or switches) in a circuit or combination of circuits, the saving in production costs is considerable to a manufacturer who mass-produces electronic devices. Therefore, an important step in arranging combinations of circuits is *simplification*.

SIMPLIFICATION OF CIRCUITS

Consider that four AND gates are combined with three OR gates. This arrangement can be simplified as in the algebra of numbers.

Example 1

$$AC + AD + BC + BD = A(C + D) + B(C + D) \qquad \text{(property 3(a))}$$
$$= (A + B)(C + D) \qquad \text{(property 3(a))}$$

The next expression requires several other Boolean properties to simplify.

Example 2

$$A(A + B) + B(\bar{B} + C) + C = AA + AB + B\bar{B} + BC + C \qquad \text{(property 3(a))}$$
$$= AA + AB + 0 + BC + C \qquad \text{(property 5(b))}$$
$$= A + AB + BC + C \qquad \text{(property 6(b), 4(a))}$$
$$= A + C + BC \qquad \text{(property 8(a), 1(a))}$$
$$= A + C \qquad \text{(property 8(a))}$$

Another way of reducing this expression is

$$A(A + B) + B(\bar{B} + C) + C = A + B(\bar{B} + C) + C \qquad \text{(property 8(b))}$$
$$= A + B\bar{B} + BC + C \qquad \text{(property 3(a))}$$
$$= A + 0 + BC + C \qquad \text{(property 5(b))}$$
$$= A + C \qquad \text{(property 1(a), 4(a), 8(a))}$$

The next examples illustrate the properties of Boolean algebra and the simplification of combinations of logic circuits. Digital logic design is outside the scope of this text, but other minimization methods may be referenced by the student as ancillary reading.

Example 3

Simplify (proof of property 8(a)):

$$A + AB$$

$$A + AB = A \cdot 1 + AB \qquad \text{(property 4(b))}$$
$$= A(1 + B) \qquad \text{(property 3(a))}$$
$$= A \cdot 1 \qquad \text{(property 7(a))}$$
$$A + AB = A \qquad \text{(property 4(b))}$$

Networks that illustrate this simplification are shown in Figure 14.17.

Figure 14.17

Example 4

Simplify (from Exercise 14-1, 6(a):

$$A + \bar{A}B$$

The second distributive law will help to simplify this circuit.

$$A + \bar{A}B = (A + \bar{A})(A + B) \qquad \text{(property 3(b))}$$
$$= 1(A + B) \qquad \text{(property 5(a))}$$
$$A + \bar{A}B = A + B \qquad \text{(property 4(b))}$$

Networks that illustrate this simplification are shown in Figure 14.18.

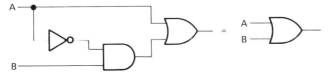

Figure 14.18

Example 5

Simplify

$$A + B + \bar{A}$$

$$A + B + \bar{A} = A + \bar{A} + B \qquad \text{(property 1(a))}$$
$$= 1 + B \qquad \text{(property 5(a))}$$
$$= 1 \qquad \text{(property 7(a))}$$

Networks that illustrate this simplification are shown in Figure 14.19.

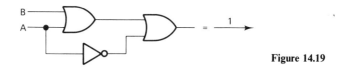

Figure 14.19

Example 6

Simplify

$$\bar{A}(B + C) + AB$$

$$
\begin{aligned}
\bar{A}(B + C) + AB &= \bar{A}B + \bar{A}C + AB && \text{(property 3(a))} \\
&= \bar{A}B + AB + \bar{A}C && \text{(property 1(a))} \\
&= B\bar{A} + BA + \bar{A}C && \text{(property 1(b))} \\
&= B(\bar{A} + A) + \bar{A}C && \text{(property 3(a))} \\
&= B \cdot 1 + \bar{A}C && \text{(property 5(a))} \\
&= B + \bar{A}C && \text{(property 4(b))}
\end{aligned}
$$

Networks that illustrate this simplification are shown in Figure 14.20.

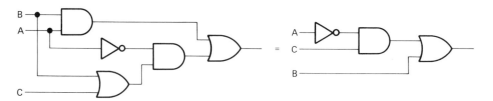

Figure 14.20

DEMORGAN'S LAWS

Properties 9(a) and 9(b) are known as DeMorgan's laws and may also be used to simplify circuits:

$$9(\text{a}) \qquad \overline{AB} = \bar{A} + \bar{B} \qquad 9(\text{b}) \qquad \overline{A + B} = \bar{A}\bar{B}$$

In property 9(a), the complement of a product is equal to the sum of the complements. In property 9(b), the complement of the sum is equal to the products of the complements. In the following truth table (Table 14.11), the last two columns contain the same values and verify 9(a):

TABLE 14.11

A	$\bar{A}$	B	$\bar{B}$	AB	$\overline{AB}$	$\bar{A} + \bar{B}$
1	0	1	0	1	0	0
1	0	0	1	0	1	1
0	1	1	0	0	1	1
0	1	0	1	0	1	1

This equivalence is shown in the following circuits (see Figure 14.21). (Refer to the circuits given in Exercise 14-1, question 15 if necessary.)

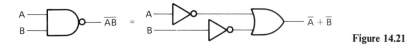

Figure 14.21

As an exercise, write the truth table that verifies property 9(b) and draw the equivalent circuits.

Note that

$$\overline{ABC} = \bar{A} + \bar{B} + \bar{C}$$

and

$$\overline{A + B + C} = \bar{A}\bar{B}\bar{C}$$

Further

$$\overline{ABCD}\ldots = \bar{A} + \bar{B} + \bar{C} + \bar{D} + \ldots$$

and

$$\overline{A + B + C + D} + \ldots = \bar{A}\bar{B}\bar{C}\bar{D}\ldots$$

Example 1

$$\bar{C} + \overline{(A + B)} = \bar{C} + (\bar{A}\bar{B}) \qquad \text{(property 9(b))}$$
$$= \bar{C} + \bar{A}\bar{B} \qquad \text{(removing parentheses)}$$

Example 2

$$\overline{\overline{AB}} = \overline{\bar{A} + \bar{B}} \qquad \text{(property 9(a))}$$
$$= A + B; \qquad \bar{\bar{B}} = B \text{ and } \bar{\bar{A}} = A$$

A variable contains the same value as its "double" complement or

$$\bar{\bar{A}} = A$$

Example 3

$$\overline{A + \overline{B}} = \overline{A}\overline{\overline{B}} \qquad \text{(property 9(b))}$$

$$= \overline{A}B; \qquad \overline{\overline{B}} = B$$

Example 4

$$\overline{AB\overline{C}} = \overline{A} + \overline{B} + \overline{\overline{C}} \qquad \text{(property 9(a))}$$

$$= \overline{A} + \overline{B} + C; \qquad \overline{\overline{C}} = C$$

Example 5

$$\overline{(AB)}\overline{(A + B + \overline{C})} = (\overline{A} + \overline{B})(\overline{A}\overline{B}\overline{\overline{C}}) \qquad \text{(properties 9(a), 9(b))}$$

$$= \overline{A}\overline{A}\overline{B}C + \overline{B}\overline{A}\overline{B}C \qquad \text{(property 3(a)); } \overline{\overline{C}} = C$$

$$= \overline{A}\overline{A}\overline{B}C + \overline{B}\overline{B}\overline{A}C \qquad \text{(property 2(b))}$$

$$= \overline{A}\overline{B}C + \overline{A}\overline{B}C \qquad \text{(property 6(b))}$$

$$= C(\overline{A}\overline{B} + \overline{A}\overline{B}) \qquad \text{(property 3(a))}$$

$$= C\overline{A}\overline{B} \qquad \text{(property 6(a))}$$

Care must be taken when simplifying some Boolean expressions. For example

$$A\overline{B}\overline{C} + \overline{A}\overline{B}\overline{C} = A\overline{(B + C)} + \overline{(A + B + C)} \qquad \text{(property 9(b))}$$

is really a false, complicated start. In this case, the first distributive law will yield the best simplification:

$$A\overline{B}\overline{C} + \overline{A}\overline{B}\overline{C} = \overline{B}\overline{C}(\overline{A} + A) \qquad \text{(property 3(a), 1(a))}$$

$$= \overline{B}\overline{C}(1) \qquad \text{(property 5(a))}$$

$$= \overline{B}\overline{C} \qquad \text{(property 4(b))}$$

EXERCISES 14-2

1. Simplify and list the appropriate property for each step.
   (a) $AB + \overline{A}$
   (b) $B(AB)$
   (c) $A(A + AB)$
   (d) $X + \overline{X}Y + Z$
   (e) $A + A\overline{B} + A\overline{B}\overline{C}$
   (f) $A(B + C) + A + AB$

2. Draw the original circuit and its simplification in 1(a) and (d) above.

3. What Boolean properties make the following expressions equal?

$$C[(\overline{A} + B)(\overline{A} + C)] = C(\overline{A} + B)$$

4. $(AB)(\overline{A} + \overline{B}) = ?$

5. $AB + (\overline{A} + \overline{B}) = ?$

6. Find an equivalent Boolean expression for the following:
   (a) $(A + B)(\bar{A} + \bar{B})$, _____
   (b) $(A + B + C)(A + \bar{B})$, _____
   (c) $(\bar{A} + \bar{B} + \bar{C})(AC)$, _____
   (d) $\bar{A}BC + A\bar{B}C + AB\bar{C}$, _____
   (e) Draw the circuits for your result in (a) and (c) above.
7. Can the variables A, B, C, represent three distinct values?
8. Does $A + \bar{A}B = A + B$?
9. (a) Does $\overline{AB}(\bar{A} + \bar{B}) = \bar{A} + \bar{B} + \bar{A}\bar{B}$?
   (b) Draw the circuits.
10. Simplify the following using DeMorgans laws.
    (a) $\overline{\bar{B} + C}$
    (b) $\overline{A + BC}$
    (c) $\overline{\bar{A} + B + C}$
    (d) $\overline{(A + B)(\bar{A} + \bar{B})}$
    (e) $\overline{A\bar{C} + A\overline{BC}}$
    (f) $\overline{CD + \bar{C}\bar{D}}$
11. When $AC = BC$ and $A\bar{C} = B\bar{C}$, does $A = B$? (*Hint:* Use a truth table.)
12. Write the Boolean expression for the function of the following truth table (Table 14.12). Is the function similar to the conditional or biconditional truth table?

TABLE 14.12

A	B	$\bar{A}$	$\bar{B}$	Function
1	1	0	0	1
1	0	0	1	0
0	1	1	0	0
0	0	1	1	1

13. (a) Complete the following table (Table 14.13):

TABLE 14.13

A	B	C	$\bar{A}$	$\bar{B}$	—	—	—	—
1	1	1	0	0	1	0	0	1
1	1	0	0	0	0	0	0	0
1	0	1	0	1	0	1	0	1
1	0	0	0	1	0	0	0	0
0	1	1	1	0	0	0	0	0
0	1	0	1	0	0	0	0	0
0	0	1	1	1	0	0	1	1
0	0	0	1	1	0	0	0	0

(b) Simplify the expression found for the result field.

(c) Draw the equivalent circuits.

14. Consider a data processing situation where an application for a credit card will be approved only under the following conditions:

    (1) The applicant is over 21 years of age.

    (2) The applicant has a good record for paying bills.

    (3) The applicant is employed or has a source of income greater than $9,500 a year.

       (a) Draw the appropriate circuit diagram.

       (b) What basic property of circuits allows this circuit diagram to be simplified?

15. An insurance company has male and female policy holders. It wants to search its data base for each of these two groups and determine how many policy holders have over $100,000 insurance with a double indemnity clause for accidental death. Draw the appropriate circuit diagram and then simplify it, giving the properties that help in simplifying.

16. This problem leads into the next section of this chapter.

    A hallway light has a downstairs and an upstairs switch. When either but not both switches are pressed, the condition of the light is changed.

    (a) Write the truth table.

    (b) Write the Boolean expression.

COUNTING—ARITHMETIC CIRCUITS

The circuit for *exclusive or* provides a method for counting. Consider the Boolean expression $\bar{A}B + A\bar{B}$ and its truth table. The last column in Table 14.14 is taken from the "Exclusive or Truth Table" in Exercise 13-3, problem 1, and shows an equivalence with the next to last column in Table 14.14.

TABLE 14.14

A	B	$\bar{A}$	$\bar{B}$	$A\bar{B}$	$\bar{A}B$	$A\bar{B} + \bar{A}B$	XOR
1	1	0	0	0	0	0	0
1	0	0	1	1	0	1	1
0	1	1	0	0	1	1	1
0	0	1	1	0	0	0	0

Refer to the following circuit (see Figure 14.22) and use 1 and 0 as inputs for A and B tracing the circuit to verify that $A\bar{B} + \bar{A}B$ is true only when A or B (but not both) have an input value of 1.

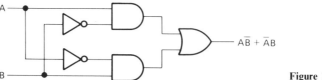

Figure 14.22

Another way of representing *exclusive or* is found in the following symbol (see Figure 14.23). Note that $\oplus$ is read "exclusive or."

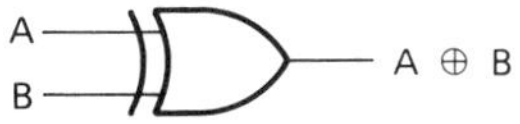

A —⟫D— $A \oplus B$
B —

Figure 14.23

Table 14.15 describes the results for addition where all the possible binary inputs for A and B are given in the first two columns, the sum and carry in the last two columns.

TABLE 14.15 TRUTH TABLE FOR
THE SUM AND CARRY

A	B	Sum	Carry
1	1	0	1
1	0	1	0
0	1	1	0
0	0	0	0

From this table we derive the Boolean expressions for the sum and carry:

$$\text{SUM} = A\bar{B} + \bar{A}B$$
$$= A \oplus B$$
$$\text{CARRY} = AB$$

Note that Sum = 1 only when either but not both A and B have a value of 1 and Carry = 1 only when both A and $B = 1$. Trace all the inputs for A and B in the next circuit diagram (Figure 14.24), the *half adder* to verify Table 14.15.

Figure 14.24 Half adder.

Table 14.15 is satisfactory when adding binary $1 + 1$ and providing for an output carry digit. If we want to find the sum of two binary bits *and* the carry bit, we need two half adders, a circuit for the sum of the three bits A, B, and the carry bit, C. To begin, we must first create a truth table showing the desired results. Refer to Table 14.16, where $C_{(i)}$ is an input carry digit and $C_{(o)}$ is the carry output.

TABLE 14.16

A	B	$C_{(i)}$	Sum	$C_{(o)}$
1	1	1	1	1
1	1	0	0	1
1	0	1	0	1
1	0	0	1	0
0	1	1	0	1
0	1	0	1	0
0	0	1	1	0
0	0	0	0	0

The circuit that performs these functions is called the *full adder* and is shown in Figure 14.25. As an exercise, verify this circuit using Table 14.16.

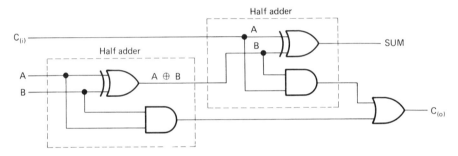

Figure 14.25 Full adder.

Letting $0 = \bar{A}, 0 = \bar{B}, 0 = \bar{C}_{(i)}$ in Table 14.16, we can write the Boolean expressions for these functions:

$$\text{SUM} = \bar{A}B\bar{C}_{(i)} + A\bar{B}\bar{C}_{(i)} + \bar{A}\bar{B}C_{(i)} + ABC_{(i)}$$

$$\text{CARRY}_{(o)} = AB\bar{C}_{(i)} + \bar{A}BC_{(i)} + A\bar{B}C_{(i)} + ABC_{(i)}$$

Subtraction can be performed in circuits called *half subtractors* and *full subtractors*.

SUBTRACTION

Circuits for subtraction are similar to those for addition. However, minuends must be distinguished from subtrahends and instead of a carry digit, a *borrow* digit must be provided for. In the examples that follow, we assume that the subtrahend size is not larger than that of the minuend. Rotating a truth table to clarify the process, Table 14.17 illustrates the *half-subtractor* process with binary digits.

TABLE 14.17

	Minuend	0	1	0	1
minus	Subtrahend	0	0	1	1
equals	Difference	0	1	1	0
	Borrow	0	0	1	0

Writing A for the minuend and B for the subtrahend, we derive from Table 14.17 the following functions:

$$\text{Difference} = A\bar{B} + \bar{A}B \quad \text{or simply written as } A \oplus B$$

$$\text{Borrow} = \bar{A}B$$

where $\bar{A}$ represents 0 in the minuend and B represents 1 in the subtrahend. The circuit for this process is shown in Figure 14.26.

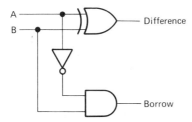

Figure 14.26   Half subtractor.

Trace these circuits to verify

$$\begin{array}{cccc} 1 & 1 & 0 & {}^{1}0 \leftarrow \text{borrow 1} \\ -1 & -0 & -0 & -1 \\ \hline 0, & 1, & 0, & 1 \end{array}$$

A *full subtractor* shown in Figure 14.27 provides for two borrows. A "borrow out," or $B_{(o)}$, when the digit in the subtrahend is greater than the digit in the minuend. A "borrow in," or $B_{(i)}$, from a previous operation. Consider the following binary subtraction example:

$$\begin{array}{r} {}_{1}\leftarrow \text{borrow out} \\ 10 \\ -01 \\ \hline 01 \end{array}$$

Subtraction in the ones column where $1 > 0$ causes a borrow out of the twos column in the minuend and results in a difference of 1. See the sixth line in Table 14.18.

Subtraction in the twos column must account for the borrow from the previous operation. See the third line in Table 14.18.

Indicating borrowing by subscripting the letter B, we use A for the minuend, B for the subtrahend, D for the difference, and write the following truth table (Table 14.18).

TABLE 14.18

A	B	$B_{(i)}$	$B_{(o)}$	D
1	1	1	1	1
1	1	0	0	0
1	0	1	0	0
1	0	0	0	1
0	1	1	1	0
0	1	0	1	1
0	0	1	1	1
0	0	0	0	0

As an exercise, write the Boolean expressions for difference and borrow out from Table 14.18 and verify Figure 14.27 using Table 14.18.

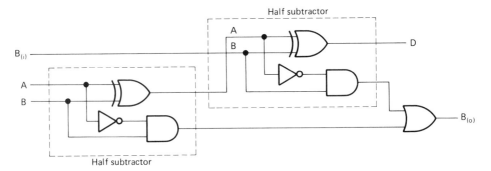

Figure 14.27 Full subtractor.

In many microcomputers, subtraction is performed by using complement arithmetic with signed numbers. This reduces the complexity of the arithmetic unit of the computer.

EXERCISES 14-3

1. Write the Boolean expressions for Sum and Carry from Figure 14.25, the full adder using the symbol $\oplus$ for Exclusive Or.

2. In the following circuit (Figure 14.28)
   (a) Can addition be performed?

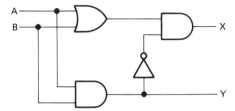

Figure 14.28

   (b) Write the Boolean expression for X and Y in Figure 14.28.
3. Show that
   (a) $(A + B)(\bar{A} + \bar{B}) = A\bar{B} + \bar{A}B$
   (b) $\overline{(\bar{A} + \bar{B})} = AB$
4. The following are Boolean expressions for Table 14.18:
   (a) $D = ABB_{(i)} + A\bar{B}\bar{B}_{(i)} + \bar{A}B\bar{B}_{(i)} + \bar{A}\bar{B}B_{(i)}$
   (b) $B_{(o)} = ABB_{(i)} + \bar{A}BB_{(i)} + \bar{A}B\bar{B}_{(i)} + \bar{A}\bar{B}B_{(i)}$
   If either or both can be simplified, show the result. (See Figure 14.27.)
5. Using truth tables determine whether
   (a) $(A + B)(\overline{AB}) = A\bar{B} + \bar{A}B$
   (b) $\overline{AB} = \bar{A}\bar{B}$
6. Simplify $\overline{(A\bar{B} + \bar{A}B)(AB + \bar{A}\bar{B})}$
7. Complete the following table (Table 14.19):

TABLE 14.19

A	B	Difference	Borrow
1	1		
1	0		
0	1		
0	0		

8. The mode switches on a printer have been set so that all characters will be monospaced and print words only in italics or with underline. Draw the appropriate circuit.
9. Give the Boolean expressions for X and Y for the following circuits.

   (a)

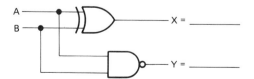

X = _____

Y = _____

(b)

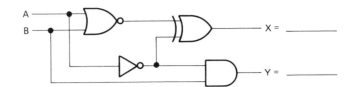

(c)

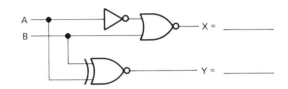

(d)

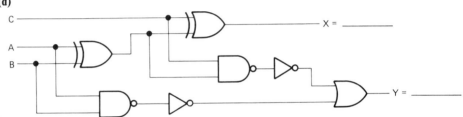

15

Graphing Linear Equations

When programming computers it is often necessary to translate a problem statement into a mathematical equation. Our study of equations begins with ordered pairs.

ORDERED PAIRS

Up to now the order of elements in a set had no effect on our operations. In operations on ordered pairs, however, the order of elements in a set is of importance.

Definition 15-1. An ordered pair (x, y) is formed by taking x from a set and designating it as the *first* element and taking y from a set and designating it as the *second* element. x and y may come from different sets or from the same set.

An ordered pair can be represented by a point on a graph. First, to construct the two axes of a graph, draw two perpendicular lines. The point at which these axes intersect is called the origin. The horizontal line is usually called the x-axis. The vertical line is usually called the y-axis.

To locate points on a graph, we use a pair of numbers called the x- and y-coordinates of the point. The x-coordinate is sometimes called the abscissa; the y-coordinate is sometimes called the ordinate. The plane on which we draw these points is called the *Cartesian coordinate system*.

In Figure 15.1, A has the coordinates (2, 3), B has the coordinates $(-4, 1)$, and C has the coordinates (3, 0). In the parentheses the x, or horizontal distance, is always given first, and the y, or the vertical distance, is given second. Any point on the graph is represented by one unique ordered pair. The rectangular lattice of points in Figure 15.2 is formed from the set of points (or coordinates) {(1, 1), (1, 2), (1, 3), (2, 1), (2, 2), (2, 3), (3, 1), (3, 2), (3, 3)}. The origin has the coordinates (0, 0).

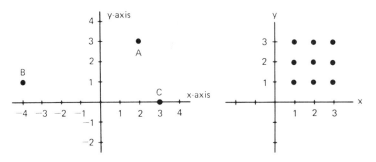

Figure 15.1   **Figure 15.2**

We note that two ordered pairs (x, y) and (a, b) are equal if and only if $x = a$ and $y = b$.

It is clear that (3, 2) is not the same ordered pair as (2, 3). However, if $a = 3$ and $x = 3$ and $b = 2$ and $y = 2$. (x, y) is the same as (a, b) and is not equal to any other ordered pair.

Definition 15-2.   A Cartesian product, designated by $A \times B$, of sets A and B, is the set of all the ordered pairs (x, y) where $x \in A$ and $y \in B$. (Thus, the first element is taken from set A; the second from set B.)

If

$$A = 1, 2, 3, 4$$
$$B = 5, 6, 7, 8$$

then

$$A \times B = \begin{bmatrix} (1, 5)(1, 6)(1, 7)(1, 8) \\ (2, 5)(2, 6)(2, 7)(2, 8) \\ (3, 5)(3, 6)(3, 7)(3, 8) \\ (4, 5)(4, 6)(4, 7)(4, 8) \end{bmatrix}$$

where each ordered pair is contained in parentheses and the entire Cartesian product is enclosed within the brackets. For ease in reading, we have grouped the Cartesian product set of ordered pairs of $A \times B$ so that the left member of the pair, or first element, is the same for each horizontal row and the right member of the pair, or second element, is the same for each vertical column.

Definition 15-1 stated that both x and y may come from either different sets or the *same set*. If

$$A = \{a, b\}$$

then

$$A \times A = \{(a, a), (a, b), (b, a), (b, b)\}$$

EXERCISES 15-1

1. If $A = \{1, 2\}$ and $B = \{4, 5\}$, write the Cartesian products for
   (a) $A \times B$
   (b) $B \times A$
   (c) $A \times A$

2. Given $A = \{1, 2, 3\}$, $B = \{1, 2\}$, $C = \{2, 3\}$. Let $U = \{1, 2, 3\}$ and tabulate
   (a) $A \times (B \cup C)$
   (b) $B \times (A \cap C)$
   (c) $(A \cap B) \times (A \cap C)$
   (d) $(A \times B) \cup (A \times C)$
   (e) $(A \times B) \cap (A \times C)$
   (f) $(\bar{B} \cup A) \times C$

3. (a) In Exercise 2 are (b) and (e) the same?
   (b) In Exercise 2 are (b) and (c) the same?
   (c) If set B has n elements and set C has m elements, how many elements are in $B \times B$? $C \times B$? $C \times C$?
   (d) Which is true?

$$A \times (B \cap C) = (A \times B) \cap (A \times C)$$

   or

$$A \times (B \cap C) = (A \cup B) \times (A \cup C)$$

   where A, B, and C are not empty sets?

4. Given $A = \{2, 4, 5\}$. Draw a lattice picture similar to Figure 15-2 of $A \times A$.

FIRST-DEGREE EQUATIONS

Definition 15-3.   A first degree equation in two variables is an equation that can be written in the form

$$ax + by + c = 0$$

where a and b cannot both be zero at the same time. This kind of equation can be

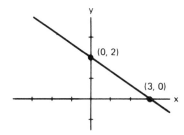

Figure 15.3

graphed as a straight line. Because a straight line can be determined by two unique points, only two ordered pairs are needed to graph the straight line. Thus, the equation for the straight line in Figure 15.3 is

$$2x + 3y = 6$$

If $y = 0$, then $x = 3$, and if $x = 0$, then $y = 2$.

If the first and second pairs of coordinates have zero for x and y, respectively, the solution set is easy to find. For example, in (0, 2) and (3, 0), we can quickly plot the line shown in Figure 15.3 by setting each variable, in turn, to zero and determining the value of the other variable.

The x-coordinate of the point at which the line crosses the x-axis is called the x-intercept, and the y-coordinate of the point at which the line crosses the y-axis is called the y-intercept. In Figure 15.3, the x-intercept is 3 and the y-intercept is 2.

Example 1

The equation $y - 5 = 0$ can be expressed in the general format $ax + by + c = 0$ by writing $0x + 1y + (-5) = 0$.

Note that for every x, $y = 5$. The graph of this equation, a line parallel to the x-axis and 5 units above it, is shown in Figure 15.4a.

The ordered pairs for this equation are found as $(x, 5)$, where $x \in R$. Only one value is found for y, but any value can be assigned to x.

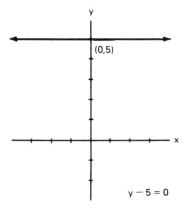

$y - 5 = 0$ **Figure 15.4a**

Example 2

The equation $x - 3 = 0$ can be expressed in the general format of $ax + by + c = 0$ by writing $1x + 0y - 3 = 0$.

Note that for every y, $x = 3$. The graph of this equation, a line parallel to the y-axis and 3 units to the right of it, is shown in Figure 15.4b.

The ordered pairs for this equation are found as $(3, y)$ where $y \in R$. Only one value is found for x, but any value can be assigned to y.

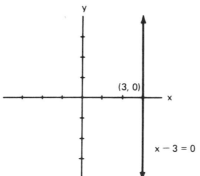

Figure 15.4b

Example 3

The equation $y = 2x - 5$ can be expressed in general format as $-2x + 1y + 5 = 0$. When $x = 0$, $y = -5$, and we have the ordered pair $(0, -5)$. When $y = 0$, $x = 2.5$. These two points, $(0, -5)$ and $(2.5, 0)$, are enough to determine the graph of the line $y = 2x - 5$, Figure 15.5.

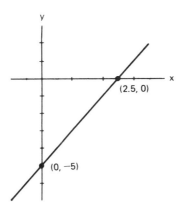

Figure 15.5

RELATIONS AND FUNCTIONS

Definition 15-4.   A relation is any subset of $U \times U$, where U is a nonempty set.

We can show examples of a relation in each of the following, where $U = \{-5, -2, -\frac{1}{2}, 3, 4, 6\}$:

1. In the listing format (where R means relation) a subset is

$$R = \{(3, -\tfrac{1}{2}), (4, -2), (6, -5)\}$$

2. In set builder notation:

$$R = \{(x, y)|3x + 2y = 8, \text{ where } x = 3, 4, \text{ and } 6\}.$$

3. In tabular form:

x	y
3	$-\tfrac{1}{2}$
4	-2
6	-5

4. In graphic form (Figure 15.6):

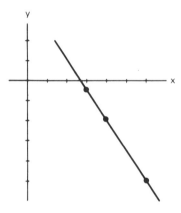

Figure 15.6

Because the members of the ordered pairs in the relation R are elements in U, the relation is a subset of $U \times U$.

Definition 15-5. The set of all the first coordinates of the ordered pairs in a relation is called the *domain* of the relation. The set of all the second coordinates of the ordered pairs is called the *range* of the relation.

Example 1

$R = \{(2, -3), (3, -4), (4, -5)\}$, where $U = \{-5, -4, -3, -2, -1, 0, 1, 2, 3, 4, 5\}$.

The set of all first members of ordered pairs in this relation is $\{2, 3, 4\}$; therefore, this set is denoted as the domain.

The set of all second members of ordered pairs in this relation is $\{-3, -4, -5\}$; therefore, this set is denoted as the range.

Example 2

$U = \{0, 1, 2\}$. Draw the graph of the relation $R = \{(x, y)|x < y\}$.

Since $U \times U = \{(0, 0), (0, 1), (0, 2), (1, 0), (1, 1), (1, 2), (2, 0), (2, 1), (2, 2)\}$, then $R = \{(0, 1), (0, 2), (1, 2)\}$, because these are the only coordinates that satisfy $x < y$. (See Figure 15.7.)

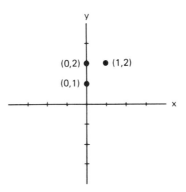

Figure 15.7

Definition 15-6.   An *inverse* of a relation is another relation obtained by the interchange of the order of the coordinates of all the ordered pairs of the original relation. The inverse of a relation R is denoted by R^{-1}.

Example

If $R = \{(4, 5), (-2, 3), (0, 1)\}$, then $R^{-1} = \{(5, 4), (3, -2), (1, 0)\}$.

Before defining a function, consider a car moving at 55 miles per hour. To know the distance traveled, we must first know the total amount of time it was driven. The idea of one variable, such as distance, depending on another variable, such as time, is such a common occurence in mathematics that there is a special name for it, a *function*. We can state that when two variables are so related that assigning a value to one determines a value for the other, the second variable is said to be a function of the first. More formally, we have the following definition.

Definition 15-7.   A *function* is a relation in U such that for each first coordinate, there is one and only one second coordinate. Thus, a function is a special type of relation that associates each element, x, in its domain with one and only one element, y, in its range.

Example 1

Let

$$U = \{1, 2, 3, 4\}$$

Then

$$S = \{(1, 2), (2, 3), (3, 4)\} \text{ is a function.}$$

Example 2

Table 15.1 does not describe a function because 3 appears twice as a first coordinate. (Compare with Definition 15-7.)

TABLE 15.1

x	y
1	2
2	3
3	4
3	5

Example 3

Figure 15.8 is a graph of a function. *Any* nonvertical straight line is a graph of a function. (Figures 15.4(b) and 15.7 are not graphs of functions—they are graphs of relations.) Note that Figure 15.4(a) is a graph of a *constant function*.

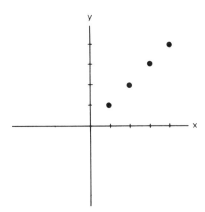

Figure 15.8

Example 4

Let

$$U = \{x, y \,|\, x \in S, \; y \in S\}$$

Then

$$S = \{(x, y) \,|\, y = 2x + 5\}$$

is a function since any x gives a unique value for y.

To simplify all of this, we write

$$f(x) = 2x + 5$$

where the symbol $f(x)$ is read as "the function of x" or "f of x."

The symbol $f(x)$ can be used to specify the y-coordinate of the ordered pair whose first member is x. Therefore, $y = f(x)$. We can now write $(x, f(x))$ is in f, or the function. In

$f = \{(x, y)|y = 5 - 2x\}$, if $x = 3$, then $y = f(3) = -1$. The value for y is obtained by substituting 3 for x in $y = 5 - 2x$. Hence, $(3, -1)$ is a member of the function f.

Definition 15-8.   The *inverse function* f^{-1} is the set of ordered pairs obtained by the interchange of the coordinates of all the ordered pairs of the original function, such that the result itself is a function.

The result of interchanging coordinates is a function only if Definition 15-7 holds true for that result. Thus, $\{(-1, 1), (0, 0), (1, 1)\}$ is a function, but $\{(1, -1), (0, 0), (1, 1)\}$ is *not* a function.

Example 1

In $f_1 = \{(3, 6), (4, 7), (5, 8)\}$, the interchange of coordinates yields $\{(6, 3), (7, 4), (8, 5)\}$. Because Definition 15-7 holds true after the interchange of coordinates, f_1 has an inverse function. Figure 15.9 contains the graph of f_1 and f_1^{-1}.

Example 2

In $f_2 = \{(0, 4), (1, 4), (2, 5)\}$, the interchange of coordinates yield $\{(4, 0), (4, 1), (5, 2)\}$. As an exercise plot the points in f_2 and f_2^{-1}.

Because Definition 15-7 does not hold true after the interchange of coordinates, f_2 does not have an inverse function.

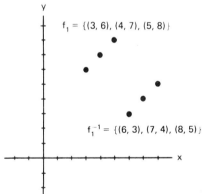

Figure 15.9

EXERCISES 15-2

1. Use the listing format and denote the domain and range for the following:
   (a) $\{(3, 2), (-1, 3)\}$
   (b) $\{(-2, 1), (-1, 0), (0, -1), (1, -2)\}$
   (c) $\{(x, y)|x + 3y = 1\}$, where the universal set $= \{-2, -3, -4, 1, 2, 3\}$
   (d) What are the members of the relation in part (c)?
2. (a) Draw the points for $U \times U$, where $U = \{-2, -1, 0, 1, 2\}$.
   (b) Graph $x - y = 1$, where $U = \{-2, -1, 0, 1, 2\}$.

3. Find the inverse for the following:
   (a) $\{(3, -2), (0, 1), (1, 0)\}$
   (b) $\{(1, 0), (0, -1), (1, 1), (-1, 0)\}$
4. Identify which of the following define a function:
   (a) $x + y = 1$
   (b) $y = 3x + c$
   (c) $y = kx$
   (d) $x = 4$
   (e)

x	y
-1	2
0	3
1	4
1	5

5. Given the domain $D = \{1, 3, 5\}$ and $f(x) = 3 - 2x$, find the range.
6. Given $f(x) = x + 2$, find the domain when
   (a) $f(x) = 0$
   (b) $f(x) = 2$
   (c) $f(x) = -1$
7. Given $R = \{(1, 2), (2, 3), (3, 4)\}$, find R^{-1}.
8. Does $R = \{(x, y) | y = x + 3\}$ have an inverse function?

SLOPE AND y-INTERCEPT

There are two fundamental properties of a line on the Cartesian coordinate system, its *slope* and *y-intercept*. The slope of a line is measured as the ratio of the difference between the *y*-coordinates of any two points to the difference between the *x*-coordinates of the same two points. Letting m represent the slope, we can write

$$m = \frac{y_1 - y_2}{x_1 - x_2} = \frac{\text{difference in } y\text{-coordinates}}{\text{difference in } x\text{-coordinates}}$$

where (x_1, y_1) and (x_2, y_2) are two points on the line. We can also write

$$\text{slope} = \Delta y / \Delta x$$

where the Greek letter Δ means the "change in" or "difference in."
If the line is parallel to the *x*-axis, $y_1 - y_2 = 0$. (Why?) Then

$$m = \frac{0}{x_1 - x_2} = 0$$

If the line is parallel to the *y*-axis, $x_1 - x_2 = 0$. (Why?) Then

$$m = \frac{y_1 - y_2}{0}$$

is undefined, since division by zero is undefined.

Example 1

Find the slope of a line that joins the points (5, 4) and (7, 2). (See Figure 15.10.)

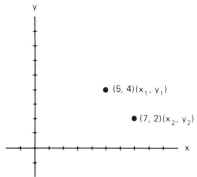

Figure 15.10

$$\text{Slope} = \frac{\Delta y}{\Delta x} = \frac{4-2}{5-7} = -1$$

Example 2

Find the slope of a line that passes through the origin and $(-4, 3)$. (The origin is denoted as $(0, 0)$.)

$$m = \frac{3-0}{-4-0} = \frac{3}{-4}$$

Using

$$m = \frac{y_1 - y_2}{x_1 - x_2}$$

we can write this expression in another manner. Thus

$$y_1 - y_2 = m(x_1 - x_2)$$

Consider the graph of a line with the slope passing through a given point on the y-axis and having the coordinates $(0, b)$. Substituting 0 and b into the formula, we obtain

$$y_1 - b = m(x_1 - 0) \text{ or } y_1 = mx_1 + b$$

Deleting the subscripts, we can write

$$y = mx + b$$

The y-intercept is the coordinate where the graph crosses the y-axis and is denoted here by the letter b. The line has a slope m, the coefficient of x. This equation is called the *slope-intercept* form. For example, $3x + 4y - 8 = 0$ can now be written as

$$y = -\tfrac{3}{4}x + 2$$

The slope of this line is $-\tfrac{3}{4}$, and the y-intercept is 2.

EXERCISES 15-3

1. Draw the graph of $x + y = 5$. To help plot the graph, obtain several values that satisfy the equation. Some of these are:

x	y
5	0
4	1
3	2

2. Draw the graph of $3x - 2y = 12$.
3. Draw the graph of $-4x + y = 8$.
4. Draw the graph of $2x - 4 = 0$.
5. Draw the graph of $2x - 3y = 0$.
   Write each of the equations in Exercises 6 through 14 in the form $y = mx + b$.
6. $x + 2y = 1$
7. $4x - 3y = 7$
8. $-5x = y - 5$
9. $x - y = 3$
10. $5x + y = 25$
11. $3x - 4y = -12$
12. $x - y = 0$
13. $2x - y = 7$
14. $x = -y + 1$
15. Draw the graph for a line with the same slope as $2x - y = 3$, but passing through the origin.
16. Draw a line through $(0, 3)$ with the slope found in $x - y = 3$.
   Use the following values to write an equation of each line in the format $y = mx + b$:
17. $(2, -3)$, $m = \frac{1}{2}$
18. $(0, 0)$, $m = 2$
19. $(2, 2)$, parallel to the y-axis
20. $(-2, -2)$, parallel to the x-axis
21. $(4, -5)$, $m = -\frac{3}{4}$
   Write a linear equation in the format $ax + by + c = 0$ for each of the following pairs of coordinates:
22. $(1, 3)$ and $(3, 1)$
23. $(1, 2)$ and $(-2, 3)$
24. $(4, 0)$ and $(0, 3)$
25. $(-4, 3)$ and $(-4, -3)$

26. Figure 15.11 represents an interstate trucker traveling from towns A to D. (Note that miles are given in hundreds.)

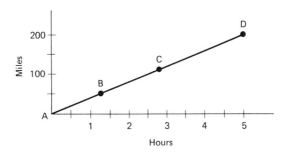

Figure 15.11

(a) What is the rate of speed?
(b) What is the time taken to travel from B to C (60 miles)?
(c) How far is C from D?
(d) Find the slope and write the formula for this exercise.

27. Write the equations in the slope-intercept form for the following graphs:

(a)   **(b)**

(c)   **(d)**

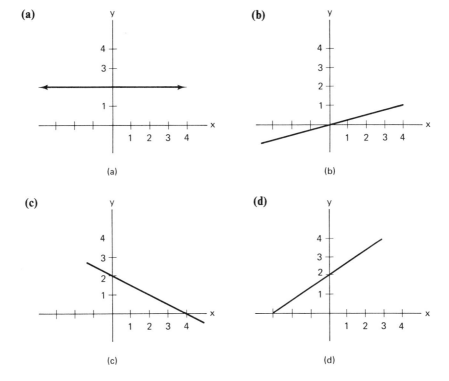

28. A truck leasing company has a minimum charge of $100 per day plus fifty cents per mile for trucks that are leased for one day only. Draw the graph that illustrates the increase in costs for each of 400 miles.

16

Systems of Linear Equations

SIMULTANEOUS EQUATIONS

When a group or system of algebraic equations can be satisfied by the same values of the variables, these equations are called *simultaneous* equations, that is, they are simultaneously true. These types of equations are often used in problems that involve time and distance and mixtures and combinations. They can be solved by one of several methods:

Substitution
Addition or subtraction
Graphing

Definition 16-1. The *solution set* for two equations in two unknowns x and y is the set of ordered pairs (x, y) that satisfy both equations.

Substitution

Simultaneous equations can be solved when one of the variables in one of the two equations can be replaced by its value in the other equation. For example

$$x = 2y + 3$$
$$x + 3y = 8$$

are two equations with $x = 5$ and $y = 1$. The solution set is $\{(5, 1)\}$. Solving these equations involves

1. Eliminating one of the variables.
2. Finding the value for the remaining variable.
3. Substituting this value into one of the original equations to find the value of the other variable.
4. Substituting the values for the variables into both original equations to check or verify the results.

Since $x = 2y + 3$ in the first equation, we can replace x by $2y + 3$ in the second equation to obtain

$$(2y + 3) + 3y = 8$$
$$5y = 5$$
$$y = 1$$

Substituting 1 for y in the first equation yields

$$x = 2 + 3$$
$$x = 5$$

Results can be verified by using these values for x and y:

$$5 = 2 + 3$$
$$5 + 3 = 8$$

Example

A candy manufacturer wants to make a 100-pound mixture of milk chocolates and peanut clusters to sell at $6.80 a pound. If milk chocolates sell at $8 per pound and peanut clusters at $5 a pound, how many pounds of each should be used?

Let

$$c = \text{pounds of milk chocolates}$$
$$p = \text{pounds of peanut clusters}$$

Then

$$c + p = 100$$

and

$$\$8c + \$5p = 6.80 \times 100$$

Substituting $100 - p$ for c in the last equation, we get

$$8(100 - p) + 5p = 680$$
$$800 - 8p + 5p = 680$$
$$-3p = -120$$
$$p = 40$$
$$c = 100 - 40 = 60$$

or 40 pounds of peanut clusters and 60 pounds of milk chocolates will make a 100-pound mixture to sell at $6.80 per pound.

Addition or Subtraction

Another way of solving simultaneous linear equations is by addition or subtraction. For example, we can solve the two equations $2x + y = 7$ and $x - y = -4$ by addition:

$$
\begin{array}{rl}
2x + y &= 7 \\
+\quad x - y &= -4 \\
\hline
3x\quad\ \ &= 3 \\
x\quad\ \ &= 1
\end{array}
$$

To obtain a value for y, substitute $x = 1$ in the first equation:

$$2(1) + y = 7$$
$$y = 5$$

With these values of x and y, we can verify that they are solutions:

$$2 + 5 = 7$$
$$1 - 5 = -4$$

Consider now the following equations:

$$2x + 3y = 11$$
$$x + 4y = 8$$

Since none of the coefficients of x or y is the same, we multiply the terms in the second equation by an appropriate coefficient and add or subtract to eliminate one of the variables.

Multiplying the second equation by 2 and recopying the first equation, we obtain

$$2(x) + 2(4y) = 2(8)$$
$$-(2x\ \ + 3y\ \ \ = 11)$$
$$5y\ \ = 5$$
$$y\ \ = 1$$

Subtracting the first equation from the second, we obtain $5y = 5$, or $y = 1$. Continuing as before, we obtain $x = 4$.

Example

A car and van are traveling on a highway and the van is ahead by 20 miles. If the van's speed is 45 miles per hour and the car is traveling at 55 miles per hour, how long will it take the car to catch up with the van? Let t represent the hours to overtake the van and d represent the distance traveled by the van in this time, then

$$45t = d$$
and
$$55t = d + 20$$

Subtracting, we get

$$55t - d = 20$$
$$-(45t - d = 0)$$
$$10t\ \ \ = 20$$

Then, $t = 2$ hours and $d = 90$ miles. The car will travel 110 miles and catch up with the van in 2 hours while the van travels 90 miles; $110 - 90 = 20$ is the original distance separating the two vehicles.

Graphing

Graphing is a third method used to solve simultaneous equations. The following steps assist in solving simultaneous equations by graphing:

1. Draw the lines for each equation by finding the slopes and the y-intercepts.
2. Identify the coordinates of the point at which the two lines intersect as the solution set. (*Note*: Equations whose graphs intersect at one point are called *consistent*, or *independent*, equations.)
3. Verify these coordinates by substituting their values into the original equations.

Example 1

Solve graphically

$$y = 4 - \tfrac{1}{2}x$$
$$y = 1 + x$$

These equations are graphed in Figure 16.1.

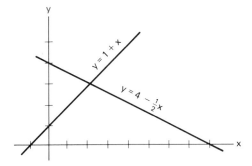

Figure 16.1

Identify the coordinates at the point where the two lines intersect as $x = 2$, $y = 3$. Verify as before:

$$3 = 4 - \tfrac{1}{2}(2)$$
$$3 = 1 + 2$$

Hence, the point at which these lines intersect is the common solution of the two equations.

Example 2

A retired mathematics teacher who was concerned that inflation will outpace his fixed income opens an automobile parts store. To keep track of expenses and revenue, he draws the following graph, Figure 16.2. As an exercise

(a) Identify the "break-even" coordinates where expenses equal revenue.

(b) Identify the areas on the graph representing profits and those representing losses.

(c) Write the equation for each line.

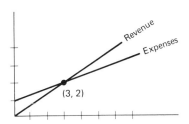

Figure 16.2

EXERCISES 16-1

Solve Exercises 1 through 9 without the use of graphs.

1. $4x + 2y = 8$
   $x - y = 5$

2. $x = y + 2$
   $3y + 5x = 8$

3. $x + 2y = 6$
    $3x + y = 3$

4. $11x + 33y = 55$
    $2x + 3y = 8$

5. $x + y = 10$
    $2x - y = 10$

6. $5x + y = 14$
    $2x = y + 2$

7. $\frac{1}{3}x + \frac{1}{2}y = 2$
    $\frac{1}{6}x + \frac{1}{3}y = \frac{2}{3}$

8. $x = y$
    $2x + y = 5$

9. $y = x + 3$
    $-x = y - 2$

10. The sum of the digits of a two-digit number is 8. If the digits are reversed, the new number is greater than the original number by 18. Find both digits.

11. A pleasure boat makes a 10-mile downstream trip in 1.5 hours. The upstream trip takes 3 hours. Find the rate of the current and the rate of the boat in still water.

Solve problems 12 through 16 by the use of graphs.

12. $x = y$
     $x + y = 8$

13. $2x + 2y = 0$
    $3x + 2y = 3$

14. $5x - 3y = 6$
    $x - 2y = 1$

15. $y = 3x + 2$
    $x = 2y + 1$

16. $3x + 6y = 33$
    $x = 3$

17. A note is discounted at 4 percent. Another note is discounted at 6 percent. The annual income from both notes is $420. If the amounts invested at each rate had been interchanged, the annual income would have been $480. What were the original amounts?

18. In the following graph (Figure 16.3), the solution set is (1, 2). Write the equations.

Figure 16.3

19. The cost to produce two fuel injection systems and three pollution-free electrical engines is $2,500, whereas the cost of producing three fuel injection systems and two pollution-free electrical engines is $3,000. Find the cost of one fuel injection system and one pollution-free electrical engine. Solve by using simultaneous equations.

20. Write the equations for Figure 16.4. What is the solution set?

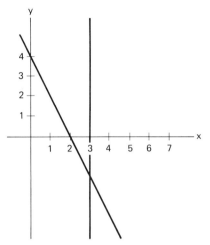

Figure 16.4

The following BASIC program can be used to demonstrate graphic solutions of simultaneous equations. Integers 1 to 9 may be used as values for x and y.

```
100 'ID = EQUAT.BAS  DRAW LINES FROM INPUT COORDINATES
110 ' INPUT INTEGER VALUES ONLY
120 SCREEN 100
130 CLS
140 WINDOW (10,10) – (80,80)
150 LOCATE 18, 70
160 PRINT "X"
170 LOCATE 4, 23
180 PRINT"Y"
190 LINE (22,30) – (70,30)
200 LINE (30,22) – (30,70)
210 FOR I = 26 to 66 STEP 4
220 LINE (I,29) – (I,31)
230 LINE (29,I) – (31,I)
240 NEXT I
250 PRINT "Enter first coordinates"
260 INPUT "X =";X1
270 X1 = X1 • 4 + 30
280 INPUT "Y =";Y1
290 Y1 = Y1 • 4 + 30
300 PRINT "Enter second coordinates"
```

(Continued)

```
310 INPUT "X=";X2
320 X2=X2·4+30
330 INPUT "Y=";Y2
340 Y2 = Y2·4 + 30
350 LINE (X1,Y1)—(X2,Y2)
360 INPUT "Draw another line (Y/N)";Y$
370 IF Y$="Y" GOTO 250
380 END
```

21. An electronics company decides to manufacture an access controlled alarm for store fronts. It has set aside $3000 in fixed costs such as rent and utilities for this venture and these fixed-costs can be shown in the following graph Figure 16.5.

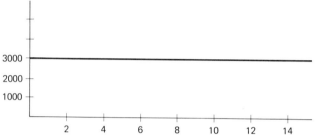

Figure 16.5

The programmer for the company has created the following graph Figure 16.6. On this graph are the line for the fixed costs, the line for sales and the line for variable costs (i.e., advertising, delivery, and other costs that change with sales volume).

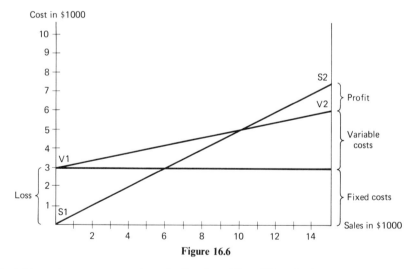

Figure 16.6

Variable costs are represented on the line from V1 to V2 and sales are represented on the line from S1 to S2.

(a) Write the equations for sales and variable costs.

(b) Find the point where revenue just covers expenses (break-even point).

22. The executives of this electronics company want to know where the break-even point will be:

   (a) If V2 were at (16,5) and sales and fixed costs were unchanged?

   (b) If fixed costs dropped by $1000 and sales and variable costs remained the same? (Hint: V1 starts at (0,2).)

   (c) If all costs were unchanged and market conditions forced the slope of the line for sales to 4/5?

SPECIAL CASES IN LINEAR EQUATIONS

In the preceding examples, we have assumed that a solution exists and have located this solution as the intersection of two lines on a graph. However, there are two cases where either many solutions exist or no solutions exist; we examine them here.

Because linear equations in two unknowns may be expressed in straight lines, we can describe the special *dependent* and *inconsistent* equations graphically.

Dependent Systems of Equations

Consider

$$2x - y = 4$$
$$-6x + 3y = -12$$

Trying to solve this system of equations by multiplication of the first equation by 3 and then adding, we obtain

$$6x - 3y = 12$$
$$+(-6x + 3y = -12)$$
$$\overline{0 = 0}$$

The statement $0 = 0$ is always true for all x and y that satisfy both of these equations. Therefore, all solutions for one equation in this system are solutions for the other. These equations are graphed in Figure 16.7.

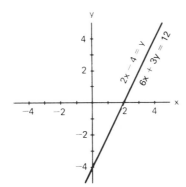

Figure 16.7

We note that the line for $2x - y = 4$ and the line for $-6x + 3y = -12$ are actually the same line. Further, we note that the slope is 2 and the y-intercept is -4 for both lines, so that both lines can be described as coincident. This means that for $x \in R$ and $y \in R$, any pair (x, y) that is a solution for one equation is a solution for the other equation. Thus, every point on the coincident lines is a solution for the equations. Systems of equations that have this property are called *dependent* or *equivalent*.

If we multiply the first equation, $2x - y = 4$, by the constant -3, we get the second equation, $-6x + 3y = -12$, and, in general, we see that where k equals some constant we can write a system of dependent equations as

$$ax + by + c = 0$$
$$kax + kby + kc = 0$$

If we solve for y in the first equation, we get

$$y = \frac{-(c + ax)}{b}$$

Substituting this expression in the second equation, we have

$$kax + kb \frac{-(c + ax)}{b} + kc = 0$$

$$kax - kc - kax + kc = 0$$

$$0 = 0$$

Thus, we find that the method of substitution will not work for dependent systems: In dependent systems, one equation is a multiple of the other, and the number of possible solutions is infinite.

Inconsistent Systems of Equations

Given

$$x + 3y = 5$$
$$2x + 6y = 8$$

Trying to solve this system of equations by multiplication and subtraction, we get

$$2x + 6y = 10$$
$$\underline{-(2x + 6y = 8)}$$
$$0 = 2$$

The statement $0 = 2$ is a contradiction. The solution set is then the *null* set.

Now suppose instead that we try to solve these equations by the method of substitution. From the first equation, we get

$$x = 5 - 3y$$

Substituting this value for x in the second equation, we obtain

$$2(5 - 3y) + 6y = 8$$
$$10 - 6y + 6y = 8$$
$$10 = 8$$

which is another contradiction.

Again, our methods for solving simultaneously will not work. The equations are graphed in Figure 16.8.

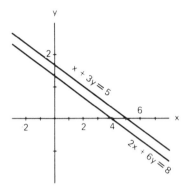

Figure 16.8

Note that the line for $x + 3y = 5$ and the line for $2x + 6y = 8$ are parallel. We define two lines as parallel if and only if they have the same slope. Further, note that although the y-intercepts are $\frac{5}{3}$ and $\frac{4}{3}$, respectively, the slopes are the same, or $-\frac{1}{3}$. Because parallel lines never intersect, there can be no common solutions (x, y) for this system of equations where $x, y \in R$. Systems of equations that have this property are called *inconsistent equations*.

Note that in $x + 3y$ and $2x + 6y$ the coefficients of x and y are multiples of each other. Therefore, we can write

$$ax + by + c = 0$$
$$kax + kby + d = 0$$

We cannot write $kax + kby + kc$ in the second equation because $kc \neq d$.

EXERCISES 16-2

Identify the following equations. Are they dependent, inconsistent, or independent? (Determine if they are coincident or parallel, or if they intersect at one point.)

1. $\begin{cases} 2x - y = 3 \\ -4x + 2y = -6 \end{cases}$

2. $\begin{cases} y = 11 + x \\ x + 2y = 8 \end{cases}$

3. $\begin{cases} x + y = 1 \\ 2x + 2y = 3 \end{cases}$

4. $\begin{cases} 5x + y = 2 \\ -15x = 3y - 6 \end{cases}$

5. **(a)** Describe the activities in the flowchart shown in Figure 16.9.

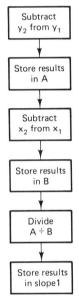

Figure 16.9

(b) Write the associated Fortran statements. Modify the flowchart to test for

   (1) Dependent equations
   (2) Inconsistent equations

Code your results in Fortran. (Refer to the IF statement in Chapter 10 and to Chapter 7 if necessary.)

6. Write a definition for the following:

   (a) Consistent equations
   (b) Inconsistent equations
   (c) Dependent equations

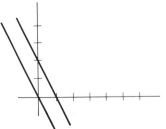

Figure 16.10

Write the definitions in terms of the graphs of these types of equations.

7. Write the equations for Figure 16.10.

8. Write two equations for Figure 16.11.

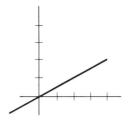

Figure 16.11

GRAPHING LINEAR INEQUALITIES

Consider the graph of the inequality $x > y$. If we wished to select some ordered pairs to satisfy this inequality, we could write

x	y
3	2
-2	-3
1	0
-4	-6
0	-3

Drawing a dotted line for $x = y$ makes it easy to locate these ordered pairs. Note that all points for $x > y$ lie in the shaded area in Figure 16.12.

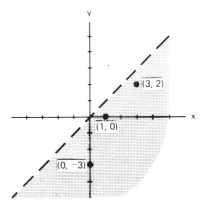

Figure 16.12

Consider the following points:

1. $(-2, 1)$ where $1 > -2$. These coordinates lie outside the shaded area.
2. $(2, 0)$ where $2 > 0$. These coordinates lie in the shaded area.

The diagonal line in Figure 16.12 has been broken to indicate that $x = y$ contains points that are not part of the solution set.

Using the general form for a straight line, $y = mx + b$, we can graph the straight line for $y = -3x + 6$, where $m =$ the slope $= -3$, and $b =$ the y-intercept $= 6$.

If we set $y = 0$, then $0 = -3x + 6$, or $x = 2$; hence, the x-intercept $= 2$. Connecting the points at $y = 6$ and $x = 2$, we have line AB in Figure 16.13.

Now consider $y \geq -3x + 6$.

Because the symbol $\geq$ means greater than *or equal to*, the line in Figure 16.13 is not broken but solid, and all the points on this line, as well as those points found in the shaded area, belong to the graph for $3x + y \geq 6$. (Note that the origin, or point $(0, 0)$, is outside the shaded area.)

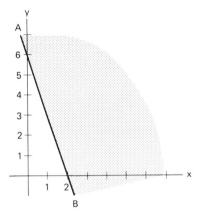

Figure 16.13

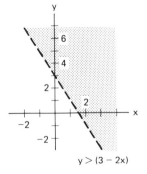

$y > (3 - 2x)$

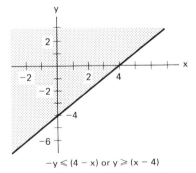

$-y \leq (4 - x)$ or $y \geq (x - 4)$

Figure 16.14

The solution set that contains ordered pairs common to *two* inequalities can be located in a region of the plane where two shaded areas overlap.

For example, in

$$y > (3 - 2x)$$
$$-y \leqslant 4 - x$$

we can plot and shade as shown in Figure 16.14. To remove the $-$ sign before y, we multiply the second inequality by -1

Thus $-1(-y \leqslant 4 - x)$

yields $y \geqslant x - 4$

and we can now write both inequalities as

$$y > 3 - 2x$$
$$y \geqslant x - 4$$

Multiplying an inequality by -1 causes the inequality sign to be reversed.

Combining these two graphs, we get Figure 16.15.

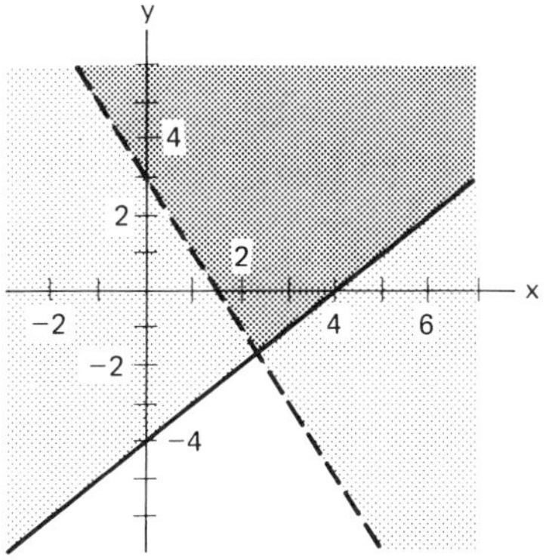

Figure 16.15

The part of the graph in which the two shaded areas overlap contains the solution set for the inequalities $y > (3 - 2x)$ and $y \geqslant (x - 4)$.

Given

$$\{(x, y)|x > 3\}$$
$$\{(x, y)|x + y \geqslant 4\}$$

Is there a solution set? To find out, we can combine graphs of these sets of ordered pairs in Figure 16.16.

The overlapping of the shaded areas contains the solution set for

$$x > 3$$
$$x + y \geqslant 4$$

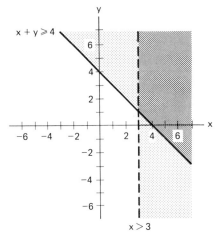

Figure 16.16

As an exercise, determine if there is a solution set for

$$\{(x, y)|x \leq 5\}$$
$$\{(x, y)|y > -2\}$$

EXERCISES 16-3

Draw the graph and shade the appropriate area for Exercises 1 through 5.

1. $x - y \geq 2$
2. $x + y < 4$
3. $3x + 2y \geq 6$
4. $y \geq 4x - 3$
5. $3x < 8 - y$

Graph and indicate the area that represents the solution set for Exercises 6 through 9.

6. $x + y > 4$
   $x - y < 5$
7. $3x + 2y > 7$
   $y + 2x < 8$
8. $y - x > 5$
   $4x + y \geq 7$
9. $2x + y \geq 6$
   $x > 2$

Draw the graphs for the following:

10. $x = |y|$
11. $y = |x + 2|$
12. $|y| > 1$

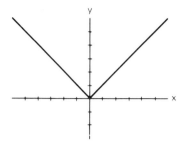

Figure 16.17

(*Hint:* In $y = |x|$ we have for positive x, $y = x$; for negative x, $y = -x$; and the graph for $y = |x|$ is shown in Figure 16.17.)

13. Suppose $y \geqslant -3x + 6$, and

   (1) y must always be equal to or greater than zero
   (2) x is the only input variable, and x must never be greater than 2.
   (3) Values for x are to be input in ascending order, beginning with the negative values.
   (4) The only outputs required are the coordinates x and y.

   To describe an appropriate algorithm for this situation, we need the DO WHILE and IF THEN control elements.

```
Set m = -3
Set b = 6
Input x
DO WHILE x is not greater than 2
    Compute y = mx + b
    IF y is equal to or greater than 0,
        THEN
                print x,y
    IF-END
    input x
DO-END
```

   Complete the following BASIC coding:

```
005 LET M = -3
010 LET B = 6
015 INPUT X
020 IF X > 2 THEN GO TO 040
025 _____
030     _____
032     _____
035    INPUT X
037 GO TO 020
040 END
```

17

Quadratic Equations

Data processing problems such as those involving the relationships between the cost and profit in the production of goods often require equations that are usually expressed as nonlinear functions, whose graphs are not straight lines.

Before considering commercial applications of nonlinear functions, we will discuss a nonlinear function called the *quadratic function*.

Definition 17-1. The function f for which $f(x) = ax^2 + bx + c$ is a *quadratic function* for $x \in R$, where a, b, c are constants in the set of real numbers, $a \neq 0$.

Note: The value of x when $f(x) = 0$ is called the *zero* of the function.

SOLVING QUADRATIC EQUATIONS

Three methods often used to solve quadratic equations are *factoring*, *completing the square*, and the *quadratic formula*.

Factoring

To find the solution set for $x^2 - 3x + 2 = 0$, factor the left-hand side of the equation to obtain $(x - 1)(x - 2) = 0$.

When the product of two factors is zero, at least one of the factors must be zero. (If $a \cdot b = 0$, then $a = 0$ or $b = 0$, or both.)

Therefore, either $(x - 1) = 0$ or $(x - 2) = 0$, or both $x - 1 = 0$ and $x - 2 = 0$.

Since both $x = 1$ and $x = 2$ satisfy the equation, the solution set for

$x^2 - 3x + 2 = 0$ is $\{1, 2\}$. In some cases, quadratic equations without a first-degree term can be solved in a similar manner. For example

$$3x^2 - 27 = 0$$
$$x^2 - 9 = 0 \qquad \text{(dividing by 3)}$$
$$(x + 3)(x - 3) = 0 \qquad \text{(factoring)}$$

and the solution set is $\{3, -3\}$.

Completing the Square

In some cases where the coefficient of x^2 is 1 (*i.e.*, $a = 1$), we may find the solution set of a quadratic equation by *completing the square.*

To get $x^2 + mx = c$ in the form where the left-hand side is a perfect square, add $m^2/4$ to both sides of the equation. Then

$$x^2 + mx + \frac{m^2}{4} = c + \frac{m^2}{4}$$

$$\left[x + \frac{m}{2} \right]^2 = c + \frac{m^2}{4}$$

where the left-hand side is a perfect square. One can determine $m^2/4$ by taking half the coefficient of x and squaring. This process is called "completing the square."

In $x^2 + 6x + 9$, we can write $x^2 + 6x + 9 = (x + 3)^2$. Then $(x + 3)^2$ is the square for $x^2 + 6x + 9$. Therefore, $x^2 + 6x + 9$ is a perfect square trinomial.

As a sample problem, assume that only $x^2 + 6x$ were given and the question was "What value for c must be added to $x^2 + 6x$ to find a perfect square trinomial?" Another way this problem may be stated is "Find c in $x^2 + 6x + c$, where $x^2 + 6x + c$ is a perfect square trinomial."

By dividing the coefficient of x by 2 and squaring the result, we obtain

$$\left(\frac{6}{2} \right)^2 = 9 = c$$

Thus, we obtain the quadratic equation

$$x^2 + 6x + 9 = 0$$

Since $x^2 + 6x + 9 = (x + 3)^2$, $x = -3$ or $\{-3\}$ is the solution set for this equation.

As another example, to find the zeros of the function $f(x) = x^2 + 6x + 3$, set $f(x) = 0$. Then add 6 to both sides in completing the square:

$$x^2 + 6x + 9 = 6$$
$$(x + 3)^2 = 6$$
$$x + 3 = \pm\sqrt{6}$$
$$x = \pm\sqrt{6} - 3$$

The Quadratic Formula

The quadratic formula is another method used to solve for x. To solve $ax^2 + bx + c = 0$ for x, we can express the solution set of a quadratic formula in terms of its coefficients (when $a \neq 0$). The solution set for x is

$$\left\{ \frac{-b + \sqrt{b^2 - 4ac}}{2a}, \frac{-b - \sqrt{b^2 - 4ac}}{2a} \right\}$$

expressed in terms of the coefficients in the quadratic equation. By Definition 17-1, the coefficients are constants in the set of real numbers. Therefore, they may be substituted for in the quadratic formula.

Step 1. Subtract c from each side of the equation:

$$ax^2 + bx = -c$$

Step 2. Divide by a:

$$x^2 + \frac{bx}{a} = -\frac{c}{a}$$

Step 3. Complete the square by adding $\left(\frac{b}{2a}\right)^2$ to both sides of the equation:

$$x^2 + \frac{bx}{a} + \frac{b^2}{4a^2} = -\frac{c}{a} + \frac{b^2}{4a^2}$$

Step 4. Find the square of left-hand side of the equation:

$$\left(x + \frac{b}{2a}\right)^2 = \frac{b^2}{4a^2} - \frac{c}{a}$$

Step 5. Express the right-hand side of the equation as one fraction:

$$\left(x + \frac{b}{2a}\right)^2 = \frac{b^2 - 4ac}{4a^2}$$

Step 6. Take the square root of both sides:

$$\left(x + \frac{b}{2a}\right) = \pm\sqrt{\frac{b^2 - 4ac}{4a^2}}$$

$$x + \frac{b}{2a} = \pm\frac{\sqrt{b^2 - 4ac}}{2a}$$

Step 7. Subtract $b/2a$ from both sides of the equation to find x:

$$x = -\frac{b}{2a} \pm \frac{\sqrt{b^2 - 4ac}}{2a}$$

Step 8. Expressing the right-hand side as one fraction, we obtain the quadratic formula:

$$x = \frac{-b \pm \sqrt{b^2 - 4ac}}{2a}$$

Example

Using the quadratic formula, find the solution set for

$$2x^2 + 3x + 1 = 0$$

$$x = \frac{-3 \pm \sqrt{3^2 - 4 \cdot 2 \cdot 1}}{2 \cdot 2}$$

$$x = \frac{-3 \pm 1}{4}$$

In this case, the solution set is $\{-\frac{1}{2}, -1\}$.

Note that in the quadratic formula the radicand, $b^2 - 4ac$, is called the *discriminant*. Because the discriminant is a radicand, it can be used to determine whether the roots of the quadratic equation will be real or complex, equal or unequal. The three possible cases are

1. If $b^2 - 4ac > 0$, the roots are real and unequal.

Example

Let $a = 1, b = 2, c = -1$. Then

$$2^2 - 4 \cdot 1 \cdot (-1) = 8, \quad \text{and } 8 > 0$$

2. If $b^2 - 4ac = 0$, the roots are real and equal (or only one root exists).

Example

Let $a = 1, b = 2, c = 1$. Then

$$2^2 - 4 \cdot 1 \cdot 1 = 0$$

3. If $b^2 - 4ac < 0$, the roots are complex and not members of the set of real numbers.

Example

Let $a = 1, b = 2, c = 3$. Then

$$2^2 - 4 \cdot 1 \cdot 3 = -8, \quad \text{and } -8 < 0$$

EXERCISES 17-1

1. Describe the nature of the roots of the following:
   (a) $2x^2 - 4x - 6 = 0$
   (b) $x^2 - x + \frac{1}{4} = 0$

(c) $x^2 + .5x - .1875 = 0$
(d) $x^2 = -3$
(e) $x^2 + 4x + 4 = 0$

2. Solve for x in the following (factoring for a, b, c, and d):
   (a) $16x^2 - 1 = 0$ (e) $3 - [(x + 2)(x - 2)] = 6$
   (b) $x^2 - 5x - 6 = 0$ (f) $3x^2 + 9x = 27$
   (c) $4x^2 - 1 = 0$ (g) $x^2 + 2.5x - 1.5 = 0$
   (d) $6x^2 - 2x - 8 = 0$ (h) $x^2 = 1$

3. Solve the following by completing the square:
   (a) $x^2 - 6x = 0$
   (b) $x^2 + mx + n = 0$
   (c) $x^2 - 10x + 21 = 0$
   (d) Given $x^2 + 10x$; complete the square and find a value for c that yields a perfect square trinomial.
   (e) Is $x^2 + 2x + 3$ a perfect square trinomial?

4. Solve the following using the quadratic formula:
   (a) $2x^2 + 5x - 1 = 0$
   (b) $x^2 + 3x + 1 = 0$
   (c) $2x^2 + 7x - 1 = 0$
   (d) $x^2 + dx + f = 0$
   (e) $3x^2 - 3 = 0$

5. Find the quadratic equation for the following roots:
   (a) $2, -5$
   (b) $4, -1$
   (c) $\sqrt{5}, -\sqrt{5}$
   (d) -1

6. Write the quadratic equations in standard form for the following:

   (a) $\dfrac{-5 + \sqrt{5^2 - 4 \cdot 3 \cdot 4}}{2 \cdot 3}$

   (b) $\dfrac{-\frac{1}{2} + \sqrt{(\frac{1}{2})^2 - 4 \cdot 1 \cdot 2}}{2}$

7. The quadratic formula yields two roots for x:

$$\frac{-b + \sqrt{b^2 - 4ac}}{2a} \quad \text{and} \quad \frac{-b - \sqrt{b^2 - 4ac}}{2a}$$

   (a) Find the sum of these two roots.
   (b) Complete by finding the product of the roots.

$$x_1 \cdot x_2 = \frac{-b + \sqrt{b^2 - 4ac}}{2a} \cdot \frac{-b - \sqrt{b^2 - 4ac}}{2a}$$

$$= \frac{b^2 - (b^2 - 4ac)}{4a^2}$$

$$=$$

8. Find the sums and products of the roots in the following:
   (a) $(x + 3)(x - 2)$
   (b) $x^2 + x - 42$
9. Write one Fortran statement to test for both a negative discriminant and a discriminant of zero.
10. Assume that we have used the coding in the answer to Exercise 9 to make certain that we only take the square root of real numbers greater than zero. Write the Fortran statements that will solve for x in $ax^2 + bx + c = f(x)$, where $f(x) = 0$.

GRAPHING ORDERED PAIRS

With linear equations in two variables, we found solutions to be ordered pairs (x, y). Quadratic equations in two variables also have solutions that are ordered pairs. A general format for this type of quadratic equation is $y = ax^2 + bx + c$.

In $y = x^2 - 3$ (where $a = 1$, $b = 0$ and $c = -3$), we can create a partial table of *replacement values* for x and y, or $f(x) = ax^2 + bx + c$. Ordered pairs are found by arbitrarily assigning values to x and computing the appropriate values for y.

TABLE 17.1

x	$f(x) = y$
-3	6
-2	1
-1	-2
0	-3
1	-2
2	1
3	6

Assigning -3 to x, we find

$$y = (-3)^2 - 3$$
$$y = 6$$

and the ordered pair for this value of x is $(-3, 6)$. In a similar manner, we can find other values for y in Table 17.1 and write the ordered pairs as follows:

$$(-3, 6), \quad (-2, 1), \quad (-1, -2), \quad (0, -3), \quad (1, -2), \quad (2, 1), \quad (3, 6)$$

Connecting these points by a smooth curve, we find a shape called a *parabola*, see Figure 17.1. Note that the curve has been drawn intuitively without plotting any more than these few points on the graph.

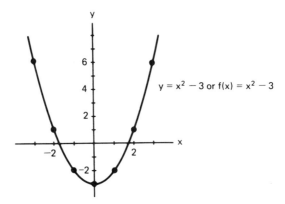

Figure 17.1

In general, we can say that the graph of the points that make up the solution set of a parabola are in the form of $y = ax^2 + bx + c$, where a, b, $c \in R$ and $a \neq 0$. (Whenever $a = 0$, a straight line will contain the points in the solution set.) The parabola is a graph of a function, since for each x there is only one value for y.

Drawing lines parallel to the y-axis to determine the point(s) of intersection is a way of testing to see if a relation is or is not a function. In Figure 17.2, the dashed line parallel to the y-axis crosses the curve twice at points A and B. Because points A and B have the same x-coordinate and different y-coordinates, this relation is not a function. More specifically, y is not a function of x in Figure 17.2.

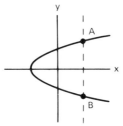

Figure 17.2

In $y = x^2 - 3$, we used a value for a greater than zero. Whenever $a > 0$, the legs of the parabola extend upward. If $a < 0$, the legs of the parabola will extend downward. (See Figure 17.3.)

$-x^2 - y - 3 = 0$

x	y
3	-12
2	-7
1	-4
0	-3
-1	-4
-2	-7
-3	-12

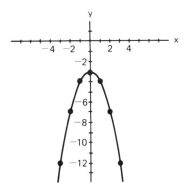

Figure 17.3

Compare the graphs of $x^2 - y - 3 = 0$, Figure 17.1, and $-x^2 - y - 3 = 0$, Figure 17.3. Note the effect of -3 in both Figure 17.1 and Figure 17.3. When $x = 0$ in $x^2 - y - 3 = 0$, the lowest point of the curve is at $y = -3$. When $x = 0$ in $-x^2 - y - 3 = 0$, the highest point of the curve is at $y = -3$.

x-Intercepts

In the graph of the function $f(x) = ax^2 + bx + c$, we can also write $y = ax^2 + bx + c$. Note that any value for x where $f(x) = 0$ will be an x-intercept (the point on the x-axis where $y = 0$) and therefore a point in the solution set of this form of the equation.

As noted earlier, the values of x for $f(x) = 0$ are called *zeros* of the function. To illustrate the zeros of the function, draw the graph for $y = x^2 - 7x + 6$ and locate $f(1) = 0$, $f(6) = 0$. (Set $f(x) = 0$; see Figure 17.4.)

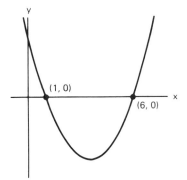

(1, 0)

(6, 0)

Figure 17.4

The solution set for this equation can be verified by using the quadratic formula. Let the first root be called x_1 and the second root x_2. Then

$$x_1 = (+7 + \sqrt{49 - 4(1)(6)}) \div 2(1)$$
$$= 6$$

and

$$x_2 = (+7 - \sqrt{49 - 4(1)(6)}) \div 2(1)$$
$$= 1$$

If one side of the quadratic equation can be factored, the zeros of the function may be located quickly. For example, in $0 = x^2 + x - 2$, we can solve as follows:

$$(x - 1)(x + 2) = 0$$
$$x = 1, \quad x = -2$$

Now, using the form $y = ax^2 + bx + c$, we note that when $x = -2$ or $x = 1$, $y = 0$ (where $y = f(x)$); the zeros of the function are -2, 1, and this is precisely where the graph crosses the x-axis. Figure 17.5 is the graph of $y = x^2 + x - 2$.

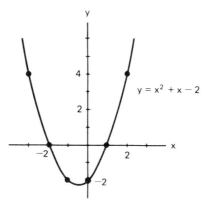

Figure 17.5

x	y
-3	4
-2	0
-1	-2
0	-2
1	0
2	4

When the graph crosses the x-axis, two roots exist. Next, consider

$$x^2 - 4x + 4 = y$$

Factoring $(x - 2)(x - 2)$ yields one root, $x = 2$, for this quadratic equation. The graphic illustration for this equation with equal roots touches the x-axis at the point (2, 0) at its lowest point (see Figure 17.6).

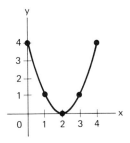

Figure 17.6

As an exercise, show that in the following graph (Figure 17.7) for $y = x^2 + 2$, no root exists in the set of real numbers. (Use the quadratic formula.)

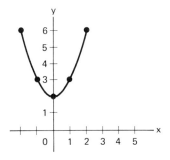

Figure 17.7

Highest and Lowest Points

A method for finding the lowest or highest point on the graph of $y = ax^2 + bx + c$ can be obtained by considering the constants a, b, and c ($a \neq 0$).

If $a > 0$, then $(x, y) = \left(\dfrac{b}{2a}, \ -\dfrac{b^2 - 4ac}{4a} \right)$ is the lowest point.

If $a < 0$, then $(x, y) = \left(\dfrac{-b}{2a}, \ -\dfrac{b^2 - 4ac}{4a} \right)$ is the highest point.

To see how this is derived, consider

$$y = ax^2 + bx + c \quad \text{or} \quad \frac{y}{a} = x^2 + \frac{bx}{a} + \frac{c}{a}$$

Completing the square, we get

$$\frac{y}{a} + \frac{b^2}{4a^2} = \left(x^2 + \frac{bx}{a} + \frac{b^2}{4a^2}\right) + \frac{c}{a}$$

$$\frac{y}{a} + \frac{b^2}{4a^2} - \frac{c}{a} = \left(x + \frac{b}{2a}\right)^2$$

$$\frac{y}{a} + \frac{b^2 - 4ac}{4a^2} = \left(x + \frac{b}{2a}\right)^2 \qquad (1)$$

where $\left(\dfrac{y}{a} + \dfrac{b^2 - 4ac}{4a^2}\right)$ is $\geqslant 0$ since $\left(x + \dfrac{b}{2a}\right)^2$ is $\geqslant 0$. (Any number squared is equal to or greater than zero.)

If $a > 0$, the parabola extends upward. In equation (1), then, when $x = \dfrac{-b}{2a}$, $y = -\dfrac{b^2 - 4ac}{4a}$. Hence, if $a > 0$, then $(x, y) = \left(\dfrac{-b}{2a}, -\dfrac{b^2 - 4ac}{4a}\right)$ is the lowest point of the graph of $y = ax^2 + bx + c$. In a similar manner, if $a < 0$, then $(x, y) = \left(\dfrac{-b}{2a}, -\dfrac{b^2 - 4ac}{4a}\right)$ is the highest point of the graph of $y = ax^2 + bx + c$, and the parabola extends downward. (If $a = 0$, then the graph is for $y = mx + b$.) Thus, $x = \dfrac{-b}{2a}, y = -\dfrac{b^2 - 4ac}{4a}$ are solutions for equation (1).

Example

In the graph of $y = x^2 - 5x + 6$

$$x = \frac{-b}{2a} = \frac{5}{2}$$

$$y = -\frac{b^2 - 4ac}{4a} = -\frac{25 - 24}{4}$$

When $x = \frac{5}{2}$, y has a minimum value of $-\frac{1}{4}$, and the coordinates of this point are $\frac{5}{2}, -\frac{1}{4}$.

EXERCISES 17-2

1. Graph the following:
   (a) $-x^2 + 7x - 6 = y$
   (b) $x^2 - 4x + 3 = f(x)$
   (c) $.5x^2 + 2x = f(x)$
   (d) $y = x^2$

2. Find the x-intercepts or zeros of the functions in parts (a) and (b), exercise 1.

3. In $x^2 = y$, is this a function?

4. Graph $y^2 = x$. Is this a function?

5. Graph $2x^2 + 3x + 7 = y$. Is the discriminant < 0?

6. Find the maximum or minimum points on the graphs for the following:
   (a) $y = x^2 - 9x + 8$
   (b) $y = -x^2 + 9x - 8$
   (c) $y = x^2 - 5x + 4$
   (d) $y = x^2 - 2x + 1$

7. In $y = x^2 + 1$, can y ever equal zero?

8. Graph $x = y^2 - 9$.

9. Graph $x = y^2 - 6y + 9$.

10. Write the Fortran IF statements to test the coefficient of x^2 for $ax^2 + bx + c = 0$. If it is positive go to statement 30; if zero, go to statement 20; if negative, go to statement 10.

11. The following program in BASIC illustrates Newton's method of finding a square root by successive approximations.

		BASIC
	Set number = 625	10 NUM = 625
	Set divisor = number	20 DIV = NUM
	Set quotient = number ÷ divisor	30 QUOT = NUM/DIV
	┌ DO WHILE	
	quotient ≠ divisor	40 IF QUOT = DIV THEN GOTO 80
	Set divisor = quotient + divisor	50 DIV = QUOT + DIV
Loop	Set divisor = divisor ÷ 2	60 DIV = DIV/2
	Set quotient = number ÷ divisor	65 QUOT = NUM/DIV
	└ DO-END	70 GOTO 40
	WRITE quotient, divisor, number	80 PRINT QUOT,DIV,NUM
	STOP	90 END

The process begins by setting the divisor equal to the dividend:

$$\frac{1}{625\overline{)625}}$$

The loop, or repeated sequence of instructions, determines the square root by averaging the sums of quotients and divisors.

Trace each instruction in the program by writing out the activity of each arithmetic instruction until QUOTIENT equals DIVISOR. (Truncate decimal fractions, using integers only for quotients.) Next, as an exercise, write the Fortran program to find the square root of any real number. You as the programmer must keep track of the decimal positions and use the correct variable names for floating-point variables. (See page 87.) Describe the algorithm first in pseudo-code, then write the Fortran program.

12. Graph quadratic inequalities as follows:
   (a) Using the graph in Figure 17.7, redraw a graph for $y < x^2 + 2$. Use a broken line and shade the appropriate area.
   (b) In a similar manner, draw the graph for $y \geq x^2$.

13. Given the following graphs (Figure 17.8), write the quadratic equations.

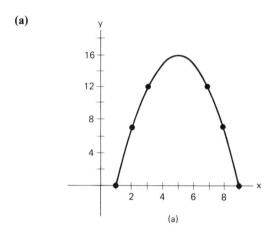

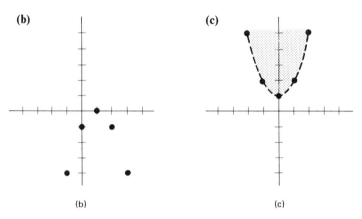

Figure 17.8

COMMERCIAL APPLICATIONS

The quadratic function may be used in commercial computer programming to determine relationships between prices, profits, and the production of goods.

Example 1

Letting P represent profit and x represent production units (such as one yard, one pound, one item, etc.) we can demonstrate an example of a functional relationship between production units and profits in the following quadratic function:

$$f(x) = P = -10x^2 + 60x - 50$$

Assuming no negative values for x (no negative production units), we can write a table of values for P and x:

x	P
0	-50
1	0
2	30
3	40

It is evident from the table of values that to operate at a profit, at least 2 or at most 4 units must be produced. Continuing our table and graphing these points, we find

x	P
4	30
5	0
6	-50

Figure 17.9 shows a graph of these points. If maximum profit is to be reached, three production units must be realized.

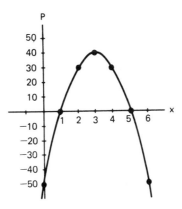

Figure 17.9

To find the zeros of this function, we solve for x in the equation for $f(x)$:

$$-10x^2 + 60x - 50 = 0$$
$$+10x^2 - 60x + 50 = 0$$
$$(x - 1)(x - 5) = 0$$

Then $f(x) = 0$ at $x = 1$ and $x = 5$.

Relationships also exist between costs and production.

Example 2

Let C *represent* *cost* *in* *dollars*, and let x represent production units. Given $C = x^2 - 4x + 9$, and again assuming no negative production units, we can construct the graph shown in Figure 17.10. The minimum cost is found at two production units.

In cost production relationships, it is important to determine minimum costs, and the point $(2, 5)$ in Figure 17.10 shows this minimum cost. Comparing this graph to the last Figure 17.9, note that the curve in Figure 17.10 never crosses the x-axis. This means that $f(x) \neq 0$.

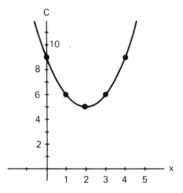

Figure 17.10

Relationships among profit, costs, and production units are discussed further in Chapter 20.

EXERCISES 17-3

1. If the relationship between profit and daily units of production for a manufacturer of computer disks is expressed as $P = -x^2 + 8x - 7$,
   (a) Graph the quadratic equation
   (b) Find the highest point on the graph
   (c) Find the zeros of the function
2. If a manufacturer of farm equipment knows that:
   $P = 0$ at $x = 2$ and $x = 6$, find the point for maximum profit using $-1((x - 2)(x - 6))$.
3. If COST $= W^2 - 3W + 4$ and W represents work units, find the corresponding number of work units at the minimum cost and draw the graph.
4. Write the Fortran statements to find the highest and lowest points.
5. The graph created by the following BASIC program will fit conveniently on the screen of many microprocessors and computer terminals. The program plots the points in Figure 17.1 and can be modified to plot points in several other graphs in this chapter by substituting other integer values in the DATA statement, changing the upper limit in a FOR statement as needed and/or rewriting the equation in statement number 310. For exercise 1 above:

(a) Give the DATA statement.
(b) Recode the formula and modify a FOR statement if necessary.

```
100 'ID = QUADR.BAS DRAW PARABOLA FROM INPUT COORDINATES
110 'INPUT INTEGER VALUES ONLY
120 DATA -3,-2,-1,0,1,2,3
130 FOR I = 1 TO 7
140 READ XARAY(I)
150 NEXT I
160 SCREEN 100
170 CLS
180 WINDOW (10,10) - (80,80)
190 LOCATE 18, 70
200 PRINT "X"
210 LOCATE 4, 23
220 PRINT"Y"
230 LINE (22,30) - (70,30)
240 LINE (30,22) - (30,70)
250 FOR I = 26 TO 66 STEP 4
260 LINE (I,29) - (I,31)
270 LINE (29,I) - (31,I)
280 NEXT I
290 FOR I = 1 TO 7
300 X = XARAY(I)
310 Y = X^2 -3
320 X = X • 4 + 30
330 Y = Y • 4 + 30
340 PSET (X,Y)
350 NEXT I
360 END
```

18

Logarithms

Logarithms can be used to reduce the complexity of certain types of calculations involving multiplication, division, and exponentiation, and thus reduce computer time. To study logarithmic functions, we need to combine what we have learned about relations, functions, and inverse functions with the basic laws of exponents.

LOGARITHMIC FUNCTIONS

Consider the following examples.

1. If $b > 1$ and $x \in N$ (x is a member of the set of positive natural numbers) then $b^x > 1$.

Example

Let $b = 2$, $x = 3$; then $2^3 > 1$.

2. If $0 < b < 1$, then $0 < b^x < 1$ (where $x \in N$).

Example

Let $b = .5$, $x = 2$; then $0 < .5^2 < 1$.

3. If $b^{1/x} = a$, then $a^x = b$ (where $x \in N$).

Example

Let $b = 8$, $x = 3$, then $8^{1/3} = 2$, and $2^3 = 8$.

Exponential functions can be easily visualized by drawing their graphs. Let $b = 2$ in Figure 18.1a and $b = \frac{1}{2}$ in Figure 18.1b.

Study these two graphs and note the ordered pairs listed next to each graph.

Figure 18.1 contains graphs of functions since there is only one y associated with each x, for $f(x) = b^x$.

Notes on Figure 18.1 follow:

1. The domain of the function is the set of all real numbers.
2. The range of the function is the set of all positive real numbers.
3. The function $f(x) = b^x$ always passes through the point $(0, 1)$.
4. In Figure 18.1a, the curve for $f(x) = 2^x$ goes *up* to the right and can be described as an increasing function.
5. In Figure 18.1b, the curve for $f(x) = (\frac{1}{2})^x$ goes *down* to the right and can be described as a decreasing function.
6. Where $b > 1$, the graph has the general appearance as shown in Figure 18.1a.
7. Where $0 < b < 1$, the graph has the general appearance as shown in Figure 18.1b.

Powers expressed in the form of b^x, where $x \in R$, $b \in R$, and $b > 0$, $b \neq 1$, can define functions, and we can define the exponential functions for the base b as $f(x) = b^x$. (If $b = 1$, then 1^x defines a constant function.)

x	$f(x)$
-2	$\frac{1}{4}$
-1	$\frac{1}{2}$
0	1
1	2
2	4

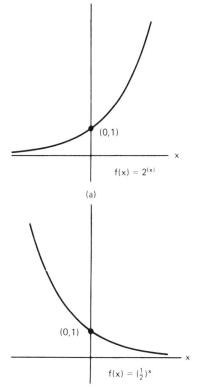

(a)

x	$f(x)$
-2	4
-1	2
0	1
1	$\frac{1}{2}$
2	$\frac{1}{4}$

(b)

Figure 18.1

Inverse Functions

Substituting y for $f(x)$ in $f(x) = b^x$, we get $y = b^x$. To find the inverse of this function, we interchange x and y and write $x = b^y$. The relationship of the function to its inverse is shown in graphic form in Figure 18.2, where $b > 1$.

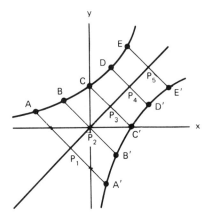

Figure 18.2

To produce the graph, draw the line for $y = x$. Draw $y = b^x$ and mark off points A, B, C, D, E. Draw a line from A perpendicular to the line $y = x$ and extend this line to its own length to A'. Continue this procedure for B, C, D, and E. Then draw a smooth curve connecting these points and representing $x = b^y$. (Note that $AP_1 = P_1A'$, $BP_2 = P_2B'$, etc.)

Observe that

1. The domain of the function $x = b^y$ is the set of all positive real numbers.

2. The range of the function is the set of all real numbers.

As an exercise, draw the graph for $x = b^y$, where $0 < b < 1$. Does the graph of $x = b^y$ always pass through $(1, 0)$ when

$y \in J$ (or integer)
x is a positive real number, and
$b > 1$ or $0 < b < 1$?

Definition 18-1.   The symbolism that expresses y in terms of x for this inverse function is $y = \log_b x$ and is read "y is the logarithm of the number x to the base b." The logarithm is the exponent to which b is raised to obtain the number x.

$x = b^y$ is called the exponential form.

$y = \log_b x$ is called the logarithmic form.

The following example can be performed on a hand calculator

$$3.5 = 10^{0.544068} \qquad \text{exponential form}$$
$$0.544068 = \log_{10} 3.5 \qquad \text{logarithmic form}$$

where $x = 3.5$, $b = 10$ and $y = 0.544068$. Then

$$x = b^{\log_b x} \text{ and } y = \log_b b^y.$$

since

$$x = b^y \text{ if and only if } y = \log_b x.$$

Properties of Logarithms

Because logarithms can be considered as exponents, the laws governing the operations of logarithms have their basis in the laws of exponents. Restating two of these laws of exponents:

I. $b^m \times b^n = b^{m+n}$

II. $\dfrac{b^m}{b^n} = b^{m-n} = \dfrac{1}{b^{n-m}}$

A third law that we are concerned with involves roots and exponents:

III. $\sqrt[n]{b^m} = (\sqrt[n]{b})^m = b^{m/n}$

Logarithms are useful in computations involving multiplication, division, exponentiation, and roots. Let us consider the properties of logarithms for $x, y > 0$ and $x, y \in R$.

1. Applying Law I, we can state that the logarithm of a product is equal to the sum of the logarithms, or $\log_b x + \log_b y = \log_b x \cdot y$.
2. Applying Law II to logarithms, we can state that the logarithm of a quotient is equal to the difference of the logarithms, or $\log_b x/y = \log_b x - \log_b y$.
3. In $\sqrt[n]{x^m}$, we can write the following for logarithms: $\log_b \sqrt[n]{x^m} = m/n \log_b x$, where $n \neq 0$, $m \in J$ (or, $n \neq 0$ and m and n are integers).
4. A special case of property 3 states that $\log_b (x)^m = m \log_b x$ (where $m \in J$), or that the logarithm of a power of x is equal to the product of the power times the logarithm of x. Using Law III, we can now write

$$\log_b \sqrt[n]{x^m} = \log_b x^{m/n} = m/n \log_b x$$

Example 1

$\log_2 32 = 5$ is read, "the log of 32 to the base 2 is 5," and the $\log_2 32 = 5$ is equivalent to the exponential form $2^5 = 32$.

Example 2

$\log_3 \frac{1}{27} = -3$, is read, "the log of $\frac{1}{27}$ to the base 3 is -3," and $\log_3 \frac{1}{27} = -3$ is equivalent to the exponential form $3^{-3} = \frac{1}{27}$.

EXERCISES 18-1

Given the following equations, find the second member of the ordered pairs (example: $y = 2^x$; (0, 1), (1, 2), (2, 4)):

1. $y = 3^x$; $(-2, \quad)$, $(2, \quad)$, $(0, \quad)$
2. $y = -2^x$; $(-1, \quad)$, $(0, \quad)$, $(1, \quad)$
3. $y = (\frac{1}{2})^x$; $(-2, \quad)$, $(-1, \quad)$, $(3, \quad)$
4. $y = 10^x$; $(-3, \quad)$, $(2, \quad)$, $(4, \quad)$

Graph the following functions and their corresponding inverse functions:

5. $y = 3^x$
6. $y = 2^{-x}$
7. $y = (\frac{1}{2})^x$
8. $y = (\frac{1}{3})^{-x}$

Express the following in exponential notation:

9. $\log_2 32 = 5$
10. $\log_{10} 100 = 2$
11. $\log_{10} 0.001 = -3$
12. $\log_{1/2} 4 = -2$
13. $\log_{16} 1 = 0$
14. $\log_5 125 = 3$

Express the following in logarithmic notation:

15. $4^3 = 64$
16. $8^{-1/3} = \frac{1}{2}$
17. $5^0 = 1$
18. $10^{-3} = 0.001$
19. $(\frac{1}{4})^2 = \frac{1}{16}$
20. $1000^{-1/3} = \frac{1}{10}$

Find x, y, or b in the following:

21. $\log_2 16 = y$
22. $\log_{10} 0.01 = y$
23. $\log_b 0.1 = -1$
24. $\log_5 x = 3$
25. $\log_b 32 = -5$

26. $\log_{10} \frac{1}{100} = y$

27. $\log_2 x = -3$

28. Draw the graph for $y = b^x$, where y is the set of positive real numbers, $x \in J$, and $b = 1$.

LOGARITHMS TO THE BASE TEN

The properties of logarithms are given in general terms in the preceding section with no requirements for the base except that it is positive. In computations and in computer languages, base ten and base e are the most commonly used. (Where e is an irrational number, e is equal to approximately 2.7182818.)

Logarithms to base ten are called *common* logarithms.

Logarithms that have base e are called *natural* logarithms.

Our study is concerned with logarithms to base ten expressed in the general form $y = \log_{10} x$.

Using Logarithmic Tables

Table 18.1 is taken from Appendix A, where a reference is provided for $\log_{10} x$ for each value of x, where $1 \leqslant x < 10$. Each number in the column headed x represents the first two significant digits of x.

TABLE 18.1   COMMON LOGARITHMS*

x	0	1	2	3	4	5	6	7	8	9
4.0	.6021	.6031	.6042	.6053	.6064	.6075	.6085	.6096	.6107	.6117
4.1	.6128	.6138	.6149	.6160	.6170	.6180	.6191	.6201	.6212	.6222
4.2	.6232	.6243	.6253	.6263	.6274	.6284	.6294	.6304	.6314	.6325
4.3	.6335	.6345	.6355	.6365	.6375	.6385	.6395	.6405	.6415	.6425
4.4	.6435	.6444	.6454	.6464	.6474	.6484	.6493	.6503	.6513	.6522
4.5	.6532	.6542	.6551	.6561	.6571	.6580	.6590	.6599	.6609	.6618
4.6	.6628	.6637	.6646	.6656	.6665	.6675	.6684	.6693	.6702	.6712
4.7	.6721	.6730	.6739	.6749	.6758	.6767	.6776	.6785	.6794	.6803

*Log tables can be obtained by calculus with the aid of a computer. Many computer manufacturers supply *functions*, or prepared programs that aid in the solution of problems involving logarithms.

The numbers in the same row as x contain a third significant digit in x. The digits located in the table at the intersection of rows and columns form the logarithms of x.

Example 1

Find the logarithm of 4.73. Look for the row next to 4.7 and move right to the column under 3, and we find

$$\log_{10} 4.73 = 0.6749$$

We can also find

$$\log_{10} 4.08 = 0.6107$$

$$\log_{10} 4.10 = 0.6128$$

Because the numbers in the logarithm table are usually irrational, they are only approximations and do not exactly equal $\log_{10} x$ for some x. However, it is conventional to use the equal sign as shown.

Example 2

Assume we needed to find $\log_{10} x$ for values of $x \geqslant 10$. Scientific notation makes it possible to represent any number $x \geqslant 10$ as a product of a number between 1 and 10 and a power of 10. Thus

$$\log_{10} 32.1 = \log_{10} (3.21 \times 10^1)$$

$$= \log_{10} 3.21 + \log_{10} 10^1$$

$$= 0.5065 + 1$$

$$= 1.5065$$

The decimal fraction portion of the logarithm is nonnegative and called the *mantissa*. The whole number part is simply the exponent on 10 when the number is written in scientific notation. It is called the *characteristic*. The characteristic can be positive or negative. Thus, in 1.5065, 1 is the characteristic and .5065 is the mantissa. $\text{Log}_{10} 32.1 = 1.5065$.

Consider the following:

$$\log_{10} 10 = \log_{10} 10^1 = 1$$

$$\log_{10} 100 = \log_{10} 10^2 = 2$$

$$\log_{10} 1 = \log_{10} 10^0 = 0$$

$$\log_{10} 0.1 = \log_{10} 10^{-1} = -1$$

$$\log_{10} 0.01 = \log_{10} 10^{-2} = -2$$

$$\log_{10} 0.001 = \log_{10} 10^{-3} = -3$$

Example 3

Find $\log_{10} 673000$

$$\log_{10} 673000 = \log_{10} (6.73 \times 10^5)$$

$$= \log_{10} 6.73 + \log_{10} 10^5$$

$$= 0.8280 + 5$$

$$= 5.8280$$

Example 4

Find $\log_{10} 0.00891$ (where $0 < x < 1$)

$$\log_{10} 0.00891 = \log_{10} (8.91 \times 10^{-3})$$
$$= \log_{10} 8.91 + \log_{10} 10^{-3}$$
$$= 0.9499 + (-3)$$

However,

$$\begin{array}{r} -3.0000 \\ +0.9499 \\ \hline \log_{10} 0.00891 = -2.0501 \end{array}$$

To write the logarithm in a form in which the *decimal fraction is positive*, we let

$$\log_{10} 0.00891 = 0.9499 - 3$$
$$= 0.9499 + (7 - 10)$$
$$= 7.9499 - 10$$

This conventional format makes it possible to subtract a multiple of 10 and to represent the logarithm in a manner whereby the decimal fraction is not a negative number. (Further, the original mantissa is retained.)

We can find a value for x in $\log_{10} x$ by reversing these procedures. For example, $\text{antilog}_{10} 2.7767$ can be found by locating the mantissa 0.7767 in Appendix A and noting that the corresponding value for x is 5.98. Because the characteristic is 2, we multiply as follows: $5.98 \times 10^2 = 598$. Therefore, $\text{antilog}_{10} 2.7767 = 598$, or $x = 598$.

Arithmetic with Logarithms

The operations of multiplication, division, and exponentiation are possible with logarithms because of basic relationships between logarithmic and exponential functions. (Examples for common logarithms follow).

Multiplication.   Refer to Appendix A and note that the logarithm of

$$4 = .6021$$
$$2 = .3010$$

We can write $\log 4 \times 2 = \log 4 + \log 2$ by the first property of logarithms. Thus

$$\log 4 \times 2 = .6021 + .3010$$
$$= .9031$$

To find the value for .9031, refer to Appendix A. The number corresponding to that logarithm is 8. This process is called finding the *antilogarithm* and is the reverse for finding a logarithm. Stated in other terms: .9031 is the log of 8, and 8 is the antilog of .9031.

Division.   The second property of logarithms states that

$$\log_b x/y = \log_b x - \log_b y$$

Using this property, we can write

$$\log 8 \div 4 = \log 8 - \log 4$$
$$= .9031 - .6021$$
$$= .3010$$

From Appendix A we get the antilog $.3010 = 2$.

Exponentiation.   With the special case of the third property of logarithms

$$\log_b (x)^m = m \log_b x$$

we can write

$$\log 3^2 = 2 \cdot \log 3$$
$$= 2(.4771)$$
$$= .9542$$

and the antilog of $.9542 = 9$.

Finding roots.   Using the third property of logarithms, find the third root of 8.

$$\text{Root} = \sqrt[3]{8^1} = 2$$
$$\text{Log root} = \tfrac{1}{3} \log 8$$
$$= \tfrac{1}{3}(.9031)$$
$$= .3010$$

and the antilog of $.3010$ is 2.

Linear Interpolation

Because of space limitations, logarithm tables are sometimes given in three digits for x. To find the common logarithm of a four-digit number, we use a method called linear interpolation. Consider

$$\frac{y_1}{y_2} = \frac{x_1}{x_2}$$

If we know three of these numbers, we can find the fourth.

Assume that we wish to find the logarithm of 5.662. We know that $5.660 < 5.662 < 5.670$. (Note that we have written the four-digit numbers 5.660 and 5.670 instead of the three-digit numbers 5.66 and 5.67.) We can now denote the 2 in

5.662 as $\frac{2}{10}$ of the distance between 5.660 and 5.670. This distance can be expressed as a ratio using logarithms. Thus, in

$$\frac{5.662 - 5.660}{5.670 - 5.660} = \frac{y}{0.7536 - 0.7528}$$

note that

$$\frac{5.662 - 5.660}{5.670 - 5.660} = \frac{0.002}{0.010}$$

$$= \frac{0.002 \times 10^3}{0.010 \times 10^3} = \frac{2}{10}$$

Using a more conventional method where 2 has the same number of significant digits as .002

$$10 \left\{ 2 \begin{cases} 5.660 \\ 5.662 \end{cases} \quad \begin{matrix} 0.7528 \\ \end{matrix} \left. \right\} y \\ 5.670 \quad\quad 0.7536 \end{matrix} \right\} 0.0008$$

$$\begin{array}{ccc} & x & \log_{10} x \end{array}$$

To find the difference between the logs of 5.66 and 5.67, we subtract

$$\begin{array}{r} 0.7536 \\ -0.7528 \\ \hline 0.0008 \end{array}$$

It follows that

$$\frac{2}{10} = \frac{y}{0.0008}$$

and $2/10(0.0008) = y = 0.00016$. Adding 0.00016 to 0.7528, we get 0.7530 (after rounding). This represents an approximation of the required logarithm, or $\log_{10} 5.662 = 0.7530$.

Sample Logarithmic Calculations

Solve the following four problems using logarithms.

1. $\dfrac{(2.37) \times (7.18)}{(4.50)}$

$$[\log_{10} (2.37) + \log_{10} (7.18)] - \log_{10} (4.50)$$
$$= [0.3747 + 0.8561 - 0.6532]$$
$$= 1.2308 - 0.6532$$

$0.5776 =$ the logarithm of the answer. To find the antilog_{10} 0.5776, we interpolate as follows:

$$11\left\{\begin{array}{l}\begin{array}{ccc}\quad & \text{log} & \text{antilog} \\ 1\left\{\begin{array}{l}.5775 \\ .5776\end{array}\right. & \begin{array}{l}3.780 \\ \end{array}\}x \\ \quad .5786 & 3.790\end{array}\end{array}\right\}0.010$$

$$\frac{1}{11} = \frac{x}{0.010}$$

$$.001 = x \text{ and } 3.780 + 0.001 = 3.781$$

Thus, antilog $0.5776 = 3.781$. The antilog provides a way of expressing the answer to $[(2.37) \times (7.18)]/(4.50) = 3.781$

2. $\dfrac{(3.75)^2 \times (8.16)^{1/2}}{(7.56)^{-3}}$

$2 \log_{10} (3.75) + \frac{1}{2} \log_{10} (8.16) - (-3) \log_{10} (7.56)$
$= 2(0.5740) + \frac{1}{2}(0.9117) + 3(0.8785)$
$= 1.1480 + 0.4558 + 2.6355 = 4.2393$

$$25\left\{\begin{array}{l}13\left\{\begin{array}{l}.2380 \\ .2393\end{array}\right. \begin{array}{l}1.730 \\ \end{array}\}x \\ \quad .2405 \quad 1.740\end{array}\right\}0.010$$

$$\frac{13}{25} = \frac{x}{0.010}$$

$.005 = x$
$\text{antilog}_{10}\ 4.2393 = 17{,}350$ (or 1.735×10^4)

3. $(580) \times (11.2)^5 \times (3.75)^{-7}$
$\log_{10} (580) + 5 \log_{10} (11.2) + (-7) \log_{10} (3.75)$
$= 2.7634 + 5(1.0492) - 7(0.5740)$
$= 2.7634 + 5.2460 - 4.0180$
$= 8.0094 - 4.0180$
$= 3.9914$

$$5\left\{\begin{array}{l}2\left\{\begin{array}{l}.9912 \\ .9914\end{array}\right. \begin{array}{l}9.800 \\ \end{array}\}x \\ \quad .9917 \quad 9.810\end{array}\right\}0.010$$

$$\frac{2}{5} = \frac{x}{0.010}$$

$.004 = x$

$\text{antilog}_{10}\ 3.9914 = 9804$

4. $\dfrac{(5.77)^3 \times \sqrt[3]{(7.23)^2}}{(20.9)^{1/3}}$

$3 \log_{10} (5.77) + \frac{2}{3} \log_{10} (7.23) - \frac{1}{3} \log_{10} (20.9)$
$= 3(0.7612) + \frac{2}{3}(0.8591) - \frac{1}{3}(1.3201)$
$= 2.2836 + 0.5727 - 0.4400$
$= 2.8563 - 0.4400$
$= 2.4163$

$$16 \left\{ 13 \left\{ \begin{array}{ll} .4150 & 2.600 \\ .4163 & \\ .4166 & 2.610 \end{array} \right\} x \right\} 0.010$$

$\dfrac{13}{16} = \dfrac{x}{0.010}$

$.008 = x$

$\text{antilog}_{10}\ 2.4163 = 260.8$

EXERCISES 18-2

Find each logarithm from the table in Appendix A:

1. $\log_{10} 4.25$
2. $\log_{10} 62.0$
3. $\log_{10} 7.21$
4. $\log_{10} 0.00512$
5. $\log_{10} 0.127$
6. $\log_{10} 32400$
7. $\log_{10} 295$

Find each of the following:

8. $\text{antilog}_{10}\ 0.5478$
9. $\text{antilog}_{10}\ 0.9786$
10. $\text{antilog}_{10}\ 2.8722$
11. $\text{antilog}_{10}\ (1.7709 - 2)$
12. $\text{antilog}_{10}\ (4.6522 - 3)$
13. $\text{antilog}_{10}\ 4.6522$
14. $\text{antilog}_{10}\ 0.7042$
15. $\text{antilog}_{10}\ 3.8887$

Interpolate and find the following:

16. $\log_{10} 6437$

17. $\log_{10} 73.82$

18. $\log_{10} 0.1235$

19. $\log_{10} 26.41$

20. $\log_{10} 7.398$

21. $\log_{10} 534.6$

22. $\log_{10} 0.04891$

23. antilog$_{10}$ $(6.7051 - 8)$

24. antilog$_{10}$ 2.9958

25. antilog$_{10}$ 1.7240

Compute each of the following using logarithms:

26. $(12.4)(7.91)$

27. $\dfrac{4.12}{1.25}$

28. $(6.41)^3$

29. $\sqrt[5]{7.61}$

30. $\dfrac{(14.8)(0.021)}{394}$

31. $\dfrac{(3.45)^3(\sqrt[2]{6.71})}{8.55}$

32. Is there any real number y where b^y is not positive? $(b > 0)$.

LOGARITHMS AND COMPUTERS

A typical problem for computers deals with compound interest and amortization. Problems of these types were given in Chapter 11 and logarithms are another important method of solving problems that involve exponents.

Example 1

In a formula given earlier

$$A = P(1 + i)^n$$

where A = the final amount, P = principal, i = rate of interest, and n = number of years. This can be converted to a problem using logarithms as follows. Given $P = 1000$, $i = 5.25\%$, and $n = 10$. Taking logarithms for both sides of the equation, we obtain

$$\log A = \log 1000 + 10 \times \log 1.0525$$

$$= 3 + .2222$$

and the antilog of 3.2222 is = 1668. Further, since $x = b^{\log_b x}$ (from page 287), we can also write

$$10.0^{3.2222} = 1668$$

Suppose that the programmer already knew the original principal, the interest rate, and the final amount but did not know the number of years. Logarithms can also be used to find an exponent:

$$1668 = 1000(1.0525)^n$$

$$\log(1668/1000) = n \times \log 1.0525$$

$$n = \log 1.668 \div \log 1.0525$$

$$n = 9.9988 \text{ or } 10 \text{ years (after rounding)}$$

A hand calculator can be used to demonstrate the following example.

Example 2

In a mercury barometer, the average atmospheric pressure at sea level is expressed as 29.92 inches or 760 millimeters of mercury. To measure variations in pressure with respect to altitude, a manufacturer of mercury barometers uses the formula

$$P = p_0 e^{-mh}$$

where
$$P = \text{pressure}$$
$$p_0 = \text{pressure at sea level}$$
$$h = \text{altitude in meters}$$
$$m = .0001232$$
$$e = 2.7182$$

If your home is 250 meters (about 820 feet) above sea level, then atmospheric pressure in terms of millimeters of mercury is

$$P = 760(2.7182)^{-mh}$$

$$\log P = \log 760 + ((-.0001232 \times 250) \times \log 2.7182)$$

$$= 2.8808136 - (.0308 \times .4343)$$

$$\log P = 2.8674372$$

and the antilog of $\log P = 736.95$ or $10.0^{2.8674372} = 736.95$. (Note that the negative exponent caused subtraction.)

The value for e closely approximates the base of the natural logarithms, or approximately 2.7182818. If a programmer uses a system that has only natural logs available, this problem and other problems involving logarithms can be easily coded as shown in the following BASIC code.

```
10 P = LOG(760) + (−.0001232*250)*LOG(2.7182)
20 ANS = 2.7182818^P
30 PRINT ANS
```

where P is the exponent on e.

The following equates the logarithms of base e to base 10.

$y = \log_b x$
and $b^y = x$ From Definition 18-1
$\log_n b^y = \log_n x$ Take logs of both sides of equation
$y \log_n b = \log_n x$ Special case of 3rd law of logarithms
$y = \log_n x / \log_n b$

Therefore, if $y = \log_e x$ we can write $y = \log_{10} x / \log_{10} e$. Since

$$\log_{10} e = \log_{10} 2.7182 = .4343$$

then

$$\log_e x = \log_{10} x / .4343$$

Example

$$\log_e 7 = \log_{10} 7 / .4343$$
$$= .8451 / .4343$$
$$= 1.9459$$

Exponents and logarithms can be evaluated by computers in so-called "library" routines, or special programs written by the computer manufacturers. These special programs can be referenced by the coding shown in Table 18.2.*

TABLE 18.2

	Function	Coding
Fortran	Exponent	EXP(X)
	Logarithm	ALOG(X)
BASIC	Exponent	EXP(X)
	Logarithm	LOG(X)

Example 3

Given a Fortran example

$$a = e^2$$

Coded: A = EXP(2)

After the statement A = EXP(2) has been executed, A will contain the base of the natural logarithm system raised to the power of 2.

---

*Students should reference the manual for the computer they are using.

Example 4

Given a Fortran example

$$C = \log_{10} A - \log_{10} B \text{ (or } A \div B)$$

Coded:

$$C = \text{ALOG10(A)} - \text{ALOG10(B)}$$

or

$$C = \text{ALOG10(A/B)}$$

The value of the common logarithm is assigned to C, where A and $B > 0$.

Antilogarithms can be found by using the logarithm as an exponent on the base as shown in the preceding examples 1 and 2 or by using the EXP function for base e.

EXERCISES 18-3

1. A bank pays 5.25 percent interest per year compounded quarterly. Let

P = the amount of money deposited in a savings account
m = the number of interest periods per year
n = the number of years the amount of money is in the bank
r = the rate of interest
A = the final amount (or current amount)

The formula used to compute interest compounded quarterly is

$$A = P\left(1 + \frac{r}{m}\right)^{mn}$$

(a) Using logarithms, find the amount to be paid a depositor whose original (and only) deposit was $200.00 made exactly ten years ago.
(b) Write the Fortran statement(s) to compute the depositor's interest using ALOG10.

2. (a) In 1626, Peter Minuit purchased Manhattan Island for about $24.00. If the Indians invested this money at 4 percent compounded semiannually, what would the amount be 360 years later?
(b) Assume the Indians desired a computer print out of A for every ten-year period since 1626. Flowchart the logic used to compute and print out A for every such ten-year period.

3. Solve part 2(a) with a Fortran statement(s) using logarithms.

4. Find n in the following:

$$3.7^n = 6.2$$

5. (a) The number of bacteria in a culture is a function of time such that from one generation to

the next, the number of bacteria doubles. Consider one thousand bacteria growing in a petri dish. If we wanted to find out the number of generations that would be required to produce a count of one billion (or 10^9) bacteria, we could use the formula $a = b \times 2^n$, where

$$b = \text{the original bacteria count}$$
$$a = \text{the final bacteria count}$$
$$n = \text{the number of generations}$$

Solve this problem using logarithms.

(b) If the production of each generation requires 30 minutes, how much time is needed to produce the number of generations found in part (a)?

19

Matrix Algebra

BASIC CONCEPTS

It is often useful to group real numbers (or other suitable items) into a rectangular array called a matrix. Consider, for example, a situation where some items in a shoe store are to be discounted. We could enter the costs of these items into an array as follows:

SIZES

	6	7	8	9	10
Shoes	40.00	40.50	41.00	42.00	43.00
Sandals	8.50	9.00	9.50	10.00	10.50
Boots	52.50	54.00	55.00	56.00	56.50
Sneakers	24.00	24.30	24.80	25.10	25.50

If each of these items were to be reduced in price by 20%, each entry in the array would be multiplied by .80. For size 6 shoes, this works out as $.80 \times 40.00 = 32.00$.

Definition 19-1. A *matrix* is a rectangular array of elements (usually real numbers displayed in brackets) and often identified by upper case letters.

Examples of matrices are

$$A = \begin{bmatrix} 1 & 4 & 7 \\ 2 & 5 & 8 \\ 3 & 6 & 9 \end{bmatrix} \qquad B = \begin{bmatrix} 1 & 2 & 3 \end{bmatrix} \qquad C = \begin{bmatrix} 1 \\ 2 \\ 3 \end{bmatrix}$$

$$\text{(a)} \qquad\qquad\qquad \text{(b)} \qquad\qquad \text{(c)}$$

A matrix consisting of a single row is referred to as a *row matrix* (see (b) of the preceding illustration). A matrix consisting of a single column is referred to as *column matrix* (see (c) of the preceding illustration).

The *dimension*, or *order*, of a matrix is denoted first by its number of rows and then by its number of columns. In the illustration, the three matrices A, B, and C are described as 3×3 (three rows by three columns) or simply "three by three," 1×3 ("one by three"), and 3×1 ("three by one"), respectively.

Matrix entries can be represented by subscripted lower-case letters. Generally, one of two formats is used.

Single Subscript Method

$$A = \begin{bmatrix} a_1 & b_1 & c_1 \\ a_2 & b_2 & c_2 \\ a_3 & b_3 & c_3 \end{bmatrix}$$

In this 3×3 matrix called A, we used a different lower-case letter for each entry in a row, but kept the same subscript denoting the row in which the element appears. Column entries are denoted by the same letter with different subscripts.

Double Subscript Method

$$A = \begin{bmatrix} a_{11} & a_{12} & a_{13} \\ a_{21} & a_{22} & a_{23} \\ a_{31} & a_{32} & a_{33} \end{bmatrix} \qquad B = \begin{bmatrix} b_{11} & b_{12} & b_{13} \\ b_{21} & b_{22} & b_{23} \end{bmatrix}$$

In the double subscript method, a single lower-case letter with two integer subscripts is used to denote each entry. The first subscript indicates the row, and the second subscript denotes the column.

Subscripts can be represented by lower-case letters, and conventionally, i is used to represent rows and j to represent columns. Thus, we can refer to the ith row or the jth column.

In much of the work in this chapter, we concentrate on square matrices, or matrices of the order $n \times n$. Although many of the ideas discussed are applicable to matrices of any order, we apply the notion to most of those usually found in data processing situations.

Equal Matrices

Definition 19-2.   Two matrices are said to be *equal* if and only if they are both of the same dimension or order and corresponding entries are equal.

$$\begin{bmatrix} 1 & 3 & 4 \\ 0 & -2 & 6 \end{bmatrix} = \begin{bmatrix} 1 & \frac{6}{2} & \frac{-12}{-3} \\ x - x & -2 & 3 \cdot 2 \end{bmatrix}$$

In general, for each ith row and jth column, $a_{ij} = b_{ij}$. This also applies to single-row and single-column matrices, where $a_{1j} = b_{1j}$ for row matrices and $a_{i1} = b_{i1}$ for column matrices. Thus

$$[4 \quad 9 \quad 5] = [2^2 \quad 3^2 \quad \sqrt{25}]$$

$$\begin{bmatrix} 3^{-2} \\ 8^{1/3} \\ 5^2 \end{bmatrix} = \begin{bmatrix} \frac{1}{9} \\ 2 \\ 25 \end{bmatrix}$$

One of the objectives of this chapter is to provide the student with another tool for solving linear equations. Before we can use matrices in solving linear equations, we must learn how to perform certain manipulations on matrices.

MATRIX OPERATIONS

Transpose of a Matrix

Definition 19-3. The *transpose* of a matrix is a manipulation in which the rows are exchanged with the columns of the same matrix.

If the entries in A are A_{ij}, the entries in A transpose are A_{ji}. For example

$$\begin{bmatrix} \sqrt{2} & 3 \\ -4 & 0 \end{bmatrix} \quad \text{transposed becomes} \quad \begin{bmatrix} \sqrt{2} & -4 \\ 3 & 0 \end{bmatrix}$$

The transpose of a matrix is denoted by a lower-case t as shown here. Thus

$$\begin{bmatrix} 1 & 2 & -4 \\ 0 & 1 & 3^2 \end{bmatrix}^t = \begin{bmatrix} 1 & 0 \\ 2 & 1 \\ -4 & 3^2 \end{bmatrix}$$

Addition of Matrices

Definition 19-4. Matrices of the *same dimension or order* can be added, and the sums consist of the sums of the corresponding entries or elements.

Thus, given

$$A = [1 \quad 2 \quad 3]$$
$$B = [-4 \quad 5 \quad 0.5]$$

Then
$$A + B = [-3 \quad 7 \quad 3.5]$$

(Column matrices with the same number of entries or elements can also be added together.)

In

$$A = \begin{bmatrix} 1 & 6 \\ 4 & -2 \end{bmatrix} \quad \text{and} \quad B = \begin{bmatrix} 14 & 0 \\ 8 & 4 \end{bmatrix}$$

$$A + B = \begin{bmatrix} 1 & 6 \\ 4 & -2 \end{bmatrix} + \begin{bmatrix} 14 & 0 \\ 8 & 4 \end{bmatrix} = \begin{bmatrix} 1 + 14 & 6 + 0 \\ 4 + 8 & -2 + 4 \end{bmatrix} = \begin{bmatrix} 15 & 6 \\ 12 & 2 \end{bmatrix}$$

Note that the sums are placed in a third matrix of the same dimension. In a general way, we can write

$$\begin{bmatrix} a_1 & b_1 \\ a_2 & b_2 \\ a_3 & b_3 \end{bmatrix} + \begin{bmatrix} x_1 & y_1 \\ x_2 & y_2 \\ x_3 & y_3 \end{bmatrix} = \begin{bmatrix} a_1 + x_1 & b_1 + y_1 \\ a_2 + x_2 & b_2 + y_2 \\ a_3 + x_3 & b_3 + y_3 \end{bmatrix}$$

The addition of matrices of different dimensions is not defined.

Multiplication by a Constant

Definition 19-5.   A matrix can be multiplied by a constant or a variable. The product of the matrix and the constant or variable is another matrix whose entries contain the products of the constant or variable, and corresponding entries of the original matrix.

Examples

$$5 \times \begin{bmatrix} \frac{1}{5} \\ 2 \\ 0.5 \end{bmatrix} = \begin{bmatrix} 1 \\ 10 \\ 2.5 \end{bmatrix}$$

$$3 \times \begin{bmatrix} 4 & \frac{1}{3} \\ 6 & -1 \end{bmatrix} = \begin{bmatrix} 12 & 1 \\ 18 & -3 \end{bmatrix}$$

In general, we can write

$$k \times \begin{bmatrix} a_1 & b_1 & c_1 \\ a_2 & b_2 & c_2 \\ a_3 & b_3 & c_3 \end{bmatrix} = \begin{bmatrix} ka_1 & kb_1 & kc_1 \\ ka_2 & kb_2 & kc_2 \\ ka_3 & kb_3 & kc_3 \end{bmatrix}$$

Let

$$A = \begin{bmatrix} 3 & 7 \\ -1 & .5 \end{bmatrix}$$

Suppose that it is desirable to multiply matrix A by the constant -1. Then

$$-1 \times \begin{bmatrix} 3 & 7 \\ -1 & .5 \end{bmatrix} = \begin{bmatrix} -3 & -7 \\ 1 & -.5 \end{bmatrix}$$

and we can write $-A = (-1) \cdot A$.

Subtraction of Matrices

The negative of a matrix is formed by replacing each entry by its *additive inverse*. Thus, if

$$A = \begin{bmatrix} 3 & -2 & 1 \\ 4 & 8 & -5 \end{bmatrix}$$

then

$$-A = \begin{bmatrix} -3 & 2 & -1 \\ -4 & -8 & 5 \end{bmatrix}$$

Definition 19-6. The sum of a matrix and the negative of another matrix of the same dimension is represented as $A + (-B)$ or $A - B$. The resulting matrix contains entries representing the differences between corresponding entries.

In general, we can write

$$\begin{bmatrix} a_{11} & a_{12} \\ a_{21} & a_{22} \end{bmatrix} - \begin{bmatrix} b_{11} & b_{12} \\ b_{21} & b_{22} \end{bmatrix} = \begin{bmatrix} a_{11} & a_{12} \\ a_{21} & a_{22} \end{bmatrix} + \begin{bmatrix} -b_{11} & -b_{12} \\ -b_{21} & -b_{22} \end{bmatrix}$$

If

$$A = \begin{bmatrix} 1 & 3 \\ 0 & 4 \end{bmatrix} \quad \text{and} \quad B = \begin{bmatrix} -8 & 11 \\ 9 & 2 \end{bmatrix}$$

then

$$A + (-B) = A - B = \begin{bmatrix} 9 & -8 \\ -9 & 2 \end{bmatrix}$$

EXERCISES 19-1

1. Write a matrix equal to

$$\begin{bmatrix} 1 & 0 & 2^2 \\ 4 & 1 & \frac{1}{2} \\ 3 & .06 & -4 \end{bmatrix}$$

2. Name the order of the following:

(a) $\begin{bmatrix} a_{11} & a_{12} \\ a_{21} & a_{22} \\ a_{31} & a_{32} \end{bmatrix}$ (b) $\begin{bmatrix} a \\ b \\ c \end{bmatrix}$ (c) $[-4 \quad 3 \quad .05]$

3. Find the transpose of each of the following:

(a) $\begin{bmatrix} 1 & -2 \\ 3 & \frac{6}{7} \end{bmatrix}$

(b) $\begin{bmatrix} 2 & 1 \\ 3 & -4 \\ 0 & 6 \end{bmatrix}$

(c) $[1 \quad 2 \quad 3]$

(d) $\begin{bmatrix} 1 & 2 & 3 & 4 \\ 5 & 6 & 7 & 8 \\ 9 & 10 & 11 & 12 \\ 13 & 14 & 15 & 16 \end{bmatrix}$

4. Add the following matrices:

(a) $\begin{bmatrix} 1 & 2 & 6 \\ 4 & 0 & \frac{1}{2} \end{bmatrix} + \begin{bmatrix} 3 & -2 & 8 \\ -1 & -1 & -2 \end{bmatrix}$

(b) $\begin{bmatrix} 1 & -\frac{1}{3} \\ 2 & \frac{7}{6} \\ 3 & 0 \\ 4 & -1 \end{bmatrix} + \begin{bmatrix} 3 & -\frac{2}{3} \\ -6 & \frac{5}{6} \\ 4 & 1 \\ \frac{1}{2} & 0 \end{bmatrix}$

(c) Let $A = \begin{bmatrix} 1 & -3 \\ 6 & 2 \end{bmatrix}$ and $B = \begin{bmatrix} 7 & 14 \\ 0 & -1 \end{bmatrix}$

Is addition of matrices commutative; that is, does $A + B = B + A$?

5. Let a matrix whose entries or elements are all equal to zero be called a zero matrix.
  (a) Does the zero matrix function as an identity matrix for addition?
  (b) Give an example to determine whether or not $A + 0 = 0 + A = A$.

6. Find the negative of each of the following:

(a) $\begin{bmatrix} 1 & -3 & 6 \\ 4 & 7 & -2 \\ -3 & -1 & 6 \end{bmatrix}$

(b) $\begin{bmatrix} 3 & 7 \\ -6 & 9 \\ 4 & -2 \\ \frac{1}{3} & -1 \end{bmatrix}$

7. Subtract the following matrices:

(a) $\begin{bmatrix} 3 & 4 \\ 2 & 1 \end{bmatrix} - \begin{bmatrix} 2 & 4 \\ 1 & 3 \end{bmatrix}$

(b) $\begin{bmatrix} 4 \\ 0 \\ 1 \end{bmatrix} - \begin{bmatrix} 3 \\ 6 \\ 0 \end{bmatrix}$

8. Solve the following for C:

(a) $C + \begin{bmatrix} 1 & -3 \\ 2 & 0 \end{bmatrix} = \begin{bmatrix} 1 & 2 \\ 1 & 4 \end{bmatrix}$

(b) $C - \begin{bmatrix} 4 & 8 & -11 \\ 15 & \frac{1}{3} & 4 \end{bmatrix} = \begin{bmatrix} 2 & 6 & -9 \\ 13 & 1 & 0 \end{bmatrix}$

(c) $C + \begin{bmatrix} 2 & 4 & 7 \\ 3 & -1 & 9 \\ 2 & 0 & 1 \end{bmatrix}^t = \begin{bmatrix} 0 & 0 & 0 \\ 0 & 0 & 0 \\ 0 & 0 & 0 \end{bmatrix}$

9. Given $A = \begin{bmatrix} -3 & 6 \\ -2 & 1 \end{bmatrix}$

$B = \begin{bmatrix} 1 & 0 \\ 3 & 1 \end{bmatrix}$

Find C in $A + B = C$ and show that $B = C - A$.

10. Multiply the following:

(a) $-3 \times \begin{bmatrix} -4 & \frac{1}{3} \\ 2 & 0 \end{bmatrix}$

(b) $y \times [a \quad -1 \quad \frac{2}{3}]$

11. J-Mart, a retailer, operates two stores in a small city and displays monthly costs in matrix form.

	Garden Supplies	
	Store A	Store B
Wholesale cost	2000	1500
Labor cost	4000	3300

	Sporting Goods	
	Store A	Store B
Wholesale cost	1800	1250
Labor cost	3800	3000

Display in matrix form the total costs for garden supplies and sporting goods by store.

MULTIPLICATION OF MATRICES

The product of two matrices A and B is a resulting matrix with entries determined as follows:
if

$$A = \begin{bmatrix} a_{11} & a_{12} \\ a_{21} & a_{22} \end{bmatrix}$$

and

$$B = \begin{bmatrix} b_{11} & b_{12} \\ b_{21} & b_{22} \end{bmatrix}$$

then

$$AB = \begin{bmatrix} (a_{11}b_{11} + a_{12}b_{21}) & (a_{11}b_{12} + a_{12}b_{22}) \\ (a_{21}b_{11} + a_{22}b_{21}) & (a_{21}b_{12} + a_{22}b_{22}) \end{bmatrix}$$

or

$$AB = C, \qquad \text{where } C = \begin{bmatrix} c_{11} & c_{12} \\ c_{21} & c_{22} \end{bmatrix}$$

c_{11} is determined by multiplying a_{11} and b_{11} and adding this product to the product of a_{12} and b_{21}, note that

$$c_{11} = a_{11}b_{11} + a_{12}b_{21}$$
$$c_{21} = a_{21}b_{11} + a_{22}b_{21}$$
$$c_{12} = a_{11}b_{12} + a_{12}b_{22}$$
$$c_{22} = a_{21}b_{12} + a_{22}b_{22}$$

It is often useful to describe the dimensions of a matrix using variables. Thus, in $A_{m \times n}$, the matrix A contains m rows and n columns.

Definition 19-7. The product of the matrices $A_{m \times n}$ and $B_{n \times p}$ is the matrix $(AB)_{m \times p}$, with entries developed as follows:

The entry c_{ij} in the product of A and B is determined by multiplying the first entry in the ith row of matrix A by the first entry in the jth column of matrix B and adding this product to the product formed by multiplying the second element in the ith row of A with the second element in the jth column of B, and so on.

In 3×3 matrices this works out as follows. Let

$$A = \begin{bmatrix} 1 & 2 & -3 \\ 4 & 0 & 1 \\ 6 & \frac{1}{2} & -1 \end{bmatrix} \qquad B = \begin{bmatrix} 0 & 1 & 1 \\ \frac{1}{2} & -2 & -4 \\ 1 & 2 & 1 \end{bmatrix}$$

Then

$$AB = \begin{bmatrix} 0+1-3 & 1-4-6 & 1-8-3 \\ 0+0+1 & 4+0+2 & 4+0+1 \\ 0+\frac{1}{4}-1 & 6-1-2 & 6-2-1 \end{bmatrix} = \begin{bmatrix} -2 & -9 & -10 \\ 1 & 6 & 5 \\ -\frac{3}{4} & 3 & 3 \end{bmatrix}$$

Unlike matrix addition, matrix multiplication is not limited to matrices having the same dimensions. Where the first matrix has the same number of columns as the second matrix has rows, we say that the two matrices are conformable for multiplication. For example

$$\begin{bmatrix} 1 & 2 & -4 \\ 3 & 7 & 5 \end{bmatrix} \times \begin{bmatrix} 3 & -1 \\ 1 & 2 \\ 2 & 3 \end{bmatrix} = \begin{bmatrix} 3+2+(-8) & -1+4+(-12) \\ 9+7+10 & -3+14+15 \end{bmatrix}$$

$$= \begin{bmatrix} -3 & -9 \\ 26 & 26 \end{bmatrix}$$

Notice that our resulting matrix is 2×2. In general, we can say that the outer two-dimension numbers of the original matrices form the dimensions of the resulting matrix. We can illustrate our last example as follows:

If our original matrices were 3×2 and 2×3, they would be conformable for multiplication. In

$$\overline{3 \times 2 \quad \underline{2 \times 3}}$$

our resulting matrix would have the dimensions of 3×3. An example of two matrices *not* conformable for multiplication is

$$\begin{bmatrix} 1 & 2 & 3 \\ 4 & 5 & 6 \end{bmatrix} \cdot \begin{bmatrix} 7 \\ 8 \end{bmatrix}$$

Since the first matrix does not have the same number of columns as the second matrix has rows, these two matrices are not conformable for multiplication.

EXERCISES 19-2

1. Multiply the following:

(a) $3 \times \begin{bmatrix} 4 & 6 \\ -2 & \frac{1}{3} \end{bmatrix}$

(b) $.02 \times \begin{bmatrix} 10.32 & 31.8 & 6.00 \\ 64.71 & 4.09 & -4.13 \end{bmatrix}$

2. Division in matrix algebra has not been defined, but we can multiply a matrix by a constant rational number. Accordingly, find

$$\frac{1}{2} \times \begin{bmatrix} 6 & -3 \\ 2 & 0 \\ 4 & 8 \end{bmatrix}$$

3. The XYZ Company owns a motel. In order to meet the rising costs of living, a 5% salary increase has been given each of 16 employees. If

four earn $9,500 yearly
six earn $10,000 yearly
three earn $11,000 yearly
two earn $11,500 yearly
one earns $13,000 yearly

display their respective salary increases in matrix form.

4. Multiply the following:

(a) $\begin{bmatrix} 4 & 7 \\ 3 & 5 \end{bmatrix} \cdot \begin{bmatrix} 1 & -2 \\ 0 & 4 \end{bmatrix}$

(b) $\begin{bmatrix} 3 & 2 & -4 \\ 0 & 5 & 6 \\ 1 & 2 & 2 \end{bmatrix} \cdot \begin{bmatrix} 1 & -1 & 1 \\ -1 & 1 & -1 \\ 1 & -1 & 1 \end{bmatrix}$

(c) $\begin{bmatrix} 2 & 0 & 4 \\ 1 & 1 & -1 \end{bmatrix} \cdot \begin{bmatrix} 1 & 3 \\ 0 & -2 \\ 4 & 1 \end{bmatrix}$

5. (a) Let $A = \begin{bmatrix} 1 & -1 \\ 2 & -2 \\ 3 & -3 \end{bmatrix}$

$B = \begin{bmatrix} 1 & 2 & 3 \\ -1 & -2 & -3 \end{bmatrix}$

Does $AB = BA$? Is the multiplication of matrices (generally) commutative?

(b) Let $A = \begin{bmatrix} 1 & 0 \\ 2 & 4 \end{bmatrix}$

$B = \begin{bmatrix} 1 & 4 \\ 2 & 1 \\ 0 & -2 \end{bmatrix}$

Does $AB = BA$?

(c) $\begin{bmatrix} 1 & -2 & 4 \end{bmatrix} \cdot \begin{bmatrix} 2 \\ -1 \\ 3 \end{bmatrix} = ?$

6. Let $A = \begin{bmatrix} 3 & 2 \\ 1 & -1 \end{bmatrix}$

$B = \begin{bmatrix} 2 & 1 \\ -1 & 1 \end{bmatrix}$

Find **(a)** AB **(e)** $B^t \cdot A^t$
(b) BA^t **(f)** $(AB)^t$
(c) B^2A or $B \cdot B \cdot A$ **(g)** Does $B^t \cdot A^t = (BA)^t$? If not, what is $(BA)^t$?
(d) A^2B or $A \cdot A \cdot B$

7. Given

$$A = \begin{bmatrix} a_{11} & a_{12} \\ a_{21} & a_{22} \end{bmatrix}$$

$$B = \begin{bmatrix} b_{11} & b_{12} \\ b_{21} & b_{22} \end{bmatrix}$$

$$C = \begin{bmatrix} c_{11} & c_{12} \\ c_{21} & c_{22} \end{bmatrix}$$

Does **(a)** $A \cdot (B + C) = AB + AC$

   (b) $A \cdot (B \cdot C) = (A \cdot B) \cdot C$ (Is the multiplication of matrices associative?)

Perform the operations enclosed in parentheses first.

8. Write your own example to show that if $CA = CB$, then A is not equal to B or that Theorem 6-4 (cancellation law for multiplication) does not hold true for matrices.

9. Special cases when a row matrix is multiplied by a column matrix result in a single number. For example

$$[1 \quad 2 \quad 3] \cdot \begin{bmatrix} 1 \\ 2 \\ 3 \end{bmatrix} = (1 \times 1) + (2 \times 2) + (3 \times 3) = 14$$

(a) A gasoline service station orders

   20 containers of brake fluid at \$1.50 each
   50 cans of dry gas at .30 each and
   100 quarts of oil at 1.25 each

Using matrix multiplication, find the total cost of this order.

(b) A manufacturer wants to produce three products, A, B, and C.

   100 items of A require 6 units of material and 8 hours of labor per item
   50 items of B require 4 units of material and 10 hours of labor per item
   80 items of C require 10 units of material and 24 hours of labor per item

If each unit of material costs the manufacturer \$2.50 and labor costs are 12.50 per hour find total costs for A, B, and C using matrix multiplication. (Include units and hours in a matrix having 3 rows and 2 columns.)

DETERMINANTS

Each square matrix (or $n \times n$ matrix) containing real number entries has associated with it another real number called the determinant.

Definition 19-8.   The *determinant* of the 2×2 square matrix A given by

$$\begin{vmatrix} a_{11} & a_{12} \\ a_{21} & a_{22} \end{vmatrix}$$

is the real number $a_{11} \cdot a_{22} - a_{12} \cdot a_{21}$, where $a_{11}, a_{12}, a_{21}, a_{22} \in R$.

The symbol for the determinant of A is $|A|$. Let

$$A = \begin{bmatrix} 2 & -1 \\ 3 & 4 \end{bmatrix}$$

Then

$$|A| = \begin{vmatrix} 2 & -1 \\ 3 & 4 \end{vmatrix} = 2 \cdot 4 - (-1) \cdot 3 = 11$$

Determinants are a useful tool in solving simultaneous equations. Consider the following general format for a linear system in two variables, x and y. Let a, b, d, and e represent the coefficients on these variables. Let c and f represent values for these equations.

$$ax + by = c \tag{19.1}$$
$$dx + ey = f \tag{19.2}$$

To solve these two equations for y,

Step 1. Multiply equation (19.1) by $-d$.

$$-dax + (-dby) = -dc \tag{19.3}$$

Step 2. Multiply equation (19.2) by a:

$$adx + aey = af \tag{19.4}$$

Step 3. Add equation (19.3) to equation (19.4):

$$aey - dby = af - dc$$

Step 4. Factor out y:

$$y(ae - db) = af - dc$$

Step 5. Solve for y:

$$y = \frac{af - dc}{ae - db}, \text{ provided } (a \cdot e - d \cdot b) \neq 0$$

In a similar manner, we can solve for x:

Step 1. Multiply equation (19.1) by e.

$$eax + eby = ec \tag{19.5}$$

Step 2. Multiply equation (19.2) by $-b$.

$$-bdx - bey = -bf \tag{19.6}$$

Step 3. Add equation (19.5) to (19.6).

$$eax - bdx = ec - bf$$

Step 4. Factor out x.

$$x(ea - bd) = ec - bf$$

Step 5. Solve for x.

$$x = \frac{ec - bf}{ea - bd}, \text{ provided } (a \cdot e - b \cdot d) \neq 0$$

If the coefficients of x and y are not zero, we can find values for x and y in terms of the values expressed on the right-hand side of the equals sign. (These values are typically real numbers.)

Recall that the determinant of matrix $\begin{bmatrix} a_{11} & a_{12} \\ a_{21} & a_{22} \end{bmatrix}$ is

$$\begin{vmatrix} a_{11} & a_{12} \\ a_{21} & a_{22} \end{vmatrix} = a_{11} \cdot a_{22} - a_{12} \cdot a_{21}$$

Using the coefficients from equations (19.1) and (19.2), let $a_{11} = a$, $a_{12} = b$, $a_{21} = d$, and $a_{22} = e$. Then we have the determinant

$$|A| = \begin{vmatrix} a & b \\ d & e \end{vmatrix} = ae - bd$$

Further, we can also get

$$|B| = \begin{vmatrix} c & b \\ f & e \end{vmatrix} = ce - bf$$

$$|C| = \begin{vmatrix} a & c \\ d & f \end{vmatrix} = af - cd$$

Then the denominators for x and y in

$$x = \frac{ec - bf}{ae - bd}, \quad y = \frac{af - dc}{ae - db} \tag{19.7}$$

are equal to the determinant of A and are the coefficients on x and y in equations (19.1) and (19.2).

The determinant for B is equal to the numerator for x and the determinant for C is equal to the numerator for y. Further, the entries in the three determinants are the coefficients of the variables x and y and the values of these equations.

A system of two linear equations does not always have unique solutions. As stated in Chapter 16, some systems are dependent or inconsistent. The use of determinants makes it a simple matter to examine systems of equations for these possibilities. Consider $x = \dfrac{|B|}{|A|}$, and $y = \dfrac{|C|}{|A|}$.

In

$$\left. \begin{array}{l} 3x - y = 2 \\ -x + \frac{1}{3}y = -\frac{2}{3} \end{array} \right\} \quad \text{a dependent system of equations}$$

we can express x in terms of determinants as

$$x = \frac{\begin{vmatrix} c & b \\ f & e \end{vmatrix}}{\begin{vmatrix} a & b \\ d & e \end{vmatrix}} = \frac{\begin{vmatrix} 2 & -1 \\ -\frac{2}{3} & \frac{1}{3} \end{vmatrix}}{\begin{vmatrix} 3 & -1 \\ -1 & \frac{1}{3} \end{vmatrix}}$$

or

$$x = \frac{\frac{2}{3} - (+\frac{2}{3})}{1 - 1} = \frac{0}{0}$$

This example illustrates that when a system of linear equations is dependent, the determinant of the coefficients on x and y [the denominators in equations (19.7)] is zero, and we need not go any further in looking for a solution.

The following system contains inconsistent equations.

$$x - y = 2$$
$$2x - 2y = 3$$

Examining the determinant of the coefficients on x and y, we find

$$|A| = \begin{vmatrix} 1 & -1 \\ 2 & -2 \end{vmatrix} = -2 - (-2) = 0$$

and therefore no unique solution is possible. (The denominator would be zero.)

Consider the next system of equations:

$$x + 2y = 4$$
$$3x + y = 8$$

Since

$$\begin{vmatrix} 1 & 2 \\ 3 & 1 \end{vmatrix} = 1 - 6 = -5 = |A|$$

the determinant of the coefficients on x and y is not zero, and we can continue to solve for x and y, as follows:

$$x = \frac{\begin{vmatrix} 4 & 2 \\ 8 & 1 \end{vmatrix}}{\begin{vmatrix} 1 & 2 \\ 3 & 1 \end{vmatrix}} = \frac{4 - 16}{1 - 6} = \frac{12}{5}$$

$$y = \frac{\begin{vmatrix} 1 & 4 \\ 3 & 8 \end{vmatrix}}{\begin{vmatrix} 1 & 2 \\ 3 & 1 \end{vmatrix}} = \frac{8 - 12}{1 - 6} = \frac{4}{5}$$

As an exercise, set up the matrices and find the determinants for the *dependent* system of equations found on page 259 of Chapter 16.

The Three-by-Three Matrix

Using the double subscript method, we can write the following 3×3 matrix:

$$A = \begin{bmatrix} a_{11} & a_{12} & a_{13} \\ a_{21} & a_{22} & a_{23} \\ a_{31} & a_{32} & a_{33} \end{bmatrix}$$

The determinant of this matrix can be evaluated by the method of expansion by minors. A minor of an element or entry in a determinant is the determinant formed by deleting the row and column in which the entry appears. Thus, the minor of a_{11} is formed by deleting the first row and first column.

$$\begin{vmatrix} a_{11} & a_{12} & a_{13} \\ a_{21} & a_{22} & a_{23} \\ a_{31} & a_{32} & a_{33} \end{vmatrix} = \begin{vmatrix} a_{22} & a_{23} \\ a_{32} & a_{33} \end{vmatrix} = \text{minor of } a_{11}$$

The minor of a_{31} is $\begin{vmatrix} a_{12} & a_{13} \\ a_{22} & a_{23} \end{vmatrix}$, the minor of a_{22} is $\begin{vmatrix} a_{11} & a_{13} \\ a_{31} & a_{33} \end{vmatrix}$, and so on.

Definition 19-9.   The *minor* of an element a_{ij} in a determinant is the determinant that remains after the ith row and jth column have been deleted.

Definition 19-10.   The *cofactor* of an element in a square matrix is the minor of that element multiplied by -1 or $+1$. If the sum of the digits in the subscript is an even number, multiply the minor by $+1$. If the sum of the digits in the subscript is an odd number, multiply the minor by -1.

Example 1

Refer to matrix A. The cofactor of a_{13} is

$$\begin{vmatrix} a_{21} & a_{22} \\ a_{31} & a_{32} \end{vmatrix}$$

because a_{13} contains the subscripts 1 and 3 that, when added, yield an even number ($1 + 3 = 4$).

Example 2

The cofactor of a_{12} is

$$- \begin{vmatrix} a_{21} & a_{23} \\ a_{31} & a_{33} \end{vmatrix}$$

or the negative of the minor of a_{12}, because $1 + 2$ yields an odd number. The cofactor is therefore a minor with a $+$ or $-$ sign. Generally, we can state that for an $n \times n$ matrix, the following pattern for alternating signs of minors holds true:

$$\begin{vmatrix} + & - & + & \cdot & & \cdot \\ - & + & - & \cdot & & \cdot \\ + & - & + & \cdot & & \cdot \\ \cdot & \cdot & \cdot & \cdot & & \cdot \\ \cdot & \cdot & \cdot & \cdot & & \cdot \end{vmatrix}$$

Evaluating the determinant of a 3×3 matrix can now be described using cofactors and an expansion by minors.

Definition 19-11. The value of the determinant of a 3×3 square matrix is the sum of the products formed by multiplying all the entries in a single row or a single column by their cofactors (or minors with a prefixed sign).

The determinant of a square matrix is expanded on the row or column chosen. Given

$$\begin{vmatrix} a_{11} & a_{12} & a_{13} \\ a_{21} & a_{22} & a_{23} \\ a_{31} & a_{32} & a_{33} \end{vmatrix}$$

if we choose to expand on the first column to find the determinant, we obtain

$$(A) \quad a_{11}\left(+\begin{vmatrix} a_{22} & a_{23} \\ a_{32} & a_{33} \end{vmatrix}\right) + a_{21}\left(-\begin{vmatrix} a_{12} & a_{13} \\ a_{32} & a_{33} \end{vmatrix}\right) + a_{31}\left(+\begin{vmatrix} a_{12} & a_{13} \\ a_{22} & a_{23} \end{vmatrix}\right)$$

If we choose to expand on the second row, we obtain

$$(B) \quad a_{21}\left(-\begin{vmatrix} a_{12} & a_{13} \\ a_{32} & a_{33} \end{vmatrix}\right) + a_{22}\left(+\begin{vmatrix} a_{11} & a_{13} \\ a_{31} & a_{33} \end{vmatrix}\right) + a_{23}\left(-\begin{vmatrix} a_{11} & a_{12} \\ a_{31} & a_{32} \end{vmatrix}\right)$$

As an exercise, show that (A) and (B) yield the same result.
Given

$$A = \begin{bmatrix} 3 & 6 & -2 \\ 1 & 4 & 5 \\ -2 & 0 & 1 \end{bmatrix}$$

find the determinant for A by expansion on the second column. (We chose the second column because the zero in the third row will simplify our calculations. For the same reason, we could have evaluated this determinant using the third row.)

Expanding yields

$$6\left(-\begin{vmatrix} 1 & 5 \\ -2 & 1 \end{vmatrix}\right) + 4\left(+\begin{vmatrix} 3 & -2 \\ -2 & 1 \end{vmatrix}\right) + 0\left(-\begin{vmatrix} 3 & -2 \\ 1 & 5 \end{vmatrix}\right)$$

$$6(-(1 + 10)) + 4(3 - 4) + 0$$

$$-66 + (-4)$$

Therefore, the value of the determinant is -70

EXERCISES 19-3

1. Find the values of the following determinants:

(a) $\begin{vmatrix} 3 & 1 \\ 4 & 6 \end{vmatrix}$

(b) $\begin{vmatrix} \frac{1}{2} & -3 \\ -2 & 6 \end{vmatrix}$

(c) $\begin{vmatrix} .75 & -2 \\ .5 & -1 \end{vmatrix}$

(d) $\begin{vmatrix} m & r \\ -s & 0 \end{vmatrix}$

2. Find the matrix for the following expressions:
   (a) $(2)\cdot(-3) - (4)\cdot(2)$
   (b) $(-1)\cdot(0) - (2)\cdot(-1)$
   (c) $mn - pq$
   (d) $(a)\cdot(b) + cd = (a)\cdot(b) - (-c)\cdot(+d)$

3. Solve the following using determinants. First determine if a unique solution exists:

(a) $\begin{cases} y = 4 + 2x \\ x + 3y = 7 \end{cases}$

(b) $\begin{cases} \dfrac{3y + x}{2} = 4 \\ x - y = 7 \end{cases}$

(c) $\begin{cases} 3x + \frac{1}{2}y = 3 \\ -6x - 3y = -6 \end{cases}$

(d) $\begin{cases} 2x + 3y = 4 \\ y - 3x = 7 \end{cases}$

(e) $\begin{cases} .5x - .75y = .25 \\ x - 1.5y = .3 \end{cases}$

(f) $\begin{cases} 3y = 2 \\ 3x + y = 7 \end{cases}$

4. Find the determinant for the following by expanding upon any row or column.

(a) $\begin{bmatrix} 1 & 0 & 0 \\ -1 & 2 & 1 \\ 3 & -2 & 1 \end{bmatrix}$

(b) $\begin{bmatrix} 0 & 1 & 2 \\ 1 & 0 & 3 \\ 2 & -1 & 0 \end{bmatrix}$

(c) $\begin{bmatrix} 1 & 2 & 3 \\ -2 & 1 & 4 \\ 1 & 2 & 1 \end{bmatrix}$

5. Solve for a in

(a) $\begin{vmatrix} a & 2 \\ -1 & 1 \end{vmatrix} = 3$

(b) $\begin{vmatrix} 1 & 0 & a \\ -2 & a & -1 \\ 0 & 1 & 1 \end{vmatrix} = 14$

THE IDENTITY MATRIX

Matrix algebra includes the identity matrix for multiplication, usually denoted by I. For 2×2 matrices the identity matrix is

$$I = \begin{bmatrix} 1 & 0 \\ 0 & 1 \end{bmatrix}$$

For 3×3 matrices the identity matrix is

$$I = \begin{bmatrix} 1 & 0 & 0 \\ 0 & 1 & 0 \\ 0 & 0 & 1 \end{bmatrix}$$

The 1's appear on a line known as the major or main diagonal.

Definition 19-12.   The *identity matrix* for multiplication is the matrix denoted by I such that $A \cdot I = I \cdot A = A$. A demonstration of the proof is left to the student.

MULTIPLICATIVE INVERSE OF SQUARE MATRICES

Recall from Chapter 6 the inverse property for a real number $1/a$ such that $a \times a^{-1} = 1$ or $a \times 1/a = 1$ $(a \neq 0)$. Matrix algebra likewise includes the inverse property that for a square matrix A there exists an inverse matrix A denoted by A^{-1} (if the determinant of $A \neq 0$).

Definition 19-13. The *multiplicative inverse* of a square matrix is the matrix, denoted by A^{-1}, such that $A \cdot A^{-1} = A^{-1} \cdot A = I$ whenever $|A| \neq 0$.

Two-by-Two Matrices

$$\begin{bmatrix} a_{11} & a_{12} \\ a_{21} & a_{22} \end{bmatrix}$$

To write the inverse of a 2×2 square matrix:

Step 1. Find the value of the determinant of the matrix. (If the value of the determinant $= 0$, no further work is needed.)

Step 2. Interchange the entries on the main diagonal.

Step 3. Change a_{12} and a_{21} to their additive inverse.

Step 4. Multiply the resulting matrix by the multiplicative inverse of the determinant.

Example 1

Let

$$|A| = \begin{vmatrix} 2 & 5 \\ 1 & -2 \end{vmatrix}$$

The steps to be followed are illustrated below:

Step 1. The determinant of A is $(-4) - (5) = -9$

Step 2. $\begin{vmatrix} -2 & 5 \\ 1 & 2 \end{vmatrix}$

Step 3. $\begin{vmatrix} -2 & -5 \\ -1 & 2 \end{vmatrix}$

Step 4. $-\frac{1}{9} \times \begin{bmatrix} -2 & -5 \\ -1 & 2 \end{bmatrix} = \begin{bmatrix} \frac{2}{9} & \frac{5}{9} \\ \frac{1}{9} & -\frac{2}{9} \end{bmatrix} = A^{-1}$

We observed in Exercise 19-2, problem 5(a) that the multiplication of matrices is not *generally* commutative. As an exercise, show that $A \cdot A^{-1} = A^{-1} \cdot A = I$.

Example 2

In

$$\begin{bmatrix} 4 & 10 \\ 2 & 5 \end{bmatrix}$$

the determinant $= 0$; therefore, no inverse of this matrix exists.

Three-by-Three Matrices

To write the inverse of a 3×3 square matrix A:

Step 1. Find the value of the determinant of A. (If the determinant of $A = 0$, no further work is needed.)

Step 2. Find the cofactors of the entries in A and replace each entry with its cofactor.

Step 3. Find the transpose of the new matrix.

Step 4. Multiply the transpose by the multiplicative inverse of the determinant of A.

Example 3

Let

$$A = \begin{bmatrix} 1 & 1 & -2 \\ 2 & 0 & 1 \\ 1 & -1 & 1 \end{bmatrix}$$

Step 1. Expanding on the first column, the value of the determinant of A is

$$1\left(+\begin{vmatrix} 0 & 1 \\ -1 & 1 \end{vmatrix}\right) + 2\left(-\begin{vmatrix} 1 & -2 \\ -1 & 1 \end{vmatrix}\right) + 1\left(+\begin{vmatrix} 1 & -2 \\ 0 & 1 \end{vmatrix}\right)$$

$$= 1(1) + 2(-(-1)) + 1(1) = 4$$

Since this value does not equal zero, continue on.

Step 2. Find cofactors of each entry and replace entries by cofactors.

$$\begin{bmatrix} 1 & -1 & -2 \\ 1 & 3 & 2 \\ 1 & -5 & -2 \end{bmatrix}$$

Step 3. Transpose

$$\begin{bmatrix} 1 & 1 & 1 \\ -1 & 3 & -5 \\ -2 & 2 & -2 \end{bmatrix}$$

Step 4.

$$A^{-1} = \tfrac{1}{4}\begin{bmatrix} 1 & 1 & 1 \\ -1 & 3 & -5 \\ -2 & 2 & -2 \end{bmatrix}$$

$A^{-1} \cdot A = I$; therefore, we can check our results as follows:

$$\tfrac{1}{4}\begin{bmatrix} 1 & 1 & 1 \\ -1 & 3 & -5 \\ -2 & 2 & -2 \end{bmatrix} \cdot \begin{bmatrix} 1 & 1 & -2 \\ 2 & 0 & 1 \\ 1 & -1 & 1 \end{bmatrix} = \tfrac{1}{4}\begin{bmatrix} 4 & 0 & 0 \\ 0 & 4 & 0 \\ 0 & 0 & 4 \end{bmatrix} = \begin{bmatrix} 1 & 0 & 0 \\ 0 & 1 & 0 \\ 0 & 0 & 1 \end{bmatrix}$$

EXERCISES 19-4

1. Find the inverse if it exists.

(a) $\begin{bmatrix} 2 & 5 \\ -1 & 1 \end{bmatrix}$

(b) $\begin{bmatrix} 1 & 3 \\ 2 & 6 \end{bmatrix}$

(c) $\begin{bmatrix} x & 3 \\ 0 & 2 \end{bmatrix}$ $(x \neq 0)$

2. If $A = \begin{bmatrix} 2 & 5 \\ 1 & -2 \end{bmatrix}$

(a) Show that $A \cdot A^{-1} = I = A^{-1} \cdot A$.
(b) Is $(A^t)^{-1} = (A^{-1})^t$?

3. Find the inverse if it exists.

(a) $\begin{bmatrix} 1 & 2 & -1 \\ 0 & 2 & 3 \\ 1 & 0 & 1 \end{bmatrix}$

(b) $\begin{bmatrix} 2 & -1 & 2 \\ 1 & -1 & 4 \\ 2 & 0 & 0 \end{bmatrix}$

(c) $\begin{bmatrix} 3 & -1 & 2 \\ 1 & -1 & 0 \\ 2 & 0 & 1 \end{bmatrix}$

4. If $A = \begin{bmatrix} 1 & 3 & 2 \\ -1 & 2 & 1 \\ 2 & 1 & 0 \end{bmatrix}$

(a) Is $A \cdot A^{-1} = I = A^{-1} \cdot A$?
(b) Is $(A^t)^{-1} = (A^{-1})^t$?

5. Given $C = \begin{bmatrix} 1 & 2 \\ -1 & 4 \end{bmatrix}$, find C^{-1}.

6. Given $A = \begin{bmatrix} 3 & 2 & 6 \\ 1 & 1 & 2 \\ 2 & 2 & 5 \end{bmatrix}$ and $B = \begin{bmatrix} 1 & 2 & -2 \\ -1 & 3 & 0 \\ 0 & -2 & 1 \end{bmatrix}$, determine whether or not $B = A^{-1}$.

LINEAR SYSTEMS IN TWO AND THREE VARIABLES

Using matrices, we can find the solution set for a system of linear equations by the procedures outlined in the following examples (procedures that are useful in computer programming).

Matrix Reductions

Reduction, sometimes called *elimination* (or elementary row operations) is a method of finding the solution set for a system of linear equations. The following algorithm, which is suitable for use on computers, yields the identity matrix and the values for members of the solution set. Before proceeding, recall that

$$A^{-1} \cdot A = I, \text{ whenever } |A| \neq 0.$$

We need

$$\begin{bmatrix} a_{11} & a_{12} & | & b \\ a_{21} & a_{22} & | & c \end{bmatrix}$$

In the form

$$\begin{bmatrix} 1 & 0 & | & x \\ 0 & 1 & | & y \end{bmatrix}$$

To get a_{11} and $a_{22} = 1$, and a_{12} and $a_{21} = 0$, we can use the following steps:

Step 1. Divide row 1 by a_{11}, which yields 1 at a_{11}.

Step 2. To get $a_{21} = 0$; multiply row 1 by $-a_{21}$ and add the products to the values in row 2, replacing the second row with the sums.

Step 3. Divide row 2 by a_{22}, which yields 1 at a_{22}.

Step 4. To get $a_{12} = 0$; multiply row 2 by $-a_{12}$ and add the products to the values in row 1, replacing the first row with the sums.

Example

$$2x + 2y = 0$$
$$3x + 2y = 3$$

Put the coefficients and the resulting values 0 and 3 in the form

$$\begin{bmatrix} 2 & 2 & | & 0 \\ 3 & 2 & | & 3 \end{bmatrix}$$

Step 1. $\begin{bmatrix} 2/2 & 2/2 & | & 0/2 \\ 3 & 2 & | & 3 \end{bmatrix} = \begin{bmatrix} 1 & 1 & | & 0 \\ 3 & 2 & | & 3 \end{bmatrix}$

Step 2. $\begin{bmatrix} 1 & 1 & | & 0 \\ (-3)1 + 3 & (-3)1 + 2 & | & (-3)0 + 3 \end{bmatrix} = \begin{bmatrix} 1 & 1 & | & 0 \\ 0 & -1 & | & 3 \end{bmatrix}$

Step 3. $\begin{bmatrix} 1 & 1 & | & 0 \\ 0/(-1) & -1/(-1) & | & 3/(-1) \end{bmatrix} = \begin{bmatrix} 1 & 1 & | & 0 \\ 0 & 1 & | & -3 \end{bmatrix}$

Step 4. $\begin{bmatrix} (-1)0 + 1 & (-1)1 + 1 & | & (-1)(-3) + 0 \\ 0 & 1 & | & -3 \end{bmatrix} = \begin{bmatrix} 1 & 0 & | & 3 \\ 0 & 1 & | & -3 \end{bmatrix}$

and $x = 3$, $y = -3$.

In cases where a coefficient on x is 1, the process can be simplified when that 1 is entered as a_{11}, for example, in

$$4x + 2y = 8$$
$$x - y = 5$$

Reverse the equations and proceed as before.

Definitions 19-12 and 19-13 can help find the solution set for a system of three equations in three unknowns. Consider:

$$x + y - 2z = 2$$
$$2x + z = 3$$
$$x - y + z = 1$$

The coefficients of the three variables x, y, and z are the entries found in the following 3×3 matrix. (In the second equation, the coefficient of y is 0.)

Multiplying the entries by the variables, we get

$$\begin{bmatrix} 1 & 1 & -2 \\ 2 & 0 & 1 \\ 1 & -1 & 1 \end{bmatrix} \cdot \begin{bmatrix} x \\ y \\ z \end{bmatrix} = \begin{bmatrix} x + y - 2z \\ 2x + 0y + z \\ x - y + z \end{bmatrix}$$

Thus, the 3×3 matrix and the 3×1 matrix are both conformable for multiplication and yield the left-hand side of the three linear equations under consideration.

The 3×3 matrix yields a determinant not equal to 0, and therefore a solution exists for these equations. Note that the original 3×3 matrix is identical to the one given in example 3, page 320.

We further note that

$$\begin{bmatrix} 1 & 1 & -2 \\ 2 & 0 & 1 \\ 1 & -1 & 1 \end{bmatrix} \cdot \begin{bmatrix} x \\ y \\ z \end{bmatrix} = \begin{bmatrix} 2 \\ 3 \\ 1 \end{bmatrix}, \qquad \text{where} \quad \begin{bmatrix} 2 \\ 3 \\ 1 \end{bmatrix}$$

is found on the right-hand side of the equal signs in the three given equations.

Recall that

$$A^{-1} = \frac{1}{4} \cdot \begin{bmatrix} 1 & 1 & 1 \\ -1 & 3 & -5 \\ -2 & 2 & -2 \end{bmatrix}$$

We have verified in Exercise 19-4, problem 4 that $A^{-1} \cdot A = I$. Now if

$$\begin{bmatrix} 1 & 1 & -2 \\ 2 & 0 & 1 \\ 1 & -1 & 1 \end{bmatrix} \cdot \begin{bmatrix} x \\ y \\ z \end{bmatrix} = \begin{bmatrix} 2 \\ 3 \\ 1 \end{bmatrix}$$

we can express this in symbolic notation as $A \cdot B = C$, where $A =$ the matrix of the coefficients, $B =$ the unknown matrix and $C =$ the constant matrix. To solve for B, we can write $B = A^{-1} \cdot C$. Since $A \cdot B = C$, then explain

$$A^{-1}(A \cdot B) = A^{-1} \cdot C$$
$$(A^{-1} \cdot A) \cdot B = A^{-1} \cdot C$$
$$I \cdot B = A^{-1} \cdot C$$
$$B = A^{-1} \cdot C$$

Expressing $B = A^{-1} \cdot C$ in terms of their corresponding matrices, we have

$$\begin{bmatrix} x \\ y \\ z \end{bmatrix} = \tfrac{1}{4} \begin{bmatrix} 1 & 1 & 1 \\ -1 & 3 & -5 \\ -2 & 2 & -2 \end{bmatrix} \cdot \begin{bmatrix} 2 \\ 3 \\ 1 \end{bmatrix} = \tfrac{1}{4} \begin{bmatrix} 6 \\ 2 \\ 0 \end{bmatrix} = \begin{bmatrix} \tfrac{3}{2} \\ \tfrac{1}{2} \\ 0 \end{bmatrix}$$

and the solution set for this system of linear equations is $\{\tfrac{3}{2}, \tfrac{1}{2}, 0\}$, where $x = \tfrac{3}{2}$, $y = \tfrac{1}{2}$, and $z = 0$. Substitution of these values for x, y and z into the system of linear equations is left to the student.

Using a method of elimination, we can also find the solution set for a system of three equations in three variables.

Example

$$3x + 2y - 4z = -5$$
$$x + y + z = 6$$
$$x - y - z = -4$$

First-Column Operations

We can write using upright curved lines:

$$\begin{array}{c} \text{Pivotal} \\ \text{column} \end{array}$$

$$\begin{array}{c} \text{Pivotal} \to \\ \text{row} \end{array} \begin{pmatrix} 3 & 2 & -4 \\ 1 & 1 & 1 \\ 1 & -1 & -1 \end{pmatrix} \begin{pmatrix} -5 \\ 6 \\ -4 \end{pmatrix}$$

First, we need 1 at a_{11}.

$$\begin{pmatrix} 3 & 2 & -4 & \vdots & -5 \\ 1 & 1 & 1 & \vdots & 6 \\ 1 & -1 & -1 & \vdots & -4 \end{pmatrix}$$ Divide 1st row by a_{11}.

$$\begin{pmatrix} 1 & \tfrac{2}{3} & -\tfrac{4}{3} & \vdots & -\tfrac{5}{3} \\ 1 & 1 & 1 & \vdots & 6 \\ 1 & -1 & -1 & \vdots & -4 \end{pmatrix}$$ We now want zero at a_{21}. Multiply 1st row by $-a_{21}$, add it to 2nd row, and replace entries in the 2nd row with the answer. (We multiply by a

$$\begin{pmatrix} 1 & \frac{2}{3} & -\frac{4}{3} & \vdots & -\frac{5}{3} \\ 0 & \frac{1}{3} & \frac{7}{3} & \vdots & \frac{23}{3} \\ 1 & -1 & -1 & \vdots & -4 \end{pmatrix}$$

negative of the entry where we need a zero in the identity matrix.)

$$\begin{pmatrix} 1 & \frac{2}{3} & -\frac{4}{3} & \vdots & -\frac{5}{3} \\ 0 & \frac{1}{3} & \frac{7}{3} & \vdots & \frac{23}{3} \\ 0 & -\frac{5}{3} & \frac{1}{3} & \vdots & -\frac{7}{3} \end{pmatrix}$$

We now need zero at a_{31}. Multiply 1st row by $-a_{31}$ and add to 3rd row. Then replace 3rd row with the answer.

Second-Column Operations

Now the pivotal row is the second row, and the pivotal column is the second column.

$$\begin{pmatrix} 1 & \frac{2}{3} & -\frac{4}{3} & \vdots & -\frac{5}{3} \\ 0 & 1 & 7 & \vdots & 23 \\ 0 & -\frac{5}{3} & \frac{1}{3} & \vdots & -\frac{7}{3} \end{pmatrix}$$

To change a_{22} to 1, divide 2nd row by a_{22}.

$$\begin{pmatrix} 1 & 0 & -\frac{18}{3} & \vdots & -\frac{51}{3} \\ 0 & 1 & 7 & \vdots & 23 \\ 0 & -\frac{5}{3} & \frac{1}{3} & \vdots & -\frac{7}{3} \end{pmatrix}$$

To get zero at a_{12}, multiply the 2nd row by $-a_{12}$, add to 1st row, and replace 1st row with the answer.

$$\begin{pmatrix} 1 & 0 & -\frac{18}{3} & \vdots & -\frac{51}{3} \\ 0 & 1 & 7 & \vdots & 23 \\ 0 & 0 & 12 & \vdots & 36 \end{pmatrix}$$

To get zero at a_{32}, multiply 2nd row by $-a_{32}$, add to 3rd row, and replace 3rd row with answer.

Third-Column Operations

Now the pivotal row is third row, and the pivotal column is the third column

$$\begin{pmatrix} 1 & 0 & -6 & \vdots & -17 \\ 0 & 1 & 7 & \vdots & 23 \\ 0 & 0 & 1 & \vdots & 3 \end{pmatrix}$$

For a 1 at a_{33}, divide 3rd row by a_{33}.

$$\begin{pmatrix} 1 & 0 & 0 & \vdots & 1 \\ 0 & 1 & 7 & \vdots & 23 \\ 0 & 0 & 1 & \vdots & 3 \end{pmatrix}$$

For a zero at a_{13}, multiply 3rd row by $-a_{13}$, add to 1st row, and replace 1st row with answer.

$$\begin{pmatrix} 1 & 0 & 0 & \vdots & 1 \\ 0 & 1 & 0 & \vdots & 2 \\ 0 & 0 & 1 & \vdots & 3 \end{pmatrix}$$

Finally, we need a zero at a_{23}. Multiply the 3rd row by $-a_{23}$, add the result to the 2nd row, and replace the 2nd row with the answer.

Identity   values
matrix   for x, y
             and z

Thus , the solution set for

$$3x + 2y - 4z = -5$$
$$x + y + z = 6$$
$$x - y - z = -4$$

is $\{1, 2, 3\}$, where $x = 1$, $y = 2$, and $z = 3$.

Note that it is sometimes possible for the element a_{11} to contain a zero coefficient of x. To get an element $a_{11} \neq 0$, it is possible to exchange the first row with a row that has an x whose coefficient is not zero. For example, given

$$\begin{pmatrix} y + 3z \\ 2x + 3y - z \\ -x + z \end{pmatrix}$$

we may exchange the 1st and 2nd rows, yielding

$$\begin{pmatrix} 2x + 3y - z \\ 0 + y + 3z \\ -x + 0 + z \end{pmatrix}$$

EXERCISES 19-5

1. Given

$$x + y - z = -1$$
$$2x - y + z = 2$$
$$x + y + 2z = 0$$

   (a) If the preceding system is written in terms of matrices A, X, and B, where $AX = B$, identify A, X, and B.
   (b) Find A^{-1}.
   (c) Solve the system using A^{-1}.

2. Find the solution sets of the following. (If the solution set is the null set, identify it.) Use either method discussed previously.

   (a) $4x + 6y = 14$ (d) $y + 2z = 3$
       $3x + 2y = 8$ $3x + z = 4$
                                 $x + y = 2$

   (b) $y = 2x + 3$ (e) $x - y + z = 3$
       $y + 3x = 8$ $2y - x - 2z = 2$
                                 $x - y + 2z = 4$

   (c) $y = x + 3$ (f) $y - x + 2z = 3$
       $-x = y - 2$ $z - x = 2$
                                 $x + 2y + z = 8$

3. In this chapter, we have described several methods for solving simultaneous equations. Study the BASIC program that follows and describe how it solves these types of equations.

The REM, or REMarks, statement contains hints on how this program executes. The REM statement may be separated from another BASIC statement by a colon (:). A REM statement is not executable, being typically used for comments about other statements in the program.

Look at statement 130. A GOSUB instruction transfers program control to a subroutine that begins at a specified line number (in this case, 1000). When the computer encounters a RETURN statement (1130 in this program), the program will return to the statement that directly follows the GOSUB.

```
10 REM PROGRAM TO SOLVE 3 SIMULTANEOUS EQUATIONS
20 PRINT "ENTER THE THREE COEFFICIENTS IN ORDER X,Y,Z"
30 PRINT "NEXT ENTER THE CONSTANT"
40 DIM A(5,5), X(5,5)
45 INPUT "FIRST EQUATION      ";A(1,1),A(1,2),A(1,3),A(1,4)
50 INPUT "SECOND EQUATION ";A(2,1),A(2,2),A(2,3),A(2,4)
60 INPUT "THIRD EQUATION     ";A(3,1),A(3,2),A(3,3),A(3,4)
70 REM LOAD ARRAY X
80 FOR I = 1 to 4
90 FOR J = 1 to 4
100 X(I,J) = A(I,J): REM SET UP A MEMORY MATRIX FOR REFERENCE
110 NEXT J
120 NEXT I
130 GOSUB 1000
140 REM FIND THE DETERMINANT
150 D = Q: REM RETURN VALUE OF SUBROUTINE AT LINE 1000
160 A(1,1) = A(1,4)
170 A(2,1) = A(2,4)
180 A(3,1) = A(3,4)
190 GOSUB 1000: REM SOLVING MATRIX WITH ROW 1 SUBSTITUTED
200 X = Q/D: REM X IS NUMERATOR DIVIDED BY DETERMINANT
210 A(1,2) = A(1,4)
220 A(2,2) = A(2,4)
230 A(3,2) = A(3,4)
240 GOSUB 1000
250 Y = Q/D
255 A(1,3) = A(1,4)
260 A(2,3) = A(2,4)
270 A(3,3) = A(3,4)
290 GOSUB 1000
300 Z = Q/D
310 REM OUTPUT ROUTINE
320 PRINT
330 PRINT "THE ORIGINAL EQUATIONS WERE"
340 PRINT
350 PRINT X(1,1);"X+ ";X(1,2);"Y+ ";X(1,3);"Z =";A(1,4)
355 PRINT
```

```
360 PRINT X(2,1);"X+ ";X(2,2);"Y+ ";X(2,3);"Z= ";A(2,4)
365 PRINT
370 PRINT X(3,1);"X+ ";X(3,2);"Y+ ";X(3,3);"Z= ";A(3,4)
375 PRINT
377 PRINT "SOLUTION"
380 PRINT "X= ";X;" Y= ";Y;" Z= ";Z
390 END
1000 D1=A(1,1)*A(2,2)*A(3,3):REM MULTIPLY
1010 D2=A(1,2)*A(2,3)*A(3,1)
1020 D3=A(1,3)*A(2,1)*A(3,2)
1030 D4=A(1,3)*A(2,2)*A(3,1)
1040 D5=A(1,2)*A(2,1)*A(3,3)
1050 D6=A(1,1)*A(2,3)*A(3,2)
1060 Q=D1+D2+D3-D4-D5-D6
1070 REM RESTORE ORIGINAL MATRIX
1080 FOR I=1 to 4
1090 FOR J=1 TO 4
1100 A(I,J)=X(I,J)
1110 NEXT J
1120 NEXT I
1130 RETURN
1140 REM****END OF SUBROUTINE
```

(a) Why is a subroutine useful in finding the solution set to simultaneous equations?

(b) In Statement 40 we set up two matrices in one statement. Why do we need the second matrix?

(c) When entering data and running the program, you must use commas to separate the coefficients and the constant. If you have a computer available, type in this program, run it, and verify the answers to exercises 19-5, 2(d), (e), and (f). What message did you get from the program when running Exercise 19-5, problem 2(f)?

ARRAYS AND COMPUTERS

Most commonly used computer languages provide techniques for operations on arrays. An *array* is a collection of elements, each of which has attributes identical to the rest of the elements in the array. If

$$A = \begin{bmatrix} 1.3 & 4.1 \\ 0.8 & -6.2 \end{bmatrix}$$

we can describe A as a 2×2 array containing decimal numbers, each of which contains one decimal fraction.

Using the subscript notation employed earlier in this chapter to identify each element in a matrix, we can write for array A

$$a_{11} = 1.3 \qquad a_{12} = 4.1$$
$$a_{21} = 0.8 \qquad a_{22} = -6.2$$

To access any of the elements in this array, we can simply write into the computer program the array name followed by the appropriate subscripts enclosed in parentheses. Thus, $A(1,2)$ is a reference to the element a_{12}, or the number 4.1.

If a matrix appeared as

$$[1, 2, 3, 4]$$

or

$$\begin{bmatrix} 1 \\ 2 \\ 3 \\ 4 \end{bmatrix}$$

it could be expressed as a one-dimensional array containing integers.

Two- and Three-Dimensional Arrays

In an array named ARRAY $(2, 4)$, the data items would be collected and coded for the computer in the following manner:

	COLUMNS			
ROWS	ARRAY (1, 1)	ARRAY (1, 2)	ARRAY (1, 3)	ARRAY (1, 4)
	ARRAY (2, 1)	ARRAY (2, 2)	ARRAY (2, 3)	ARRAY (2, 4)

The first subscript refers to rows, and the second subscript refers to columns.

We can think of ARRAY $(1, 2)$ as an element that resides in the first row, second column. If the following values were assigned,

$$1 \;\; ②\;\; 3 \;\; 4$$
$$5 \;\; 6 \;\; 7 \;\; 8$$

then ARRAY subscripted by $(1, 2)$ would be a reference to the 2 circled above.

Another way of expressing a two-dimensional array is through the use of a "tree" diagram as shown in Figure 19.1, which could be dimensioned TABLE $(3,4)$. For TABLE $(3,4)$, we would have as elements

TABLE (1,1)	TABLE (1, 2)	TABLE (1, 3)	TABLE (1, 4)
TABLE (2, 1)	TABLE (2, 2)	TABLE (2, 3)	TABLE (2, 4)
TABLE (3, 1)	TABLE (3, 2)	TABLE (3, 3)	TABLE (3, 4)

A three-dimensional array requires three subscripts. For example, an array dimensioned as AVE $(2, 2, 3)$ can be considered as an array containing two groups separated into two lists with each list containing three data items:

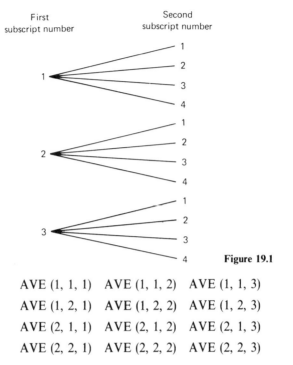

Figure 19.1

$$AVE\ (1,\ 1,\ 1)\quad AVE\ (1,\ 1,\ 2)\quad AVE\ (1,\ 1,\ 3)$$
$$AVE\ (1,\ 2,\ 1)\quad AVE\ (1,\ 2,\ 2)\quad AVE\ (1,\ 2,\ 3)$$
$$AVE\ (2,\ 1,\ 1)\quad AVE\ (2,\ 1,\ 2)\quad AVE\ (2,\ 1,\ 3)$$
$$AVE\ (2,\ 2,\ 1)\quad AVE\ (2,\ 2,\ 2)\quad AVE\ (2,\ 2,\ 3)$$

This is expressed in tree diagram form as shown in Figure 19.2. Using the array AVE, we can present a practical application of Figure 19.2 in average test scores for students in the last three years of two secondary schools:

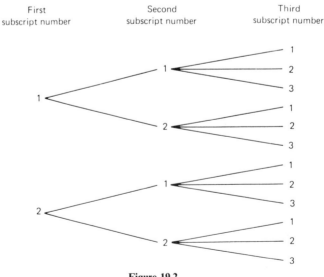

Figure 19.2

	School A Average			School B Average	
Year	Midterm	Final	Year	Midterm	Final
10	80.0	80.4	10	83.1	83.2
11	81.2	81.3	11	82.0	82.5
12	82.0	82.1	12	82.6	83.0

Arranging these data in another manner, we have

	School A Average				School B Average		
Year	10	11	12	Year	10	11	12
Midterm	80.0	81.2	82.0	Midterm	83.1	82.0	82.6
Final	80.4	81.3	82.1	Final	83.2	82.5	83.0

Note that the School A, School B, years 10, 11, 12, midterm, and final are not elements in either array The only elements in the arrays are average grades. These are given as homogeneous elements—in this case, numbers containing decimal fractions.

The eleventh year final average for School A is referenced as AVE(1, 2, 2), or first group, second row, second column. How is the twelfth year midterm average for School B referenced in AVE?

Manipulating Data in Arrays

In Fortran, the DIMENSION statement is used to reserve an area in the computer's storage for arrays of the size specified by the information found in the statement. Consider, for example,

DIMENSION A(5),B(2, 5),C(2, 3, 4).

When the statement is executed, the computer will reserve 5 storage locations to array A, 10 (or 2×5) storage locations to array B, and 24 (or $2 \times 3 \times 4$) storage locations to array C.

Next consider:

```
DIMENSION A(10), B(10), C(10)
    DO 15 I=1, 10
15 C(I)=A(I)+B(I)
```

The number 15 is the number of a Fortran statement that is to be executed 10 times. Each time, the Ith element in C will be replaced by the sum of the Ith element in A plus the Ith element in B.

EXERCISES 19-6

1. The following Fortran code contains a DO loop and an IF statement. Explain the activities of this coded routine.

```
DIMENSION IARRAY(50)
DO 20 K = 1, 50
    IF (IARRAY(K)) 10, 20, 20
10 IARRAY(K) = IARRAY(K)·(−1)
20 CONTINUE
```

(The CONTINUE statement is a "dummy" statement, providing a common finishing point in a DO loop.)

2. *Matrix Addition Problem.* Given three one-dimensional arrays (e.g., IARAY1, IARAY2, IANS) each of which contains ten elements, do the following, using FORTRAN:

(a) Initialize the values into the first two arrays so that the first elements = 1, the second elements = 2, and so on.

(b) Sum up corresponding elements of the first two arrays, and place the result in the corresponding position of the third array.

3. *Reverse Elements in a Matrix.* Given a one dimension array (IARRAY) consisting of ten elements, do the following:

(a) Initialize IARRAY so that IARRAY(1) = 1, IARRAY(2) = 2, and so on.

(b) Invert IARRAY; that is, reverse IARRAY(1) and IARRAY(10), IARRAY(2) and IARRAY(9), and so on.

4. The COBOL programming language uses its OCCURS clause to create arrays. Following is a bank depositor's record containing an array of 20 elements, each representing a possible deposit or withdrawal made within a given month.

```
01 DEPOSITOR-RECORD.
    02 NAME                        PICTURE X(19).
    02 SOCIAL-SECURITY-NUMBER      PICTURE X(11).
    02 ADDRESS                     PICTURE X(30).

    02 TRANSACTION OCCURS 20 TIMES.
        03 DEPOSIT                 PICTURE 9999V99.
        03 WITHDRAWAL              PICTURE 9999V99.
```

What is accomplished by the programmer in the following routine?

```
        MOVE 20 TO N.
LOOP.   MOVE ZEROS TO DEPOSIT(N).
        SUBTRACT 1 FROM N.
        IF N = ZERO GO TO NEXT-LINE.
        GO TO LOOP.
```

NEXT-LINE.

———————

———————

———————   other statements in program

———————

———————

If you are familiar with the PERFORM verb in COBOL, you can simplify the preceding coding.

5. The following chart gives rough approximations of wind chill values for selected Fahrenheit temperatures and wind velocities in miles per hour. The formula used for these approximations is

$$\text{Wind chill} = .0817(3.71\sqrt{v} + 5.81 - .25v)(t - 91.4) + 91.4$$

where v = velocity in miles per hour and t = Fahrenheit degrees.

Column headings and row captions are to be read into arrays W and T, respectively, before printing. Complete the BASIC coding given in the program listing that follows the WIND CHILL CHART. Note that the semicolons at the end of lines 127, 140, 197, and 210 suppress a carriage return.

By changing the PRINT commands to LPRINT, we can make a copy of the chart on the computer's printer.

WIND CHILL CHART

TMP	Velocity						
	5	10	15	20	25	30	35
+35	+32	+22	+15	+11	+7	+5	+3
+30	+26	+15	+8	+4	+0	−3	−4
+25	+21	+9	+2	−4	−7	−10	−12
+20	+16	+3	−5	−11	−15	−18	−20
+15	+11	−3	−12	−18	−22	−25	−28
+10	+5	−9	−18	−25	−30	−33	−36
+5	+0	−15	−25	−32	−37	−41	−43
+0	−5	−21	−32	−39	−44	−48	−51
−5	−10	−28	−38	−46	−52	−56	−59
−10	−16	−34	−45	−53	−59	−63	−67
−15	−21	−40	−52	−60	−67	−71	−74
−20	−26	−46	−59	−67	−74	−79	−82
−25	−31	−52	−65	−75	−81	−86	−90
−30	−37	−58	−72	−82	−89	−94	−98
−35	−42	−64	−79	−89	−96	−101	−105

```
10  DIM W(7)
20  DIM T(15)
25  DIM CHILL(15,7)
30  DATA 5,10,15,20,25,30,35
40  DATA 35,30,25,20,15,10,5,0,−5,−10,−15,−20,−25,−30,−35
50  _____
60  _____
70  _____
80  _____
90  _____
100 _____
110 PRINT "                      WIND CHILL CHART"
115 PRINT
120 PRINT "                         VELOCITY"
125 PRINT
127 PRINT "TMP";
130 FOR I = 1 TO 7
140 PRINT USING "# # # # # # # #";W(I);
150 NEXT I
160 PRINT:PRINT
170 FOR J = 1 TO 15
180 FOR I = 1 TO 7
190 CHILL _____ = _____
195 NEXT I
197 PRINT USING "+ # #";T(J);
200 FOR I = 1 TO 7
210 PRINT USING "+ # # # # # # #";INT(CHILL(_____));
215 NEXT I
220 PRINT
240 NEXT J
250 END
```

20

Linear Programming

In this chapter we will apply the algebraic, matrix, and graphing methods studied earlier, as problem-solving tools in linear programming.

Software companies provide standardized products that are frequently inadequate for some business situations and must be modified or new programs written to meet special and individual needs. Linear programming problems are one example.

THE CHARACTERISTICS OF LINEAR PROGRAMMING

Linear programming in this chapter is concerned with nonnegative solutions to systems of linear equations. Problems in linear programming have the following characteristics:

1. A desired objective, such as maximum profit, minimum cost, or minimum time.
2. A large number of variables to be manipulated at the same time, such as ingredients in a gasoline mixture, money, plant space, products, man- or machine-hours.
3. Constraints or restrictions upon variables, such as the number of man-hours allowable by union contract, output possible from a machine, the demand for a product in an open market. (Without restrictions on the variables, most problems are trivial.)
4. Interaction among the variables; for example, in determining which products to

manufacture, the maximum profits, man-hours, plant capacity, and costs for all products must be considered. Plants have limited capacities, some types of skilled labor are more costly than others, certain kinds of raw materials are more difficult to acquire than others, and so on. For reasons such as these, products *compete* for resources, and linear programming methods can be used to determine the most profitable approach to production.

The word "linear" in linear programming implies that the variables are linear, that is, they can be expressed in the relationships found in linear equations. Some typical problems in linear programs are

1. *Mixture Problems.* (Example: Food prices vary from week to week and a housewife must purchase foods that meet nutritional requirements as well as financial limitations.)
2. *Production Problems.* (Example: Scheduling machines to get the greatest output for the least cost.)
3. *Transportation Problems.* (Example: Products are stored in several warehouses, from which they must be distributed to various retail stores and individual customers in the minimum amount of time and in the least expensive manner.)

Linear programming is an important tool in finding the optimum values of linear functions subject to specified constraints.

MAXIMIZING PROFIT

Using nonnegative values, consider a manufacturer of fuel-injection systems making two different types of systems: system A for power boats and system B for automobiles. There are two separate plants, plant 1 and plant 2, each capable of producing both types of fuel-injection systems. After the parts are produced, they are packaged and shipped to another plant for product-test and assembly. Assume that

1. System A requires 60 hours in plant 1 or 70 hours in plant 2.
2. System B requires 80 hours in plant 1 or 40 hours in plant 2.
3. Under union rules, for a labor force of constant size, only 480 hours of work can be performed in plant 1 and 280 hours of work in plant 2 each week.
4. For present market conditions, it is possible to realize a profit of 30 dollars on system A and 20 dollars on system B.

Table 20.1 shows the relationship of hours to profits for each of the two systems in each of the two plants.

TABLE 20.1

	System A	System B	Union hours
Plant 1 hours	60	80	480
Plant 2 hours	70	40	280
Profits	30	20	

Let

A = the number of marine fule-injection systems produced

B = the number of automobile fuel-injection systems produced

P = total profit

Because the number of fuel-injection systems produced is a nonnegative number, $A \geqslant 0$ and $B \geqslant 0$. Then for plant 1

$$60A + 80B \leqslant 480$$

where system A requires $60A$ hours of labor, system B requires $80B$ hours of labor, and 480 represents a limitation in terms of hours imposed by union rules. For plant 2, this works out as

$$70A + 40B \leqslant 280$$

For both plants, total profit can be expressed as

$$30A + 20B = P$$

To realize maximum profit, how many of each of the fuel-injection systems should each plant manufacture?

Because we are interested only in nonnegative numbers, we can examine these considerations in the first quadrant of a graph. Let the x-axis represent system A and the y-axis system B. To plot the line for plant 1, set the number of systems produced equal to 480, or

$$60A + 80B = 480$$

Next, set $A = 0$ and $B = 6$; then set $B = 0$ and $A = 8$. Next, connect the two points $(0, 6)$ and $(8, 0)$. Thus

If system $A = 0$, then system $B = 6$.

If system $B = 0$, then system $A = 8$.

The shaded area in Figure 20.1 contains all the points that satisfy the inequality $60A + 80B \leqslant 480$ and describes the constraints or restrictions on the production in plant 1 that are also given in the inequality.

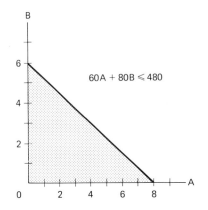

60A + 80B ≤ 480

Figure 20.1

In a similar manner, we can plot a graph for plant 2.

The shaded area in Figure 20.2 contains all the points that satisfy the inequality $70A + 40B \leqslant 280$ and describes the constraints for plant 2.

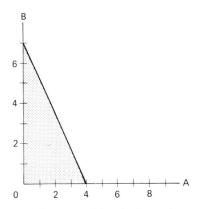

Figure 20.2

In Figure 20.3 we have combined Figure 20.1 with Figure 20.2.

The heavily shaded portion now contains all the solutions common to both in-equalities. This area will be called the feasible region and represents the combination of fuel-injection systems produced by both plants under the given constraints.

Our objective in graphing these inequalities is to find a combination that provides the greatest profit (or the highest value for P) in

$$30A + 20B = P$$

In other words, we will try to maximize profits under the two constraints given.

Expressing our profit equation in terms of the formula for a straight line $y = mx + b$, we can substitute B for y and write

$$B = -\tfrac{3}{2}A + \tfrac{P}{20}$$

The slope $-\tfrac{3}{2}$ is a constant that can be moved across the feasible region. The lines S_1, S_2, and S_3 (Figure 20.4) are parallel and all have the slope $-\tfrac{3}{2}$.

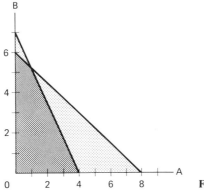

Figure 20.3

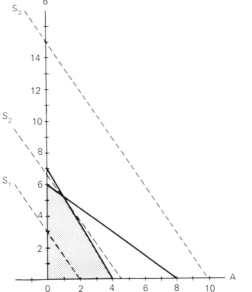

Figure 20.4

S_1 lies entirely within the feasible region. However, there are many points outside S_1 that also lie within the feasible region and represent a greater value for P than those points on S_1. S_3 contains no points in the feasible region and therefore represents no realistic value for P. All points on the line S_3 are beyond the production capability of both plants.

As the line with the slope $-\frac{3}{2}$ moves out from the origin, the maximum profit will be reached when that line touches the last feasible point in the solution set. S_2 represents the maximum feasible profit line and contains a point that can be found by solving the two simultaneous equations

$$60A + 80B = 480$$

$$70A + 40B = 280$$

Solving, we obtain $A = 1$ and $B = 5.25$. This answers the question, "How many of each of the fuel-injection systems per week should each plant manufacture?" (Consider that one-fourth of the work will be done toward a complete fuel-injection system B near the end of each week and that every four weeks we will have 21 automobile fuel-injection systems.)

Substituting 1 for A and 5.25 for B in

$$30A + 20B = P$$

we get

$$30 \cdot 1 + 20 \cdot 5.25 = P$$

Thus, $P = \$135.00$, which is the maximum profit under the given constraints.

Observe that the line with slope $-\frac{3}{2}$ will also touch points $(0, 6)$ and $(4, 0)$. As an exercise, determine whether there would be a gain in dropping production for either system A or system B.

EXERCISES 20-1

1. Using Figure 20.4, locate the following points and determine whether or not they are in the feasible region. (Let the first number represent a value for system A, the second number represent a value for system B.)

   (a) $(1, 2)$ **(b)** $(5, 5)$ **(c)** $(3, 4)$ **(d)** $(2, 3)$ **(e)** $(6, 4)$

2. If the number of unused and overtime hours for each plant is as given in Table 20.2, complete the tables for A and B.

(a)   **TABLE 20.2**

	Unused Hours	A (Units)	B
Plant 1	40	2	
Plant 2	30		1

(b)

	Over Time Hours	A (Units)	B
Plant 1	100		5
Plant 2	80	4	

(*Hint:* For plant 1, $A + B = 480$ – unused hours; for plant 2, $A + B = 280$ – unused hours.)

3. Using the same intersection of the simultaneous equations for Figure 20.1 and Figure 20.2, find P (the profit) if
   (a) $10A + 20B = P$
   (b) $15A + 10B = P$
   (c) $70A + 80B = P$

4. Graph the following, shade the feasible region, draw the maximum profit line, and solve the simultaneous equations to maximize. (Find the maximum value for P.)
   (a) $7x + 3y = P$
   where the constraints are
   $2x + 4y \leqslant 80$
   $5x + 3y \leqslant 150$
   (b) $3x + 4y = P$
   where the constraints are
   $x + y \leqslant 120$
   $x + 2y \leqslant 160$

5. Two induction motors are made in three plants. The time requirements for each plant are shown in Table 20.3.

TABLE 20.3

	Plant*			Profit per Unit
	1	2	3	
Motor A	4	5	7	$20
Motor B	8	5	4	$25
Max. hr. available	320	250	280	—

*Hours to make a unit.

Graph the three equations and, using $P = 20A + 25B$, indicate the best possible combination of manufacturing these two motors that will yield the maximum profit. (A and B are units to be manufactured.)

6. Assume the profit on item A is $5 and the profit on item B is $7 and a maximum production is 15 for item A and 9 for item B; using matrix algebra, we can then find the maximum profit as follows:

$$\begin{bmatrix} 15 & 9 \end{bmatrix} \begin{bmatrix} 5 \\ 7 \end{bmatrix} = 75 + 63 = \$138$$

   (a) Using matrix multiplication, show the profit involved in the manufacture of the fuel-injection systems described on page 336.
   (b) In the same problem recall that

$$60A + 80B = 480$$
$$70A + 40B = 280$$

and complete

$$[1 \quad 5.25] \begin{bmatrix} \ \\ \ \end{bmatrix} = 480$$

$$[1 \quad 5.25] \begin{bmatrix} \ \\ \ \end{bmatrix} = 280$$

(c) Write the appropriate Fortran statement to perform the multiplication indicated in part (b).

7. Refer to Figure 20.4 for the following problems.
   (a) If S_2 in Figure 20.4 had the slope $-\frac{3}{4}$, where would the maximum profit be found?
   (b) If the slope S_2 were almost vertical (very large) and were moved on the Cartesian plane from right to left, which point would it touch first?

MINIMIZING COSTS

A factory decides to dispose of its waste in a large nearby holding pond. To avoid creating a toxic dump site and reduce pollution, its management has decided to treat the waste with two standard products. Each of these products contains three important antipollutants in varying amounts.

The respective amounts per gallon of the three antipollutants in product A are 10-9-2 and in product B, 5-15-9. Minimum hourly requirements for each antipollutant are, respectively, 30-45-18. Product A costs 80 cents per gallon and Product B costs 60 cents per gallon. The management wishes to find the most inexpensive mixture of A and B that meets the minimum requirements.

Table 20.4 displays the antipollution problem, showing the amounts of antipollution items for each product, the hourly requirements of each of the three items, and the cost per gallon. Again, we are interested only in nonnegative numbers. Therefore, $A \geqslant 0$ and $B \geqslant 0$.

While it would be desirable to get a mixture of A and B that contains the exact hourly requirement, the management is willing to accept an excess, rather than a deficiency, of one or two antipollutants. Therefore, we can write

1. $10A + 5B \geqslant 30$
2. $9A + 15B \geqslant 45$
3. $2A + 9B \geqslant 18$

TABLE 20.4 ANTIPOLLUTANTS*

Product	Item 1	Item 2	Item 3	Cost
A	10	9	2	0.80
B	5	15	9	0.60
Required/hour	30	45	18	

*By units per gallon.

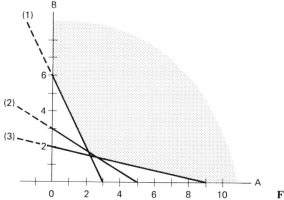

Figure 20.5

Figure 20.5 expresses the problem in graphical form.
In the figure, the line

1. Connecting points (3, 0) and (0, 6) represents the equation $10A + 5B = 30$ (item 1)
2. Connecting points (5, 0) and (0, 3) represents the equation $9A + 15B = 45$ (item 2)
3. Connecting points (9, 0) and (0, 2) represents the equation $2A + 9B = 18$ (item 3)

The line drawn for item 1 indicates that three gallons of product A or six gallons of product B provide the exact minimum for item 1. But three gallons of product A yield 27 units of item 2, which represent a deficiency of 18 units for the hourly requirement, and six gallons of product B yield 90 units of item 2, which represent a 45-unit excess for the hourly requirement.

An analysis of the other two lines yields similar results.

The shaded area represents a feasible region that contains points that represent combinations of the three items yielding, at the very least, the minimum hourly requirements. The shaded area contains all those points that represent solutions to all three inequalities. The feasible region is bounded in part by the lines JK, KL, and LM in Figure 20.6.

Our objective in graphing these three lines is to find a combination that provides the least possible cost, or lowest value, for C where $.80A + .60B = C$. Stated in other terms, minimize $.80A + .60B = C$ under the following constraints:

$$10A + 5B \geqslant 30$$
$$9A + 15B \geqslant 45$$
$$2A + 9B \geqslant 18$$

Expressing our cost equation in terms of the formula for a straight line (and substituting B for y in $y = mx + b$), we have

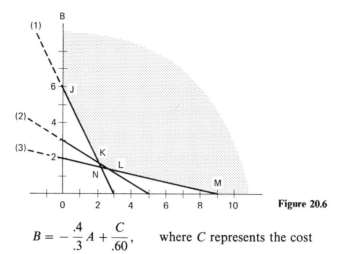

Figure 20.6

$$B = -\frac{.4}{.3}A + \frac{C}{.60}, \qquad \text{where } C \text{ represents the cost}$$

Drawing three lines with a slope of $-\frac{4}{3}$, we note that the minimum cost should be the point that is as close as possible to the origin, but still intersects the feasible region. This eliminates consideration of line S_3 in Figure 20.7. In other words, as the line with a slope of $-\frac{4}{3}$ moves in toward the origin, the minimum will be reached when that line touches the last feasible point in the solution set.

In Figure 20.7, the point P on line S_1 represents 4 gallons of B and 3 gallons of A. Expressing the items in products A and B as two 1×3 matrices where column 1 contains the entry for item 1, column 2 the entry for item 2 and so on, we have

$$A = [10 \quad 9 \quad 2]$$
$$B = [\,5 \quad 15 \quad 9]$$

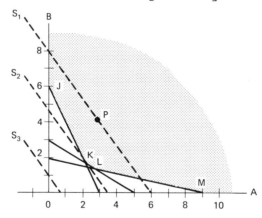

Figure 20.7

Next, multiply each by the appropriate number of gallons:

$$3 \times [10 \quad 9 \quad 2] = [30 \quad 27 \quad 6] \quad (3 \text{ gallons for } A \text{ at point } P)$$
$$4 \times [\,5 \quad 15 \quad 9] = [20 \quad 60 \quad 36] \quad (4 \text{ gallons for } B \text{ at point } P)$$

Inspection reveals $30 + 20 = 50$, or an excess of 20 units for item 1; further, there is an excess of 42 units for item 2 and 24 units for item 3.

Since we are trying to minimize cost at the same time that we are trying to get the best possible mixture, we can move the slope $-\frac{4}{3}$ closer to the origin. Inspection reveals that point K seems to be the closest point to the origin that still lies within the feasible region. To find this point, we solve the simultaneous equations obtained by the two intersecting straight lines:

$$10A + 5B = 30$$
$$9A + 15B = 45$$

Solving yields

$$A = \tfrac{15}{7} \quad \text{and} \quad B = \tfrac{12}{7}$$

Replacing A and B with $\frac{15}{7}$ and $\frac{12}{7}$, respectively, we compute

$$10A + 5B \tag{1}$$
$$9A + 15B \tag{2}$$
$$2A + 9B \tag{3}$$

For item 1: $\dfrac{15 \cdot 10}{7} + \dfrac{12 \cdot 5}{7} = 30$ gallons (exact requirement)

For item 2: $\dfrac{15 \cdot 9}{7} + \dfrac{12 \cdot 15}{7} = 45$ gallons (exact requirement)

For item 3: $\dfrac{15 \cdot 2}{7} + \dfrac{12 \cdot 9}{7} = 19.7$ gallons, or 1.7 gallons in excess of requirements

Referring to Table 20.4, we note that the exact requirements are met for items 1 and 2 and that we have a small excess of 1.7 gallons for item 3 in the least expensive mixture of antipollutants at point K on S_2. As stated previously, our objective in graphing these three inequalities is to find a combination that provides the least cost for

$$C = .80A + .60B$$

in other words, to minimize C under the three constraints given. Hence, substituting $\frac{15}{7}$ for A and $\frac{12}{7}$ for B, we find that

$$C = .80(\tfrac{15}{7}) + .60(\tfrac{12}{7})$$
$$C = 2.74$$

EXERCISES 20-2

Refer to Figure 20.7 for problems 1 through 4.

1. (a) Find the appropriate solution set at L.
   (b) Use the values for A and B at L, and compute
      (1) $10A + 5B$
      (2) $9A + 15B$
      (3) $2A + 9B$

2. Using values for A and B at L,
   (a) Refer to Table 20.4 and list any excess or deficiency.
   (b) Find the cost of products A and B at L using matrix algebra.

3. At what point on the graph are the requirements best met for
   (a) Items 1 and 3
   (b) Items 2 and 3

4. (a) Find the costs of products A and B at J.
   Assume that there are different vendors for products A and B and that the costs for these products vary with each vendor. Let A remain equal to $\frac{15}{7}$ and B remain equal to $\frac{12}{7}$.
   (b) Use matrix algebra and compute costs for
      (1) $COST = .49A + .56B$
      (2) $COST = .50A + .70B$

   Note: For all linear programming problems, it is always best first to graph the constraints, find the slope, and shade the feasible region and then
   (a) For maximizing, move the slope out from the origin and determine the last feasible point in the solution set.
   (b) For minimizing, move the slope in the feasible region in toward the origin and determine the last feasible point in the solution set.
      These points may lie at the intersection of two lines or on the x or y axis.

5. In problems 5(a) and 5(c) first draw the graphs as previously described, and then minimize. (Find the minimum value for C.)
   (a) $.30x + .20y = C$
   where the constraints are
      (1) $6x + 5y \geqslant 30$
      (2) $10x + 14y \geqslant 70$
      (3) $6x + 20y \geqslant 60$
   (b) How many points must be examined in order to minimize C in problem a?
   (c) $x + y = COST$
   where the constraints are
      (1) $3x + 2y \geqslant 30$
      (2) $x + 3y \geqslant 36$
      (3) $3x + 5y \geqslant 60$
   (d) If $COST = 5x + 2y$ in problem 5(c), at what point on the graph is the minimum cost found?
   (e) Design your own problem to find C *at its minimum* on one of the axes of the Cartesian plane. Approach the solution to this problem by first drawing the graph.

6. Refer to page 344 and write the Fortran statements to multiply a matrix by the appropriate number of gallons.

7. A builder plans to construct two types of homes. Type x, with 2 floors requires 300 units of wood, 200 units of concrete, and 80 units of roofing. Type y, a ranch type home requires 100 units of wood, 100 units of concrete, and 160 units of roofing. At least 1200 units of wood, 1000 units of concrete, and 640 units of roofing are to be used. If COST $= 80x + 60y$, how many homes of each type can be built where the cost of construction is at a minimum?

8. Given: COST $= \$150x + \$200y$ and the constraints:

$$3x + y \geqslant 6$$
$$x + y \geqslant 3$$
$$x + 3y \geqslant 6$$

Find the minimum amount for COST.

21

Statistical Measurements

Frequently, programmers are asked to write computer programs that will provide management with statistical information. This information generally falls into two categories:

1. Measures of central tendency
2. Measures of dispersion

Many of the formulas that provide this information can be quickly coded into computer languages such as Fortran, COBOL, and BASIC. These formulas are given here as problem-solving tools only; their proofs lie outside the scope of this text.

ORGANIZING THE DATA

The collection of numerical information can lead to massive quantities of data items. If these numerical data items are to be understood easily, they must be displayed and summarized effectively. There are three basic methods of doing this:

1. The report method, which summarizes data
2. The tabular method, which arranges data items in columns and rows
3. The pictorial method, which arranges quantitative information in graphical form

The Report Method

The report method is typical in data processing. Reports such as the Trial Balance are often prepared by programmers to present information in summary form. Table 21.1 summarizes information found in an accounting ledger and is a report indicating that debits and credits are equal.

TABLE 21.1   TRIAL BALANCE

	Debits	Credits
Cash	3,000	
Accounts Receivable	4,800	
Supplies	3,500	
Prepaid Rent	2,000	
Equipment	50,000	
Accumulated Depreciation Equipment		4,000
Accounts Payable		10,100
Owner Capital		50,000
Owner Drawing	1,000	
Sales		3,000
Salary Expense	1,800	
Miscellaneous Expense	1,000	
	67,100	67,100

The Tabular Method

TABLE 21.2   ABC COLLEGE ENROLLMENT

Year	Enrollment
1966	1850
1967	1950
1968	2500
1969	2800
1970	3000

In Table 21.2 the arrangement of data items in rows and columns makes it easy to note certain characteristics of the data under consideration. In the previous example, we can determine that the student enrollment at College *ABC* has steadily increased from 1966 to 1970. The largest increase took place in the interval of time from January 1, 1968 to December 31, 1968. Since 1968, the enrollment has increased, but at a slower rate for each successive period.

Definition 21-1. An *interval* is a measured distance between real numbers. The outside limits of an interval are real numbers greater than, less than, or excluding other real numbers.

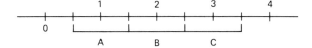

On the number line marked off in units of 1, 2, 3, and 4, the intervals marked *A*, *B*, and *C* are intervals of .5–1.5, 1.5–2.5, and 2.5–3.5, respectively. The interval *A*, for example, contains the set of real numbers from .5 to 1.5 (real numbers $\geq$ .5 and $\leq$ 1.5).

Definition 21-2. A *class* is a group of individual measurements that can be found within a given interval.

Definition 21-3. The data items or individual measurements are called *variates*.

Definition 21-4. The number of variates falling within a given class interval is called the *frequency*, or class frequency.

The pictorial method illustrates this concept.

The Pictorial Method

Using the enrollment figures given earlier for College *ABC*, we can create a vertical bar graph, having no space between bars. This type of vertical bar graph (Figure 21.1) is called a *histogram*, with intervals or class boundaries for each period as points on the horizontal axis and frequencies on the vertical axis. Enrollment, the range, is expressed as a function of time, the domain.

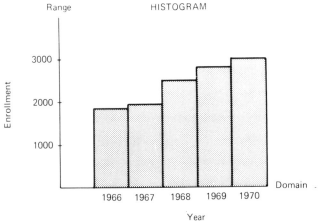

Figure 21.1

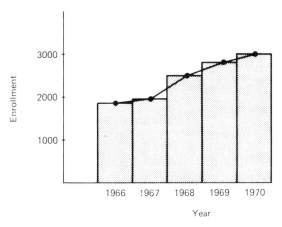

Figure 21.2

By marking a midpoint at the top of each bar and connecting these midpoints, we can construct the *frequency polygon* shown in Figure 21.2. The line graph in Figure 21.2 that forms the frequency polygon is placed on top of the histogram of Figure 21.1.

We can also separate the bars, rotate our histogram 90° clockwise, and present the same information in a horizontal bar graph. The bar graph dramatizes enrollment growth and provides a summary of the numerical information that is easily understood. Figure 21.3 no longer expresses a function; rather, it graphically illustrates the dispersion of the data.

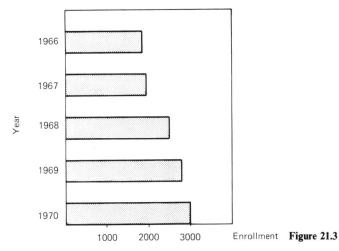

Enrollment **Figure 21.3**

Figure 21.4 shows a relationship of boys to girls in a component bar graph (a bar graph divided into two parts).

If we wished to make a closer comparison between the male and female enrollment figures, we could group the component bars as in Figure 21.5. The grouped bar graph indicates that the increase in enrollment is greater for girls than for boys.

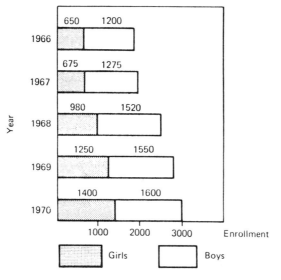

Figure 21.4

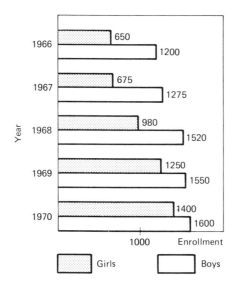

Figure 21.5

Figure 21.6 is a simple display showing the universe of all students in a district. This type of graphic presentation is called a pie graph, another pictorial method, Figure 21.6 illustrates that half the students are elementary school students.

The selection and construction of a pictorial summary depends on the manner in which data items are to be displayed, measured, or compared. Such data items as

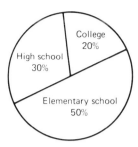

Figure 21.6

the number of students in a city, the number of persons over 65 years of age, and the amount of dollars paid for school taxes, are measured and expressed in integers and are called *discrete variables*.

A data item or variable that assumes any real number value within certain limits is called a *continuous variable*. Data items such as temperatures, average rainfalls, airplane speeds, and those dealing with weight, time and length are called continuous variables. These data items reflect continuous variations or changes.

Continuous data items are usually expressed in the pictorial form of a smooth curve. Figure 21.7 displays a continuous variable.

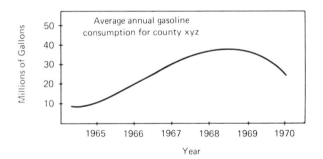

Figure 21.7

EXERCISES 21-1

1. **(a)** Give an example of a discrete variable.
   (b) Give an example of a continuous variable.
2. Of all transactions at the *XYZ* Hotel chain, 20% were cash, 60% were by one of the major credit cards, and the rest were by personal check. Draw a pie graph to show these different types of transactions.

3. The number of persons insured for a ten-year period by the *ABC* Insurance Company is

Year	Life insurance	Property insurance
1971	10,000	8,000
1972	12,000	10,000
1973	15,000	11,000
1974	20,000	15,000
1975	26,000	21,000
1976	32,000	26,000
1977	37,000	30,000
1978	41,000	36,000
1979	47,000	42,000
1980	52,000	48,000

From these data items construct a component or grouped bar graph for this company.

4. The average daily temperatures at *XYZ* Airport are given as follows:

Temperatures		Number of days in year for temperature
Low	High	
20°	30°	5
30	40	35
40	50	30
50	60	65
60	70	80
70	80	70
80	90	55
90	100	25

For example, the average daily temperature ranged from 20° to 30° for five days and from 30° to 40° for 35 days. Construct the following:

(a) A histogram

(b) A frequency polygon over the histogram

5. The *ABC* Products Company has two different products in three areas. The products, known as *X* and *Y*, both have the same potential sales demand, but each requires a different product knowledge. Product *X* is the easiest for a salesperson to understand and to explain to a customer. The estimated profit is $10 for *X* and $7 for *Y*.

Each of the three market areas has three salespeople, one of whom functions as a regional sales manager who

(1) Coordinates the activities of the other two

(2) Coordinates paper work

(3) Trains new salespeople

(4) Makes calls on customers as time allows.

Salesperson *C* has been with the company for only four months. The remaining eight salespeople have over two years experience. Given the following table:

SALES REPORT

Region	Salesperson	Product	Units
I	A Manager	X	100
		Y	95
	B	X	190
		Y	170
	C	X	100
		Y	75
II	D Manager	X	225
		Y	75
	E	X	200
		Y	100
	F	X	175
		Y	125
III	G Manager	X	115
		Y	105
	H	X	215
		Y	210
	I	X	200
		Y	190

Prepare a more meaningful report reflecting the following:
(a) Profit in dollars by region
(b) Manager D's low sales for product Y
(c) Manager G's performance in dollar amounts.

SUMMATION NOTATION

With large amounts of data it is necessary to simplify the notation for grouping and summation. If a universe of terms is under consideration, such as all the students' grades in one class, we may designate the universe as X and the individual student grades as X_1 (read as "X sub one"), X_2, X_3, and so on. Then X_N denotes the last term in the universe when that universe has N terms, N being a positive integer. X_i is generally referred to as the ith term.

The symbol $\sum$ is the *summation symbol* and indicates a sum of N terms. Thus

$$\sum_{i=1}^{N} X_i = X_1 + X_2 + X_3 + \ldots + X_N$$

is the sum of all the terms in the universe X. We read this as "The summation of X_i where i assumes all integral values from 1 to N, inclusive," The subscript i is called the *summation index*. Let

$$X_1 = 2, X_2 = 4, X_3 = 8, X_4 = 16$$

Then

$$\sum_{i=1}^{4} X_i = X_1 + X_2 + X_3 + X_4 = 2 + 4 + 8 + 16 = 30$$

The summation index functions like other indices. It points at the items under consideration. Let

$$N = 5, \ X_1 = -4, \ X_2 = 3, \ X_3 = 0, \ X_4 = -2, \text{ and } X_5 = 1$$

Then

$$\sum_{i=2}^{N} X_i = X_2 + X_3 + \ldots + X_N = 3 + 0 + (-2) + 1 = 2$$

Examples

Given $X_1 = 3, \ X_2 = -4, \ X_3 = 6, \ X_4 = 7$,

find 1. $\displaystyle\sum_{i=1}^{4} (X_i)^2$ 2. $\displaystyle\sum_{i=2}^{3} (X_i - 3X_i^2)$ 3. $\displaystyle\sum_{i=1}^{4} (X_i - 2)^2$ 4. $\displaystyle\left(\sum_{i=3}^{4} X_i\right)^2$

1. $\displaystyle\sum_{i=1}^{4} (X_i)^2 = (X_1)^2 + (X_2)^2 + (X_3)^2 + (X_4)^2$

$$= 9 + 16 + 36 + 49$$

$$= 110$$

2. $\displaystyle\sum_{i=2}^{3} (X_i - 3X_i^2) = (X_2 - 3X_2^2) + (X_3 - 3X_3^2)$

$$= (-4 - 48) + (6 - 108)$$

$$= -154$$

3. $\displaystyle\sum_{i=1}^{4} (X_i - 2)^2 = (X_1 - 2)^2 + (X_2 - 2)^2 + (X_3 - 2)^2 + (X_4 - 2)^2$

$$= (3 - 2)^2 + (-4 - 2)^2 + (6 - 2)^2 + (7 - 2)^2$$

$$= 78$$

4. $\displaystyle\left(\sum_{i=3}^{4} X_i\right)^2 = (X_3 + X_4)^2$

$$= (6 + 7)^2$$

$$= 169$$

EXERCISES 21-2

1. Express the following in summation notation.
   (a) $X_1 + X_2 + X_3 + \ldots + X_N$

(b) $(X_2 + 2X_2) + (X_3 + 2X_3)$

(c) $(X_1 - p)^3 + (X_2 - p)^3 + \ldots + (X_N - p)^3$

(d) $(cX_2)^2 + (cX_3)^2 + (cX_4)^2$

(e) $(X_5 + X_6)^2$

2. Write out all the terms for the following:

(a) $\sum\limits_{j=2}^{N} X_j$

(b) $\sum\limits_{i=1}^{4} X_i^2$

(c) $\left(\sum\limits_{i=5}^{6} Y_i - 2 \right)^2$

(d) $\sum\limits_{i=2}^{3} (X_i + 2X_i)X_i$

(e) $\sum\limits_{k=1}^{N} (aX_k + b)$

3. If $X_1 = 2$, $X_2 = -3$, $X_3 = 0$, $X_4 = 9$, and $c = 4$, find the numerical values for the following:

(a) $\sum\limits_{i=1}^{4} X_i$

(b) $\sum\limits_{j=2}^{3} (X_j + c)$

(c) $\left[\sum\limits_{i=1}^{2} (2X_i - c) \right]^2$

(d) $\sum\limits_{i=3}^{4} (X_i^2 - 2X_i)$

(e) $\sum\limits_{i=1}^{4} (cX_i)$

4. Does

$$\sum\limits_{i=1}^{2} (X_i)^2 = \left(\sum\limits_{i=1}^{2} X_i \right)^2$$

SCORES

A *score* is a count or tally and suggests order and relationship to other scores, that is, the highest score, the lowest score, or the average score. A single score can be described as a raw score or single variate. A grade of 85 on an examination, for example, can be termed a raw score. Assume that a class of ten made the following raw scores: 63, 65, 73, 75, 81, 83, 85, 91, 95, 100. These scores, as listed, can be described as *ungrouped*. If we listed scores by arranging them as follows:

Class	Frequency
61–70	2
71–80	2
81–90	3
91–100	3

we would be discussing *grouped scores.*

The remainder of this chapter contains a discussion of the measures of central tendency and dispersion for ungrouped and grouped scores.

UNGROUPED SCORES

Measures of central tendency are measurements that indicate the center of a distribution of scores. In this chapter, we are concerned about the mean, the median, and the range.

The Median

Definition 21-5.   The *median* is that number on a scale that divides the number of scores into two equal parts.

Example 1

Assume the following to be the variates or raw scores on an aptitude test made by nine job applicants: 93, 90, 88, 86, 85, 77, 68, 64, 60. The median is the raw score 85, as there are four scores greater than 85 and four scores less than 85.

If the number of raw scores were an even number, such as 10, we could compute the median as

$$\frac{X_{N/2} + (X_{N/2+1})}{2} \quad \text{or} \quad \frac{X_5 + X_6}{2} \quad (N = 10 \text{ in this example.})$$

Example 2

Assuming the ten raw scores to be

$X_1 = 93, X_2 = 90, X_3 = 88, X_4 = 86, X_5 = 85, X_6 = 77, X_7 = 68, X_8 = 64, X_9 = 60,$
$X_{10} = 40$

then

$$\frac{85 + 77}{2} = \frac{162}{2} = 81$$

The median in this case is 81. It should be noted that the median of 81 is *not* one of the ten raw scores, but the mean of the two middle scores.

The Mean

Definition 21-6.   The *mean* (or arithmetic mean) denoted by m for a set of N variates is defined as

$$m = \frac{X_1 + X_2 + X_3 + \ldots + X_N}{N} \quad \text{or} \quad m = \frac{\sum_{i=1}^{N} X_i}{N}$$

Considering our sample of nine raw scores presented in Example 1 (where $N = 9$), we can compute m as follows:

$$m = \frac{\sum_{i=1}^{N} X_i}{N} = 79$$

or

$$\frac{93 + 90 + 88 + 86 + 85 + 77 + 68 + 64 + 60}{9} = 79$$

If several of the raw scores were 40 or below, they would have noticeably lowered the test mean. Similarly, if several of test scores were above 93, they would have significantly raised the mean. In such situations, the median has a significance as a measure of central tendency.

The Range

Definition 21-7.   For a set of N numbers, the *range* is a computed distance between the largest and smallest numbers, that is, the difference.

The range of the scores in the last example is:

median

93, 90, 88, 86, 85, 77, 68, 64, 60

range $= 93 - 60 = 33$

Or, stated in another manner, the scores range from 60 to 93. Note that within the range there is a scattering of scores about a central point, such as the mean or median.

Measure of Dispersion

The arithmetic mean is a helpful measure of a central tendency, and the median is useful when extremely high or low scores occur as noted earlier. The range gives some measure of the dispersion of scores about the mean. However, none of these three measurements indicates the deviations from the mean or the distribution of the variates either at the extremes of the range or at the center.

Consider the following three sets of raw scores:

Example 1

$$20, 50, 80, 90, 100$$
$$\text{Median} = 80$$
$$\text{Mean} \ = 68$$
$$\text{Range} \ = 80$$

Example 2

$$30, 45, 80, 85, 90$$
$$\text{Median} = 80$$
$$\text{Mean} \ = 66$$
$$\text{Range} \ = 60$$

Example 3

$$15, 65, 75, 80, 95$$
$$\text{Median} = 75$$
$$\text{Mean} \ = 66$$
$$\text{Range} \ = 80$$

Examples 1 and 2 have the same median. Examples 1 and 3 have the same range. Examples 2 and 3 have the same mean. Examination of

Examples 1 and 2 shows that the median does not describe these two sets of raw scores equally well

Examples 1 and 3 shows that the range does not describe these two sets of raw scores equally well

Examples 2 and 3 shows that the mean does not describe these two sets of raw scores equally well

We need, therefore, some method to describe the spread or dispersion of a set of raw scores about their mean. This measure of the spread of all scores is called the *standard deviation*.

Before studying the standard deviation, we must first consider the *deviation* and the *variance*, which are required to compute standard deviation.

Definition 21-8.   A *deviation* of a score X_i is the difference between X_i and m. A deviation is denoted as d, where $d = X_i - m$.

In Example 1 (above) this works out for X_5 as

$$d = X_5 - m$$
$$d = 100 - 68$$
$$d = 32$$

Note that in Example 1, $\sum (X - m) = 0$:

$$\sum_{i=1}^{5} (X_i - m) = (X_1 - m) + (X_2 - m) + (X_3 - m) + (X_4 - m) + (X_5 - m)$$

$$= (20 - 68) + (50 - 68) + (80 - 68) + (90 - 68) + (100 - 68)$$

$$= (-48) + (-18) + (12) + (22) + (32)$$

$$= 0$$

As an exercise, show that $\sum (X - m) = 0$ for examples 2 and 3.

Definition 21-9. A *variance* is the sum of the deviations squared divided by N, that is

$$\text{Variance} = \frac{\sum_{i=1}^{N} (X_i - m)^2}{N}$$

and is denoted by σ^2.

Examine Table 21.3.

TABLE 21.3

Score	f	$X_i - m = d$	d^2
93	1	$93 - 79 =$ 14	$(14)^2$
90	1	$90 - 79 =$ 11	$(11)^2$
88	1	$88 - 79 =$ 9	$(9)^2$
86	1	$86 - 79 =$ 7	$(7)^2$
85	1	$85 - 79 =$ 6	$(6)^2$
77	1	$77 - 79 =$ -2	$(-2)^2$
68	1	$68 - 79 =$ -11	$(-11)^2$
64	1	$64 - 79 =$ -15	$(-15)^2$
60	1	$60 - 79 =$ -19	$(-19)^2$

Scores are found in the left column in descending order. (They may also be presented in ascending order.) The second column from the left contains the frequency (f) for each score. (Since in this example we are using raw scores, only one frequency can be written for each score achieved.) Marking off the deviations from the mean gives us the column, d.

At this point we wish to find the average dispersion of scores from a central point. But notice that, in adding up the column under d, negative and positive values cancel each other out. To avoid $+$ and $-$ designations, we square the deviation and take the mean of the squares. This may be represented by the formula

$$\frac{\sum_{i=1}^{N} d_i^2}{N}$$

In our example, this works out as $\frac{1194}{9} = 132.7$. But 132.7 is a measure of variance as a square. To find this variance as a linear measurement, we take the square root of 132.7, or $\sqrt{132.7} = 11.52$.

Definition 21-10. The square root of the variance is called the *standard deviation*.

The symbol σ is used to denote the *standard deviation*. The following is the formula to find the standard deviation for ungrouped scores and illustrates taking the square root of the sum of the deviations squared, divided by N, or the square root of the variance.

$$\sigma = \sqrt{\frac{\sum_{i=1}^{N} d^2}{N}}$$

GROUPED SCORES

Table 21.4 contains the deposits made in 100 banks for one year. The deposits are expressed in millions of dollars (50.5 = $50,500,000). The amounts have been placed in descending numerical order.

TABLE 21.4 DEPOSITS

50.5	46.8	42.2	39.2	38.4	36.2	32.1	27.1	21.4	15.3
50.3	46.6	41.6	39.1	38.3	36.1	31.6	25.9	21.3	14.4
50.0	45.5	41.6	39.1	38.3	36.1	31.5	25.7	20.3	13.9
48.6	45.0	41.5	39.0	38.2	35.6	30.7	25.6	20.1	12.7
48.5	44.8	41.3	39.0	38.0	35.6	30.6	25.0	19.6	11.7
47.3	44.7	41.1	38.8	37.9	34.8	28.4	24.7	18.4	10.2
47.1	44.5	40.7	38.8	37.9	34.2	28.3	24.6	17.9	9.6
47.0	43.7	40.6	38.8	37.7	32.9	27.5	23.2	16.2	7.1
46.9	43.2	40.0	38.6	37.4	32.4	27.4	23.0	15.6	7.0
46.9	42.3	39.8	38.5	37.3	32.3	27.2	22.5	15.5	5.5

This arrangement of the distribution of variates is cluttered and bulky. Table 21.5 shows the distribution of these variates in a more compact format that is easier to visualize. The data now can be easily manipulated and measured because the interval of measurement includes not just one variate, but a group of variates. We refer to such a group of scores as a *class*. Each class has its own upper and lower boundary and contains those values that properly belong in their respective class intervals.

Classes are arranged in ascending numerical order in the first column in Table 21.5.

TABLE 21.5

Class Boundaries (in millions)	Class Midpoints	Tallied Frequencies	Class Frequency	Cumulative Frequency
5.5–10.5	8	ЖГ	5	5
10.5–15.5	13	ЖГ,	5	10
15.5–20.5	18	ЖГ |||	8	18
20.5–25.5	23	ЖГ |||	8	26
25.5–30.5	28	ЖГ ||||	9	35
30.5–35.5	33	ЖГ ЖГ	10	45
35.5–40.5	38	ЖГ ЖГ ЖГ ЖГ ЖГ ||	27	72
40.5–45.5	43	ЖГ ЖГ ЖГ	15	87
45.5–50.5	48	ЖГ ЖГ |||	13	100

Note that the last column, cumulative frequency, is computed by adding up the class frequencies row by row. For example, for the first class the cumulative frequency is 5. For the second class the cumulative frequency is $5 + 5 = 10$. For the third class the cumulative frequency is $10 + 8 = 18$, and so on. The cumulative frequency is shown graphically in Figure 21.10.

The range for grouped scores is the computed distance between the upper boundary of the highest class and the lower boundary of the lowest class. As an exercise, compute the range for Table 21.5.

The nine class boundaries in the left-hand column include all the dollar amounts found in Table 21.4. The *class midpoint* is halfway between the upper and lower boundary. The number of data items falling within any class is called the *class frequency*. In this chapter, any data item falling on a class boundary shall be placed in the higher class.[1] (Class boundaries could be specified to the hundredths place to avoid variates falling on them.)

In this example, the class interval was determined by taking the difference of the endpoints of the range ($50.5 - 5.5 = 45.0$), dividing by 10, ($\frac{45}{10} = 4.5$), and rounding to the nearest integer.

It is sometimes useful to display grouped scores in graphic form. Graphs and

---

[1]Except for 50.5, which is the greatest variate in Table 21.4.

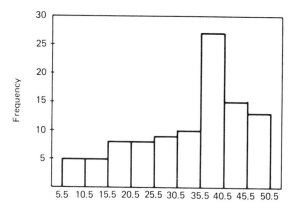

Figure 21.8 Histogram

histograms display information in a compact form and differences in magnitude are easy to recognize. (See Figure 21.8.)

The term *mode of the distribution* is used to describe that part of the scale at which more variates are found than at any other place. It is a characteristic of the concentration of scores that cannot be expressed by any other measure of central tendency. In Figure 21.8, we can see that the mode of the distribution occurs in the class bounded by 35.5 and 40.5.

In grouped scores or variates, a true mode requires several computations and is used to express the place (or places) on a scale where frequencies occur most often.

If we rotate Table 21.5, 90° counterclockwise, we are able to create a histogram (Figure 21.8) or vertical bar graph, with class boundaries on the horizontal axis and frequencies on the vertical axis. By connecting class midpoints (second column in Table 21.5), we can then draw the frequency polygon shown in Figure 21.9. The broken lines in the frequency polygon of Figure 21.9 connect the midpoints of the tops of the rectangles of Figure 21.8.

To illustrate graphically the accumulation of monies deposited in the one hundred banks, we create a cumulative frequency polygon or broken line graph. Take the first column from Table 21.5 as our horizontal axis, and use the last column in

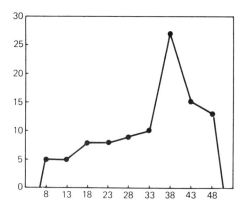

Figure 21.9 Frequency polygon

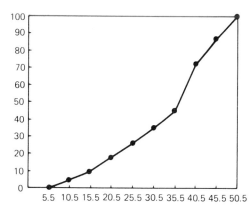

Figure 21.10   Cumulative frequency polygon

Table 21.5 as our vertical axis. (See Figure 21.10.) Upper-class boundaries are indicated by points on the graph, and these points are connected by line segments.

The Mean

One method of calculating the mean for grouped scores assumes that the data items in each class are uniformly distributed about that class midpoint, where

$$m = \frac{\sum_{i=1}^{K} X_i f_i}{N}$$

for

N = the total of all the frequencies for all classes

X_i = the ith midpoint

f_i = the ith frequency

K = the number of classes

m = the mean

For the data given in Table 21.6, the mean for the grouped scores (Xf column) can be computed as

$$\frac{8(5) + 13(5) + 18(8) + 23(8) + 28(9) + 33(10) + 38(27) + 43(15) + 48(13)}{100}$$

$$= \frac{40 + 65 + 144 + 184 + 252 + 330 + 1026 + 645 + 624}{100}$$

$$= \frac{3310}{100}$$

$$= 33.10$$

TABLE 21.6

Class Boundaries	X	f	Xf
5.5–10.5	8	5	40
10.5–15.5	13	5	65
15.5–20.5	18	8	144
20.5–25.5	23	8	184
25.5–30.5	28	9	252
30.5–35.5	33	10	330
35.5–40.5	38	27	1026
40.5–45.5	43	15	645
45.5–50.5	48	13	624

The Median

It was a simple operation to find the median for ungrouped scores. However, to find the median for grouped scores requires more computation. In grouped scores, the median is found in the *median class*, or in the lowest class in which the cumulative frequency is greater than $N/2$. Let

N = the total of all the frequencies for all classes

L = the mean of the lower boundary of the median class and the upper boundary of the next lower class

c = the difference between two adjacent class midpoints

fm = the frequency of the median class

F_c = the cumulative frequency for the class before the median class in Table 21.5 (specifies all the variates up to but not including L)

M_d = the median for grouped scores

Assume that the data items in the median class are distributed uniformly throughout the interval. (Refer to Table 21.5; the last column implies that the median class is $35.5 - 40.5$.) Then

$$c\left(\frac{N/2 - F_c}{fm}\right)$$

is the distance from L to the median, or the correction added to L to find the median. Therefore

$$M_d = L + c\left(\frac{N/2 - F_c}{fm}\right)$$

$$M_d = 35.5 + 5\left(\frac{100/2 - 45}{27}\right)$$

$$= 35.5 + 5(.185)$$

$$= 36.425$$

Note that when N is even, the formula for the median considers the first of the two middle numbers, not their mean. (See page 358.) This is satisfactory, since a frequency distribution of grouped scores will usually contain enough variates so that the middle numbers differ by very little.

Consider that the number of variates equal to F_c is subtracted from half of the total number of variates. Divide this difference by the frequency of the median class. The resulting number is equivalent to the number derived by subtracting the mean of the lower boundary of the median class and the upper boundary of the next lower class from the median and dividing this difference by the difference between two adjacent class midpoints, or

$$\frac{N/2 - F_c}{fm} = \frac{M_d - L}{c}$$

Standard Deviation

The standard deviation for grouped scores can be computed easily if we drop the fourth column in Table 21.6 and add four new columns to get Table 21.7. (Note that $|X - m|$ means the absolute value of $X - m$.)

TABLE 21.7

Class Boundaries	X	f	$|X - m|$	$|X - m|f$	$(X - m)^2$	$(X - m)^2 f$
5.5–10.5	8	5	25.1	125.5	630.01	3150.05
10.5–15.5	13	5	20.1	100.5	404.01	2020.05
15.5–20.5	18	8	15.1	120.8	228.01	1824.08
20.5–25.5	23	8	10.1	80.8	102.01	816.08
25.5–30.5	28	9	5.1	45.9	26.01	234.09
30.5–35.5	33	10	.1	1.0	.01	.10
35.5–40.5	38	27	4.9	132.3	24.01	648.27
40.5–45.5	43	15	9.9	148.5	98.01	1470.15
45.5–50.5	48	13	14.9	193.7	222.01	2886.13

By modifying the formula used earlier for ungrouped scores, we obtain the following formula for grouped scores:

$$\sigma_g = \sqrt{\frac{\sum_{i=1}^{K} (X_i - m)^2 f_i}{N}}$$

σ_g is the symbol used to denote the standard deviation for grouped scores, and $K =$ the number of classes. Thus, for the data in our table

$$\sigma_g = \sqrt{\frac{13049}{100}}$$

$$= 11.423$$

EXERCISES 21-3

1. Given the set of numbers

$$4.9, \ 1.5, \ 3.9, \ 0.1, \ 6.2, \ 8.4, \ 9.5, \ 7.8, \ 2.3$$

find the following to two decimal places.
(a) The median
(b) The mean
(c) The standard deviation

2. Given

Class Boundaries	Frequencies
6.5– 9.5	3
9.5–12.5	7
12.5–15.5	8
15.5–18.5	17
18.5–21.5	24
21.5–24.5	18
24.5–27.5	11
27.5–30.5	4

Find

(a) The mean
(b) The median class
(c) The median
(d) The standard deviation

3. Describe the following Fortran statements.

(a) SUM = A + B + C + D + E
(b) DIFF = (XN/2) − FC

4. Code a Fortran statement to find the averages of the variables A, B, C, D, and E in problem 3(a).

5. Write Fortran statements to find the following.
(a) The mean for grouped scores in four classes, where

$$XM = \text{the mean}$$

$$XI = \text{the } i\text{th midpoint}$$

$$FI = \text{the } i\text{th frequency}$$

$$XK = \text{the number of classes}$$

$$XN = \text{the total numbers of frequencies for all classes}$$

(b) The median for grouped scores. Create your own variable names, but remember that letters $I - N$ are used as the first letter in a variable name for integers only.

   (c) The standard deviation for
      (1) Ungrouped scores
      (2) Grouped scores

6. The following contains sorted normal monthly temperatures in Fahrenheit degrees from
   ten airports.

SORTED TEMPERATURES

30.1	32.1	32.7	34.7	36.0	36.5	37.6	39.2	41.1	41.3
42.4	43.5	44.3	44.6	45.2	45.3	45.5	45.6	46.1	46.5
49.9	50.5	50.6	50.9	51.7	52.1	53.2	53.6	53.8	54.6
54.6	55.1	55.2	55.8	56.5	57.5	58.6	58.6	59.6	60.5
60.7	60.8	61.3	61.5	61.9	62.3	62.5	62.7	62.7	63.4
63.7	63.7	63.7	63.8	63.9	64.2	64.3	64.7	64.8	64.8
64.9	65.0	65.0	66.5	66.6	66.9	67.3	68.3	68.3	68.7
68.9	69.6	70.3	70.5	71.0	71.1	71.4	72.0	73.0	73.4
73.5	74.7	75.4	75.5	75.8	75.9	77.5	77.6	77.9	78.2
78.6	79.0	80.3	80.5	81.5	81.8	82.0	82.7	83.4	84.2
85.0	85.0	85.8	85.9	86.2	86.3	86.5	86.8	87.0	87.4
88.2	88.4	89.7	91.2	91.4	91.9	92.0	92.4	92.7	93.4

   (a) From the temperature data given, complete a table using the headings

   Class
   Boundaries X f Xf $|X - m|$ $|X - m|f$ $(X - m)^2$ $(X - m)^2 f$

   (A method for determining class boundaries for grouped scores may be found on page 363
   of this chapter.)
   (b) Find the following:
      (1) The mean
      (2) The median
      (3) The standard deviation
   (c) Draw the appropriate histogram.
   (d) Draw the frequency polygon.
   (e) Draw the cumulative frequency polygon.

7. A programming class is divided into two sections and both sections take the same test.
   Section 1 with 35 students has a mean score of 70 and section 2 with 40 students has a mean
   score of 78. Find the mean of the entire class, using

$$m = \frac{m_1 N_1 + m_2 N_2}{N_1 + N_2}$$

8. A captain of a freighter finds that the mean of 30 boxes of produce is 60 pounds and the
   mean of the entire shipment of 65 boxes of produce is 71 pounds. Find the mean of the
   remaining boxes.

9. A company gives applicants an aptitude test before an interview. If the standard deviation
   for this test is 8 and the sum of the deviation squared is 5120, find the number of applicants.

10. A stockbroker reviews portfolios of several clients and finds that in 64 stocks, the following
   appreciations (Table 21.8) occurred in a particular year.

TABLE 21.8

Stock	Appreciation %	Frequency
A	1	1
B	2	6
C	3	15
D	4	20
E	5	15
F	6	6
G	7	1

(a) Find the mean appreciation and standard deviation.
(b) The BASIC program to draw the histogram for this problem follows. It can be modified to draw other histograms in this chapter and in Chapter 22.

```
100 'ID = hist.bas DRAW histogram
110 ' INPUT INTEGER VALUES ONLY
120 SCREEN 100
130 CLS
140 WINDOW (10,10) – (80,80)
150 LOCATE 18,64
160 PRINT "X"
170 LOCATE 3, 23
180 PRINT"FREQUENCY"
190 LINE (26,30) – (66,30)
200 LINE (30,30) – (30,70)
210 FOR I = 26 TO 62 STEP 4
220 LINE (I,29) – (I,31)
230 LINE (29,I+4) – (31,I+4)
240 NEXT I
250 'DIMENSION ARRAYS
260 DIM X(7),FREQ(7)
270 ' DATA TO BE GRAPHED
280 DATA 1,1,2,6,3,15,4,20,5,15,6,6,7,1
290 ' READ IN DATA
300 FOR I = 1 TO 7
310     READ X(I),FREQ(I)
320 NEXT I
330 'DRAW GRAPH
340 INCREMENT = 31
350 FOR I = 1 TO 7
360 Y = FREQ(I)*2 + 30
370 X = X(I) + INCREMENT
380 LINE (X,30) – (X+4,Y) , ,B
390 INCREMENT = INCREMENT + 3
400 NEXT I
```

```
410 LOCATE 7,36
420 PRINT "15"
430 LOCATE·7,46
440 PRINT "15"
450 LOCATE 13,32
460 PRINT "6"
470 LOCATE 13,51
480 PRINT "6"
490 LOCATE 3,41
500 PRINT "20"
510 LOCATE 17,28
520 PRINT "1"
530 LOCATE 17,55
540 PRINT "1"
550 LOCATE 4,18
560 PRINT "20"
570 LOCATE 11,18
580 PRINT "10"
590 END
```

22

Elements of Probability and Statistics

Every day provides risk and opportunity. Probability theory provides a numerical method for expressing risks or uncertainty in conclusions, predictions, and inferences. Over the recent years, statisticians have used probability theory for the following:

Retail stores stocking inventory shelves

Insurance companies computing mortality tables

Biologists studying laws of nature

Physicists predicting the behavior of electrons

Politicians planning a campaign

Sales managers, teachers, farmers, and many others, performing professional work

MEASURING SUCCESS AND FAILURE—A RATIO

Ratios for success and failure can be easily found in activities such as tossing coins and dice, or selecting a card from a deck of playing cards, and these are convenient models for the study of other phenomena occurring in business, nature, and science. Consider that in a toss of a properly balanced coin, only one of two outcomes is possible: a head or tail will turn up. Since these are the only two possibilities, we can state that if an event can happen in s number of ways and fail to happen in f number of ways the probability, or p, of success is

$$p = \frac{s}{s + f}$$

where $s + f$ = the total number of possible outcomes.

Success can be measured as a ratio, that is, the number of successes divided by the total number of possible outcomes. Similarly, there are six likely ways an honest die can land and the probability that any one of these six outcomes will occur is $\frac{1}{6}$.

In these examples, the outcomes or events that may occur are mutually exclusive. Only one event can occur at any given time. Letting $s + f = n$, or the total number of possible outcomes, we can write

Definition 22-1.   The probability that event A may occur in n equally likely and mutually exclusive ways and if s is considered a successful way, then

$$P(A) = \frac{s}{n}$$

When $s = n$, success is 1, or inevitable. When no success is possible, $s = 0$. We will discuss situations where s/n satisfies the relation

$$0 \leqslant \frac{s}{n} \leqslant 1$$

Note that the sum of the probabilities of an event A occurring and the same event not occurring is 1, where

$$P(A) = s/n \quad \text{and} \quad P(\text{NOT } A) = 1 - s/n$$

This can easily be shown when the model is a die. For example, the probability of getting a 5 in one toss of a die is 1/6 and the probability of not getting a 5 is 5/6. Then $1/6 = 1 - \frac{5}{6}$.

INDEPENDENT AND DEPENDENT EVENTS

Definition 22-2.   Two or more events are *independent* if the probability of an occurrence of one of them is not affected by the occurrence of any other events. Otherwise, the events are *dependent*, that is, conditional on a previous event.

Example 1

If a coin is tossed twice, the occurrences of a head or tail on either throw are independent events.

Example 2

If in a jar of 50 red marbles and 50 blue marbles, a blue marble is randomly drawn first without replacement, the probability of a red marble on the second draw is dependent on the first draw or $p = 50/99$. If the first marble were replaced, then the outcome of the second draw would not be dependent on the outcome of the first, or $p = 50/100$.

COMPUTATIONS WITH PROBABILITIES

Addition

Consider that A and B represent two mutually exclusive events. The probability of one or the other of these two events occurring is

$$P(A \text{ OR } B) \text{ and can be written as } P(A) + P(B)$$

Example 1

> Assume that a jar contained 50 blue, 40 red, and 10 yellow marbles, the probability that a red or blue marble would be randomly drawn is
>
> $$P(\text{red OR blue}) = P(\text{red}) + P(\text{blue}) = 40/100 + 50/100 = 9/10$$
>
> For finite events, computations like this can be expanded to
>
> $$P(A \text{ OR } B \text{ OR } C \text{ OR } D \ldots) = P(A) + P(B) + P(C) + P(D) + \ldots$$

Example 2

> Care must be taken when events are not mutually exclusive. For example, there are three odd numbers and three even numbers on a die. What is the probability that when tossed, an even number or a number less than 4 will appear?
>
> Adding these probabilities, $3/6 + 3/6 = 1$, which says that $s = n$, or that success is certain. This is not possible since a problem lies in counting the outcome of a 2 twice (an even number *and* a number less than 4). In cases like this, our computations should be: $P(E) + P(<4) - P(2)$, subtracting out the probability that $P(E)$ and $P(2)$ (or a 2) will occur on the same toss or $3/6 + 3/6 - 1/6 = \frac{5}{6}$.

In general, we can state that a problem with mutually exclusive events that involves the occurrence of the first event *or* the second event *or* the third event, and so on is a problem of the addition of the probabilities. Problems with independent events that involve the occurrence of the first event *and* the second event, *and* the third event and so on, are problems of multiplication of probabilities.

Multiplication

Consider two independent events, tossing a coin and tossing a die where the events will have no influence on each other. The combinations of all possible outcomes make up the set O where

$$O = \{(H, 1); (H, 2); (H, 3); (H, 4); (H, 5); (H, 6); (T, 1); (T, 2); (T, 3); (T, 4); (T, 5); (T, 6)\}$$

or 12 possible outcomes, each outcome having the probability of $\frac{1}{12}$. What is the probability of getting a head and a number greater than 4? There are two ordered pairs that satisfy this condition, $(H, 5)$ and $(H, 6)$. Let $N = $ a number greater than 4, then

$$P(H \text{ and } N) = 1/2 \times 2/6 = 2/12 \quad \text{or} \quad \frac{1}{6}$$

For finite events, computations for AND can be expanded to

$$P(A \text{ AND } B \text{ AND } C \text{ AND } D\ldots) = P(A) \times P(B) \times P(C) \times P(D) \times \ldots$$

Care must be taken when a second event is dependent on a first event. Consider the jar of 50 blue marbles, 40 red marbles, and 10 yellow marbles again. What is the probability of randomly drawing two blue marbles in succession? In this situation, the probabilities are

$$P(A \text{ AND } B) = P(A) \times P(B) = 50/100 \times 49/99 = 2450/9900 = 49/198$$

EXPECTATION

If a farmer plants 100 sunflower seeds each year and 51 germinate in the first year, the next year 47 germinate, in the third year 49 germinate, and in the fourth year 48 germinate, successful germination approaches an average of nearly 49 successes a year and can be described as an *expectation* or expected result.

Sometimes expectation is described in terms of *odds* in newspaper predictions about sports and even weather. However, *odds* are measured as

$$\frac{\text{Success}}{\text{Failure}} \quad \text{or} \quad \frac{s}{f} \quad \text{not as} \quad \frac{s}{s+f} \quad \text{for probability}$$

Note that the reciprocal of odds in favor, is the odds against an event occurring. Our discussion will be concerned with the mathematical expectation that is a product of a probability and a number that may be an amount or a number of trials.

Example 1

Using dice as a simple model, consider the expectation of obtaining a sum less than 4 in each of 180 trial throws of two die. For each throw there are 3 combinations of numbers that yield a total of less than 4. Thus $s = 3$ and $s + f = 36$ (or 36 possible combinations of numbers for each throw). The expected number of occurrences or expectations that this particular event will occur in 180 tries is $180 \times 3/36$ or 15 times. In this situation, expectation can be expressed as $e = np$, where n is the number of trials and p is the probability of an event occurring in a single trial.

An expectation is not a guarantee, it is only more likely to occur than not. (The event does not *need* to occur.)

Example 2

Instead of n number of trials, consider that in an honest game $1.00 will be paid each time two heads appear on a toss of two coins. The mathematical expectation is $1.00(1/4)$ or $0.25. If $1.00 were paid for two heads, $0.50 for one head, and nothing for two tails, the mathematical expectation is

$$\$1.00(1/4) + \$0.50(1/2) + 0(1/4) = \$0.50$$

If there are several probabilities and several amounts, then

$$e = n_1 P(A) + n_2 P(B) + \ldots$$

when all possible outcomes are considered, the sum of the probabilities equals 1. For example 2 this means $1/4 + 1/2 + 1/4 = 1$.

Example 3

Life insurance companies use mortality tables to determine the rates they are willing to pay. Mortality tables are basically experience tables made from data on population figures and deaths per a particular age group. Assume that at a given time, the number of 50-year-old people living is 703,125 and the number of deaths for 50-year-olds is 9040, then the probability of the deaths for this age group measured as a ratio is

$$\frac{9040}{703125} \quad \text{or} \quad .0129$$

In a community having one hundred 50-year-old residents, the number expected to die is $100(.0129) = 1.29$.

EXERCISES 22-1

1. If an event can happen in x ways and fail to happen in y ways, then the probability of success is expressed as _____.

2. If more than one event cannot occur in the same trial, the events are said to be
   _____.

3. When $P(A) = 1$, success is _____.

4. If a die is rolled once, what is the probability of a 2 or a 3?

5. If a die is rolled twice, what is the probability that the first roll yields a 3 or 4 and the second roll will not turn up a 1?

6. In a single roll of two die, what is the probability that the same number will appear on each die or that 11 will appear?

7. Using set O on page 374 of this chapter, find the probability for the following:
   (a) A head and an even number
   (b) A tail and a number less than 3
   (c) A head and a number greater than three or a head and a 2

8. What is the probability that both parents were born on a Monday?

9. In a bag of groceries there are five oranges and five grapefruit. If they are removed randomly, one at a time and without replacement, what is the probability that they will be removed alternatively beginning with an orange?

10. Let $P(A) = $ a king, $P(B) = $ a queen.
    In a deck of 52 playing cards, what is the probability of
    (a) $P(A) \times P(B)$ (without replacement)
    (b) $P(A) + P(B)$
    (c) $P(A) \times P(A)$ (with replacement)
    (d) $P(A) + P(\text{NOT } A)$

11. In a deck of 52 playing cards when a single card is drawn, find the probability for the following:
    (a) A heart or a queen
    (b) A heart and a queen

12. A door in a vacated office may be locked. If a real estate agent has six keys, one of which is the key to the lock, what is the probability of opening that door with one of those keys selected randomly?

13. Assume that for two parents the chances of their children being boys or girls are the same. What are the probabilities for the following:
    (a) Two boys in a family of four
    (b) A boy and a girl in a family of four

14. A door prize of $100 will be given to any one of 250 ticket holders. If a ticket costs $5.00, what is the mathematical expectation given in dollars and cents.

15. With the models we have been using, when all possible outcomes have been considered, what is the sum of the probabilities?

16. After reading the Farmer's Almanac, a farmer expects that his chances for good weather in the spring and summer are 60%. After planning to raise 1000 bushels of tomatoes and computing expenses, he figures a profit of $1.50 with good weather and a loss of 30 cents with bad weather (per bushel). What is his mathematical expectation?

17. A type of plant seed comes in two look-alike varieties. These look-alikes are genetically different. For every seed planted, one will blossom red, and three will appear with pink blossoms. A housewife plants one in each of two pots. Find the probability that
    (a) Both pots will produce red blossoms
    (b) One pot will contain a red blossom, the other a pink blossom
    (c) Neither pot will contain a red blossom

18. The probability that a woman will live another ten years is 3/5 and that her husband will live the same number of years longer is 1/2. What is the probability that they can spend the next ten years together?

19. A pocket contains 2 ten-dollar bills and 3 twenty-dollar bills. What is the mathematical expectation for drawing two bills, assuming the bills are not clipped together in any order? (Consider drawing 2 tens, or 2 twenties, or (a (ten *and* a twenty), or (a (twenty *and* a ten)).

20. The following is a hypothetical mortality table (Table 22.1). The last column gives numbers for the age at 10, 20, 30,... (not numbers for the years in between).

TABLE 22.1

Age	Living	Deaths
10	1,000,000	7,038
20	933,118	6,794
30	860,634	6,765
40	786,749	7,188
50	703,125	9,040
60	583,389	14,527
70	388,499	22,468
80	145,794	19,649
90	8,531	3,617

(a) What are the probabilities of a 10-year-old living to age 50?
(b) If alive at 20, what is the probability of living to 90?
(c) What is the probability of dying at 20?
(d) What is the probability of a 50-year-old living to 80?
(e) What is the probability of dying between 50 and 60?

THE BINOMIAL EXPANSION

We note that the outcomes for tossing a coin several times (or tossing several coins once) is

1 time is HT

2 times is HH HT TH TT

3 times is HHH HHT HTH THH HTT THT TTH TTT

The probabilities for these different events can be expressed in the binomial expansion of $(q + p)^n$, where $p =$ the probability of getting a head or $p = 1/2$, and $q =$ the probability of getting a tail or $q = 1/2$, and $n =$ the number of trials. Refer to Table 22.2.

TABLE 22.2

Tosses	Possible Results	Expansions
1	$H\ T$	$(q + p)^1 = q + p$
2	$HH\ HT\ TH\ TT$	$(q + p)^2 = q^2 + 2qp + p^2$
3	$HHH\ HHT\ HTH\ THH$	$(q + p)^3 = q^3 + 3q^2p + 3qp^2 + p^3$
	$HTT\ THT\ TTH\ TTT$	
$\vdots$	$\vdots$	$\vdots$ $\vdots$
n		$(q + p)^n = q^n + nq^{n-1}p + \ldots + p^n$

A simple method for displaying the coefficients of the binomial expansion is found in Pascal's triangle, a portion of which is given here:

$$
\begin{array}{ccccccccc}
 & & & & 1 & & 1 & & \\
 & & & 1 & & 2 & & 1 & \\
 & & 1 & & 3 & & 3 & & 1 \\
 & 1 & & 4 & & 6 & & 4 & & 1 \\
1 & & 5 & & 10 & & 10 & & 5 & & 1
\end{array}
$$

After the first row, elements in succeeding rows are obtained by adding the two elements above in the previous row. For example, the coefficients 4, 6, 4 in the fourth row are obtained as follows: $1 + 3 = 4$, $3 + 3 = 6$, and $3 + 1 = 4$. Note that row 4 contains the coefficients for $(q + p)^4$ and row 5 contains the coefficients for the expression $(q + p)^5$, and

$$(q + p)^5 = q^5 + 5q^4p + 10q^3p^2 + 10q^2p^3 + 5qp^4 + p^5$$

Before reviewing the following examples that use the binomial expansion, let:

> n, an exponent on $(q + p)$ = the number of trials
>
> the exponents on q and p in the binomial expansion = the number of failures or successes
>
> the coefficient on a term in the binomial expansion = the number of ways an event may occur

We can represent 2 trials or tosses of a coin as $(q + p)^2$. Then in

$$(q + p)^2 = q^2 + 2qp + p^2$$

we expect that 1 tail and 1 head will occur 2 ways or $2qp$. Refer to Table 22.2 and note that there are 2 ways to get 1 tail and 1 head in 2 tosses of a coin.

Now if $p = 1/2 = q$ then the probability for this particular outcome is

$$2(1/2)(1/2) = 2/4$$

As an exercise find the sum of the terms for $(q + p)^3$ where $p = 1/2 = q$.

Example 1

> Find the probability of getting a 4 exactly twice in four throws of a die. The probability of getting a 4 in 1 trial is 1/6. Let 4, the number of trials be the exponent in $(q + p)^4$. Then in $(q + p)^4 = q^4 + 4q^3p + 6q^2p^2 + 4qp^3 + p^4$, we need the term that includes p^2, or the term for two successes. Thus
>
> $$p = 6(5/6)^2(1/6)^2$$
> $$= 150/1296$$

Example 2

> If 5% of a company's flashlights are defective, what is the probability that exactly 2 in a box of 5 will be defective?
>
> In this case, $p = 1/20$ and $q = 19/20$, and we need the term in $(q + p)^5$ that includes the term p^2 or $10q^3p^2$. Thus
>
> $$p = 10(19/20)^3(1/20)^2 = .0214$$

If the problem were stated as "at least 2 in a box of 5 were defective," we would need to add the terms containing p^2, p^3, p^4, p^5.

The Binomial Distribution

That successive terms of the binomial expansion can provide the probabilities for successes in n trials can also be illustrated by obtaining a frequency distribution from a binomial expansion. To demonstrate this, we can construct a hypothetical example of a frequency table and histogram for seven coins tossed 128 times. (128 is used to simplify results.)

Let p = probability of success or a head and q = the probability of failure or a tail and $p = q = 1/2$. Given

$$(q + p)^7 = q^7 + 7q^6p + 21q^5p^2 + 35q^4p^3 + 35q^3p^4 + 21q^2p^5 + 7qp^6 + p^7$$

TABLE 22.3

X	Expected f for 128 Times	Xf
0	1	0
1	7	7
2	21	42
3	35	105
4	35	140
5	21	105
6	7	42
7	1	7
Total	128	448

When $p = q = 1/2$, the histogram will appear in symmetrical form. The first column, X, in Table 22.3 contains the number of heads, 0, 1, 2, 3, 4, 5, 6, 7 in 128 sample trials. The second column, f, contains the expected frequencies for $0, 1, 2, \ldots , 7$ heads. Note that in our hypothetical example $1/128 + 7/128 + \ldots + 1/128 = 1$. The last column contains the products for X and f.

A frequency distribution obtained by using the binomial expansion is referred to as a binomial distribution.

In Figure 22.1, the boundaries on the x-axis are set at midpoints .5, 1.5, 2.5, and so on, and each rectangle has a width of 1. The area of a rectangle is equal to its height × base and is a measure of the frequency of its class.

The mean for a binomial distribution can be computed as m = number of trials times the probability of success or $m = np = 7(1/2) = 3.5$. Using the formula for the mean for grouped scores in Chapter 21, we can divide $448/128 = 3.5$. Note that the values 448 and 128 are found in Table 22.3.

The standard deviation for a binomial distribution can be computed as $\sigma = \sqrt{npq}$. For our example, $\sigma = \sqrt{7(1/2)(1/2)} = 1.32$.

As an exercise, use the standard deviation formula for grouped scores in Chapter 21 and determine whether the results are the same.

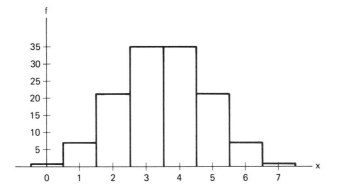

Figure 22.1

THE NORMAL DISTRIBUTION

Calculations with binomial expansions containing a larger number of trials are drudgery. A faster method is found in the *normal distribution*, a continuous probability distribution method.

Using the previous figure, connect the midpoints of the rectangles in Figure 22.2 and note that the curve approaches the *x*-axis but never touches it.

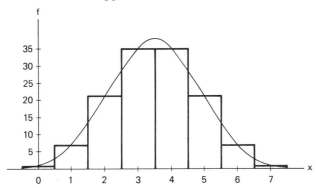

Figure 22.2

Since the sum of the probabilities is 1, we describe the total area under the curve as 1. As *n* trials increases in a binomial distribution for *S* samples, a line connecting midpoints on the vertical bars in the histogram approaches a normal or bell-shaped curve. The proof of this involves mathematical formulas outside the scope of this book. The curve is symmetrical about the vertical line at the mean, and this vertical line touches the highest point on the curve in Figure 22.3.

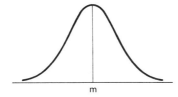

Figure 22.3

Areas Under the Normal Curve

In statistics, the normal distribution is an important method used to represent or closely approximate many practical problems. We will examine some areas under the normal curve in order to learn more about the techniques used to make predictions and assist in decision making and in determining such things as the quality of manufactured products.

The X scale is needed to measure, in units, a particular distribution we wish to represent—in our example, the tosses of a coin. Note that multiples of the standard deviation are marked off on the X scale. In order to measure $X - m$ in terms of the standard deviation, we create a new horizontal scale, the Z scale and use a new variable z. (See Figure 22.4.)

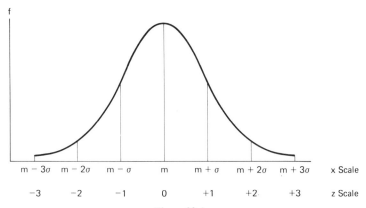

Figure 22.4

$$z = \frac{X - m}{\sigma}$$

Z equals the difference between a unit of X and the mean, divided by the standard deviation. Refer to Appendix B, Areas Under the Normal Curve, and find that the area under the curve is .3413 when $z = 1.0$. Further, we can state that from $z = -1$ to $z = +1$, or from $X = m - \sigma$ to $X = m + \sigma$ the area = .6826. In Figure 22.5(a), the probabilities indicated by the shaded area are found 1 standard deviation on each side of the mean, and are therefore equal to 2(.3413), or 68.26%. In Figure 22.5(b), the probabilities found within 2 standard deviations of the mean are .4772 + .4772 = 95.44%. In Figure 22.5(c), the total of the probabilities within 3 standard deviations of the mean are .9973, or 99.73%.

On the Z scale, the standard deviations to the left of the mean are expressed in minus terms, and those to the right in plus terms. It is also possible to find points on the Z scale that lie between standard deviations.

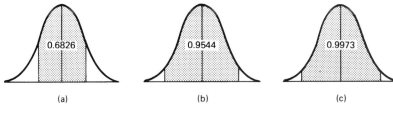

Figure 22.5

Example 1

To find the area for $z = 0$ to 1.55 refer to Appendix B and look up 1.5 under Z, then find the column headed .05 to locate .4394. Thus, $1.5 + .05$ equals 1.55 and the corresponding area is .4394.

Example 2

Find the area under the normal curve to the left of -1.72.

The table in Appendix B gives the area from $z = 0$, to $z = 1.72$ as .4573, and since the normal curve is symmetrical, the area for -1.72 is the same as that for $+1.72$. However, as the sketch in Figure 22.6 shows, we need only the area for $z \leqslant -1.72$. This means we must subtract:

$$\begin{array}{r} .5000 \\ -.4573 \\ \hline \text{Area} = \quad .0427 \end{array}$$

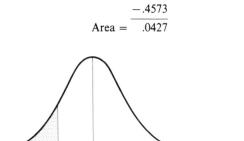

Figure 22.6

We subtract from .5000 because the area to the left of $z = 0$ is .5, or one half the total area of 1.

Example 3

Find the area under the normal curve from $z = -1.8$ to $z = 1.95$, points that fall within standard deviations.

$$\text{Area} = .4641 + .4744 = .9385$$

Example 4

Find the probability for 2 to 5 heads in a toss of 7 coins or that X is from 2 to 5 inclusive. Using midpoints in Figure 22.2, the area from $X = 1.5$ to 5.5 represents the expected number of occurrences. We need to find the z values for these corresponding X values. We have already found that

$$m = np = 7(1/2) = 3.5$$

and

$$\sigma = \sqrt{7(1/2)(1/2)} = 1.32$$

Then,   for $X = 1.5$, $z = (1.5 - 3.5)/1.32 = -1.52$ and   for $X = 5.5$, $z = (5.5 - 3.5)/1.32 = 1.52$

To find the area from $z = -1.52$ to 1.52, look up the area in the table (in Appendix B) from $z = 0$ to $z = 1.52$. Because of the symmetry of the curve, this is the same area for $z = -1.52$, and we can multiply by 2 to find the probability:

$$p = 2(.4357) = .8714$$

Example 5

Find a value for z when the area under the curve is .4953. Look up .4953 as an area under the curve, the z value is $+$ or $-$ 2.6.

Example 6

A nationwide civil service exam has an acceptable range of scores for applicants. Only 60% of the best scores will assure an interview. Assume that after the exam has been given, the mean is 410 and the standard deviation is 32, what is the lowest acceptable score?

We need to find a value for X to the left of the mean. This means taking 50% of the best scores from the right of the mean plus up to 10% of the scores to the left of the mean. The value .1 is not found as an area in the table in Appendix B, but looking in the table we find .0987 as a reasonable approximation and its corresponding z value is .25. Since we are now on the left-hand side of the mean and looking for the lowest acceptable score, $z = -.25$. We can now find a value for X. Letting $m = 410$, $\sigma = 32$, solve for the value of X as follows:

$$z = (X - m)/\sigma$$

and

$$-.25 = (X - 410)/32$$
$$X - 410 = (-.25)(32)$$
$$X = 410 + (-.25)(32)$$
$$X = 402, \qquad \text{the lowest acceptable score}$$

EXERCISES 22-2

1. (a) Find the fourth term in $(q + p)^6$
   (b) Given the BASIC code

$$40 \text{ PROB} = 21 \cdot P\hat{\ }5 \cdot Q\hat{\ }2$$

Where $P = Q = 1/2$, find the value for the variable PROB and identify the term in the binomial expansion.

2. Find the probability of getting a head exactly three times in six tosses of a coin.

3. What is the probability of getting 65 or more heads in 100 tosses of a coin?
   (a) Find $m =$ _____.
   (b) $\sigma =$ _____.
   (c) Find z by taking a midpoint between 64 and 65 on the X scale. $z =$ _____.
   (d) The area under the normal curve for 65 or more heads in 100 tosses of the coin is
       _____.

4. (a) Find the probability of getting two 5s in five throws of a die.
   (b) Find the probability of getting 0, or 1, or 2 fives in five throws of a die.

5. An instructor finds that in a certain course the failure rate is 5%. What is the probability that in five randomly selected student records, only one will contain a student that failed this course? (Let $p = \frac{1}{20}$, $q = \frac{19}{20}$, $n = 5$.)

6. A manufacturer of computer chips finds that 4% of these products are defective. What is the expectation that in a random sample of 4 that:
   (a) Exactly two will be defective
   (b) None will be defective
   (c) At least two will be defective

7. A hospital's records show that 10% of the cases of a certain disease are fatal. If six of its patients are suffering from this disease, what is the probability that
   (a) All patients will recover
   (b) Only three will die
   (c) At most two will die

8. Find the area under the normal curve for the following:
   (a) from $z = -1.5$ to $z = 1.95$.
   (b) from $z = 0$ to $z = 2.3$
   (c) from $z = -1.32$ to $z = -2.11$
   (d) from $z = -1.44$ to $z = 0$
   (e) for $z \geqslant 1.47$
   (f) for $z \leqslant -1.47$
   (g) from $z = 1.3$ to $z = 2.34$

9. Find X when $\sigma = 35$, $z = -.75$, $m = 300$.

10. Find σ, when $m = 100$, $z = 1.0$, $X = 130$.

11. A college professor using the normal curve, assigns quiz grades under the following rules:

    A for the top 6.68% of the grades, F for the lowest 8.08%,
    and estimates grades B = 27.78%, C = 31.08%, and D = 26.38%.

    If the grade A can be expressed as equal to or greater than $m + 1.50\sigma$, find values for grades B, C, D, and F in a similar manner.

12. A battery is advertised as having an average lifetime of 100 hours when a portable radio is played at a normal volume. Assuming that this lifetime follows the normal distribution with a standard deviation of 10 hours, what percent of batteries will fall between 100 and 110 lifetime hours?

13. Refer to Table 22.1. The probability for a person dying at 40 years is .01 (rounded to the nearest hundredths). In a company that has 10,000 life insurance policy holders at age 40, what is the probability that 90 claims will be made within the year? Use the normal curve to estimate.

14. Compare these two normal, or bell-shaped, curves in Figure 22.7. Without doing any arithmetic, answer the following:
 (a) Are the means the same?
 (b) Must the standard deviations be the same?

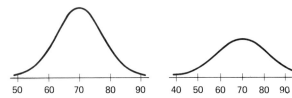

Figure 22.7

15. The following BASIC program can, with simple modifications, be converted to a Fortran program. The program creates a binomial expansion for 1 to 9 trials and computes values for terms in the expansion. Values for q and p must be entered as decimal fractions. For example, 1/6 should be entered as .1666667 and 5/6 as .8333333. Both q and p should have the same precision and when added together they must $= 1$. Write and code the algorithm in statement number 380 to find the coefficients on q and p in any binomial expansion. (The student can modify this program to process more than 9 trials.)

```
10 'ID = binom.bas
20 DIM PROB(9)
30 LPRINT CHR$(27)"T";
40 LPRINT
50 INPUT"ENTER VALUES FOR Q AND P ",Q,P
60 LPRINT"Q = ",Q
70 LPRINT"P = ",P
80 TEST = Q + P
90 IF TEST < > 1 THEN PRINT "Q + P NOT = 1" ELSE GOTO 110
100 GOTO 50
110 INPUT"ENTER VALUES FOR NUMBER OF TRIALS ",T
120 LPRINT"TRIALS = ",T
130 C = 1
140 N = T
150 M = N
160 FOR I = 0 TO N
170 PN = I
180 QN = M − I
190 IF QN = 0 THEN 310
200 IF PN = 0 THEN 240
210 C$ = STR$(C)
220 LPRINT RIGHT$(C$,3);
230 PROB(I) = C•Q^QN•P^PN
240 LPRINT "q";
```

```
250 IF PN = 0 THEN PROB(I) = Q^QN*P^PN
260 QN$ = STR$(QN)
270 QN$ = RIGHT$(QN$,1)
280 LPRINT CHR$(27)"S0" QN$;
290 LPRINT CHR$(27)"T";
300 IF PN = 0 THEN 370
310 LPRINT "p";
320 IF QN = 0 THEN PROB(I) = Q^QN*P^PN
330 PN$ = STR$(PN)
340 PN$ = RIGHT$(PN$,1)
350 LPRINT CHR$(27)"S0"PN$;
360 IF QN = 0 THEN 390
370 LPRINT CHR$(27)"T + ";
380 C = _____
390 NEXT I
400 LPRINT CHR$(27)"T"
410 FOR I = 0 TO T
420 LPRINT PROB(I)
430 NEXT I
435 LPRINT
440 PRINT"ENTER TERM IN THE BINOMIAL EXPANSION THAT YOU WANT COMPUTED"
450 PRINT"i.e., 1 for 1st term, 2 for 2nd term etc."
460 INPUT TERM
470 LPRINT"TERM = ",TERM
480 IF TERM > (T +1) OR TERM < 0 THEN PRINT "OUT OF ARRAY BOUNDS" ELSE 500
490 GOTO 440
500 RESULT = RESULT + PROB(TERM−1)
510 INPUT"DO YOU WANT TO ENTER ANOTHER TERM?(Y/N)",A$
520 IF A$ = "Y" THEN 460 ELSE 530
530 PRINT RESULT
540 LPRINT RESULT
550 END
```

Appendix A

Common Logarithms

x	0	1	2	3	4	5	6	7	8	9
1.0	.0000	.0043	.0086	.0128	.0170	.0212	.0253	.0294	.0334	.0374
1.1	.0414	.0453	.0492	.0531	.0569	.0607	.0645	.0682	.0719	.0755
1.2	.0792	.0828	.0864	.0899	.0934	.0969	.1004	.1038	.1072	.1106
1.3	.1139	.1173	.1206	.1239	.1271	.1303	.1335	.1367	.1399	.1430
1.4	.1461	.1492	.1523	.1553	.1584	.1614	.1644	.1673	.1703	.1732
1.5	.1761	.1790	.1818	.1847	.1875	.1903	.1931	.1959	.1987	.2014
1.6	.2041	.2068	.2095	.2122	.2148	.2175	.2201	.2227	.2253	.2279
1.7	.2304	.2330	.2355	.2380	.2405	.2430	.2455	.2480	.2504	.2529
1.8	.2553	.2577	.2601	.2625	.2648	.2672	.2695	.2718	.2742	.2765
1.9	.2788	.2810	.2833	.2856	.2878	.2900	.2923	.2945	.2967	.2989
2.0	.3010	.3032	.3054	.3075	.3096	.3118	.3139	.3160	.3181	.3201
2.1	.3222	.3243	.3263	.3284	.3304	.3324	.3345	.3365	.3385	.3404
2.2	.3424	.3444	.3464	.3483	.3502	.3522	.3541	.3560	.3579	.3598
2.3	.3617	.3636	.3655	.3674	.3692	.3711	.3729	.3747	.3766	.3784
2.4	.3802	.3820	.3838	.3856	.3874	.3892	.3909	.3927	.3945	.3962
2.5	.3979	.3997	.4014	.4031	.4048	.4065	.4082	.4099	.4116	.4133
2.6	.4150	.4166	.4183	.4200	.4216	.4232	.4249	.4265	.4281	.4298
2.7	.4314	.4330	.4346	.4362	.4378	.4393	.4409	.4425	.4440	.4456
2.8	.4472	.4487	.4502	.4518	.4533	.4548	.4564	.4579	.4594	.4609
2.9	.4624	.4639	.4654	.4669	.4683	.4698	.4713	.4728	.4742	.4757
3.0	.4771	.4786	.4800	.4814	.4829	.4843	.4857	.4871	.4886	.4900
3.1	.4914	.4928	.4942	.4955	.4969	.4983	.4997	.5011	.5024	.5038
3.2	5051	.5065	.5079	.5092	.5105	.5119	.5132	.5145	.5159	.5172
3.3	5185	.5198	.5211	.5224	.5237	.5250	.5263	.5276	.5289	.5302
3.4	.5315	.5328	.5340	.5353	.5366	.5378	.5391	.5403	.5416	.5428

x	0	1	2	3	4	5	6	7	8	9
3.5	.5441	.5453	.5465	.5478	.5490	.5502	.5514	.5527	.5539	.5551
3.6	.5563	.5575	.5587	.5599	.5611	.5623	.5635	.5647	.5658	.5670
3.7	.5682	.5694	.5705	.5717	.5729	.5740	.5752	.5763	.5775	.5786
3.8	.5798	.5809	.5821	.5832	.5843	.5855	.5866	.5877	.5888	.5899
3.9	.5911	.5922	.5933	.5944	.5955	.5966	.5977	.5988	.5999	.6010
4.0	.6021	.6031	.6042	.6053	.6064	.6075	.6085	.6096	.6107	.6117
4.1	.6128	.6138	.6149	.6160	.6170	.6180	.6191	.6201	.6212	.6222
4.2	.6232	.6243	.6253	.6263	.6274	.6284	.6294	.6304	.6314	.6325
4.3	.6335	.6345	.6355	.6365	.6375	.6385	.6395	.6405	.6415	.6425
4.4	.6435	.6444	.6454	.6464	.6474	.6484	.6493	.6503	.6513	.6522
4.5	.6532	.6542	.6551	.6561	.6571	.6580	.6590	.6599	.6609	.6618
4.6	.6628	.6637	.6646	.6656	.6665	.6675	.6684	.6693	.6702	.6712
4.7	.6721	.6730	.6739	.6749	.6758	.6767	.6776	.6785	.6794	.6803
4.8	.6812	.6821	.6830	.6839	.6848	.6857	.6866	.6875	.6884	.6893
4.9	.6902	.6911	.6920	.6928	.6937	.6946	.6955	.6964	.6972	.6981
5.0	.6990	.6998	.7007	.7016	.7024	.7033	.7042	.7050	.7059	.7067
5.1	.7076	.7084	.7093	.7101	.7110	.7118	.7126	.7135	.7143	.7152
5.2	.7160	.7168	.7177	.7185	.7193	.7202	.7210	.7218	.7226	.7235
5.3	.7243	.7251	.7259	.7267	.7275	.7284	.7292	.7300	.7308	.7316
5.4	.7324	.7332	.7340	.7348	.7356	.7364	.7372	.7380	.7388	.7396
5.5	.7404	.7412	.7419	.7427	.7435	.7443	.7451	.7459	.7466	.7474
5.6	7482	.7490	.7497	.7505	.7513	.7520	.7528	.7536	.7543	.7551
5.7	.7559	.7566	.7574	.7582	.7589	.7597	.7604	.7612	.7619	.7627
5.8	.7634	.7642	.7649	.7657	.7664	.7672	.7679	.7686	.7694	.7701
5.9	.7709	.7716	.7723	.7731	.7738	.7745	.7752	.7760	.7767	.7774
6.0	.7782	.7789	.7796	.7803	.7810	.7818	.7825	.7832	.7839	.7846
6.1	.7853	.7860	.7868	.7875	.7882	.7889	.7896	.7903	.7910	.7917
6.2	.7924	.7931	.7938	.7945	.7952	.7959	.7966	.7973	.7980	.7987
6.3	.7993	.8000	.8007	.8014	.8021	.8028	.8035	.8041	.8048	.8055
6.4	.8062	.8069	.8075	.8082	.8089	.8096	.8102	.8109	.8116	.8122
6.5	.8129	.8136	.8142	.8149	.8156	.8162	.8169	.8176	.8182	.8189
6.6	.8195	.8202	.8209	.8215	.8222	.8228	.8235	.8241	.8248	.8254
6.7	.8261	.8267	.8274	.8280	.8287	.8293	.8299	.8306	.8312	.8319
6.8	.8325	.8331	.8338	.8344	.8351	.8357	.8363	.8370	.8376	.8382
6.9	.8388	.8395	.8401	.8407	.8414	.8420	.8426	.8432	.8439	.8445
7.0	.8451	.8457	.8463	.8470	.8476	.8482	.8488	.8494	.8500	.8506
7.1	.8513	.8519	.8525	.8531	.8537	.8543	.8549	.8555	.8561	.8567
7.2	.8573	.8579	.8585	.8591	.8597	.8603	.8609	.8615	.8621	.8627
7.3	.8633	.8639	.8645	.8651	.8657	.8663	.8669	.8675	.8681	.8686
7.4	.8692	.8698	.8704	.8710	.8716	.8722	.8727	.8733	.8739	.8745
7.5	.8751	.8756	.8762	.8768	.8774	.8779	.8785	.8791	.8797	.8802
7.6	.8808	.8814	.8820	.8825	.8831	.8837	.8842	.8848	.8854	.8859
7.7	.8865	.8871	.8876	.8882	.8887	.8893	.8899	.8904	.8910	.8915
7.8	.8921	.8927	.8932	.8938	.8943	.8949	.8954	.8960	.8965	.8971
7.9	.8976	.8982	.8987	.8993	.8998	.9004	.9009	.9015	.9020	.9025
8.0	.9031	.9036	.9042	.9047	.9053	.9058	.9063	.9069	.9074	.9079

x	0	1	2	3	4	5	6	7	8	9
8.1	.9085	.9090	.9096	.9101	.9106	.9112	.9117	.9122	.9128	.9133
8.2	.9138	.9143	.9149	.9154	.9159	.9165	.9170	.9175	.9180	.9186
8.3	.9191	.9196	.9201	.9206	.9212	.9217	.9222	.9227	.9232	.9238
8.4	.9243	.9248	.9253	.9258	.9263	.9269	.9274	.9279	.9284	.9289
8.5	.9294	.9299	.9304	.9309	.9315	.9320	.9325	.9330	.9335	.9340
8.6	.9345	.9350	.9355	.9360	.9365	.9370	.9375	.9380	.9385	.9390
8.7	.9395	.9400	.9405	.9410	.9415	.9420	.9425	.9430	.9435	.9440
8.8	.9445	.9450	.9455	.9460	.9465	.9469	.9474	.9479	.9484	.9489
8.9	.9494	.9499	.9504	.9509	.9513	.9518	.9523	.9528	.9533	.9538
9.0	.9542	.9547	.9552	.9557	.9562	.9566	.9571	.9576	.9581	.9586
9.1	.9590	.9595	.9600	.9605	.9609	.9614	.9619	.9624	.9628	.9633
9.2	.9638	.9643	.9647	.9652	.9657	.9661	.9666	.9671	.9675	.9680
9.3	.9685	.9689	.9694	.9699	.9703	.9708	.9713	.9717	.9722	.9727
9.4	.9731	.9736	.9741	.9745	.9750	.9754	.9759	.9763	.9768	.9773
9.5	.9777	.9782	.9786	.9791	.9795	.9800	.9805	.9809	.9814	.9818
9.6	.9823	.9827	.9832	.9836	.9841	.9845	.9850	.9854	.9859	.9863
9.7	.9868	.9872	.9877	.9881	.9886	.9890	.9894	.9899	.9903	.9908
9.8	.9912	.9917	.9921	.9926	.9930	.9934	.9939	.9943	.9948	.9952
9.9	.9956	.9961	.9965	.9969	.9974	.9978	.9983	.9987	.9991	.9996

Appendix B

AREAS UNDER THE NORMAL CURVE BETWEEN THE ORDINATE AT THE MEAN
AND THE ORDINATE AT Z
(expressed as proportions of the total area under the curve)

Z	.00	.01	.02	.03	.04	.05	.06	.07	.08	.09
0.0	.0000	.0040	.0080	.0120	.0159	.0199	.0239	.0279	.0319	.0359
0.1	.0398	.0438	.0478	.0517	.0557	.0596	.0636	.0675	.0714	.0753
0.2	.0793	.0832	.0871	.0910	.0948	.0987	.1026	.1064	.1103	.1141
0.3	.1179	.1217	.1255	.1293	.1331	.1368	.1406	.1443	.1480	.1517
0.4	.1554	.1591	.1628	.1664	.1700	.1736	.1772	.1808	.1844	.1879
0.5	.1915	.1950	.1985	.2019	.2054	.2088	.2123	.2157	.2190	.2224
0.6	.2257	.2291	.2324	.2357	.2389	.2422	.2454	.2486	.2518	.2549
0.7	.2580	.2612	.2642	.2673	.2704	.2734	.2764	.2794	.2823	.2852
0.8	.2881	.2910	.2939	.2967	.2995	.3023	.3051	.3078	.3106	.3133
0.9	.3159	.3186	.3212	.3238	.3264	.3289	.3315	.3340	.3365	.3389
1.0	.3413	.3438	.3461	.3485	.3508	.3531	.3554	.3577	.3599	.3621
1.1	.3643	.3665	.3686	.3718	.3729	.3749	.3770	.3790	.3810	.3830
1.2	.3849	.3869	.3888	.3907	.3925	.3944	.3962	.3980	.3997	.4015
1.3	.4032	.4049	.4066	.4083	.4099	.4115	.4131	.4147	.4162	.4177
1.4	.4192	.4207	.4222	.4236	.4251	.4265	.4279	.4292	.4306	.4319
1.5	.4332	.4345	.4357	.4370	.4382	.4394	.4406	.4418	.4430	.4441
1.6	.4452	.4463	.4474	.4485	.4495	.4505	.4515	.4525	.4535	.4545
1.7	.4554	.4564	.4573	.4582	.4591	.4599	.4608	.4616	.4625	.4633
1.8	.4641	.4649	.4656	.4664	.4671	.4678	.4686	.4693	.4699	.4706
1.9	.4713	.4719	.4726	.4732	.4738	.4744	.4750	.4758	.4762	.4767
2.0	.4772	.4778	.4783	.4788	.4793	.4798	.4803	.4808	.4812	.4817
2.1	.4821	.4826	.4830	.4834	.4838	.4842	.4846	.4850	.4854	.4857
2.2	.4861	.4865	.4868	.4871	.4875	.4878	.4881	.4884	.4887	.4890
2.3	.4893	.4896	.4898	.4901	.4904	.4906	.4909	.4911	.4913	.4916
2.4	.4918	.4920	.4922	.4925	.4927	.4929	.4931	.4932	.4934	.4936
2.5	.4938	.4940	.4941	.4943	.4945	.4946	.4948	.4949	.4951	.4952
2.6	.4953	.4955	.4956	.4957	.4959	.4960	.4961	.4962	.4963	.4964
2.7	.4965	.4966	.4967	.4968	.4969	.4970	.4971	.4972	.4973	.4974
2.8	.4974	.4975	.4976	.4977	.4977	.4978	.4979	.4980	.4980	.4981
2.9	.4981	.4982	.4983	.4984	.4984	.4984	.4985	.4985	.4986	.4986
3.0	.49865	.4987	.4987	.4988	.4988	.4989	.4989	.4989	.4990	.4990

Answers to Exercises

EXERCISES 1-1

1. (a) $\{3, 4, 5, 6, 7, 8\}$ (d) $\{1, 2, 3\}$
   (b) $\{\ldots, -1, 0, 1, 2, 3\}$ (e) $\{0, 1, 2, 3, \ldots\}$
   (c) $\{-19, -18, -17, -16\}$ (f) $\{8, 9, 10, 11, \ldots\}$

2. (a) $\{3, 6\}$ (c) $\{3, -4, 6, -8\}$
   (b) $\{3, \sqrt{2}, -4, 6, \frac{1}{2}, -8, \pi\}$ (d) $\{3, -4, 6, \frac{1}{2}, -8\}$

3. (a) $\{n | n \in R\}$ (d) $\{n | n \geqslant 0, n \in Q\}$
   (b) $\{n | n > 6, n \in N\}$ (e) $\{n | n < 0, n \in J\}$
   (c) $\{n | \frac{1}{4} < n < \frac{5}{2}, n \in Q\}$

EXERCISES 1-2

1. Yes   2. Yes   3. Yes   4. Yes   5. No   6. No   7. No   8. No   9. Yes

EXERCISES 1-3

1. (a)

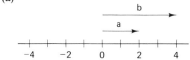

(b)

(c)

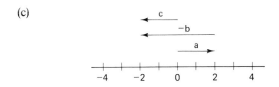

2. (a)

(b)

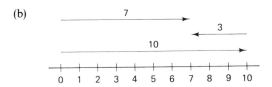

(c)

(d)

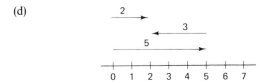

(e)

3. (a) $|7| = 7$ (b) $|\frac{3}{7}| = \frac{3}{7}$ (c) $|-.73| = .73$ (d) $|0| = 0$ (e) $|x - 2| = x - 2$

4. (a) $x > y$ (b) $x < 0 < y$ (c) $y \geqslant x$ (d) $x \neq y$

EXERCISES 1-4

1. constant   2. a letter   3. an expression   4. a term   5. a nonnegative

6. (a) 1   (b) 3   (c) -4 (d) -5

7. (a) DISCOUNT = PRICE × .10

(b) Finds the number of days in four years.

(c) TIME = MINUTES × DISTANCE ÷ MPH

EXERCISES 2-1

1. $$143 = 1(10)^2 + 4(10) + 3$$
   $$+23 = 2(10) + 3$$
   $$\overline{166 = 1(10)^2 + 6(10) + 6}$$

2. $$273 = 2(10)^2 + 7(10) + 3$$
   $$+419 = 4(10)^2 + 1(10) + 9$$
   $$\overline{692 = 6(10)^2 + 8(10) + 12}$$
   $$ = 6(10)^2 + 9(10) + 2$$

3. $$672 = 6(10)^2 + 7(10) + 2$$
   $$+981 = 9(10)^2 + 8(10) + 1$$
   $$\overline{1653 = 15(10)^2 + 15(10) + 3}$$
   $$ = 1(10)^3 + 6(10)^2 + 5(10) + 3$$

4. $$275 = 2(10)^2 + 7(10) + 5$$
   $$-63 = - (6(10) + 3)$$
   $$\overline{212 = 2(10)^2 + 1(10) + 2}$$

5. $$281 = 2(10)^2 + 7(10) + 11$$
   $$-102 = -(1(10)^2 + 0(10) + 2)$$
   $$\overline{179 = 1(10)^2 + 7(10) + 9}$$

6. $$543 = 4(10)^2 + 13(10) + 13$$
   $$-258 = -(2(10)^2 + 5(10) + 8)$$
   $$\overline{285 = 2(10)^2 + 8(10) + 5}$$

7. $$58 = 5(10) + 8$$
   $$\times 16 = \times 1(10) + 6$$
   $$\overline{348 = 30(10) + 48} = 3(10)^2 + 4(10) + 8$$
   $$58 = 5(10)^2 + 8(10) = 5(10)^2 + 8(10)$$
   $$\overline{928} = 8(10)^2 + 12(10) + 8$$
   $$ = 9(10)^2 + 2(10) + 8$$

8. $$249 = 2(10)^2 + 4(10) + 9$$
   $$\times 65 = \times 6(10) + 5$$
   $$\overline{1245 = 10(10)^2 + 20(10) + 45}$$
   $$1494 = 12(10)^3 + 24(10)^2 + 54(10)$$
   $$\overline{16185} \overline{= 12(10)^3 + 34(10)^2 + 74(10) + 45}$$
   $$ = 1(10)^4 + 6(10)^3 + 1(10)^2 + 8(10) + 5$$

9. $\quad$ 428 $=$ $\qquad$ $4(10)^2 + 2(10) + 8$
$\quad \times 101 =$ $\qquad$ $\times\ 1(10)^2 + 0(10) + 1$
$\quad \overline{428\ =}$ $\qquad$ $\overline{4(10)^2 + 2(10) + 8}$
$\quad\ 000\ =$ $\qquad$ $0(10)^3 +\ \ 0(10)^2 + 0(10)$
$\quad\ 428\ = 4(10)^4 + 2(10)^3 +\ \ 8(10)^2$
$\quad \overline{43228}\ \ \overline{4(10)^4 + 2(10)^3 + 12(10)^2 + 2(10) + 8}$
$\qquad\quad = 4(10)^4 + 3(10)^3 +\ \ 2(10)^2 + 2(10) + 8$

10. $\qquad$ 13 $\qquad\qquad\qquad\qquad$ $1(10) + 3$
$\quad 13\overline{)169} = 1(10)^1 + 3\overline{)1(10)^2 + 6(10) + 9}$
$\qquad\qquad\qquad\qquad\quad\ \underline{1(10)^2 + 3(10)}$
$\qquad\qquad\qquad\qquad\qquad\qquad 3(10) + 9$
$\qquad\qquad\qquad\qquad\qquad\qquad \underline{3(10) + 9}$

11. $\qquad$ 45 $\qquad\qquad\qquad\qquad$ $4(10) + 5$
$\quad 19\overline{)855} = 1(10)^1 + 9\overline{)8(10)^2 + 5(10) + 5}$
$\qquad\qquad\qquad\qquad\quad\ \underline{7(10)^2 + 6(10)}$
$\qquad\qquad\qquad\qquad\qquad\qquad 9(10) + 5$
$\qquad\qquad\qquad\qquad\qquad\qquad \underline{9(10) + 5}$

12. $\qquad$ 142 $\qquad\qquad\qquad$ $1(10)^2 + 4(10) + 2$
$\quad 7\overline{)1000} = 7\overline{)1(10)^3 + 0(10)^2 + 0(10) + 0}$
$\qquad \underline{7} \qquad\qquad\qquad\quad\ \underline{7(10)^2}$
$\qquad \overline{30} \qquad\qquad\qquad\ \overline{3(10)^2 + 0(10)}$
$\qquad \underline{28} \qquad\qquad\qquad\ \underline{2(10)^2 + 8(10)}$
$\qquad \overline{20} \qquad\qquad\qquad\qquad \overline{2(10) + 0}$
$\qquad \underline{14} \qquad\qquad\qquad\qquad \underline{1(10) + 4}$
$\qquad \overline{6}\ \ $ Remainder $\longrightarrow$ 6

EXERCISES 2-2

1. (a) 12   (b) 5   (c) 17
2. (a) $10101_{(B)} = (1 \times 2^4) + (0 \times 2^3) + (1 \times 2^2) + (0 \times 2^1) + (1 \times 2^0)$
   (b) $110000_{(B)} = (1 \times 2^5) + (1 \times 2^4) + (0 \times 2^3) + (0 \times 2^2) + (0 \times 2^1) + (0 \times 2^0)$
   $\qquad\qquad\quad = 32 + 16 + 0 + 0 + 0 + 0$
   $\qquad\qquad\quad = 48_{(D)}$
   (c) $101011_{(B)} = (1 \times 2^5) + (0 \times 2^4) + (1 \times 2^3) + (0 \times 2^2) + (1 \times 2^1) + (1 \times 2^0)$
   $\qquad\qquad\quad = 32 + 0 + 8 + 0 + 2 + 1$
   $\qquad\qquad\quad = 43_{(D)}$
   (d) $10110011_{(B)} = 179_{(D)}$
   (e) $11011110_{(B)} = 222_{(D)}$
3. 0, 1, power   4. an exponent

EXERCISES 2-3

1. $110110011 = 663$
2. $1010101 = 125$
3. $1110001101 = 1615$
4. $1010 = 12$
5. $11010 = 32$
6. $100000001001 = 4011$
7. $1010110111111 = 12677$
8. $10111011 = 273$

9. $1111000111011 = 17073$
10. $476 = 100111110$
11. $1045 = 001000100101$
12. $201 = 010000001$
13. $3321 = 011011010001$
14. $1001 = 001000000001$
15. $456 = 100101110$
16. $1327 = 001011010111$

17. (a) $370_{(O)} = (3 \times 8^2) + (7 \times 8^1) + (0 \times 8^0)$
      $= 192 + 56 + 0$
      $= 248_{(D)}$
    (b) $1011_{(O)} = (1 \times 8^3) + (0 \times 8^2) + (1 \times 8^1) + (1 \times 8^0)$
      $= 512 + 0 + 8 + 1$
      $= 521_{(D)}$
    (c) $3715_{(O)} = (3 \times 8^3) + (7 \times 8^2) + (1 \times 8^1) + (5 \times 8^0)$
      $= 1536 + 448 + 8 + 5$
      $= 1997_{(D)}$
    (d) $163_{(O)} = 115_{(D)}$
    (e) $2042_{(O)} = 1058_{(D)}$

EXERCISES 2-4

1. B6
2. 1E06
3. 1D
4. 5D
5. 5DD
6. 3FF

7. 2AA
8. 127B
9. 17D5
10. DEED
11. 101000010010
12. 110010101011

13. 0100111100000011
14. 111111101101
15. 11011110000101100001
16. 01000000111100001011
17. omitted

18. (a) $3F1_{(H)} = (3 \times 16^2) + (15 \times 16^1) + (1 \times 16^0)$
      $= 768 + 240 + 1$
      $= 1009_{(D)}$
    (b) $ABAD_{(H)} = (10 \times 16^3) + (11 \times 16^2) + (10 \times 16^1) + (13 \times 16^0)$
      $= 40960 + 2816 + 160 + 13$
      $= 43949_{(D)}$
    (c) $70CF_{(H)} = 28879_{(D)}$
    (d) $60FAA_{(H)} = 397226_{(D)}$
    (e) $1CE0_{(H)} = 7392_{(D)}$
    (f) $198638_{(D)}$

EXERCISES 2-5

1.
0	0	0	1	0	1	1	0	1	0	1	0

2.
0	0	0	1	1	0	1	1	0	0	0	0

3.
0	0	0	0	0	0	1	1	1	0	0	0	1	0	0	0

4.
0	0	0	0	0	1	0	0	0	0	1	1	0	0	0	0

5. 0552, 0660   6. 0388, 0430

EXERCISES 3-1

1. 10000   2. 100110
3. 100010   4. 1101110
5. 10000000   6. 100100
7. 1100111

8.
$$
\begin{array}{r}
1101 \\
+\ 1001 \\
\hline
10110
\end{array}
\qquad
\begin{array}{l}
1(10)^3 + 1(10)^2 + 0(10)^1 + \ 1 \\
1(10)^3 + 0(10)^2 + 0(10)^1 + \ 1 \\
\hline
10(10)^3 + 1(10)^2 + 0(10)^1 + 10 \\
= 1(10)^4 + \ 0(10)^3 + 1(10)^2 + 1(10)^1 + \ 0
\end{array}
$$

9.
$$
\begin{array}{r}
110110 \\
+\ 10101 \\
\hline
1001011
\end{array}
=
\begin{array}{l}
1(10)^5 + 1(10)^4 + 0(10)^3 + 1(10)^2 + 1(10)^1 + 0 \\
1(10)^4 + 0(10)^3 + 1(10)^2 + 0(10)^1 + 1 \\
\hline
1(10)^6 + 0(10)^5 + 0(10)^4 + 1(10)^3 + 0(10)^2 + 1(10)^1 + 1
\end{array}
$$

10.
$$
\begin{array}{r}
11011 \\
+\ 1011 \\
\hline
100110
\end{array}
=
\begin{array}{l}
1(10)^4 + 1(10)^3 + 0(10)^2 + 1(10)^1 + 1 \\
1(10)^3 + 0(10)^2 + 1(10)^1 + 1 \\
\hline
1(10)^5 + 0(10)^4 + 0(10)^3 + 1(10)^2 + 1(10)^1 + 0
\end{array}
$$

11. (a) 11010101   (b) 101010110

1. (a)

+	0	1
0	0	1
1	1	10

(b)

+	0	1	2	3	4	5	6	7
0	0	1	2	3	4	5	6	7
1	1	2	3	4	5	6	7	10
2	2	3	4	5	6	7	10	11
3	3	4	5	6	7	10	11	12
4	4	5	6	7	10	11	12	13
5	5	6	7	10	11	12	13	14
6	6	7	10	11	12	13	14	15
7	7	10	11	12	13	14	15	16

(c)

+	0	1	2	3	4	5	6	7	8	9	A	B	C	D	E	F
0	0	1	2	3	4	5	6	7	8	9	A	B	C	D	E	F
1	1	2	3	4	5	6	7	8	9	A	B	C	D	E	F	10
2	2	3	4	5	6	7	8	9	A	B	C	D	E	F	10	11
3	3	4	5	6	7	8	9	A	B	C	D	E	F	10	11	12
4	4	5	6	7	8	9	A	B	C	D	E	F	10	11	12	13
5	5	6	7	8	9	A	B	C	D	E	F	10	11	12	13	14
6	6	7	8	9	A	B	C	D	E	F	10	11	12	13	14	15
7	7	8	9	A	B	C	D	E	F	10	11	12	13	14	15	16
8	8	9	A	B	C	D	E	F	10	11	12	13	14	15	16	17
9	9	A	B	C	D	E	F	10	11	12	13	14	15	16	17	18
A	A	B	C	D	E	F	10	11	12	13	14	15	16	17	18	19
B	B	C	D	E	F	10	11	12	13	14	15	16	17	18	19	1A
C	C	D	E	F	10	11	12	13	14	15	16	17	18	19	1A	1B
D	D	E	F	10	11	12	13	14	15	16	17	18	19	1A	1B	1C
E	E	F	10	11	12	13	14	15	16	17	18	19	1A	1B	1C	1D
F	F	10	11	12	13	14	15	16	17	18	19	1A	1B	1C	1D	1E

2. (a) 1547   (b) 7037
   (c) 7035   (d) 73451
   (e) 617605   (f) 1622

   (g) (a)

$$1(10)^3 + 3(10)^2 + 4(10)^1 + 0$$
$$+ \qquad 2(10)^2 + 0(10)^1 + 7$$
$$\overline{1(10)^3 + 5(10)^2 + 4(10)^1 + 7}$$

       (b)

$$6(10)^3 + 4(10)^2 + 0(10)^1 + 2$$
$$+ \qquad 4(10)^2 + 3(10)^1 + 5$$
$$\overline{6(10)^3 + 10(10)^2 + 3(10)^1 + 7}$$
$$= 7(10)^3 + 0(10)^2 + 3(10)^1 + 7$$

       (c)

$$1(10)^3 + 3(10)^2 + 2(10)^1 + 6$$
$$+ 5(10)^3 + 5(10)^2 + 0(10)^1 + 7$$
$$\overline{6(10)^3 + 10(10)^2 + 2(10)^1 + 15}$$
$$= 7(10)^3 + 0(10)^2 + 3(10)^1 + 5$$

3. (a) 3DFF   (b) 10FFF
   (c) 1CDDA   (d) 529A5
   (e) BE0245   (f) 194

   (g) (a)

$$1(10)^3 + B(10)^2 + E(10)^1 + A$$
$$+ 2(10)^3 + 2(10)^2 + 1(10)^1 + 5$$
$$\overline{3(10)^3 + D(10)^2 + F(10)^1 + F}$$

      (b)

$$D(10)^3 + E(10)^2 + E(10)^1 + D$$
$$+ 3(10)^3 + 1(10)^2 + 1(10)^1 + 2$$
$$\overline{10(10)^3 + F(10)^2 + F(10)^1 + F}$$
$$= 1(10)^4 + 0(10)^3 + F(10)^2 + F(10)^1 + F$$

      (c)

$$F(10)^3 + E(10)^2 + E(10)^1 + D$$
$$+ C(10)^3 + E(10)^2 + E(10)^1 + D$$
$$\overline{1B(10)^3 + 1C(10)^2 + 1C(10)^1 + 1A}$$
$$= 1(10)^4 + C(10)^3 + D(10)^2 + D(10)^1 + A$$

4.

0	0	1	0	1	1	0	1	0	1	1	0		1326

2(c)

1	0	1	1	0	1	0	0	0	1	1	1		+ 5507
1	1	1	0	0	0	0	0	1	1	1	0	1	7035

3(a)

0	0	0	1	1	0	1	1	1	1	1	0	1	0	1	0		1BEA
0	0	1	0	0	0	1	0	0	0	0	1	0	1	0	1		+ 2215
0	0	1	1	1	1	0	1	1	1	1	1	1	1	1	1		3DFF

EXERCISES 3-3

1.
```
   3764      9999
  -1045    -1045
  ─────    ─────
            8954
         +     1
         ──────
            8955 + 3764 = +│2719
```

2.
```
   7951      9999
  -  263    -0263
  ─────    ─────
            9736
         +     1
         ──────
            9737 + 7951 = +│7688
```

3.
```
   7889      9999
  -8910    -8910
  ─────    ─────
            1089
         +     1                9999
         ──────               ─────
            1090 + 7889 = ]8979
                              1020
                           +     1
                           ──────
                            -1021
```

4.
```
   8395      9999
  -   26    -0026
  ─────    ─────
            9973
         +     1
         ──────
            9974 + 8395 = +│8369
```

5.
```
   6530      9999
  -6809    -6809
  ─────    ─────
            3190
         +     1                9999
         ──────               ─────
            3191 + 6530 = ]9721
                               278
                           +     1
                           ──────
                            -279
```

6.
```
   4096      9999
  -  185    -0185
  ─────    ─────
            9814
         +     1
         ──────
            9815 + 4096 = +│3911
```

7.
```
  67552     99999
  - 9021   -09021
  ──────   ──────
            90978
         +      1
         ───────
            90979 + 67552 = +│58531
```

8.
```
  42031     99999
  - 1940   -01940
  ──────   ──────
            98059
         +      1
         ───────
            98060 + 42031 = +│40091
```

EXERCISES 3-4

1. 1,0
2. No
3. (a)
```
   10110     11111
  -10010     10010
  ──────    ──────
             01101
          +      1
          ──────
             01110
          + 10110
          ───────
          +│00100
```

   (b)
```
   1101      1111
  -1110      1110
  ─────    ─────
              1
          +   1
          ─────
             10
          +1101
          ──────
          ]1111, 0000 + 1 = 1, -1 ans.
```

   (c)
```
   10101011     11111111
  -00111001     00111001
  ────────     ────────
               11000110
            +         1
            ─────────
               11000111
            + 10101011
            ──────────
            +│01110010
```

(d) 111011   111111
     −10110   010110
                 ──────
                 101001
              +   1
                 ──────
                 101010
              + 111011
                 ──────
              +│ 100101

(e)   364   777
     −211   211
                 ───
                 566
              +   1
                 ───
                 567
              + 364
                 ───
              +│ 153

(f) 4075   7777
    −4314   4314
                ────
                3463
              +   1
                ────
                3464
              + 4075   7777
                ────   ─────
              ⌐ 7561 = −7561
                            216
                        +   1
                        ──────
                        −217

(g) 32240   77777
    −02051   02051
                ─────
                75726
              +   1
                ─────
                75727
              + 32240
                ─────
              +│ 30167

(h)   375   777
     − 26   026
                 ───
                 751
              +   1
                 ───
                 752
              + 375
                 ───
              +│ 347

(i)   AFC   FFF
     −495   495
                 ───
                 B6A
              +   1
                 ───
                 B6B
              + AFC
                 ───
              +│ 667

(j) 403B8   FFFFF
    −014A9   014A9
                ─────
                FEB56
              +   1
                ─────
                FEB57
              + 403B8
                ─────
              +│ 3EF0F

(k) DEED   FFFF
    −FEED   FEED
                ────
                0112
              +   1
                ────
                0113
              + DEED   FFFF
                ────   ─────
              ⌐ E000 = −E000
                          1FFF
                        +   1
                        ─────
                        −2000

(l) 13FA6   FFFFF
    −10EAB   10EAB
                ─────
                EF154
              +   1
                ─────
                EF155
              + 13FA6
                ─────
              +│ 030FB

EXERCISES 3-5

1. (a)

BINARY MULTIPLICATION TABLE

×	0	1
0	0	0
1	0	1

(b)

OCTAL MULTIPLICATION

1	2	3	4	5	6	7
2	4	6	10	12	14	16
3	6	11	14	17	22	25
4	10	14	20	24	30	34
5	12	17	24	31	36	43
6	14	22	30	36	44	52
7	16	25	34	43	52	61

(c)

HEXADECIMAL MULTIPLICATION TABLE

1	2	3	4	5	6	7	8	9	A	B	C	D	E	F
2	04	06	08	0A	0C	0E	10	12	14	16	18	1A	1C	1E
3	06	09	0C	0F	12	15	18	1B	1E	21	24	27	2A	2D
4	08	0C	10	14	18	1C	20	24	28	2C	30	34	38	3C
5	0A	0F	14	19	1E	23	28	2D	32	37	3C	41	46	4B
6	0C	12	18	1E	24	2A	30	36	3C	42	48	4E	54	5A
7	0E	15	1C	23	2A	31	38	3F	46	4D	54	5B	62	69
8	10	18	20	28	30	38	40	48	50	58	60	68	70	78
9	12	1B	24	2D	36	3F	48	51	5A	63	6C	75	7E	87
A	14	1E	28	32	3C	46	50	5A	64	6E	78	82	8C	96
B	16	21	2C	37	42	4D	58	63	6E	79	84	8F	9A	A5
C	18	24	30	3C	48	54	60	6C	78	84	90	9C	A8	B4
D	1A	27	34	41	4E	5B	68	75	82	8F	9C	A9	B6	C3
E	1C	2A	38	46	54	62	70	7E	8C	9A	A8	B6	C4	D2
F	1E	2D	3C	4B	5A	69	78	87	96	A5	B4	C3	D2	E1

2. (a)   1011   (b)   101101   (c)   101110

```
   2. (a)      1011        (b)        101101      (c)        101110
           ×   111              ×      10001             ×      1010
           ─────────            ──────────────            ──────────────
              1011                    101101                   1011100
              1011                 101101000                  1011100
              1011              ──────────────            ──────────────
           ─────────            1011111101                 111001100
           1001101
```

3. 00101000, Four, Dividing, Two
4. 1000,00000011
5. (a)   137   (b) 74010   (c) 40703

```
           ×    20
           ────────
              000
               16
                6
                2
           ────────
             2760
```

6. (a)   1AD   (b) CDD2050   (c) 7925A68

```
           ×    63
           ────────
               27
             ¹1E
                3
           ────────
               4E
             ¹3C
                6
           ────────
             A5E7
```

EXERCISES 3-6

```
   1. (a)       1001
            11│11011
                11000  11 × 1000
              ────────
                0011
                  11  11 × 1
                ──────
                   0     1000 + 1 = 1001
```

(b) $11\frac{10}{110}$
(c) 10001

2. (a)
$$
\begin{array}{r}
731\frac{2}{12} \\
12\overline{)11174}
\end{array}
$$

1200	12 × 100
7774	
1200	12 × 100
6574	
1200	12 × 100
5374	
1200	12 × 100
4174	
1200	12 × 100
2774	
1200	12 × 100
1574	
1200	12 × 100
374	
120	12 × 10
254	
120	12 × 10
134	
120	12 × 10
14	
12	12 × 1
2	

(b) $144\frac{14}{45}$ (c) $543\frac{1}{37}$

3. (a)
$$
\begin{array}{r}
E \\
E\overline{)C4}
\end{array}
$$

E	E × 1
B6	
E	E × 1
A8	
E	E × 1
9A	
E	E × 1
8C	
E	E × 1
7E	
E	E × 1
70	
E	E × 1

(b) 7A6

4. 00101100, one, C0

(Continued)

$$
\begin{array}{r}
62 \\
\underline{E} \quad E \times 1 \\
54 \\
\underline{E} \quad E \times 1 \\
46 \\
\underline{E} \quad E \times 1 \\
38 \\
\underline{E} \quad E \times 1 \\
2A \\
\underline{E} \quad E \times 1 \\
1C \\
\underline{E} \quad E \times 1 \\
\underline{E} \quad E \times 1 \\
E \\
\underline{E} \quad E \times 1 \\
0
\end{array}
$$

EXERCISES 4-1

1.

	Decimal	Binary	Octal	Hexadecimal
(a)	25	11001	31	19
(b)	13	1101	15	D
(c)	81	1010001	121	51
(d)	44	101100	54	2C
(e)	121	1111001	171	79
(f)	497	111110001	761	1F1
(g)	5862	1011011100110	13346	16E6

2.

	Binary	Octal	Hexadecimal	Decimal
(a)	1011011	133	5B	91
(b)	1011001101	1315	2CD	717
(c)	1011011011011	13333	16DB	5851
(d)	100000111100101	40745	41E5	16869
(e)	10101011011101111	253357	156EF	87791
(f)	10111111110010111010	2776272	BFCBA	785594

3.

	Octal	Binary	Hexadecimal	Decimal
(a)	127	1010111	57	87
(b)	4610	100110001000	988	2440
(c)	55	101101	2D	45
(d)	103	1000011	43	67
(e)	4200	100010000000	880	2176
(f)	1111	1001001001	249	585

4.

	Hexadecimal	Binary	Octal	Decimal
(a)	DEED	1101111011101101	157355	57069
(b)	401	10000000001	2001	1025
(c)	EA2	111010100010	7242	3746
(d)	BEAD	1011111010101101	137255	48813
(e)	129CF	10010100111001111	224717	76239

5.

Decimal	Binary	Octal	Hexadecimal
242	11110010	362	F2
110	1101110	156	6E
252	11111100	374	FC
7892	1111011010100	17324	1ED4

EXERCISES 4-2

	Decimal	Binary	Octal	Hexadecimal
1.	0.92	0.111010111000	0.7270	0.EB8
2.	111.59375	1101111.100110000	157.46	6F.98
3.	1.0029296875	1.000000001100	1.0014	1.00C
4.	190.67578125	10111110.10101101	276.532	BE.AD
5.	.25	.0100	.2	.4
6.	3.421875	11.011011	3.33	3.6C
7.	.66015625	.10101001	.522	.A9
8.	1.80078125	1.11001101	1.632	1.CD

EXERCISES 5-1

1. BCD
2. 8421-BCD, 2421-BCD
3. Excess-3
4. quadruplet, decimal
5. self-complementing
6. ten is represented by two decimal digits
7. (a) 25   (b) 133
8. (a) 0001 0011   (b) 0001 0010   (c) 1001
   (d) 0001 0101   (e) 0101   0000
9. (a) 0101   (b) 0001   (c) 0001 0101   (d) 0001 0010
10. (a) 1100   (b) 0101   (c) 1000   (d) 1011 1010
11. omitted

EXERCISES 5-2

1. 64, 128
2. zero is included as a character, and $2^6 = 64$.
3. Computing business problems exactly to the penny.

4.

EBCDIC	7-bit ASCII	Character
1111 0011	011 0011	3
1100 0001	100 0001	A
1101 0111	101 0000	P
0101 1011	010 0100	$
0100 0000	010 0000	space
1110 0100	101 0101	U
1000 0010	110 0010	b
1010 1001	111 1010	z

5. F3, C1, D7, 5B, 40, E4, 82, A9
6. (a) F0F4F160F3F160F8F7F6F5
   (b) 11 bytes
7. (a) 5BF2F44BF9F5
   (b) 5BF16BF4F0F24BF9F6
   (c) F6F54BF0F0
   (d) 5CD9858789A2A38599
   (e) 4E4096994060
8. (a) 01347D
   (b) 203C
   (c) 41863C
   (d) 09600D
9. (a) Start of Table

(b)

Data Item	Address
129C	018E
100C	0192
321C	0196
204D	019A
188C	019E

(c) 40404040534C404040404040

EXERCISES 5-3

1. (a) .6875   (b) .06640625   (c) .15625
   (d) .501953125   (e) .21875

2. (a) $.010011 \times 2^4$ (b) $.00010110001 \times 2^8$
   (c) $.001000011011 \times 2^8$ (d) $.00000101 \times 2^4$
   (e) $.00001 \times 2^4$
3. (a) $-.50$ (b) 160 (c) 3584 (d) .01171875
4. (a) 1 1000001 010101000...
   (b) 0 1000000 101000000...
   (c) 0 1000001 010000000...
   (d) 0 1000011 100100000...

5.

	Value	Sign	Exponent	Binary Fraction
(a)	4 3 60 0000	+	$+3$	0110000000...
(b)	BE23 0000	$-$	-2	0010001100...
(c)	C1 54 0000	$-$	$+1$	0101010000...

EXERCISES 6-1

1. (a) 3 (c) 11 (e) 7 (g) 7 (i) 4 (k) 11 (m) 2 (o) 5
   (b) 1 (d) 9 (f) 7 (h) 11 (j) 2 (l) 10 (n) 8 (p) 10
2. (a) symmetric law (b) substitution law (c) transitive law
3. No   4. No   5. No
6. Addition is not distributive with respect to multiplication.

EXERCISES 6-2

1. omitted
2. (a) $\dfrac{1}{1/a} = a$, where $a \in R$ (b) $(-a)(-b) = c$, where $a, b, c, \in R$

   (c) $\dfrac{a}{-b} = -c$, likewise $\dfrac{-a}{b} = -c$, where $a, b, c, \in R$ (d) $a \cdot 0 = 0$, where $a \in R$
3. Yes   4. No   5. Yes   6. No   7. No   8. Yes

EXERCISES 6-3

1. $2x = 8$ $x = 4$
2. (a) $5x = 10$ (b) $2x + 3x = 10x - 5x$
3. (a) $\{\frac{20}{3}\}$ (b) $\varnothing$ (c) $\{1, -4\}$ (d) $y/2$
4. 1, 3, 5, 7, 9
5. $-10, -8, -6, -4, -2, 0, 2$
6. $\{1, -\frac{19}{3}\}$
7. (a) $\{-3, -2, -1, 0, 1, 2, 3, 4\}$ (b) $\{x|x < -2 \text{ or } x > 2\}$
8. (a) $\{x|x < -9 \text{ or } x > 9\}$ (b) $\{x|-9 < x < 9\}$

EXERCISES 6-4

1. (a) A = (X/Y)•Z   (b) D = B••2 − 4.0•A•C
   (c) X = A/(B•C)   (d) Y = 1.5/(A + S + T••2)
   (e) X = C•((A + B)•(X + Y))
2. (a) 3   (b) 3
3. (a) 8   (b) 4   (c) −3
4. (a) 15.   (b) 19.   (c) −7.5
5. (a) X = 4/3 or 1.333   (b) $X = 8/3$ or 2.666   (c) $X = \dfrac{-25}{2}$ or −12.5
6. $A^{(B^c)}$ 7. a

EXERCISES 6-5

1. (a) C = A + 2.5   (b) (I .NE. J)   (c) ((4.1 • X + 2.1) .GT. Y)
   (d) IF (BASE • HEIGHT .GT. 20.5) GO TO 50
   (e) IF (PAY .LT. 999.99) GO TO 100
2. $X = 3$, TOTAL $= 270$
3. 14
4. 10 X = 2
   20 B = X^2
   30 X = B
   40 IF B < 256 GO TO 20
5.   OVRTM = 0.0
      IF (HOURS .LT. 41.0) GO TO 5
   10 OVRTM = (HOURS − 40.0) • (1.5 • RATE)
    5 GROSS = RATE • HOURS + OVRTM

EXERCISES 7-1

1. (a) floating-point   (b) floating-point   (c) fixed-point   (d) floating-point
   (e) fixed-point   (f) floating-point   (g) fixed-point   (h) floating-point
2. (a) I3   (b) I5   (c) I4   (d) F5.1   (e) F4.0   (f) F5.4   (g) F6.3   (h) F7.3
3. (a) none   (b) none   (c) F5.2   (d) F3.1   (e) F6.4   (f) F7.4   (g) none
4. (a) 999   (b) S9V9   (c) 99V99   (d) 999V99   (e) 9V999   (f) 999
5. (a) 32105   (b) 4∧   (c) 54372−   (d) 50∧9   (e) 74∧510   (f) 0023
6. (a) F7.1   (b) F4.2   (c) F6.2   (d) F4.3   (e) I4

EXERCISES 7-2

1. (a) 576000   (b) .0001001   (c) 33345   (d) .00751   (e) 756.4   (f) .00000009
2. (a) .1003E + 6   (b) .64907E + 2   (c) .45E − 5   (d) .573467E − 2   (e) .6E + 6

3.

Number	Scientific Notation	Exponential Notation
10030	1.003×10^4	.1003E + 5
.000045	4.5×10^{-5}	.45E − 4
.321	3.21×10^{-1}	.321E + 0
.00095	9.5×10^{-4}	.95E − 3
701000	7.01×10^5	.701E + 6
.0575	5.75×10^{-2}	.575E − 1
.07	7.0×10^{-2}	.7E − 1
.005734	5.734×10^{-3}	.5734E − 2
.00000019	1.9×10^{-7}	.19E − 6
16.45	1.645×10^1	.1645E + 2

4. (a) E5.1   (b) E8.4   (c) E6.2   (d) E6.2   (e) E8.4   (f) E6.2
   (g) E7.3   (h) E9.5   (i) E7.3   (j) E7.3   (k) E5.1
5. (a) .104032E + 2   (b) −.514E − 1   (c) .10512E + 5   (d) .34906556E + 3

EXERCISES 8-1

1. (a) nn   (b) −nn.nn   (c) nnn.nnn   (d) −nnn.nn   (e) nnnn.nn   (f) −nnn.nn
2. F6.2   3. (a) No   (b) Yes   (c) Yes
4. F10.2   5. ON SIZE ERROR, IF
6. ˙ READ(1,20)BALNCE
   20 FORMAT(F8.2)
      IF (BALNCE)30,40,50
where statement 30 should contain an instruction to alert the bank of the problem.

EXERCISES 8-2

1. (a) nnnnnnnn.nnnn   (b) −n.nn   (c) nn.nnn   (d) nnn.n   (e) nnn
2. c
3. (a) 1   (b) 2   (c) 7
4. (a) 1.85714   (b) 1.22222   (c) .111111   (d) 1.63636   (e) 340.100   (f) .0000324001
   (g) F8.6
5. DIVIDEND − (QUOTIENT × DIVISOR).
6. (a) 1 = 37 − (12 × 3)
   (b) 4.5 = 14.5 − (2 × 5)
   (c) 2.5 = 19 − (5 × 3.3)
7. b
8. F6.1, C = (F − 32.0)/9.0•5.0, F6.1
9. (a) F7.2, F4.2   (b) COST = PRICE − (PRICE × RATE)
10. (a) PRICE PICTURE 99V999
       EARNINGS-PER-SHARE PICTURE 9V99
       RATIO PICTURE 99V999
    (b) DIVIDE EARNINGS-PER-SHARE INTO PRICE GIVING RATIO.

11. The entries in column 4 do not add up to 100% and therefore create an undesirable report. Procedure to create columns 5 and 6: In the third column the necessary .000500 is added in only for Monday or once at the beginning and yields the number in column 5. Unwanted decimal fractions (the last three decimal places) in the column 5 are added to the next number in column 3. Then

$$.094653 + .000500 = .095153$$
$$.038995 + .000153 = .039148$$
$$.010515 + .000148 = .010663 \text{ and so on.}$$

12. (a) .0004567 (b) .1234 (c) 679.0 (d) .1478 (e) 1271
13. (a) 347840 (b) 3478395.8 (c) 3478 (d) 34784 (e) 3 (f) 3478395.79
14. $45658760.85/10^6 = 45.65876085$

$$\frac{+ \quad .5}{\text{INT}(46.15876085)}$$

15. In (HOURS $-$ 40.0 $*$ 1.5) multiplication is performed first, reducing hours by 60. Further, NET should be changed to GROSS.

EXERCISES 9-1

1. (Answers in BASIC)
   (a) X^11 (b) 4•A^9 (c) (Y•Z)^4 (d) A^4 (e) (A/B)^X (f) 8•X (g) 1/9
   (h) 5 (i) 2•Y^7 (j) 2^24 (k) 1/A (l) 3^10 (m) x^{2n} (n) x^{2n}
2. (a) 4.278×10 (b) $(6.12 \times 10^5)/7.8$
3. 3.763×10^8
4.   READ (1,10) RADIUS,PI
   10 FORMAT(F5.2,F6.4)
        AREA = PI • RADIUS••2.
5. 747.26
6. 0.12
7. $\dfrac{2.4 \times 10^5}{5.5 \times 10^1} = .436363 \times 10^4$

   $= 4363.63$ hours
8. $\underbrace{1.3 \times 10^1}_{\text{weeks}} \times \underbrace{5}_{\text{days}} \times \underbrace{4.80 \times 10^2}_{\substack{\text{minutes} \\ \text{per day}}} = .31200 \times 10^5$

EXERCISES 9-2

1. (a) 9 (b) 56 (c) $-\sqrt{3}$ (d) $160 + \sqrt{2}$ (e) $39\sqrt{5}$ (f) $\dfrac{7}{\sqrt{3}}$ (g) x^2 (h) $\sqrt[x]{4^2}$
   (i) Let $\sqrt[n]{a} = a^{1/n}$ and $\sqrt[n]{b} = b^{1/n}$ then, $a^{1/n} \cdot b^{1/n} = (ab)^{1/n} = \sqrt[n]{ab}$ (j) $\frac{25}{4}$ (k) $\frac{1}{54}$
   (l) $\dfrac{\sqrt{2}}{2x}$ (m) x

2. (a) 6·SQRT(2.)   (b) SQRT(5.)
   (c) 5./2.   (d) 9.·(9.··(1./3.))
   (e) X·SQRT(Y)   (f) (A+B)·SQRT(C)
   (g) .25·SQRT(10.0)
3. When n is odd, $a^n = -1$.
   When n is even, $a^n = 1$.
4. (a) No   (b) Yes
5. (a) 13   (b) 256   (c) 4.125   (d) .000064
6. (a) X = A··5.0   (b) X = B··(.25)   (c) A = SQRT(X/Y)   (d) C = X··2. − 4.·X + 9.
   (e) A = (X/Y)··(1./3.)   (f) F = A··(1./5.) + B   (g) A = A··5./5.
   (h) B − (SQRT(B··2. − 4.·A·C))
7. (a) $s = \left\{ -\dfrac{61}{16} \right\}$ (b) $s = \{5\}$ (c) $s = \{26\}$
8. (a) >   (b) <,<   (c) =
9.   20 FORMAT(F4.1)
           TIME = .25 · 3.14159 · SQRT(XLEN)
           WRITE (2,30) TIME
        30 FORMAT(F6.3)
10. (a) H = (2.·M··2.)/3.   (b) V = SQRT(P/.003)
11. $2.5\sqrt{2}$ 12. 144 feet

EXERCISES 10-1

1. (a) Sums and prints previous terms until sum = 55. (Fibonacci sequence.)
   (b) Rounds positive and negative numbers. (Modify to handle 0.)
2. (a) IF applicant ⩾ 16-years-old
          THEN
                  issue driver's permit
       IF-END
   (b) Collect receipts
       Enter expenses on voucher
       Total expenses
   (c) Input number
          IF number less than 0
              THEN
                  print CREDIT
              ELSE IF number greater than 0
              THEN
                  print DEBIT
              IF-END
          IF-END
   (d) Open file
       DO WHILE there is a record in the file
          Input employee record
          print employee name
          print employee address
       DO-END
       Close file

(e) Set F = 20
   DO WHILE F less than 61
      Compute C = 5 × ((F − 32) ÷ 9)
      Add 10 to F
   DO-END
3. (a) decision (b) sequential (c) iteration (d) iteration
4. (a) See flowchart 4a.

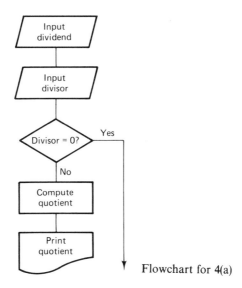

Flowchart for 4(a)

(b) Input dividend
    Input divisor
            IF divisor not equal to 0
                THEN
                    compute quotient
                    print quotient
            IF-END
5. See flowcharts 5(a), (b) and (c).

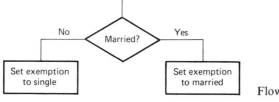

Flowchart for 5(a)

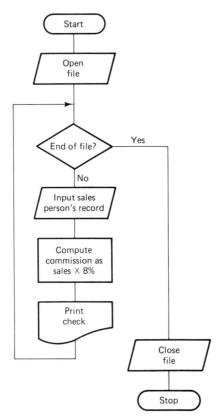

Flowchart for 5(b)

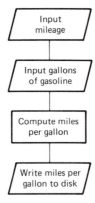

Flowchart 5(c)

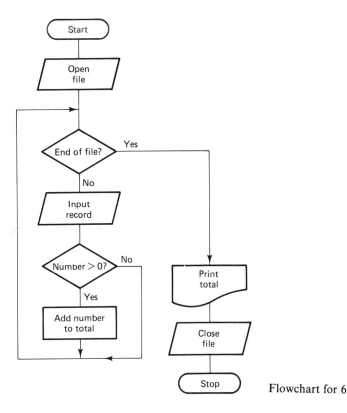

Flowchart for 6

6. See flowchart 6.
7. Open the file
   DO WHILE there is a record in the file
           Input account record
           IF account balance > 0
               THEN
                  Add balance to Debit total
               ELSE
                  IF account balance < 0
                      THEN
                              Add balance to Credit total
                  IF-END
           IF-END
   DO-END
   Multiply Credit total by −1
   IF Credit total = Debit total
   (*Continued*)

```
THEN
    Print totals
    Close file
ELSE
    Print error message
    Close file
IF-END
```

EXERCISES 11-1

1. (a) proof number   (b) hash totals   (c) record identification number   (d) records that have common characteristics or similar functions   (e) related data items

2.   READ (1,20) Q1,Q2,Q3,Q4
   20 FORMAT (F6.2,F6.2,F6.2,F6.2)

       WRITE (2,50) QT
   50 FORMAT (F8.2)

3. Numbers are placed in ascending order.

4. (a) 10   (b) 5

5. Set hash total to zero
   ```
   DO WHILE there is a record in the file
            Input inventory record
            Add part number to hash total
            IF quantity-on-hand < = reorder number
                THEN print reorder message
            IF-END
   DO-END
   ```

6. BASIC
   ```
   10 B = ARRAY(1)
   20 FOR I = 2 TO 100
   30 IF ARRAY(I) < = B THEN 50
   40 B = ARRAY(I)
   50 NEXT I
   ```

7. See flowchart 7, assume no missing entries.

8. Cost of loan

   Compute loan amount = price of home − down payment

   Compute number of payments

   Compute monthly payment amount

   Compute total amount of monthly payments for 15 years

   Compute actual cost of loan = total of monthly payments − 65,000

   Return on savings

   Compute amount in savings after 15 years

   Compute return = amount in savings − 10,000

   Compare cost of loan to return on savings

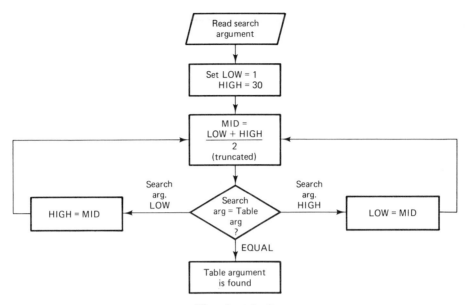

Flowchart for 7

9.   Input beginning month, day

Compute beginning date = table(month) + day

Input ending month, day

Compute ending date = table(month) + day

Compute elapsed time = ending date − beginning date

IF elapsed time < 0

      THEN add 365 to elapsed time

IF-END

print elapsed time

```
100 '...JULIAN DATE PROGRAM...
125 DIM JULIAN(12)
127 DATA 0,31,59,90,120,151,181,212,243,273,304,334
130 FOR I = 1 TO 12
137     READ JULIAN(I)
150 NEXT I
160 INPUT "ENTER FIRST MONTH ", MONTH1
165 INPUT "ENTER DATE ",DAY1
170 DATE1 = JULIAN(MONTH1) + DAY1
180 INPUT "ENTER SECOND MONTH ",MONTH2
185 INPUT "ENDING DAY ",DAY2
190 DATE2 = JULIAN(MONTH2) + DAY2
200 ELAPSED = DATE2 − DATE1
```

(*Continued*)

```
205 IF ELAPSED < 0 THEN ELAPSED = ELAPSED + 365
210 PRINT ELAPSED "Days elapsed"
215 END
```

10. A valid license plate is being searched for.
    The first record in the DRIVER-FILE is processed as the other records. After the last record is read and processed, program control is given to a paragraph named NEXT-SEARCH where a new search may begin with the next record in the LICENSE-FILE.

11. omitted

12. See flowchart 12.

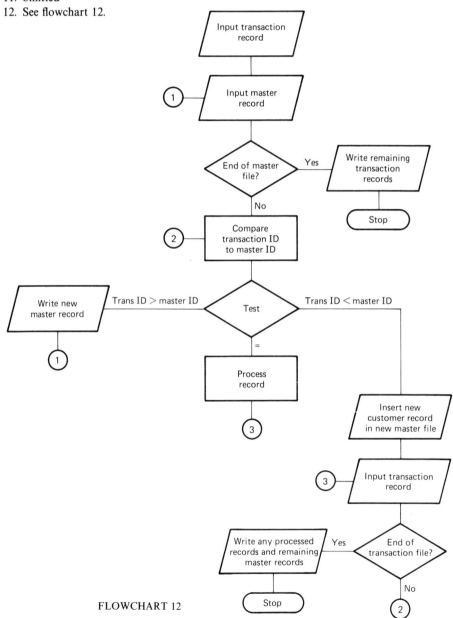

FLOWCHART 12

EXERCISES 12-1

1. (a) $A = \{$Sun., Mon., Tues., Wed., Thurs., Fri., Sat.$\}$
   (b) $A = \{8, 9, 10, 11\}$ (c) $A = \{1, 2, 9, 10, 11, 12, \ldots\}$
   (d) $A = \{2, 4, 6, 8, 10, \ldots\}$
2. (a) True   (b) False   (c) True   (d) False   (e) True   (f) False   (g) True
   (h) False   (i) False
3. (a) Infinite   (b) Finite   (c) Infinite   (d) Finite
4. $\{\$\}, \{a\}, \{?\}, \{\$, a\}, \{\$, ?\}, \{a, ?\}, \{\$, a, ?\}, \{\ \ \}$.
5. (a) equal; equivalent   (b) not equal; equivalent
   (c) not equal; equivalent   (d) not equal; not equivalent
6. (a) $B \subset U$ (b) $A \not\subset B$ (c) $7 \notin B$ (d) $1 \in A$ (e) $\varnothing \subset B$
7. (a) Yes   (b) No   (c) Yes   (d) Yes
8. (a) $\{1\}, \{2\}, \{1, 2\}, \varnothing$
   (b) $\{1\}, \{2\}, \{3\}, \{1, 2\}, \{1, 3\}, \{2, 3\}, \{1, 2, 3\}, \varnothing$
   (c) $\{1\}, \{2\}, \{3\}, \{4\}, \{1, 2\}, \{1, 3\}, \{1, 4\}, \{2, 3\}, \{2, 4\}, \{3, 4\}, \{1, 2, 3\}, \{1, 2, 4\}, \{1, 3, 4\},$
   $\{2, 3, 4\}, \{1, 2, 3, 4\}, \varnothing$
9. 32 subsets in a set of five elements. 2^n, where $n =$ the number of elements.
10. Yes, the null set.
11. (a) $\{\ \ \}$ is a set that contains no elements, the null set.
    (b) the null set
    (c) a set containing the null set
12. (a) $\{\ \ \}$ (b) $\varnothing$ (c) $\varnothing, \{\varnothing\}$

EXERCISES 12-2

1. A and B A and C A and D B and D
2.

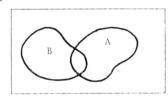 $=$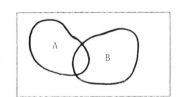

3. (a) $\{1, 2, 3, 4\}$ (b) $\{0, 3, 7, 8, 9, 80\}$ (c) $\{a, b, c, d, e\}$
4. $(A \cup B) \cup C = A \cup (B \cup C)$
   $(\{\$, \#\} \cup \{11\}) \cup \{/, \#\} = \{\$, \#\} \cup (\{11\} \cup \{/, \#\})$
   $\{\$, \#, 11\} \cup \{/, \#\} = \{\$, \#\} \cup \{11, /, \#\}$
   $\{\$, \#, 11, /\} = \{\$, \#, 11, /\}$
   $\therefore (A \cup B) \cup C = A \cup (B \cup C)$
5. See identity property.

6. $S = \{\Delta, 0\}$ $A = \{\Delta\}$
$B = \{0\}$
$\varnothing = \{\ \}$

$\cup$	S	A	B	$\varnothing$
S	S	S	S	S
A	S	A	S	A
B	S	S	B	B
$\varnothing$	S	A	B	$\varnothing$

7. (a) $A \cup D = A$ when $D \subseteq A$
   (b) $A \cup \varnothing = U$ when $A = U$
8. (a) {Name, Address, ID#, Purchases, Date, Amount, Balance}
   (b) Yes
   (c)

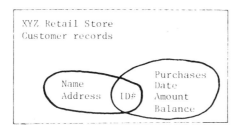

EXERCISES 12-3

1. (a) $\{1\}$ (b) $\{\#, ?\}$ (c) $\{1, 2, 3\}$ (d) $\varnothing$
2. (a) $A \cap B = \{b, d\}$ (b) $A \cup C = \{a, b, c, d, e, f, g, h\}$ (c) $\bar{A} = \{a, c, e, g\}$ (d) $\bar{B} = \{e, f, g, h\}$
   (e) $\overline{(A \cup B)} = \{e, g\}$ (f) $\bar{A} \cap C = \{a, c, e, g\}$ (g) $\bar{B} \cap \bar{C} = \{f, h\}$
   (h) $A \cup (B \cap C) = \{a, b, c, d, f, h\}$
3. $S = \{1, 2, 3, 4\}$ $E = \{1, 2\}$ $K = \{1, 2, 3\}$
   $A = \{1\}$ $F = \{1, 3\}$ $L = \{1, 2, 4\}$
   $B = \{2\}$ $G = \{1, 4\}$ $M = \{1, 3, 4\}$
   $C = \{3\}$ $H = \{2, 3\}$ $N = \{2, 3, 4\}$
   $D = \{4\}$ $I = \{2, 4\}$ $\varnothing = \{\ \}$
   $J = \{3, 4\}$

∩	S	A	B	C	D	E	F	G	H	I	J	K	L	M	N	∅
S	S	A	B	C	D	E	F	G	H	I	J	K	L	M	N	∅
A	A	A	∅	∅	∅	A	A	A	∅	∅	∅	A	A	A	∅	∅
B	B	∅	B	∅	∅	B	∅	∅	B	B	∅	B	B	∅	B	∅
C	C	∅	∅	C	∅	∅	C	∅	C	∅	C	C	∅	C	C	∅
D	D	∅	∅	∅	D	∅	∅	D	∅	D	D	∅	D	D	D	∅
E	E	A	B	∅	∅	E	A	A	B	B	∅	E	E	A	B	∅
F	F	A	∅	C	∅	A	F	A	C	∅	C	F	A	F	C	∅
G	G	A	∅	∅	D	A	A	G	∅	D	D	A	G	G	D	∅
H	H	∅	B	C	∅	B	C	∅	H	B	C	H	B	C	H	∅
I	I	∅	B	∅	D	B	∅	D	B	I	D	B	I	D	I	∅
J	J	∅	∅	C	D	∅	C	D	C	D	J	C	D	J	J	∅
K	K	A	B	C	∅	E	F	A	H	B	C	K	E	F	H	∅
L	L	A	B	∅	D	E	A	G	B	I	D	E	L	G	I	∅
M	M	A	∅	C	D	A	F	G	C	D	J	F	G	M	J	∅
N	N	∅	B	C	D	B	C	D	H	I	J	H	I	J	N	∅
∅	∅	∅	∅	∅	∅	∅	∅	∅	∅	∅	∅	∅	∅	∅	∅	∅

4. (a)

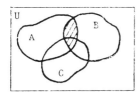

(b)

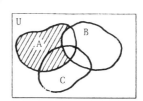

(c)

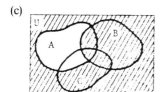

(d)

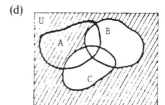

(e)

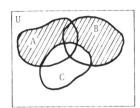

(f)

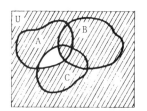

5. (a) sometimes (b) always (c) never unless A is the universal set
(d) identity property, intersection

6. $\{\Delta, 0, \square, \Diamond\} \cap \{\Delta, 0, 11\} = \{\Delta, 0\}$, and
$\{\Delta, 0, 11\} \cap \{\Delta, 0, \square, \Diamond\} = \{\Delta, 0\}$
$\therefore \{\Delta, 0\} = \{\Delta, 0\}$

7. (a) True (b) False (c) True (d) False

8. (a) $\{1, 2, 3, 4, 5, 6\}$ (b) $\{1, 4\}$ (c) $\{1\}$ (d) $\{1, 2, 3, 4, 6\}$ (e) $\{3, 5, 7\}$

9. $A \cup (B \cap C) = (A \cup B) \cap (A \cup C)$, where
$\{h\} \cup \{h, s\} = \{f, h, s\} \cap \{h, s, m\}$

EXERCISES 13-1

1. (a) $p: y = 3$, $q: x = 4$ $p \wedge q$
(b) $p: c < 1$, $q: a = c^2$ $p \vee q$
(c) $p:$ TYPE = SALARIED
$q:$ NETPAY = GROSS − TAXES $p \wedge q$
(d) $p:$ Triangle has a right angle
$q:$ Angles are equal. $\sim p \vee q$
(e) $p: z = 10$, $q: y = 9$, $r: x = 8$ $p \wedge q \wedge r$

2. (a)

p	q	$\sim q$	$p \vee \sim q$
T	T	F	T
T	F	T	T
F	T	F	F
F	F	T	T

(b)

p	q	$\sim p$	$\sim q$	$\sim p \wedge \sim q$
T	T	F	F	F
T	F	F	T	F
F	T	T	F	F
F	F	T	T	T

(c)

p	q	$p \wedge q$	$\sim p$	$\sim p \vee (p \wedge q)$
T	T	T	F	T
T	F	F	F	F
F	T	F	T	T
F	F	F	T	T

(d)

p	q	$\sim p$	$\sim q$	$(\sim p \wedge q)$	$(p \wedge \sim q)$	$(\sim p \wedge q) \vee (p \wedge \sim q)$
T	T	F	F	F	F	F
T	F	F	T	F	T	T
F	T	T	F	T	F	T
F	F	T	T	F	F	F

(e)

q	$\sim q$	$\sim \sim q$
T	F	T
F	T	F

3.

p	q	$p \veebar q$
T	T	F
T	F	T
F	T	T
F	F	F

4. (a) No

Not equivalent

p	q	$\sim p$	$\sim q$	$\sim p \vee \sim q$	$\sim(p \vee q)$
T	T	F	F	F	F
T	F	F	T	T	F
F	T	T	F	T	F
F	F	T	T	T	T

(b) No

Not equivalent

p	q	$\sim p$	$\sim q$	$\sim p \wedge \sim q$	$\sim(p \wedge \sim q)$
T	T	F	F	F	T
T	F	F	T	F	F
F	T	T	F	F	T
F	F	T	T	T	T

5.

p	q	$\sim q$	$(p \wedge q)$	$(p \wedge \sim q)$	$(p \wedge q) \vee (p \wedge \sim q)$
T	T	F	T	F	T
T	F	T	F	T	T
F	T	F	F	F	F
F	F	T	F	F	F

6. (a), (b)

p	q	r	$(p \wedge q)$	$(p \wedge q) \vee r$	$(p \vee q)$	$(p \vee q) \wedge r$
T	T	T	T	T	T	T
T	T	F	T	T	T	F
T	F	T	F	T	T	T
T	F	F	F	F	T	F
F	T	T	F	T	T	T
F	T	F	F	F	T	F
F	F	T	F	T	F	F
F	F	F	F	F	F	F

EXERCISES 13-2

1. (a) If the triangle is equilateral, then it has equal sides.
   (b) If it is Friday, then it is payday.
   (c) If you stitch in time, then you save nine.
2. (a) biconditional (b) conditional (c) conditional (d) biconditional
3. (a) $p:y = mx + b$
      $q:b = y - mx$
      $p \leftrightarrow q$
   (b) p = It is a quadrilateral.
      q = It is a polygon.
      $p \rightarrow q$
   (c) p = It is snowing.
      q = Temperature is below 33°.
      $p \rightarrow q$
   (d) $p:x^2 - x - 6 = 0$
      $q:x = 3$
      $p \leftrightarrow q$

4. (a)

p	q	$\sim p$	$\sim q$	$\sim p \rightarrow \sim q$
T	T	F	F	T
T	F	F	T	T
F	T	T	F	F
F	F	T	T	T

(b)

p	q	r	$(q \wedge r)$	$(q \wedge r) \rightarrow p$
T	T	T	T	T
T	T	F	F	T
T	F	T	F	T
T	F	F	F	T
F	T	T	T	F
F	T	F	F	T
F	F	T	F	T
F	F	F	F	T

(c)

q	r	$(q \wedge r)$	$(r \wedge q)$	$(q \wedge r) \leftrightarrow (r \wedge q)$
T	T	T	T	T
T	F	F	F	T
F	T	F	F	T
F	F	F	F	T

(d)

p	q	r	$\sim p$	$(q \vee r)$	$r \vee (q \vee r)$	$\sim p \rightarrow r \vee (q \vee r)$
T	T	T	F	T	T	T
T	T	F	F	T	T	T
T	F	T	F	T	T	T
T	F	F	F	F	F	T
F	T	T	T	T	T	T
F	T	F	T	T	T	T
F	F	T	T	T	T	T
F	F	F	T	F	F	F

(e)

p	q	r	$\sim r$	$\sim q$	$(p \to q)$	$(\sim r \vee \sim q)$	$(p \to q) \leftrightarrow (\sim r \vee \sim q)$
T	T	T	F	F	T	F	F
T	T	F	T	F	T	T	T
T	F	T	F	T	F	T	F
T	F	F	T	T	F	T	F
F	T	T	F	F	T	F	F
F	T	F	T	F	T	T	T
F	F	T	F	T	T	T	T
F	F	F	T	T	T	T	T

(f)

p	q	$\sim p$	$\sim p \to q$	$p \to (\sim p \to q)$
T	T	F	T	T
T	F	F	T	T
F	T	T	T	T
F	F	T	F	T

5. (a) No

p	q	$p \vee q$	$p \to (p \vee q)$	$(p \vee q) \to p$	$p \leftrightarrow (p \vee q)$
T	T	T	T	T	T
T	F	T	T	T	T
F	T	T	T	F	F
F	F	F	T	T	T

(b) Omitted

6. (a) $q \to p$ (b) $\sim q \to p$
    $\sim p \to \sim q$ $\sim p \to q$ or $\sim p \to \sim \sim q$
    $\sim q \to \sim p$ $q \to \sim p$ or $\sim \sim q \to \sim p$

7. $(q \to p) \wedge (p \to q)$

p	q	$p \to q$	$q \to p$	$(p \to q) \wedge (q \to p)$	$(q \to p) \wedge (p \to q)$
T	T	T	T	T	T
T	F	F	T	F	F
F	T	T	F	F	F
F	F	T	T	T	T

8. (a)

p	q	$p \wedge q$	$(p \wedge q) \to p$
T	T	T	T
T	F	F	T
F	T	F	T
F	F	F	T

(b)

p	q	$p \to q$	$p \wedge (p \to q)$	$[p \wedge (p \to q)] \to q$
T	T	T	T	T
T	F	F	F	T
F	T	T	F	T
F	F	T	F	T

(c)

p	q	$\sim p$	$\sim q$	$p \wedge q$	$\sim(p \wedge q)$	$\sim p \vee \sim q$	$\sim(p \wedge q) \to \sim p \vee \sim q$
T	T	F	F	T	F	F	T
T	F	F	T	F	T	T	T
F	T	T	F	F	T	T	T
F	F	T	T	F	T	T	T

$\sim p \vee \sim q \to \sim(p \wedge q)$	$\sim(p \wedge q) \leftrightarrow \sim p \vee \sim q$
T	T
T	T
T	T
T	T

(d)

p	q	$\sim p$	$\sim q$	$p \vee q$	$\sim(p \vee q)$	$\sim p \wedge \sim q$
T	T	F	F	T	F	F
T	F	F	T	T	F	F
F	T	T	F	T	F	F
F	F	T	T	F	T	T

$\sim(p \vee q) \to \sim p \wedge \sim q$	$\sim p \wedge \sim q \to \sim(p \vee q)$	$\sim(p \vee q) \leftrightarrow \sim p \wedge \sim q$
T	T	T
T	T	T
T	T	T
T	T	T

(e)

p	q	$\sim q$	$p \to q$	$\sim(p \to q)$	$p \wedge \sim q$
T	T	F	T	F	F
T	F	T	F	T	T
F	T	F	T	F	F
F	F	T	T	F	F

$\sim(p \to q) \to p \wedge \sim q$	$p \wedge \sim q \to \sim(p \to q)$	$\sim(p \to q) \leftrightarrow p \wedge \sim q$
T	T	T
T	T	T
T	T	T
T	T	T

9. (a) If P and Q, then print R. $(p \wedge q) \to r$
   (b) If not P and not R or if P and not Q, then print S.
      $(\sim p \wedge \sim r) \vee (p \wedge \sim q) \to s$

EXERCISES 13-3

1. EXCLUSIVE OR

Truth Value Expression$_1$	Truth Value Expression$_2$	Result
1	1	0
1	0	1
0	1	1
0	0	0

2. (a) 0 (b) 0 (c) 1 (d) 1
3. (a) 1 (b) 1 (c) 0

4.

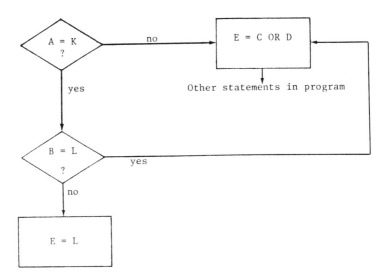

5. (a) when INVENTORY is less than a purchase order and VENDOR-ONE-PRICE is less than prices for vendors two and three.

(b) Test vendors one and two AND one and three.

Test vendors two and three AND two and one.

Test vendors three and one AND three and two.

6. IF X > Y AND X > Z GO TO 10   IF (X − Z) 70, 50, 60
   IF X < Y AND X > Z GO TO 20   OR   60 IF (X − Y) 20, 50, 10
   IF X > Y AND X < Z GO TO 30   70 IF (X − Y) 40, 50, 30
   IF X < Y AND X < Z GO TO 40

EXERCISES 13-4

1. (a) 00010100 (b) 110110 (c) 00000000
2. (a) 10111111 (b) 111111 (c) 11110101
3. (a) 00111001 (b) 001101 (c) 11000101
4. (a) omitted (b) The result is all 0's.
5. (a) AND (b) subtraction (c) EXCLUSIVE OR (d) addition (e) OR
6. (a) 4D (b) 0C (c) 17
7. DF
8. omitted
9. AND, zeros

EXERCISES 14-1

1. {0, 1}, + or sum, ·, or product
2. (a) 0 (b) 1 (c) 0 (d) 1 (e) 1

3. reverses the condition of variable A

4. (a)

A	B	C	$A + B + C$	Result
1	1	1	$1 + 1 + 1$	1
1	1	0	$1 + 1 + 0$	1
1	0	1	$1 + 0 + 1$	1
1	0	0	$1 + 0 + 0$	1
0	1	1	$0 + 1 + 1$	1
0	1	0	$0 + 1 + 0$	1
0	0	1	$0 + 0 + 1$	1
0	0	0	$0 + 0 + 0$	0

(b)

A	B	C	$A \cdot B \cdot C$	Result
1	1	1	$1 \cdot 1 \cdot 1$	1
1	1	0	$1 \cdot 1 \cdot 0$	0
1	0	1	$1 \cdot 0 \cdot 1$	0
1	0	0	$1 \cdot 0 \cdot 0$	0
0	1	1	$0 \cdot 1 \cdot 1$	0
0	1	0	$0 \cdot 1 \cdot 0$	0
0	0	1	$0 \cdot 0 \cdot 1$	0
0	0	0	$0 \cdot 0 \cdot 0$	0

5. (a) 1 (b) 0 (c) 1 (d) 1
6. (a)

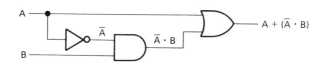

(b)

A	B	$\bar{A}$	$A + \bar{A}B$	Result
1	1	0	$1 + 0 \cdot 1$	1
1	0	0	$1 + 0 \cdot 0$	1
0	1	1	$0 + 1 \cdot 1$	1
0	0	1	$0 + 1 \cdot 0$	0

7. 2^n possible results.
8. (a) $A \cdot (B + \bar{B})$ (b) dependent upon A

9.

A	$\bar{A}$	B	$A \cdot B + \bar{A}$	Result
1	0	1	$1 \cdot 1 + 0$	1
1	0	0	$1 \cdot 0 + 0$	0
0	1	1	$0 \cdot 1 + 1$	1
0	1	0	$0 \cdot 0 + 1$	1

10.

A	B	$\bar{B}$	$B \cdot (A + \bar{B})$	Result
1	1	0	$1 \cdot (1 + 0)$	1
1	0	1	$0 \cdot (1 + 1)$	0
0	1	0	$1 \cdot (0 + 0)$	0
0	0	1	$0 \cdot (0 + 1)$	0

11. (a)

A	B	$\bar{A}$	$\bar{A}(A + B)$	Result
1	1	0	$0(1 + 1)$	0
1	0	0	$0(1 + 0)$	0
0	1	1	$1(0 + 1)$	1
0	0	1	$1(0 + 0)$	0

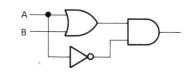

(b)

A	B	$\bar{A}$	$\bar{A}B(A + B)$	Result
1	1	0	$0 \cdot 1(1 + 1)$	0
1	0	0	$0 \cdot 0(1 + 0)$	0
0	1	1	$1 \cdot 1(0 + 1)$	1
0	0	1	$1 \cdot 0(0 + 0)$	0

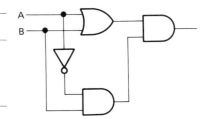

(c)

A	B	C	AB	$(B + C)$	$A(B + C)$	$AB + A(B + C)$
1	1	1	1	1	1	1
1	1	0	1	1	1	1
1	0	1	0	1	1	1
1	0	0	0	0	0	0
0	1	1	0	1	0	0
0	1	0	0	1	0	0
0	0	1	0	1	0	0
0	0	0	0	0	0	0

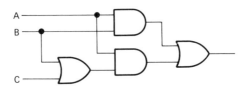

12. (a) $(A + B)(C + D)$ (b) $(A + B) + (AC)$ (c) $(A + B + C) + (DE)$
13. b

14. (a)

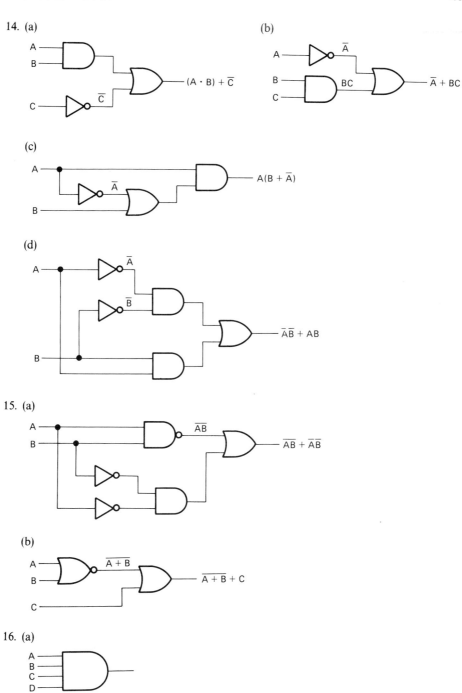

(b)

(c)

(d)

15. (a)

(b)

16. (a)

(b) 1

EXERCISES 14-2

<table>
<tr><td></td><td></td><td>Property</td></tr>
<tr><td>1. (a)</td><td>$AB + \bar{A} = (A + \bar{A})(B + \bar{A})$</td><td>3(b)</td></tr>
<tr><td></td><td>$= 1(B + \bar{A})$</td><td>5(a)</td></tr>
<tr><td></td><td>$AB + \bar{A} = B + \bar{A}$</td><td>4(b)</td></tr>
<tr><td>(b)</td><td>$B(AB) = (AB)B$</td><td>1(b)</td></tr>
<tr><td></td><td>$= A(B \cdot B)$</td><td>2(b)</td></tr>
<tr><td></td><td>$B(AB) = AB$</td><td>6(b)</td></tr>
<tr><td>(c)</td><td>$A(A + AB) = A(A)$</td><td>8(a)</td></tr>
<tr><td></td><td>$A(A + AB) = A$</td><td>6(b)</td></tr>
</table>

<table>
<tr><td></td><td></td><td>Property</td></tr>
<tr><td>(d)</td><td>$X + \bar{X}Y + Z = (X + \bar{X})(X + Y) + Z$</td><td>3(b)</td></tr>
<tr><td></td><td>$= 1(X + Y) + Z$</td><td>5(a)</td></tr>
<tr><td></td><td>$X + \bar{X}Y + Z = X + Y + Z$</td><td>4(b)</td></tr>
<tr><td>(e)</td><td>$A + A\bar{B} + A\bar{B}\bar{C} = A(1 + \bar{B} + \bar{B}\bar{C})$</td><td>3(a)</td></tr>
<tr><td></td><td>$= A(1 + \bar{B}\bar{C})$</td><td>7(a)</td></tr>
<tr><td></td><td>$\doteq A(1)$</td><td>7(a)</td></tr>
<tr><td></td><td>$A + A\bar{B} + A\bar{B}\bar{C} = A$</td><td>4(b)</td></tr>
<tr><td>(f)</td><td>$A(B + C) + A + AB = AB + AC + A + AB$</td><td>3(a)</td></tr>
<tr><td></td><td>$= A + AC + AB + AB$</td><td>1(a)</td></tr>
<tr><td></td><td>$= A + AC + AB$</td><td>6(a)</td></tr>
<tr><td></td><td>$= A(1 + C + B)$</td><td>3(a)</td></tr>
<tr><td></td><td>$= A(1 + B)$</td><td>7(a)</td></tr>
<tr><td></td><td>$= A(1)$</td><td>7(a)</td></tr>
<tr><td></td><td>$= A$</td><td>4(b)</td></tr>
</table>

2. (1a)

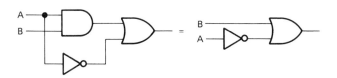

2. (1d)

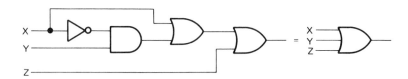

3. 3(b), 3(a), 6(b), 3(a)

4. 0

5. 1

6. (a) $(A + B)\overline{(AB)}$ (b) $A + \bar{B}C$ (c) $A\bar{B}C$ (d) $\overline{ABC}$
   Answers to 6(e)

6(a) 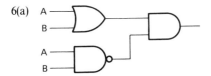 6(c)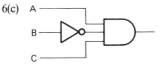

7. No
8. Yes
9. (a) Yes (b) See following diagram.

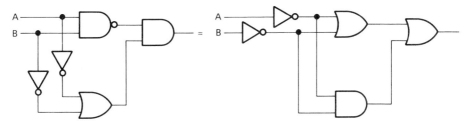

10. (a) $B\bar{C}$ (b) $\bar{A}\bar{B}\bar{C}$ (c) $A\bar{B}\bar{C}$ (d) $\bar{A}\bar{B}$ (e) $A(\bar{C} + \bar{B})$ (f) $C\bar{D} + D\bar{C}$
11. Yes
12. $AB + \bar{A}\bar{B}$, biconditional
13. (a) ABC, $A\bar{B}C$, $\bar{A}\bar{B}C$, $ABC + A\bar{B}C + \bar{A}\bar{B}C$

   (b)

		Property
$ABC + A\bar{B}C + \bar{A}\bar{B}C$	$= C(AB + A\bar{B} + \bar{A}\bar{B})$	1(b) and a generalization of 3(a)
	$= C[A(B + \bar{B}) + \bar{A}\bar{B}]$	3(a)
	$= C[A(1) + \bar{A}\bar{B}]$	5(a)
	$= C(A + \bar{A}\bar{B})$	4(b)
	$= C[(A + \bar{A})(A + \bar{B})]$	3(b)
	$= C(1)(A + \bar{B})$	5(a)
	$= C(A + \bar{B})$	4(b)

   (c)

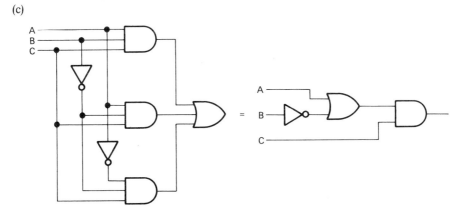

14. (a)

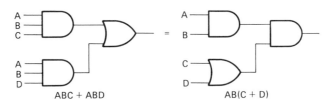

ABC + ABD   AB(C + D)

(b) first distributive law

15.

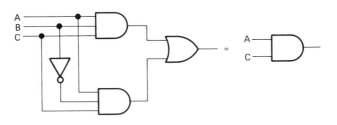

Let

$$A = > \$100,000$$
$$B = \text{male}$$
$$\bar{B} = \text{female}$$
$$C = \text{double indemnity}$$

Then

$$
\begin{array}{ll}
& \text{Property} \\
ABC + A\bar{B}C = A(BC + \bar{B}C) & 3\text{(a)} \\
\quad\quad\quad\quad\quad = A(C(B + \bar{B})) & 3\text{(a)} \\
\quad\quad\quad\quad\quad = AC(1) & 5\text{(a)} \\
\quad\quad\quad\quad\quad = AC & 4\text{(b)}
\end{array}
$$

16. (a)

A	B	$\bar{A}$	$\bar{B}$	$A\bar{B}$	$\bar{A}B$	$A\bar{B} + \bar{A}B$
1	1	0	0	0	0	0
1	0	0	1	1	0	1
0	1	1	0	0	1	1
0	0	1	1	0	0	0

(b) $A\bar{B} + \bar{A}B$

EXERCISES 14-3

1. Sum $= C_{(i)} \oplus (A \oplus B)$
   Carry $= AB + C_{(i)}(A \oplus B)$
2. (a) Yes, for two binary digits

(b) $X = (A + B)(\overline{AB})$, $Y = AB$

3. (a) properties 3(a), 5(b), 4(a), and 1(b)
   (b) property 9(b) and $\overline{\overline{A}} = A$

4. (a) $D = B_{(i)} \oplus (A \oplus B)$
   (b) $B_{(o)} = \overline{A}B + B_{(i)}(A \oplus B)$

5. (a)

A	B	$A + B$	$\overline{AB}$	$(A + B)(\overline{AB}) = A\overline{B} + \overline{A}B$
1	1	1	0	0
1	0	1	1	1
0	1	1	1	1
0	0	0	1	0

(b) $\overline{AB} \neq \overline{A}\overline{B}$

6. 1.

7.

A	B	Difference	Borrow
1	1	0	0
1	0	1	0
0	1	1	1
0	0	0	0

8.

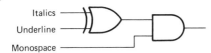

Italics
Underline
Monospace

9. (a) $X = A \oplus B$, $Y = \overline{AB}$ (b) $X = \overline{(A + B)} \oplus \overline{A}$, $Y = \overline{A}B$
   (c) $X = \overline{A} + B$, $Y = \overline{A \oplus B}$ (d) $X = C \oplus (A \oplus B)$, $Y = C(A \oplus B) + AB$

EXERCISES 15-1

1. (a) $\{(1, 4), (1, 5), (2, 4), (2, 5)\}$ (b) $\{(4, 1), (4, 2), (5, 1), (5, 2)\}$
   (c) $\{(1, 1), (1, 2), (2, 1), (2, 2)\}$

2. (a) $\{(1, 1), (1, 2), (1, 3), (2, 1), (2, 2), (2, 3), (3, 1), (3, 2), (3, 3)\}$
   (b) $\{(1, 2), (1, 3), (2, 2), (2, 3)\}$
   (c) $\{(1, 2), (1, 3), (2, 2), (2, 3)\}$
   (d) $\{(1, 1), (1, 2), (2, 1), (2, 2), (3, 1), (3, 2) \cup (1, 2), (1, 3), (2, 2), (2, 3), (3, 2), (3, 3)\}$
       $= \{(1, 1), (1, 2), (1, 3), (2, 1), (2, 2), (2, 3), (3, 1), (3, 2), (3, 3)\}$
   (e) $\{(1, 2), (2, 2), (3, 2)\}$
   (f) $\{(1, 2), (1, 3), (2, 2), (2, 3), (3, 2), (3, 3)\}$

3. (a) No (b) Yes (c) n^2, mn, m^2 (d) $A \times (B \cap C) = (A \times B) \cap (A \times C)$

4.

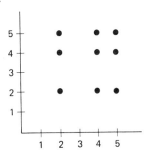

EXERCISES 15-2

1. (a) domain $\{3, -1\}$
      range $\{2, 3\}$
   (b) domain $\{-2, -1, 0, 1\}$
      range $\{1, 0, -1, -2\}$

   (c) domain $\{-2\}$
      range $\{1\}$
   (d) $(-2, 1)$

2. (a)

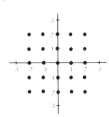

(b)

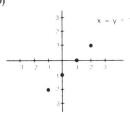

3. (a) $\{(-2, 3), (1, 0), (0, 1)\}$ (b) $\{(0, 1), (-1, 0), (1, 1), (0, -1)\}$
4. (a) Yes (b) Yes (c) Yes (d) No (e) No
5. $\{1, -3, -7\}$
6. (a) $\{-2\}$ (b) $\{0\}$ (c) $\{-3\}$
7. $\{(2, 1), (3, 2), (4, 3)\}$
8. Yes

EXERCISES 15-3

1.

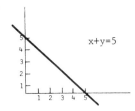

2.

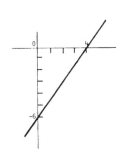

3.

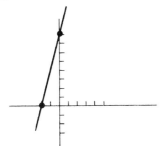

4.

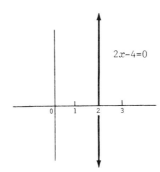

5.

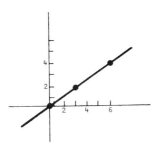

6. $y = -\frac{1}{2}x + \frac{1}{2}$
7. $y = \frac{4}{3}x - \frac{7}{3}$
8. $y = -5x + 5$
9. $y = x - 3$
10. $y = -5x + 25$
11. $y = \frac{3}{4}x + 3$
12. $y = x$
13. $y = 2x - 7$
14. $y = -x + 1$
15.

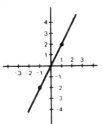

16.

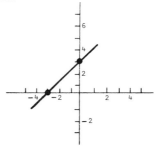

17. $y = \frac{1}{2}x - 4$
18. $y = 2x$
19. $x = 2$
20. $y = 0x - 2$

21. $y = -\frac{3}{4}x - 2$
22. $y + x - 4 = 0$
23. $3y + x - 7 = 0$
24. $4y + 3x - 12 = 0$
25. $0y + x + 4 = 0$
26. (a) 40 MPH   (b) 1.5 hours   (c) 90 miles   (d) $\frac{2}{5}$, $y = \frac{2}{5}x$
27. (a) $y = 2$ (b) $4y = x$ (c) $y = -\frac{1}{2}x + 2$ (d) $y = \frac{2}{3}x + 2$
28.

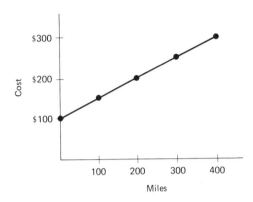

EXERCISES 16-1

1. $x = 3$, $y = -2$ 6. $x = 2\frac{2}{7}$, $y = 2\frac{4}{7}$
2. $x = 7/4$, $y = -\frac{1}{4}$ 7. $x = 12$, $y = -4$
3. $x = 0$, $y = 3$ 8. $x = \frac{5}{3}$, $y = \frac{5}{3}$
4. $x = 3$, $y = \frac{2}{3}$ 9. $x = -\frac{1}{2}$, $y = \frac{5}{2}$
5. $x = 6\frac{2}{3}$, $y = 3\frac{1}{3}$ 10. $x = 3$, $y = 5$
11.   Let x = rate of boat in still water
                       Let y = rate of current
                       Let $x + y$ = rate of boat going downstream
                       Let $x - y$ = rate of boat going upstream

$$x + y = \frac{10 \text{ miles}}{1.5 \text{ hr.}}$$

$$x - y = \frac{10 \text{ miles}}{3 \text{ hr.}}$$

rate of boat = 5.0 mi/hr
rate of current = 1.7 mi/hr   (approx.)

12.

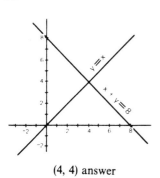

(4, 4) answer

13.

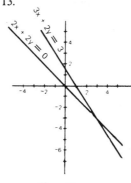

(3, −3) answer

14.

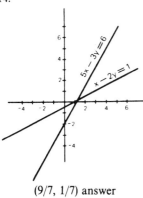

(9/7, 1/7) answer

15.

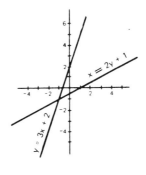

(−1, −1) answer

16.

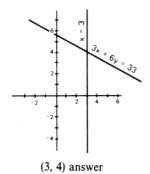

(3, 4) answer

17. Let x = the 1st note
    Let y = the 2nd note
    $.04x + .06y = 420$
    $.06x + .04y = 480$
    $x = \$6000 \quad y = \$3000$
18. $2x + y = 4, x - y = -1$
19. Let x = cost of fuel injection system
    Let y = cost of electrical engine
    $x = \$800 \quad y = \$300$
20. $x = 3, 2x + y = 4; 3, -2$
21. (a) $2y = x, 5y = x + 15$ (b) 10, 5
22. (a) 8, 4 (b) $6\frac{2}{3}, 3\frac{1}{3}$ (c) 5, 4

EXERCISES 16-2

1. Dependent, coincident
2. Independent, intersects at one point
3. Inconsistent, parallel
4. Dependent, coincident
5. (a) The flowchart determines the slope of a line.
   (b) $A = Y1 - Y2$
       $B = X1 - X2$
       SLOPE1 $= A/B$
5. (b) Repeat flowchart for second equation, then test:

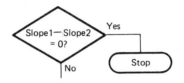

IF (SLOPE1 − SLOPE2)10,20,10
10 other statements in program
20 STOP
END

6. (a) Consistent equations are equations whose graphs intersect.
   (b) Inconsistent equations are equations whose graphs parallel.
   (c) Dependent equations are equations whose graphs determine the same line (have the same slope and the same y-intercept).
7. $y = -2x, y = -2x + 2$
8. $y = \frac{1}{2}x, 2y = x$

EXERCISES 16-3

1.

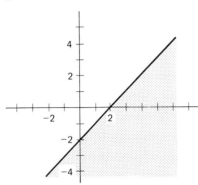

2.

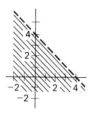

3.

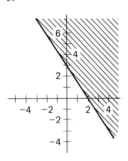

4.

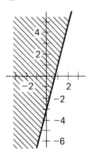

5.

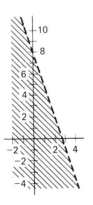

6.

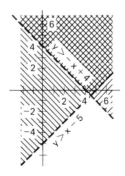

7. $y > -3/2x + 7/2$
   $y < -2x + 8$

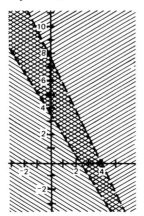

8. $y > x + 5$
   $y \geqslant -4x + 7$

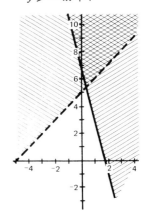

9. $y \geqslant -2x + 6$
   $x > 2$

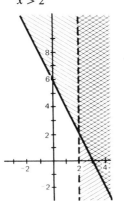

10.

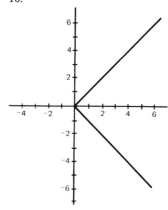

11.

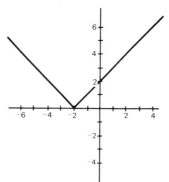

12.

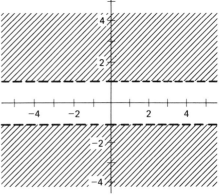

13. 005 LET M = −3
    010 LET B = 6
    015 INPUT X
    020 IF X > 2 THEN GO TO 040
    025   LET Y = M · X + B
    030   IF Y < 0 THEN GO TO 035
    032   PRINT X,Y
    035   INPUT X
    037 GO TO 020
    040 END

EXERCISES 17-1

1. (a) real, unequal   (b) real, equal   (c) real, unequal   (d) complex   (e) real, equal
2. (a) $1/4, -1/4$ (b) $-1, 6$ (c) $1/2, -1/2$ (d) $-1, 4/3$

    (e) $1, -1$ (f) $\dfrac{-3 \pm 3\sqrt{5}}{2}$ (g) $1/2, -3$ (h) $-1, 1$

3. (a) $0, 6$ (b) $\dfrac{-m \pm \sqrt{m^2 - 4n}}{2}$ (c) $7, 3$ (d) $\left(\dfrac{10}{2}\right)^2 = 25 = c$ (e) No

4. (a) $\dfrac{-5 \pm \sqrt{33}}{4}$ (b) $\dfrac{-3 \pm \sqrt{5}}{2}$ (c) $\dfrac{-7 \pm \sqrt{57}}{4}$ (d) $\dfrac{-d \pm \sqrt{d^2 - 4f}}{2}$ (e) $1, -1$

5. (a) $x^2 + 3x - 10 = 0$ (b) $x^2 - 3x - 4 = 0$ (c) $x^2 = 5$ (d) $x^2 + 2x + 1 = 0$
6. (a) $a = 3, b = 5, c = 4$
    $3x^2 + 5x + 4 = 0$
  (b) $a = 1, b = \frac{1}{2}, c = 2$
    $x^2 + \frac{1}{2}x + 2 = 0$

7. (a) $\dfrac{-b}{a}$ (b) $\dfrac{c}{a}$

8. (a) $-1, -6$ (b) $-1, -42$
9. IF(B··2 − 4.0·A·C)10,20,30
10. 30 X1 = (−B + (SQRT(B··2 − 4.0·A·C)))/2.0·A
    X2 = (−B − (SQRT(B··2 − 4.0·A·C)))/2.0·A

EXERCISES 17-2

1. (a) $-x^2 + 7x - 6 = y$ (b) $x^2 - 4x + 3 = y$ (c) $.5x^2 + 2x = y$

 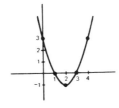 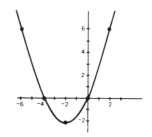

(d) $y = x^2$

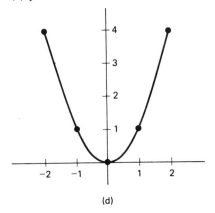

(d)

2. See graphs for 1(a) and 1(b).

3. It is a function

4. $y^2 = x$

It is not a function

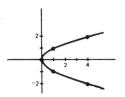

5. $2x^2 + 3x + 7$
   discriminant < 0

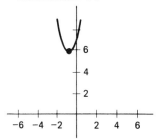

6. (a) $y = x^2 - 9x + 8$

Minimum point
(4.5, -12.25)

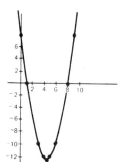

(b) $y = -x^2 + 9x - 8$

Maximum point
(4.5, 12.25)

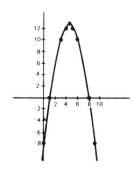

(c) $y = x^2 - 5x + 4$

Minimum point
$(2.5, -2.25)$

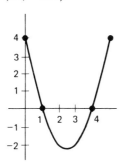

(d) $y = x^2 - 2x + 1$

Minimum point
$(1, 0)$

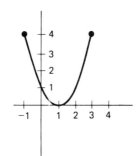

7. No

8. $x = y^2 - 9$

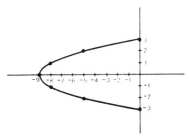

9. $x = y^2 - 6y + 9$

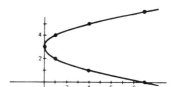

10. IF(A)10,20,30
11. omitted

12. (a) $y < x^2 + 2$

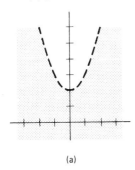

(a)

(b) $y \geqslant x^2$

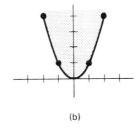

(b)

13. (a) $-x^2 + 10x - 9 = 0$ (b) $y = -x^2 + 2x - 1$ (c) $y > x^2 + 1$

EXERCISES 17-3

1. (a)

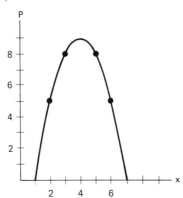

   (b) 4, 9
   (c) (1, 0), (7, 0)

2. 4, 4

3.

minimum cost at (1.5, 1.75)

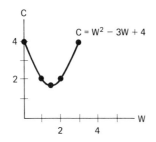

4. X = −B/(2.0•A)
   Y = −1.0•((B••2 − 4.0•A•C)/4.0•A)

5. (a) 120 DATA 1,2,3,4,5,6,7
   (b) 310 Y = −1 • (X^2) + 8 • X − 7
       130 FOR I = 1 TO 7

EXERCISES 18-1

1. $y = 3^x$; $(-2, \frac{1}{9})$, $(2, 9)$, $(0, 1)$
2. $y = -2^x$; $(-1, -\frac{1}{2})$, $(0, 1)$, $(1, -2)$
3. $y = (\frac{1}{2})^x$; $(-2, 4)$, $(-1, 2)$, $(3, \frac{1}{8})$
4. $y = (10)^x$; $(-3, \frac{1}{1000})$, $(2, 100)$, $(4, 10{,}000)$

5.

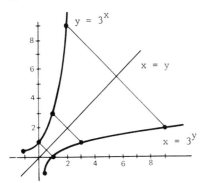

6.

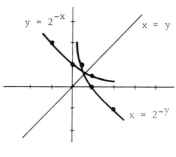

7.

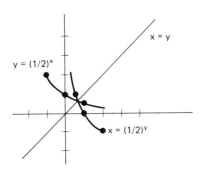

8.

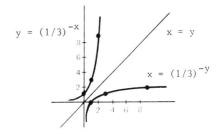

9. $2^5 = 32$
10. $10^2 = 100$
11. $10^{-3} = 0.001$
12. $(\frac{1}{2})^{-2} = 4$
13. $16^0 = 1$
14. $5^3 = 125$
15. $\log_4 64 = 3$
16. $\log_8 \frac{1}{2} = -\frac{1}{3}$
17. $\log_5 1 = 0$
18. $\log_{10} 0.001 = -3$

19. $\log_{1/4} \frac{1}{16} = 2$
20. $\log_{1000} \frac{1}{10} = -\frac{1}{3}$
21. $y = 4$
22. $y = -2$
23. $b = 10$
24. $x = 125$
25. $b = \frac{1}{2}$
26. $y = -2$
27. $x = \frac{1}{8}$
28.

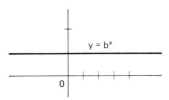

EXERCISES 18-2

1. $\log_{10} 4.25 = 0.6284$
2. $\log_{10} 62.0 = 1.7924$
3. $\log_{10} 7.21 = 0.8579$
4. $\log_{10} 0.00512 = 7.7093 - 10$
5. $\log_{10} 0.127 = 9.1038 - 10$
6. $\log_{10} 32400 = 4.5105$
7. $\log_{10} 295 = 2.4698$
8. 3.53
9. 9.52
10. 745.
11. .590

12. 44.9
13. 44900.
14. 5.06
15. 7740.
16. 3.8087
17. 1.8682
18. $9.0917 - 10$
19. 1.4218
20. 0.8691
21. 2.7280
22. $8.6894 - 10$

23. .05071
24. 990.4
25. 52.96
26. 98.08
27. 3.296
28. 263.4
29. 1.501
30. 7.888×10^{-4}
31. 12.44
32. No

EXERCISES 18-3

1. (a) \$336.94
   (b) $Y = (1.0 + (.0525/4.))$
       $X = ALOG10(200.00) + 40.0 \cdot ALOG10(Y)$
       $ANS = 10.0 \cdot \cdot X$
2. (a) \$37,353,810

(b)

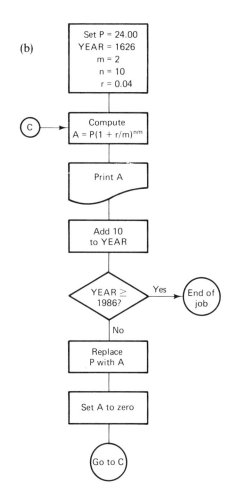

3. $X = ALOG10(24.0) + 720.0 \cdot ALOG10(1.02)$
   $ANS = 10.0 \cdot \cdot X$
4. 1.395
5. (a) $19.93 = n$ or 20 generations
   (b) $20 \cdot \frac{1}{2} = 10$ hours
   As an exercise, write the Fortran program for the preceding solution.

EXERCISES 19-1

1. omitted
2. (a) 3×2 (b) 3×1 (c) 1×3

3. (a) $\begin{bmatrix} 1 & 3 \\ -2 & \frac{6}{7} \end{bmatrix}$ (b) $\begin{bmatrix} 2 & 3 & 0 \\ 1 & -4 & 6 \end{bmatrix}$ (c) $\begin{bmatrix} 1 \\ 2 \\ 3 \end{bmatrix}$ (d) $\begin{bmatrix} 1 & 5 & 9 & 13 \\ 2 & 6 & 10 & 14 \\ 3 & 7 & 11 & 15 \\ 4 & 8 & 12 & 16 \end{bmatrix}$

4. (a) $\begin{bmatrix} 4 & 0 & 14 \\ 3 & -1 & -1\frac{1}{2} \end{bmatrix}$ (b) $\begin{bmatrix} 4 & -1 \\ -4 & 2 \\ 7 & 1 \\ 4\frac{1}{2} & -1 \end{bmatrix}$ (c) $A + B = \begin{bmatrix} 8 & 11 \\ 6 & 1 \end{bmatrix}$

$B + A = \begin{bmatrix} 8 & 11 \\ 6 & 1 \end{bmatrix}$

$\therefore A + B = B + A$

5. (a) Yes (b) omitted

6. (a) $\begin{bmatrix} -1 & 3 & -6 \\ -4 & -7 & 2 \\ 3 & 1 & -6 \end{bmatrix}$ (b) $\begin{bmatrix} -3 & -7 \\ 6 & -9 \\ -4 & 2 \\ -\frac{1}{3} & 1 \end{bmatrix}$

7. (a) $\begin{bmatrix} 1 & 0 \\ 1 & -2 \end{bmatrix}$ (b) $\begin{bmatrix} 1 \\ -6 \\ 1 \end{bmatrix}$

8. (a) $C = \begin{bmatrix} 0 & 5 \\ -1 & 4 \end{bmatrix}$ (b) $C = \begin{bmatrix} 6 & 14 & -20 \\ 28 & \frac{4}{3} & 4 \end{bmatrix}$ (c) $C = \begin{bmatrix} -2 & -3 & -2 \\ -4 & 1 & 0 \\ -7 & -9 & -1 \end{bmatrix}$

9. $A + B = C$
$\begin{bmatrix} -3 & 6 \\ -2 & 1 \end{bmatrix} + \begin{bmatrix} 1 & 0 \\ 3 & 1 \end{bmatrix} = \begin{bmatrix} -2 & 6 \\ 1 & 2 \end{bmatrix} = C$

$C - A = B$
$\begin{bmatrix} -2 & 6 \\ 1 & 2 \end{bmatrix} - \begin{bmatrix} -3 & 6 \\ -2 & 1 \end{bmatrix} = \begin{bmatrix} 1 & 0 \\ 3 & 1 \end{bmatrix}$

10. (a) $\begin{bmatrix} 12 & -1 \\ -6 & 0 \end{bmatrix}$ (b) $\begin{bmatrix} ya-y & \frac{2y}{3} \end{bmatrix}$

11. $\begin{bmatrix} 3800 & 2750 \\ 7800 & 6300 \end{bmatrix}$

EXERCISES 19-2

1. (a) $\begin{bmatrix} 12 & 18 \\ -6 & 1 \end{bmatrix}$ (b) $\begin{bmatrix} .2064 & .636 & .120 \\ 1.2942 & .0818 & -.0826 \end{bmatrix}$ 2. $\begin{bmatrix} 3 & -\frac{3}{2} \\ 1 & 0 \\ 2 & 4 \end{bmatrix}$

3. $.05 \times \begin{bmatrix} 9,500 & 9,500 & 9,500 & 9,500 \\ 10,000 & 10,000 & 10,000 & 10,000 \\ 10,000 & 10,000 & 11,000 & 11,000 \\ 11,000 & 11,500 & 11,500 & 13,000 \end{bmatrix} = \begin{bmatrix} 475 & 475 & 475 & 475 \\ 500 & 500 & 500 & 500 \\ 500 & 500 & 550 & 550 \\ 550 & 575 & 575 & 650 \end{bmatrix}$

4. (a) $\begin{bmatrix} 4 & 20 \\ 3 & 14 \end{bmatrix}$

(b) $\begin{bmatrix} -3 & 3 & -3 \\ 1 & -1 & 1 \\ 1 & -1 & 1 \end{bmatrix}$ (c) $\begin{bmatrix} 18 & 10 \\ -3 & 0 \end{bmatrix}$

5. (a) No
   (b) No, A and B are not conformable for multiplication
   (c) $[2 + 2 + 12] = [16]$

6. (a) $\begin{bmatrix} 4 & 5 \\ 3 & 0 \end{bmatrix}$ (b) $\begin{bmatrix} 8 & 1 \\ -1 & -2 \end{bmatrix}$ (c) $\begin{bmatrix} 12 & 3 \\ -9 & -6 \end{bmatrix}$

   (d) $\begin{bmatrix} 18 & 15 \\ 1 & 5 \end{bmatrix}$ (e) $\begin{bmatrix} 4 & 3 \\ 5 & 0 \end{bmatrix}$ (f) $\begin{bmatrix} 4 & 3 \\ 5 & 0 \end{bmatrix}$ (g) No, $\begin{bmatrix} 7 & -2 \\ 3 & -3 \end{bmatrix} = (BA)^t$

7. (a) Yes (b) Yes
8. omitted 9. (a) 170 (b) 44250

EXERCISES 19-3

1. (a) 14 (b) -3 (c) .25 (d) sr
2. (a) $\begin{bmatrix} 2 & 4 \\ 2 & -3 \end{bmatrix}$ (b) $\begin{bmatrix} -1 & 2 \\ -1 & 0 \end{bmatrix}$ (c) $\begin{bmatrix} m & p \\ q & n \end{bmatrix}$ (d) $\begin{bmatrix} a & -c \\ +d & b \end{bmatrix}$
3. (a) $x = -\frac{5}{7}, y = \frac{18}{7}$ (b) $x = \frac{29}{4}, y = \frac{1}{4}$ (c) $x = 1, y = 0$
   (d) $x = -\frac{17}{11}, y = \frac{26}{11}$ (e) No unique solution (f) $x = \frac{19}{9}, y = \frac{2}{3}$
4. (a) 4 (b) 4 (c) -10
5. (a) $a = 1$ (b) $a = -13$

EXERCISES 19-4

1. (a) $\begin{bmatrix} \dfrac{1}{7} & -\dfrac{5}{7} \\[2mm] \dfrac{1}{7} & \dfrac{2}{7} \end{bmatrix}$ (b) None   (c) $\begin{bmatrix} \dfrac{1}{x} & -\dfrac{3}{2x} \\[2mm] 0 & \dfrac{1}{2} \end{bmatrix}$

2. (a)
$$\overset{A}{\begin{bmatrix} 2 & 5 \\ 1 & -2 \end{bmatrix}} \cdot \overset{A^{-1}}{\begin{bmatrix} \dfrac{2}{9} & \dfrac{5}{9} \\[2mm] \dfrac{1}{9} & -\dfrac{2}{9} \end{bmatrix}} = \begin{bmatrix} \dfrac{2\cdot2}{9}+\dfrac{5\cdot1}{9} & \dfrac{2\cdot5}{9}+\dfrac{5\cdot(-2)}{9} \\[2mm] \dfrac{1\cdot2}{9}+\dfrac{-2\cdot1}{9} & \dfrac{1\cdot5}{9}+\left(-\dfrac{2\cdot2}{9}\right) \end{bmatrix} = \overset{I}{\begin{bmatrix} 1 & 0 \\ 0 & 1 \end{bmatrix}}$$

$$\overset{A^{-1}}{\begin{bmatrix} \dfrac{2}{9} & \dfrac{5}{9} \\[2mm] \dfrac{1}{9} & -\dfrac{2}{9} \end{bmatrix}} \cdot \overset{A}{\begin{bmatrix} 2 & 5 \\ 1 & -2 \end{bmatrix}} = \begin{bmatrix} \dfrac{2\cdot2}{9}+\dfrac{5\cdot1}{9} & \dfrac{2\cdot5}{9}+\dfrac{5\cdot(-2)}{9} \\[2mm] \dfrac{2\cdot1}{9}+\dfrac{-2\cdot1}{9} & \dfrac{1\cdot5}{9}+\left(-\dfrac{2\cdot2}{9}\right) \end{bmatrix} = \overset{I}{\begin{bmatrix} 1 & 0 \\ 0 & 1 \end{bmatrix}}$$

(b) Yes

3. (a) $\begin{bmatrix} \dfrac{2}{10} & -\dfrac{2}{10} & \dfrac{8}{10} \\[2mm] \dfrac{3}{10} & \dfrac{2}{10} & -\dfrac{3}{10} \\[2mm] -\dfrac{2}{10} & \dfrac{2}{10} & \dfrac{2}{10} \end{bmatrix}$ (b) $\begin{bmatrix} 0 & 0 & \dfrac{1}{2} \\[2mm] -2 & 1 & \dfrac{3}{2} \\[2mm] -\dfrac{1}{2} & \dfrac{1}{2} & \dfrac{1}{4} \end{bmatrix}$ (c) $\begin{bmatrix} -\dfrac{1}{2} & \dfrac{1}{2} & 1 \\[2mm] -\dfrac{1}{2} & -\dfrac{1}{2} & 1 \\[2mm] 1 & -1 & -1 \end{bmatrix}$

4. (a) Yes   (b) Yes

5. $C^{-1} = \begin{bmatrix} \dfrac{2}{3} & -\dfrac{1}{3} \\[2mm] \dfrac{1}{6} & \dfrac{1}{6} \end{bmatrix}$

6. $\begin{bmatrix} 3 & 2 & 6 \\ 1 & 1 & 2 \\ 2 & 2 & 5 \end{bmatrix} \cdot \begin{bmatrix} 1 & 2 & -2 \\ -1 & 3 & 0 \\ 0 & -2 & 1 \end{bmatrix} = \begin{bmatrix} 1 & 0 & 0 \\ 0 & 1 & 0 \\ 0 & 0 & 1 \end{bmatrix}$

$\therefore B = A^{-1}$

EXERCISES 19-5

1. (a) $A = \begin{bmatrix} 1 & 1 & -1 \\ 2 & -1 & 1 \\ 1 & 1 & 2 \end{bmatrix}$ $X = \begin{bmatrix} x \\ y \\ z \end{bmatrix}$ $B = \begin{bmatrix} -1 \\ 2 \\ 0 \end{bmatrix}$ (c) $x = \dfrac{1}{3}$

$y = -1$

$z = \dfrac{1}{3}$

(b) $\begin{bmatrix} \dfrac{1}{3} & \dfrac{1}{3} & 0 \\ \dfrac{1}{3} & -\dfrac{1}{3} & \dfrac{1}{3} \\ -\dfrac{1}{3} & 0 & \dfrac{1}{3} \end{bmatrix}$

2. (a) $\{2, 1\}$ (b) $\{1, 5\}$ (c) $\{-\frac{1}{2}, \frac{5}{2}\}$
   (d) $\{1, 1, 1\}$ (e) $\{8, 6, 1\}$ (f) the null set
3. (a) to repeat the algorithm without rewriting the instructions
   (b) reference matrix, and for printing original equations
   (c) division by zero in statement 200

EXERCISES 19-6

1. Sets negative elements in IARAY to positive.
2.   DIMENSION IARAY1(10),IARAY2(10),IANS(10)
       DO 10 I = 1, 10
       IARAY1(I) = I
   10 IARAY2(I) = I
       DO 15 I = 1, 10
   15 IANS(I) = IARAY1(I) + IARAY2(I)
3.   DIMENSION IARRAY(10)
       DO 5 I = 1, 10
     5 IARRAY(I) = I
       DO 15 I = 1, 5
       ITEMP = IARRAY(I)
       IEND = 11 − 1
       IARRAY(I) = IARRAY(IEND)
   15 IARRAY(IEND) = ITEMP
       STOP
       END
4. Sets deposits to zero.

5. 50 FOR I = 1 TO 7
   60 READ W(I)
   70 NEXT I
   80 FOR I = 1 TO 15
   90 READ T(I)
   100 NEXT I
   190 CHILL(J,I) = .0817•(3.71•SQR(W(I)) + 5.81 − .25•W(I))•(T(J) − 91.4) + 91.4

EXERCISES 20-1

1. (a) Yes   (b) No   (c) No   (d) Yes   (e) No
2. (a) Plant 1 $60(2) + 80B = 480 − 40, B = 4$
      Plant 2 $70A + 40(1) = 280 − 30, A = 3$
   (b) Plant 1 $60A + 80(5) = 480 + 100, A = 3$
      Plant 2 $70(4) + 40B = 280 + 80, B = 2$
3. (a) 115.00   (b) 67.50   (c) 490.00
4. (a) 201.43   (b) 400
5. Maximum profit is at the intersection of lines for plants 1 and 3.
6. (a) $[1 \quad 5.25] \cdot \begin{bmatrix} 30 \\ 20 \end{bmatrix} = 30 + 105.00 = 135$

   (b) $[1 \quad 5.25] \begin{bmatrix} 60 \\ 80 \end{bmatrix} = 60 + 420 = 480$

   $[1 \quad 5.25] \begin{bmatrix} 70 \\ 40 \end{bmatrix} = 70 + 210 = 280$

   (c) HOURS = (ARAY(1)•ARAYB(1)) + (ARAY(2)•ARAYB(2))
7. (a) Maximum profit is found on an infinite number of points from (0, 6) and the intersection of the lines

$$60A + 80B = 480$$
$$70A + 40B = 280$$

   (b) (8, 0)

EXERCISES 20-2

1. (a) $A = 2.7 \quad B = 1.4$ or $S = \{2.7, 1.4\}$
   (b) (1) $10 \cdot (2.7) + 5 \cdot (1.4) = 27 + 7.0 = 34$
      (2) $9 \cdot (2.7) + 15 \cdot (1.4) = 24.3 + 21.0 = 45.3$
      (3) $2 \cdot (2.7) + 9 \cdot (1.4) = 5.4 + 12.6 = 18.0$
2. (a) Item 1 − 4 gallons in excess
      Item 2 − 0.3 gallons in excess
      Item 3 − exact requirements
   (b) $[.80 \quad .60] \begin{bmatrix} 2.7 \\ 1.4 \end{bmatrix} = 2.16 + .84 = \$3.00$

3. (a) at N, Fig. 20.6 (b) at L
4. (a) $A = 0, B = .60 \times 6 = 3.60$
   (b) (1) 2.01
       (2) 2.27
5. (a) 1.20 (b) 4 points (c) $13\frac{5}{7}$ (d) $(0, 15)$ (e) omitted
6.   DIMENSION K(3)
       DO 10 I = 1,3
       IPROD = K(I) • 3
       WRITE(2,2) IPROD
    2 FORMAT(I4)
   10 CONTINUE
7. 4 of x, 2 of y
8. $525

EXERCISES 21-1

1. omitted
2.

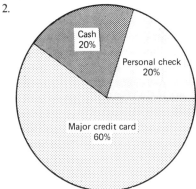

3.

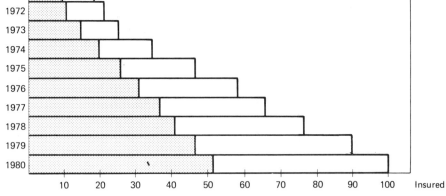

4. Frequency in days (365 days per year)

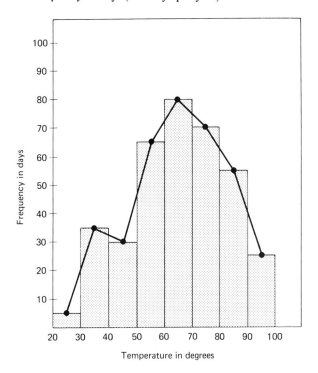

Frequency in days

Temperature in degrees

5. .

MONTHLY SALES REPORT

Region	Salesperson	Product X	Product Y	Total Sales
I	A-Mgr	1000	665	1665
	B	1900	1190	3090
	C	1000	525	1525
Region total		3900	2380	6280
II	D-Mgr	2250	525	2775
	E	2000	700	2700
	F	1750	875	2625
Region total		6000	2100	8100
III	G-Mgr	1150	735	1885
	H	2150	1470	3620
	I	2000	1330	3330
Region total		5300	3535	8835
Company total		15200	8015	23215

EXERCISES 21-2

1. (a) $\sum\limits_{i=1}^{N} X_i$ (c) $\sum\limits_{i=1}^{N} (X_i - p)^3$ (e) $\left(\sum\limits_{i=5}^{6} X_i\right)^2$

   (b) $\sum\limits_{i=2}^{3} (X_i + 2X_i)$ (d) $\sum\limits_{i=2}^{4} (cX_i)^2$

2. (a) $X_2 + X_3 + X_4 + \ldots + X_N$
   (b) $X_1^2 + X_2^2 + X_3^2 + X_4^2$
   (c) $[(Y_5 - 2) + (Y_6 - 2)]^2$
   (d) $(X_2 + 2X_2)X_2 + (X_3 + 2X_3)X_3$
   (e) $(aX_1 + b) + (aX_2 + b) + (aX_3 + b) + \ldots + (aX_N + b)$

3. (a) $X_1 + X_2 + X_3 + X_4 = 8$ (d) $(X_3^2 - 2X_3) + (X_4^2 - 2X_4) = 63$
   (b) $(X_2 + c) + (X_3 + c) = 5$ (e) $cX_1 + cX_2 + cX_3 + cX_4 = 32$
   (c) $[(2X_1 - c) + (2X_2 - c)]^2 = 100$

4. No

EXERCISES 21-3

1. (a) 4.9   (b) 4.96   (c) 3.09
2. (a) 19.5   (b) $18.5 - 21.5$ (c) 19.9   (d) 5
3. (a) Finds the sum of the variables A, B, C, D, and E.
   (b) Subtracts FC from the value of XN/2.
4. $AVER = (A + B + C + D + E)/5.0$
5. (a) SUM = XI1 ∗ FI1 + XI2 ∗ FI2 + XI3 ∗ FI3 + XI4 ∗ FI4
      XM = SUM/XN
   (b) XMD = XL + C ∗ ((XN/2.0 − FC)/FM)
   (c) 1. Let D = sum of deviations squared, XN = number of scores then the standard
          deviation = SQRT(D/XN)

      2. Let $XMF = \sum\limits_{i=1}^{K} (X_i - m)^2 f_i$, then the standard deviation = SQRT(XMF/XN)

6. (a)

Class Boundaries	F	X	Xf	$\|X - m\|$	$\|X - m\|f$	$(X - m)^2$	$(X - m)^2 f$
$30.08 - 38.08$	7	34.08	238.56	31.72	222.04	1006.1584	7043.1088
$38.08 - 46.08$	11	42.08	462.88	23.72	260.92	562.6384	6189.0224
$46.08 - 54.08$	11	50.08	550.88	15.72	172.92	247.1184	2718.3024
$54.08 - 62.08$	16	58.08	929.28	7.72	123.52	59.5984	953.5744
$62.08 - 70.08$	27	66.08	1784.16	.28	7.56	.0784	2.1168
$70.08 - 78.08$	17	74.08	1259.36	8.28	140.76	68.5584	1165.4928
$78.08 - 86.08$	15	82.08	1231.20	16.28	244.20	265.0384	3975.5760
$86.08 - 94.08$	16	90.08	1441.28	24.28	388.48	589.5184	9432.2944

(b) mean = 65.8, median = 66.5, standard deviation = 16.2

(c)

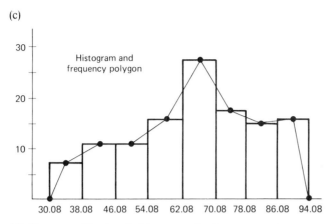

(d) Connect midpoints in histogram for frequency polygon.

(e)

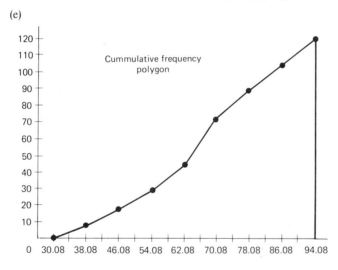

7. 74.27   8. 80.43   9. 80   10. 4%, 1.2

EXERCISES 22-1

1. $p = \dfrac{x}{x + y}$ 2. mutually exclusive

3. 1, certain   4. $\dfrac{1}{3}$

5. $\dfrac{5}{18}$ 6. $\dfrac{2}{9}$

7. (a) $\dfrac{3}{12}$ (b) $\dfrac{2}{12}$ (c) $\dfrac{4}{12}$ 8. $\dfrac{1}{49}$

9. .0039683

10. (a) .0060332   (b) .1538462   (c) .00591716   (d) 1

11. (a) $\dfrac{4}{13}$ (b) $\dfrac{1}{52}$

12. $\dfrac{4}{6}$ 13. (a) $\dfrac{1}{4}$ (b) $\dfrac{1}{2}$

14. .40   15. 1

16. $780   17. (a) $\dfrac{1}{16}$ (b) $\dfrac{3}{16}$ (c) $\dfrac{9}{16}$

18. $\dfrac{3}{10}$ 19. $32

20. (a) .703125 (b) .0091 (c) .0073 (d) .2074 (e) .1703

EXERCISES 22-2

1. (a) $20q^3p^3$ (b) .1640625, $21q^2p^5$ 2. $\dfrac{5}{16}$

3. (a) 50 (b) 5 (c) 2.9 (d) .0019

4. (a) .16075 (b) .9645062

5. .2036266

6. (a) $\dfrac{3456}{390625}$ (b) $\dfrac{331776}{390625}$ (c) $\dfrac{3553}{390625}$

7. (a) $\dfrac{531441}{1000000}$ (b) $\dfrac{14580}{1000000}$ (c) $\dfrac{984150}{1000000}$

8. (a) .9076 (b) .4893 (c) .0760 (d) .4251 (e) .0708 (f) .0708 (g) .0872

9. 273.75   10. 30

11. $A \geqslant m + 1.5\sigma(.5000 - .4332 = .0668)$
    B between $m + .4\sigma$ and $m + 1.5\sigma$ (.4332 − .2778 = .1554)
    C between $m - .4\sigma$ and $m + .4\sigma(.1554 + .1554 = .3108)$
    D between $m - 1.4\sigma$ and $m - .4\sigma(.4192 - .1554 = .2638)$
    $F \leqslant m - 1.4\sigma(.5000 - .0808 = .4192)$

12. 34.13%   13. .3438   14. (a) Yes (b) No

15. (C*QN)/(PN + 1)

Index

459